D1328570

# THE WORKS
# AND CORRESPONDENCE OF
# DAVID RICARDO

## VOLUME VI

# PLAN OF THE EDITION

A General Index of the whole work is in preparation.

# THE WORKS
# AND CORRESPONDENCE OF
# DAVID RICARDO

EDITED BY

### PIERO SRAFFA

WITH THE COLLABORATION OF

### M. H. DOBB

VOLUME VI

## LETTERS 1810–1815

CAMBRIDGE
## AT THE UNIVERSITY PRESS
FOR THE ROYAL ECONOMIC SOCIETY
1962

PUBLISHED BY
THE SYNDICS OF THE CAMBRIDGE UNIVERSITY PRESS

Bentley House, 200 Euston Road, London, N.W. 1
American Branch: 32 East 57th Street, New York 22, N.Y.
West African Office: P.O. Box 33, Ibadan, Nigeria

*First printed* 1952
*Reprinted* 1962

*First printed in Great Britain at the University Press, Cambridge*
*Reprinted by offset-lithography by Bradford & Dickens Ltd, London, W.C. 1*

# CONTENTS OF VOLUME VI

## LETTERS 1810–1815

*\* denotes letters not previously published*

*N.B.* The date of five letters to Malthus, formerly published as of 1810, has been corrected to 1813.

PLATE

56, Upper Brook Street, Grosvenor Square, Ricardo's house
in London, 1812–1823 (photograph taken in 1932) . *facing p.* 1

# PREFACE
## TO VOLUMES VI–IX

THESE four volumes, now published together and containing Ricardo's Correspondence, complete the nine which in the preface to Vol. I were promised for early publication. They contain proportionately more new material than any of the previous volumes: of the 555 letters included, 317 are hitherto unpublished. Information about the various series of letters which make up the Correspondence and about the personalities concerned will be found in the Introductory Notes which open this volume. Readers whose chief interest is in the unpublished material can go directly to the Contents or the Index of Correspondents in each volume, where new letters are marked with an asterisk.

Acknowledgement is due to the late Lord Keynes who took an active part in the search for letters and went through these volumes in proof at an early stage; to Professor Jacob Viner and Professor F. A. Hayek who also saw the proofs and made valuable suggestions; and to the late Dr James Bonar and the late Professor J. H. Hollander who allowed use to be made of the introductions and notes to their editions of Ricardo's letters.

Acknowledgement is also due to Mr Frank Ricardo, Mr C. K. Mill, the late Mr F. E. Cairnes and Mr Robert Malthus, who, as owners of the main collections of letters, have generously placed them at the disposal of the editor; to Sir John Murray, Lady Langman, M. Edgar Raoul-Duval, Mrs Harriet J. Butler and the late Professor H. E. Butler, the Hon. Mrs Eustace Hills, Lady Charnwood and Lt.-Col. O. E. d'Avigdor Goldsmid, who have kindly made available groups of letters or single letters in their possession; to the Trustees of the British Museum, to the Librarians of University College, London, of the National Library of Scotland, of the Overstone Library of the University of Reading, of the Goldsmiths' Library of the University of London, of the Seligman Library of Columbia University, of the

Baker Library of Harvard University, of the Biblioteca Comunale
di Pescia, of the Bibliothèque Publique et Universitaire de
Genève, and to the Moscow Historical Museum, for permission
to use letters in their keeping; also to the Delegates of the Oxford
University Press, to the American Economic Association and to
The Johns Hopkins Press for permission to reproduce letters
previously published by them.

Among those who have helped to find letters, special thanks are
due to Professor Arthur H. Cole, Professor Hayek, Messrs
Maggs Bros., M. E. de Nalèche, Professor George O'Brien and
Mr G. W. Zinke. Finally, the editor must thank the innumerable
other persons of whom he has made enquiries while seeking for
Ricardo's letters and who, even though without result, have
taken trouble on his behalf.

P. S.

TRINITY COLLEGE
CAMBRIDGE
*February 1952*

# INTRODUCTORY NOTES TO THE CORRESPONDENCE

## I. *Ricardo's Correspondence*

THE economic correspondence of Ricardo opens in 1810 when he is in his thirty-eighth year and covers the whole of his productive life as a political economist. Ricardo had four main correspondents with whom he was in constant communication over a period of years—James Mill, Malthus, M<sup>c</sup>Culloch and Trower; while he maintained a less frequent exchange with Jean-Baptiste Say. By an extraordinary piece of good fortune both sides of each of the five series of letters have come down to us substantially complete.[1]

The Mill correspondence is of special interest as being entirely new and as throwing a vivid light on Ricardo's apprenticeship as a writer and on the development of his thought. The correspondence with Malthus however, Ricardo's side of which has long been known, and which is now completed, is of greater economic importance. It has the character of a sustained discussion, with a constant clash of two opposite viewpoints; and it is with reference to these letters that Keynes has written: 'This friendship will live in history on account of its having given rise to the most important literary correspondence in the whole development of Political Economy.'[2] The M<sup>c</sup>Culloch letters,

---

[1] The letters which, from the internal evidence of those extant, can be inferred to be missing do not exceed one-tenth of the total number.

[2] 'Robert Malthus', in *Essays in Biography*, 1933, p. 137.

which cover a shorter period of years, reflect a relation almost of disciple to master, within which differences of opinion only occasionally arise on particular points; being mostly written previous to personal acquaintance, they are more exclusively devoted to economic matters. Finally, the correspondence with Trower has a peculiar interest as exhibiting an attempt to explain to a comparative layman the economic discussions in which Ricardo was engaged. All these, together with the letters exchanged with other persons with whom Ricardo discussed mainly subjects of an economic or political character, are given in these volumes in full.

In contrast with previously published collections, the letters to and from the various correspondents have been arranged in a single chronological series. The reader is thus placed as it were behind Ricardo's desk at Gatcomb Park and reads the letters as Ricardo writes them or receives them. On the other hand those who wish to follow through one individual series of letters can do so with the help of the Index of Correspondents appended to each volume. (In Vol. IX the Index of Correspondents is cumulative and covers the four volumes.)

## LETTERS

| Year | To MILL | From MILL | To MALTHUS | From MALTHUS | To TROWER | From TROWER | To McCULLOCH | From McCULLOCH | To SAY | From SAY | To Other Correspondents | From Other Correspondents | To All Correspondents | From All Correspondents |
|---|---|---|---|---|---|---|---|---|---|---|---|---|---|---|
| 1810 | | 1 | | | | | | | | | 3 | | 3 | 1 |
| 1811 | 2 | 3 | 7 | 10 | | | | | | | 4 | 2 | 13 | 15 |
| 1812 | | | 3 | 2 | | | | | | | 1 | | 4 | 2 |
| 1813 | | | 6 | | 1 | | | | | | | | 7 | |
| 1814 | | 4 | 8 | 7 | 1 | 1 | | | 1 | | 2 | 3 | 12 | 15 |
| 1815 | 5 | 5 | 19 | 23 | 2 | 4 | | | 2 | 2 | 1 | 14 | 29 | 48 |
| 1816 | 7 | 7 | 10 | 7 | 3 | 6 | 2 | 1 | | | 2 | 2 | 24 | 23 |
| 1817 | 6 | 4 | 14 | 5 | 7 | 7 | | | 1 | 2 | 2 | 2 | 30 | 20 |
| 1818 | 10 | 7 | 4 | 4 | 6 | 5 | 2 | 5 | | | 5 | 5 | 27 | 26 |
| 1819 | 5 | 7 | 2 | 2 | 7 | 5 | 6 | 5 | | 1 | 7 | 5 | 27 | 25 |
| 1820 | 6 | 6 | 5 | 6 | 7 | 6 | 10 | 7 | 1 | 2 | 3 | 3 | 32 | 30 |
| 1821 | 7 | 4 | 7 | 6 | 7 | 6 | 8 | 7 | 1 | 1 | 4 | 5 | 34 | 29 |
| 1822 | 5 | | 1 | | 7 | 1 | 7 | 6 | 1 | 2 | 6 | 3 | 27 | 12 |
| 1823 | 5 | 1 | 6 | 3 | 6 | 4 | 6 | 4 | | | 4 | 1 | 27 | 13 |
| Totals | 58 | 49 | 92 | 75 | 54 | 45 | 41 | 35 | 7 | 10 | 44 | 45 | 296 | 259 |
| | 107 | | 167 | | 99 | | 76 | | 17 | | 89 | | 555 | |

The distribution of the letters between the main correspondents and their frequency at various periods can be seen at a glance from the table above. It will be noticed from the table that in each of the four main series the letters from Ricardo are more numerous than those written to him. To some extent this is probably explained by Ricardo having been less methodical in keeping letters than his correspondents were. But it may also have been due to his greater activity as a letter writer. For example, the initiative in resuming a correspondence when it had been interrupted mostly came from Ricardo's side (notably in the case of Mill).

More detailed information about the arrangement and annotation of the letters is provided at the end of this Introduction, after some account has been given of the individual correspondents.

## II. *The Main Correspondents*

JAMES MILL (1773–1836). Ricardo and James Mill were first brought together as a result of the publication of Mill's early pamphlet *Commerce Defended* in 1808: 'the first of his writings which attained any celebrity' (as John Stuart Mill writes) 'and which he prized more as having been his first introduction to the friendship of David Ricardo, the most valued and most intimate friendship of his life.'[1] Their intimacy, Ricardo tells us, however, was the consequence of the part which Ricardo took in the Bullion controversy of 1810;[2] and when their correspondence begins, at the end of 1810, we find them already on terms of close friendship. Mill characteristically came to adopt the role of educator, and Ricardo always acknowledged a large debt to him for urging him on and encouraging him to write.

Mill, who had come to London from Scotland in 1802, lived at Newington Green and later, in 1814, moved to Queen Square in Westminster (where he rented a house from Bentham). In London they met regularly, at one time taking 'almost daily'

---

[1] J. S. Mill, *Principles of Political Economy*, Bk. III, Chap. XIV, § 4; Ashley's ed., 1909, p. 563.

[2] Letter to Trower, 26 Jan. 1818, below, VII, 246.

walks together in the park,[1] so that there was little occasion for letter writing. From 1814 onwards, however, both Ricardo and Mill used to be away from London during half of each year, between July and January; Ricardo going to Gatcomb Park, while Mill, together with his family, was the guest of Bentham at Ford Abbey in Devonshire, on the border of Somerset near Chard. Their correspondence has accordingly a highly seasonal character and is confined almost entirely to that period of each year.

Mill up to 1817 was engaged in writing his *History of British India*, and made a living by contributing to the reviews. His friends, however, were anxious to find him a regular position which would secure him a steady income and independence. It was at one time intended that he should be head of the projected 'Chrestomatic School', which however never materialized.[2] In 1819, as a result of the appearance of his *History* and with the assistance of Ricardo and other friends, he secured an appointment with the East India Company as assistant examiner of correspondence.[3] From that time he was so occupied at the office that his meetings with Ricardo were usually confined to Sundays.[4] For the period of his vacation in the summer he went first to Marlow and from 1822 to Dorking. On several occasions he visited Ricardo at Gatcomb; in October 1814 going there (as he wrote) with 'all my incumbrances, consisting of a wife, and five brats, and a maid';[5] in August 1818 he was there alone for ten days;[6] in August and September 1820 'for more than three weeks';[7] and he was expecting to spend at Gatcomb the second half of September 1823, the month of Ricardo's death.[8]

Much of the discussion in Ricardo's correspondence with Mill arises from their reading one another's manuscripts. We find Ricardo reporting on his work and on his reading to Mill, and

---

[1] Letter to Malthus, 25 May 1818, below, VII, 263.
[2] See below, VII, 182, n. 1.
[3] For details on Mill's post, see below, VIII, 40, n.
[4] See letter to Trower, 13 March 1820, below, VIII, 162.

[5] Below, p. 137. Four more children were born subsequently; in all four sons and five daughters.
[6] Below, VII, 285, 292, 293, n.
[7] Below, VIII, 231, and cp. 241, n.
[8] Below, IX, 329, 333.

Mill in return giving him advice on his writing and suggestions for reading. While the sterner side of James Mill's character is well-known from the description in John Stuart Mill's *Autobiography*, these letters show another and more genial aspect of him.

There are in these letters several indications of Ricardo's friendly interest in Mill's eldest son, John Stuart Mill, such as Ricardo's invitation that he should come by himself to stay at Gatcomb in the summer of 1821, when he was fifteen years old.[1] These are borne out by the passage in J. S. Mill's *Autobiography*, in which he speaks of his connection with Ricardo: 'My being an habitual inmate of my father's study made me acquainted with the dearest of his friends, David Ricardo, who by his benevolent countenance, and kindliness of manner, was very attractive to young persons, and who after I became a student of political economy, invited me to his house and to walk with him in order to converse on the subject.'[2] There are, however, no letters between them,[3] although Ricardo's last letter to James Mill of 5 September 1823 can be regarded as virtually directed to John, since it is entirely devoted to the discussion of a paper written by him on the measure of value.

The letters of James Mill to Ricardo are in the Ricardo Papers.[4] The letters which he received from Ricardo were carefully filed and docketed by James Mill. Together with the papers which were sent to him at Ricardo's death (among them unpublished manuscripts and two letters from Malthus and one from McCulloch received by Ricardo a short time before) they form what we have called the Mill-Ricardo papers.[5] These were inherited by John Stuart Mill, and from him (it is not clear whether before or after his death) they passed to his friend John Elliot

---

[1] Below, IX, 44 and 104, and cp. 48 and 115.
[2] *Autobiography*, 1873, p. 54.
[3] What was believed to be 'a juvenile note by John Stuart Mill' addressed to Ricardo (*Minor Papers*, ed. by J. H. Hollander, 1932, p. 229) turns out to be a postscript by James Mill to one of his own letters (see below, IX, 331, n. 3).
[4] Two of these (letters 413 and 539), found earlier, were printed in Ricardo's *Minor Papers*, ed. by J. H. Hollander, Baltimore, The Johns Hopkins Press, 1932.
[5] With the exception of letter 370, which is among the Bentham MSS at University College, London.

Cairnes, the economist;[1] it was among the Cairnes family possessions that they were found by Mr C. K. Mill in 1943 and made available for the present edition (as has been described in the General Preface in Volume I).

By the time these letters to Mill were found, however, the rest of the correspondence had been annotated and made up into page. The newly-found letters were inserted in their proper chronological order, efforts being made to disturb as little as possible the work already done; in particular avoiding the transfer of notes from the old to the new letters unless essential. As a result the letters of Ricardo to Mill are less fully annotated than the others: for example, in the case of letters 506 to 509, written from abroad in 1822, no biographical notes are given about the persons whom Ricardo met, since notes had already been attached to the *Journal of a Tour on the Continent* (to be included in Vol. X), where the same persons recur.

THOMAS ROBERT MALTHUS (1766–1834). The correspondence between Malthus and Ricardo began in June 1811, when, immediately following their first meeting, both of them, independently, started to write to one another. Malthus's letter, however, reached Ricardo before Ricardo had sent his own, which he had to adapt accordingly. Malthus's letter and the first draft of Ricardo's opened with curiously similar words, to the effect that, 'as we are *mainly* on the same side of the question', as Malthus wrote, or 'as we are so nearly agreed on the principles', as Ricardo put it, they should endeavour to remove the few points of difference between them by 'amicable discussion in private', as they both said in identical words.[2]

---

[1] A parallel is found in the fate of the copy of the first edition of the *Principles* (1817) which Ricardo presented to James Mill and which is now in the Library of the London School of Economics. It is inscribed (not in Ricardo's hand) 'From the Author', and contains the following note written by Lord Courtney on the inside of the cover: 'This volume was presented by the author to James Mill, from whom it passed to John Stuart Mill, by whom it was given to John Elliot Cairnes, on whose death I selected it from his books in accordance with his death bed request July 1875   Leonard H. Courtney'.
[2] Below, pp. 21 and 24, n. 1. The subject of discussion was Bullion,

This first meeting had taken place on Malthus's initiative and perhaps through the intermediary of their mutual friend Richard Sharp, who is frequently mentioned in these early letters as a participant in joint breakfast parties at which Ricardo and Malthus met.

At the time of their first meeting, while Ricardo had only just appeared in print, Malthus had long been known to the public as the author of the *Essay on Population*, which, having been first published in 1798, was now in its fourth edition. Malthus had been educated at Jesus College, Cambridge, where he succeeded to a Fellowship in 1793. His College tutor had been William Frend, who in the same year became the centre of a storm in the University, being attacked for Jacobinism and irreverence to religion.[1] Later Malthus took orders and in 1798 obtained a curacy at Albury in his native county of Surrey. From 1806, and throughout the period of his correspondence with Ricardo, he was Professor of History and Political Economy at the East India College at Haileybury, Hertfordshire, which was a residential establishment for the training of cadets for the Company's service. The College was well-known for the unruliness of its students: a matter which is often referred to in the letters. The Professors lived in with their families and Malthus occupied the house under the college clock-turret.[2]

Ricardo from time to time paid week-end visits to Haileybury to stay with Malthus, and Malthus made frequent visits to London where he invariably had meetings with Ricardo, sometimes staying at his house, first at Mile End and then in Upper Brook Street. Later, on several occasions Malthus, who regularly spent his vacations at Bath with the Eckersalls, his wife's relatives, on his way visited Ricardo at Gatcomb Park in Gloucestershire.

While the Malthus-Ricardo letters are less influenced than the other series by the passing events of the day, and approach more

on which they had been having a 'controversy in print', as Malthus calls it in his first letter. On that stage, see above, III, 10–12.

[1] Frend will be noticed again, in Volume X, as an early acquaintance of Ricardo.

[2] *Memorials of Old Haileybury College*, by F. C. Danvers and others, Westminster, 1894, p. 199.

nearly to a systematic discussion, yet they range over the whole wide field of their disagreement and do not lend themselves to a classification by subjects. However, at some periods one topic becomes dominant. Thus in the early period of 1811–12 the correspondence is exclusively devoted to currency and foreign exchange; the crowded letters of the spring of 1815 are concerned with rent, profits and the price of corn; those of 1820 and the early summer of 1821, with the causes of stagnation and the possibility of a general glut; and the final group of 1823, with the revived controversy upon the measure of value.

Although Malthus had a son and two daughters, none of these left any children; so that Ricardo's letters passed to the descendants of Malthus's elder brother, Sydenham.[1] It was the latter's grandson, Col. Sydenham Malthus, who placed them at the disposal of Dr Bonar for his original publication. Col. Malthus's son, Mr Robert Malthus, formerly of Albury, Surrey, has made the MSS available for the present edition.

Ricardo's letters were known to William Empson, who as Professor of Law had been for many years Malthus's colleague at Haileybury, and he quoted a number of passages in his biographical article on Malthus in the *Edinburgh Review* of January 1837. The letters were published under the title of *Letters of David Ricardo to Thomas Robert Malthus 1810–1823*, edited by James Bonar, Oxford, Clarendon Press, 1887.[2]

The letters of Malthus, on the other hand, remained for a long time undiscovered. Dr Bonar caused the representatives of Ricardo, as he says in his preface, 'to make search for the corresponding letters of Malthus, but without success'. These finally came to light with the Ricardo Papers, which Mr Frank Ricardo made available for the present edition.[3]

---

[1] On the other hand his library (after passing into the possession of his son, the Rev. Henry Malthus) went to the descendants of his sister, Mrs Bray, and in 1949 was presented by Mr R. A. Bray to Jesus College, Cambridge.

[2] Letter 454 from Ricardo came only recently to light and was published by Professor Viner in 1933. Letters 12 and 14 have not been previously published.

[3] Malthus's letter 62 was published by Professor Foxwell in the *Economic Journal* in 1907, and letter 540 was included in *Letters to M<sup>c</sup>Culloch*, 1895. For the location of the MSS of these separated letters

There are in Bonar's edition a number of mistakes in the dating of letters; these have had the effect of muddling the sequence of development of Ricardo's thought and have stood in the way of a proper study of that development. The first instance is that of the letters attributed to 1810, which turn out to belong to 1813.[1] This has had the consequence (apart from antedating the beginning of the friendship between Ricardo and Malthus) of advancing by three years the formation of Ricardo's theory of profits, which is first outlined in those letters, and of concealing the fact that up to 1813 Ricardo's concern was almost exclusively with monetary questions.[2] No less serious has been the misdating of Ricardo's letter to Malthus of 5 March 1817, which in that edition is given as of 1816.[3] Since this letter mentions the last chapter of Ricardo's *Principles* as being ready to go to the printers, this error has made it seem that that work had already been completed at a time when the writing of it was in fact in the initial phase, and it has accordingly made it difficult to reconstruct the stages in which the book was put together. Two other errors are of minor importance: the letter of 8 May 1815 is there misdated Oct. 1815, and that of 3 April 1817 is misdated 3 June 1817.[4]

Numerous short passages of a personal nature were omitted in Bonar's edition; these have been restored in the present edition without specific mention.

JOHN RAMSAY McCULLOCH (1789–1864). Ricardo's connection with McCulloch had its beginning in 1816 when McCulloch sent him from Edinburgh successively two pamphlets on the National Debt. But the real start of their correspondence was when McCulloch reviewed the *Principles of Political Economy* in the *Edinburgh Review* for June 1818. In this review, which was decisive in establishing Ricardo's fame and popularizing his

(among them letters 536 and 545, in the Mill-Ricardo papers) see footnotes to the letters.

[1] This no doubt arose from Ricardo's '3' in those cases being written like a broken 'O'. These are letters 39, 40, 41, 42 and 43.

Similar in form, though unimportant, is the misdating of letter 76 as of 10 (instead of 13) Feb. 1815.

[2] Cp. above, IV, 3.

[3] Letter 206. This arose from a slip of the pen in the original MS.

[4] Letters 96 and 213.

doctrines, he showed himself the most complete convert and disciple of Ricardo's theories, as he was to become the main defender of his doctrines against criticism. Over the next five years they corresponded regularly; but it was not until 1823 that they met, when M^cCulloch came to London for a visit of six weeks in May and June and a number of discussions took place between them during these weeks.

M^cCulloch's chief occupation at this time was on the staff of the *Scotsman* newspaper. This had been founded by a group of Reformers as a weekly in 1817 (becoming bi-weekly in 1823) in order to oppose the dominance of the Scottish Tories. M^cCulloch became at first a contributor and later for a time the editor. He wrote all the political economy in the paper, often devoting to it the leading article, or 'disquisition', which occupied the whole front page. As the *Edinburgh Review* said: 'Scotland boasts but one original newspaper, the *Scotsman*, and that newspaper but one subject—Political Economy.—The Editor, however, may be said to be king of it.'[1] At the end of 1819 Ricardo was induced to become a regular subscriber, and thereafter comment on these articles was a frequent subject of their correspondence.

After Ricardo's death M^cCulloch came to be regarded as the main representative of the Ricardian tradition. At the end of 1823 a committee of Ricardo's friends was formed to institute a series of lectures on Political Economy in London in his memory; and M^cCulloch was chosen as lecturer in 1824. He was author of the most widely known biography of Ricardo; and in 1846 the editor of his *Works*.

Passages from Ricardo's letters were quoted by M^cCulloch in his *Literature of Political Economy*, 1845 (p. 177–8), in the 'Life' prefixed to his edition of Ricardo's *Works*, 1846 (p. xxvi), with some additional quotations in the reprint of the 'Life' in M^cCulloch's *Treatises and Essays* (2nd ed. 1859, pp. 559 and 562), and later by Hugh G. Reid in the Biographical Notice of M^cCulloch in the 1869 edition of the latter's *Dictionary of Commerce*.

[1] 'The Periodical Press' in *Edinburgh Review*, May 1823, p. 369. This article (which is frequently quoted in notes to these volumes) is attributed to William Hazlitt.

After M$^c$Culloch's death the letters passed into the possession of his executors, and the last survivor of them, his biographer and son-in-law Reid, presented them to the British Museum in 1894, where they are entered under the class-mark Add. MSS. 34,545. They were published under the title of *Letters of David Ricardo to John Ramsay M$^c$Culloch 1816–1823*, edited by J. H. Hollander, in the 'Publications of the American Economic Association', vol. x, Nos. 5–6, Sept. and Nov. 1895.

The letters of M$^c$Culloch to Ricardo were found among the Ricardo Papers.[1] Some of M$^c$Culloch's letters however (17 out of 35) were in the bundle found earlier (1919) by Mr Frank Ricardo and these were published as a pamphlet in the series 'A Reprint of Economic Tracts', edited by J. H. Hollander, under the title *Letters of John Ramsay M$^c$Culloch to David Ricardo 1818–1823*, Baltimore, The Johns Hopkins Press, 1931. The others were found in 1930 and are published here for the first time.

HUTCHES TROWER (1777–1833). Unlike the other main correspondents of Ricardo, Trower has no claim to literary fame in his own right; he is only remembered because of this correspondence. He was, like Ricardo, a stockbroker and their friendship had been formed in the early years of the century, when they were accustomed to meet daily and to pursue their discussions amid 'the tumultuous scenes' of the Stock Exchange. They found common ground as admirers of the work of Adam Smith and of the articles on political economy which had appeared in the early numbers of the *Edinburgh Review* from 1802.[2] As we have seen,[3] they found themselves on opposite sides in the early stages of the Bullion controversy in 1809, when both contributed anonymously to the *Morning Chronicle*; and it was only after publication that Ricardo discovered the identity of his critic.

Trower's mother was a Miss Smith, aunt of Sydney Smith, the essayist; he was born at Clapton on 2 July 1777 and was adopted by a Mr Palmer who made him his heir. He became a member of

---

[1] Except letter 541 which came to light with the Mill-Ricardo papers.
[2] See the reminiscent passages in

Ricardo's letter to Trower of 26 Jan. 1818, below, VII, 246.
[3] Above, III, 4–5.

the new Stock Exchange on its foundation in 1802, and retired in 1812, when his partnership with his brother, John Trower, was dissolved; the business being thereafter carried on by the latter until his own retirement in 1822.[1] In 1813 he married Penelope Frances, daughter of Gilbert Slater or Sclater. The following year he purchased as a country residence Unsted Wood, at Godalming, Surrey. This was the same year as Ricardo acquired Gatcomb Park; and thereafter the correspondence between them settled down to a fairly regular exchange at roughly monthly intervals.[2] Trower never visited Gatcomb, despite repeated invitations; and when at last he agreed to come, Ricardo's death intervened before the date arranged for the visit. Trower himself died on 5 June 1833 from an injury to the spine. He left four daughters, and his widow lived until 1875.

(The information in the preceding paragraph, except that relating to the Stock Exchange, was supplied by his daughter, Miss Frances Trower, in 1895, a year before her death, to Bonar and Hollander, and it is here taken from the Introduction to their edition of Ricardo's *Letters to Trower*.)

After Trower's death Ricardo's letters appear to have become divided into two groups. The first group was composed of the last 24 letters addressed by Ricardo to Trower (together with the two letters of Anthony Austin), and was donated by Mrs Trower 'through Mr Greenough'[3] to the Library of University College, London (according to an entry dated 22 Feb. 1844 in 'Additions to the Library'). The second group, consisting of the 30 earliest letters to Trower, remained undiscovered among Trower's papers until in 1895 they were found by Miss Trower. Eventually this second group of letters also was presented to the Library of University College by the executors of Miss Trower; and the whole was published in *Letters of David Ricardo to Hutches*

[1] 'List of the Members of the Stock Exchange from its Establishment in 1802', compiled by George Webb, Sec., 1855, and Minutes of the Stock Exchange Committee for General Purposes, entry of 6 July 1812 (MSS in the possession of the Stock Exchange; quoted by kind permission of the Secretary).

[2] See Trower's reference to 'our ordinary course of correspondence', below, IX, 315.

[3] This was George Bellas Greenough, the geologist, a friend of Ricardo and Trower.

*Trower and Others 1811–1823*, edited by James Bonar and J. H. Hollander, Oxford, Clarendon Press, 1899.

Trower's letters to Ricardo came to light with the Ricardo Papers.[1]

JEAN-BAPTISTE SAY (1767–1832) was given a commercial education in France and England, but his prospects of a business career were brought to an end by his father's ruin in the collapse of the Assignats. He turned to literary activities, and in 1803 published his *Traité d'Économie politique*. This work, however, found no favour with the authorities, and Say went into industry, establishing a spinning mill of 400 workers in the country near Paris. Shortly before the fall of Napoleon he sold his interest to his partner, and returned to Paris. In 1814, following the change of government, he was enabled to publish a second edition of his *Traité*. In the autumn of the same year he was sent to England on a government mission to report upon the progress of industry. Here he was introduced by William Godwin to Francis Place, and through Mill to Ricardo, whom he visited at Gatcomb Park. From Gatcomb Ricardo and Say went together to visit Bentham at Ford Abbey.[2] This was the beginning of Say's correspondence with Ricardo, which was from time to time revived by the publication of their respective works which they sent to one another. They met again on the occasion of Ricardo's visits to Paris in 1817 and 1822, but Ricardo did not find him a ready talker on economic subjects.[3] In 1821 Say was appointed to the Chair of Industrial Economy newly established at the Conservatoire des Arts et Métiers in Paris. While from this time he devoted himself mainly to academic and literary pursuits, he was also occasionally concerned with projects of commercial speculation, in which in his letters he tried to interest Ricardo without success.[4]

Of Ricardo's regular correspondents, Say is the one who more nearly seems to be writing with an eye to eventual publication (on

[1] Of these, two (letters 534 and 547), which had become separated from the rest, were published by Hollander in Ricardo's *Minor Papers*, Baltimore, 1932.

[2] See below, pp. 156–61.
[3] See below, IX, 244 and cp. below, p. 161.
[4] See below, VII, 166 and 224–6.

one occasion he suggested that his letter should be communicated to the Political Economy Club by Ricardo).[1] It is therefore not surprising to find him soon after Ricardo's death making tentative arrangements for publication, although these came to nothing. The first hint was in his 'Examen critique du discours de M. Mac-Culloch sur l'économie politique' which appeared in the *Revue Encyclopédique* for September 1825. This was a general attack on Ricardo's theories and in order, as he says, to forestall the reproach of not having before made known his opinion of the doctrines of Ricardo, he writes: 'on verra peut-être quelque jour, par notre correspondance, que, si j'ai evité de le combattre sous les yeux du public, je soutenais néanmoins à huis clos contre lui, quelques combats dans l'interêt de la vérité.'[2] It would seem that Say had intended actually to publish his own letters as an appendix to the article (and possibly also a translation of Ricardo's letters), since the following MS notice is appended to his own copy of it: 'Les lettres originales de David Ricardo qui font partie de cette correspondance sont déposées au bureau de la Revue Encyclopédique, rue D'Enfer-St-Michel Numéro 18 à Paris, où l'on peut en prendre connaissance.'[3]

It is unlikely that this publication by 'deposit' did in fact take place. But a few weeks later (in November 1825) we find Say writing to Francis Place[4] with a view to the translation and publication in English of a small volume containing his correspondence with Ricardo and a few other pieces. However, in January 1826, after receiving a specimen of Place's translation, Say seems to have changed his mind; and in a letter of 18 January, written partly in English and partly in French, he writes that while comparing Place's English with his own French 'some scruples got into my head', among them the question, 'What will Ricardo's family think of the publication?' He announces his intention of abandoning the project, and expresses regret for the wasted work

[1] See below, IX, 36.
[2] *Revue Encylopédique*, vol. 27, p. 719. Reprinted under the above title in Say's *Œuvres diverses*, p. 279.
[3] MS in Say's papers; kindly communicated (with another note quoted below, p. xxvii) by M. Raoul-Duval.
[4] Letters from Say to Place, 11 and 27 Nov. 1825 (unpublished MSS in British Museum, Add. 35,153, fols. 229–33).

of Place and himself—as regards the latter, adding a significant phrase on the trouble he has taken about his correspondence with Ricardo: 'Je regrette d'avoir pris la peine de mettre au net ma correspondance avec Ricardo';[1] which perhaps explains some of the discrepancies that are noticeable between the version of Say's letters which was subsequently published and the original MSS in the Ricardo Papers.[2]

Besides his scruples, a more decisive reason may have been Say's dissatisfaction with what he had seen of Place's translation; for on the folder containing the sample MS which he had received, and which is among his papers, he noted: 'Il s'y trouve la traduction anglaise que Francis Place avait essayé d'en faire, et qui ne vaut rien.'

Despite these *contretemps*, Ricardo's letters to Say were among his first to be published: they appeared (in French translation), with some of Say's replies, in Say's *Mélanges et Correspondance d'économie politique*, a posthumous collection edited by his son-in-law, Charles Comte (Paris, Chamerot, 1833), and were re-printed in Say's *Œuvres diverses* (Paris, Guillaumin, 1848), a volume in the 'Collection des principaux économistes'.

In the present edition Ricardo's letters to Say are published in the original English from the MSS. These letters are among J.-B. Say's papers, and were placed at the disposal of the editor before the war by their owner, M. Edgar Raoul-Duval, of le Havre, a great-grandson of J.-B. Say.

The MSS of Say's letters to Ricardo are among the Ricardo Papers. A number of them are here published for the first time in the original version[3] as they were received by Ricardo.[4]

---

[1] Say to Place, 18 Jan. 1826 (*ib.* fol. 235). See also letters of 7 March and 5 April 1826 (*ib.* fols. 236–7) and Say's letter to Tooke, 14 May 1826 (misdated 1825) in *Œuvres diverses*, p. 525.

[2] See below, p. 273 and IX, 31, n. and 188, n.

[3] Say's letter 356 however, since the MS is not extant, has had to be reprinted from the published version.

[4] Exceptions regarding the location of MSS are Ricardo's letter 108, which is in the Moscow Historical Museum, and Say's letters 347, which is in the library of Professor Hollander, and 393 which is in the Baker Library of Harvard University. The original versions of letters 446, 496 and 498 and a copy of 488, which were in the bundle of Ricardo Papers found in 1919, were published in Ricardo's *Minor Papers*, ed. by J. H. Hollander, Baltimore, 1932.

## III. *Other Correspondents*

JEREMY BENTHAM (1748–1832). At the time of this correspondence Bentham had ceased for some years to be occupied
with economic questions and had become absorbed in projects of
law reform. When exactly he first met Ricardo is uncertain; but it
is clear that it was Mill, with whom both had been acquainted for
some time, who introduced them to one another not long after
the summer of 1811.[1] The letters between them are in the nature
of occasional notes and are clearly not part of a continuous
correspondence. These, together with other pieces of evidence,
give a picture, however, of fairly close personal contact between
them over the years, this contact being maintained mainly through
Mill. Once, in 1814, Ricardo visited Bentham at Ford Abbey
with Say; on occasions, in London he dined with Bentham at his
house in Queen Square Place, and they went for walks together,
as is shown, for instance, by the allusion in a letter of 1820 to
meeting in the Green Park 'at the usual hour'.[2] Bowring records
that Bentham used to boast: 'I was the spiritual father of Mill,
and Mill was the spiritual father of Ricardo: so that Ricardo was
my spiritual grandson.'[3]

A few letters exchanged between Ricardo and Bentham have
been omitted in these volumes as being of insufficient interest: they
concern details of the abortive business of setting up the Chrestomathic School planned by Bentham. This was intended to be an

---

[1] They had not yet met in the
winter of 1810–11 when Ricardo at
the request of Mill wrote his *Notes
on Bentham* (which have been
given in Volume III); nor in
August 1811 when Bentham invited Ricardo to take a house near
Barrow Green, in Surrey, where he
was spending the summer together
with Mill: see Ricardo's first letter,
below, p. 46.
[2] Below, VIII, 191. Cp. also
Bentham's reference to Ricardo:
'We used to walk together in Hyde
Park, and he reported to me what

passed in the House of Commons'.
(Quoted in 'Memoirs of Bentham',
by J. Bowring, in Bentham's
*Works*, 1843, vol. x, p. 498.)
[3] *ib.* p. 498. Bowring, in his own
memoirs written many years later,
seems to have confused their relations when, after saying that it
was *Ricardo* who introduced Mill
to Bentham, gives Bentham's dic-
tum as: 'I begot Ricardo and
Ricardo begot Mill'. (*Autobio-
graphical Recollections* of Sir John
Bowring, 1877, p. 68.)

extension to higher (*i.e.* secondary) education of the Lancaster System, which was a method of instruction based on the teaching of lessons by a master to 'monitors', who in turn taught the other pupils. A nation-wide association had been started in 1810, the Royal Lancastrian Association, to which 'the existing system of popular education in England can be traced directly back'.[1] Bentham wrote a plan for a Chrestomathic School and sent it to Ricardo in 1814 to elicit his support, which Ricardo promised to give in the form of a subscription. In 1816 a committee was formed to further the project, with Francis Place as secretary and Ricardo and Mill among its members. In 1817 it was proposed that Ricardo should buy the ground in the centre of Leicester Square and make it available for building the school. Ricardo had almost completed the purchase at a price of £3300,[2] when, on hearing that the shopkeepers in the square had threatened legal action to stop any building on this site, he refused to proceed with the purchase rather than become involved in litigation, and the proposal was abandoned. An alternative project was to build the School in Bentham's garden in Queen Square Place. Prolonged negotiations ensued on the clauses of the lease which Bentham was to grant to the School, negotiations in which Ricardo took part. Bentham, however, became increasingly difficult to satisfy, and no agreement could be reached. This was soon followed by the abandonment of the whole scheme. The committee was wound up in 1821, and the sums contributed were returned to the subscribers.

These fruitless negotiations over a period of six or seven years have left their trace in a number of letters and papers in which Ricardo is concerned. The MSS of these letters are in various places: (i) The British Museum Newspaper Library, Place Collection of Newspaper Cuttings, vol. 60, 'Chrestomathic School' (which includes *inter alia* the Minutes Book of the Committee of the School); (ii) University College, London, Bentham MSS, case 165; (iii) the Ricardo Papers. Of these letters only those which contain passages referring to other matters have been

---

[1] Graham Wallas, *Life of Francis Place*, 1898, p. 93.

[2] See letter to Mill of 12 Sept. 1817, below, VII, 190.

ncluded in the present volumes (although every letter, if included, has been given in full). All the others are unpublished. It may be convenient to list the letters in which Ricardo is involved, with their location:

Ricardo to Bentham and Mill, 15 July 1814. MS at University College, London. Letter 52 in the present edition. (Promises subscription.)

Ricardo to Place, from Upper Brook St., 5 April 1816. MS in Place Collection of Newspaper Cuttings, vol. 60, No. 11, fol. 2. (Accepts office as a manager of the School.)

Ricardo to Place, from Upper Brook St., 10 July 1816. MS in Place Collection of Newspaper Cuttings, vol. 60, No. 13, fol. 8. (Apologises for being unable to attend a meeting of the committee and announces collection of £1000 for the fund.)

Ricardo to Place, from Gatcomb Park, 7 Aug. 1817. MS in Place Collection of Newspaper Cuttings, vol. 60, No. 14, fol. 4. (Intimates his willingness to buy a piece of ground in the centre of Leicester Square and to lease it to the School.)

Ricardo to Place, from Gatcomb Park, 17 Aug. 1817. MS in Place Collection of Newspaper Cuttings, vol. 60, No. 14, fol. 6. (Announces that he is proceeding with the purchase of the ground in Leicester Square.)

Ricardo to Place, from Gatcomb Park, 18 Sept. 1817. MS in Place Collection of Newspaper Cuttings, vol. 60, No. 14, fol. 8. (Informs him that he has received news from his solicitors 'that the shopkeepers of the Square are resolved by every means in their power to prevent the Ground being built on', and that he has replied that unless the right to build was guaranteed he would decline the purchase.)

Bentham to Ricardo, from Queen Square Place, 16 May 1820. MS in *R.P.* (Asks him for details of a lease of land for a building for the Geological Society, as a precedent for the Chrestomathic School.)

Ricardo to Bentham, from Upper Brook St., 17 May 1820. MS at University College, London. (Replies that the lease to the Geological Society, of which he is one of the trustees, was not of land but of a house.)

Ricardo to Bentham, 18 May 1820. MS at University College, London. Letter 367 in the present edition. (Postpones a meeting.)

Bentham to Ricardo, 17 June 1820. MS in *R.P.* Letter 369 in the present edition. (Wishes the School to be in his garden so as to be under the inspection of James Mill; refers to the education of J. S. Mill.)

Bentham to Ricardo, from Queen Square Place, 2 July 1820. MS in *R.P.*; copy at University College, London. (Discusses details of the draft agreement for the lease of his garden for building the School [A letter from Mill to Ricardo which was enclosed is not extant].)

Ricardo to Mill, 3 July 1820. MS at University College, London; a partial copy in Bentham's handwriting in Place Collection of Newspaper Cuttings, vol. 60, No. 25. Letter 370 in the present edition. (On the draft agreement for the lease, in reply to the missing letter from Mill mentioned under the preceding item.)

Bentham to Ricardo, from Queen Square Place, 6 July 1820. MS in *R.P.* (Arranging for a meeting of the committee.)

Bentham to Ricardo, from Queen Square Place, 7 July 1820. MS in *R.P.* (Continues discussion of the details of the agreement.)

Ricardo to Place, from Gatcomb Park, 4 Aug. 1821. MS in Place Collection of Newspaper Cuttings, vol. 60, No. 26, fol. 8. (Concerns the winding-up of the committee; expresses anxiety 'that the money should be divided amongst the subscribers according to their respective claims with as little delay as possible'.)

Place to Ricardo, from London, 21 Sept. 1821. MS in *R.P.* A postscript concerning Place's book is quoted below, IX, 58, n. (Sends the final accounts of the School.)

Ricardo to Place, from Gatcomb Park, 23 Sept. 1821. MS in Place Collection of Newspaper Cuttings, vol. 60, No. 26, fol. 11. (Deals with the winding-up of the fund and repayment to the subscribers.)

In addition to the letters, there is in the Place Collection of Newspaper Cuttings, vol. 60, No. 25, a series of observations, in Ricardo's handwriting, on Bentham's draft agreement for the lease of his garden for the building of the school; each observation is followed by a reply in Bentham's handwriting. This paper is undated, but is referred to in Ricardo's letter to Mill of 3 July 1820 and is clearly contemporary with it.

MARIA EDGEWORTH (1767–1849). At the time of these letters Miss Edgeworth was at the height of her fame as a novelist. When her correspondence with Ricardo begins, we find them on terms of established friendship; and in writing they are accustomed to refer to one another as 'cousins'.[1] In fact, the first letter between her and Ricardo is some weeks after she had been staying, with her two sisters, Fanny and Harriet, at Gatcomb Park in November 1821 as the guests of the Ricardos.[2] Yet there is no earlier evidence of their acquaintance than a reference in a letter of Maria Edgeworth to her half-sister Honora of 26 Dec. 1820 (when she was staying with the Smiths[3] at Easton Grey), which is franked by Ricardo. 'Why I asked for a frank at all I cannot tell' (she writes) 'except for the honour and glory of having one from David Ricardo. He has been here one whole day and is exceedingly agreeable'.[4] In 1822 she was again in London with her sisters; and in her letters home she refers repeatedly to 'our delightful breakfasts at Mr Ricardos'.[5]

Both sides of the correspondence with Maria Edgeworth (with the exception of one letter) are among the few letters which had long been known to be in the possession of the Ricardo family at Bromesberrow Place, Ledbury. Ricardo's side of the correspondence must have been returned to his family after his death by Maria Edgeworth or her heirs. In 1907 the *Economic Journal*, to which they had been made available, published in its issue of September 1907 extensive extracts from Ricardo's letters and from two (out of five) of Maria Edgeworth's. The MSS of these letters are referred to in these volumes as part of the Ricardo Papers.

One letter from Ricardo (letter 502), however, remained among Maria Edgeworth's papers which are in the possession of

---

[1] See below, IX, 240, 274, 295. There is no indication that they were actually related, either directly or through Mrs Ricardo.
[2] Her own description of this visit will be given in Volume X.
[3] See below, p. 135, n.
[4] *A Memoir of Maria Edgeworth*, by Mrs Edgeworth [her stepmother] 'Not Published', London 1867,

vol. II, p. 136. (Much of the material of the *Memoir* is reproduced in the published *Life and Letters of Maria Edgeworth*, ed. by A. J. C. Hare, 2 vols., London, Arnold, 1894.)
[5] Letter of 9 March 1822, *Memoir*, vol. II, p. 180; and cp. letter dated Feb. 1822, *ib*. p. 175. See also below, IX, 230.

her niece, Mrs Harriet J. Butler. This was made available through the kindness of Mrs Butler's son, Professor H. E. Butler.

PASCOE GRENFELL (1761–1838) was one of the leading speakers on financial subjects in the House of Commons. After Ricardo's entry into Parliament Grenfell often sided with him on economic questions, although he strongly disagreed with the radicalism of Ricardo's political views. He had a large business in the City as a metal merchant, and his country seat was Taplow House in Buckinghamshire. It was at his suggestion that Ricardo undertook in 1815 to write a pamphlet attacking the policy of the Bank of England, which took shape in *Proposals for an Economical and Secure Currency*. Most of Grenfell's letters belong to that period and consist of promptings and information for the proposed pamphlet.[1]

The letters of Ricardo to Grenfell have not been found, although in 1933 searches were made, at the request of Lord Keynes, by the representatives of the two branches of the Grenfell family (both descended from the eldest son of Pascoe Grenfell): Lord Desborough, of Taplow Court, and Mr E. C. Grenfell, M.P. for the City of London.

GEORGE GROTE (1794–1871), the historian of Greece, was partner in the banking house of Grote and Prescott. He became acquainted with Ricardo in 1817,[2] and through him was introduced to the Benthamite circle.[3] We have only a fragment of a letter of Ricardo to him; but he was one of the young students of political economy to whom what John Stuart Mill says of himself (in the passage quoted above, p. xvii) with reference to Ricardo's kindliness to young persons could well be applied. Like John Mill, Grote used to be invited to Ricardo's house and to walk and converse on the

---

[1] One letter from Grenfell, dated 8 Aug. 1823, which is like the others in the Ricardo Papers, has been by exception omitted since it has no connection with the others and deals purely with the appointment of Ricardo as umpire in connection with the purchase of a process for manufacturing copper.

[2] *Personal Life of George Grote*, by Mrs Grote, London, Murray, 1873, p. 12.

[3] J. S. Mill, *Autobiography*, 1873, p. 72.

subject, as it appears from his diary for 1819, of which the following are extracts:[1]

'*Tuesday, March 23rd.* Rose at 6. Read Kant, and ate a little bread and butter, till ½ past 8, when I went up to Brook Street to breakfast with Mr Ricardo; was very politely received by him; walked with him and Mr Mill in St. James's Park until near 12, when I went into the City; my mother in town this day. Between 4 and 5 read some more Kant; dined at ½ past 5; wrote out again in the evening some of my remarks upon Foreign trade, and arranged them in a different manner. Bed at 11.

'*Saturday, March 27th.* Rose at 6. Finished my remarks on Foreign trade, and enclosed them to Ricardo. Studied some more of Kant...I read a chapter in Ricardo's "Pol. Econ." Bed at 11.

'*Sunday, March 28th.* Rose at ½ past 5. Studied Kant until ½ past 8, when I set off to breakfast with Mr. Ricardo. Met Mr. Mill there, and enjoyed some most interesting and instructive discourse with them, indoors and out (walking in Kensington Gardens), until ½ past 3, when I mounted my horse and set off to Beckenham. Was extremely exhausted with fatigue and hunger when I arrived there, and ate and drank plentifully, which quenched my intellectual vigour for the night. Bed at ½ past 10.'

Grote's 'remarks upon Foreign trade' referred to in the diary can be identified with an unsigned MS essay on the theory of comparative costs which is among the Ricardo Papers. This consists of twelve pages under the title 'Foreign Trade': it is in the same handwriting and has the same general appearance as Grote's papers on political economy in the British Museum,[2] which belong to this period.

FRANCIS HORNER (1778–1817) had been one of the founders of the *Edinburgh Review*, and was the chairman of the Bullion Committee in 1810. Ricardo's first letter to him, which opens this collection, is in the nature of a supplement to his own *High*

---

[1] *Personal Life*, p. 36–7.    [2] Add. MSS. 29,530.

*Price of Bullion.*[1] It was written a few days after Horner's motion in the House of Commons which led to the appointment of the Bullion Committee. From the formal style of this letter, it would seem that they were not well acquainted. Subsequently, they must have come into closer contact as active protagonists on the same side of the bullion controversy and owing to the many friends they had in common.

Ricardo's letters to Horner are in the possession of Lady Langman, a great-granddaughter of Francis Horner's brother Leonard.

JOHN MURRAY (1778–1843), the founder of the firm, was Ricardo's publisher, or 'bookseller' as it was then called, first in Fleet Street and after 1812 in Albemarle Street. Of his relations with Ricardo a contemporary says that, as an author, 'Mr Ricardo never made anything. He gives his works to Murray'.[2] That Ricardo claimed no royalties is confirmed by another contemporary, who says that he surrendered the *Principles* 'into the hands of his bookseller, without thinking of that remuneration which, in this day, the highest have not been found to despise'.[3] In the case of one of his pamphlets, on which he feared that Murray might make a loss, he even insisted on himself bearing any deficiency.[4]

The MSS of Ricardo's letters are in the possession of Sir John Murray, the great-grandson of Ricardo's publisher.

FRANCIS PLACE (1771–1854), the radical tailor of Charing Cross, organiser of the Westminster Reformers, was a disciple of Bentham and a friend of James Mill; and it was presumably through the latter that he became acquainted with Ricardo. His correspondence with Ricardo turned on two subjects upon which Place had concentrated his efforts, the Sinking Fund and popula-

---

[1] Several passages of the letter were actually embodied in the third edition of the *High Price of Bullion.*

[2] J. L. Mallet, in a diary entry of 14 Jan. 1820, quoted more fully below, VIII, 152, n.

[3] Obituary of Ricardo in *Windsor Express*, Sept. 1823 (by James Hitchings, who had been tutor of Ricardo's children).

[4] Below, VII, 14. On his scruples about accepting payment for his article in the *Encyclopædia Britannica*, see below, VIII, 242–3.

tion. When Ricardo was commissioned to write an article on the
Funding System in 1819, Mill asked Place to comment on the
manuscript, which led to some correspondence between them.
Ricardo's letters on that occasion were first published in the
*Economic Journal* for June 1893.[1] In 1821 Place wrote a book in
defence of Malthus against Godwin, which Ricardo read in
manuscript. On this Ricardo wrote an extensive commentary
(letter 451)[2] and recommended it to Murray for publication.
Some letters between Ricardo and Place on the business of the
committee of the proposed Chrestomathic School, which are
not included in the present collection, have been described above
in the section on Bentham.[3]

RICHARD SHARP (1759–1835) was known as 'Conversation
Sharp' and enjoyed a great reputation in Whig society and in
literary circles.[4] He was a considerable person in the City, where
'his interests were divided between the wholesale trade in hats,
carried on in Fish St., and a connection with the West Indies—
also a family one—which he developed into an extensive and
successful business, with its headquarters in Mark Lane.'[5] His
partners in Mark Lane were Samuel Boddington and George
Philips, who were also his intimate friends and are occasionally
mentioned in these volumes. He was at various times a member
of Parliament, and was Ricardo's immediate predecessor as
member for Portarlington. In 1810 he was a member of the
Bullion Committee. Although we have only two of their letters,
Sharp appears to have been among Ricardo's friends since the

---

[1] These MSS are in the British
Museum, 'Place Papers' (a collection which is distinct from the
'Place Collection of Newspaper
Cuttings', where are the Chrestomathic School letters).
[2] The MS of this is in the Seligman
Library of Columbia University.
[3] A draft letter from Place to Ricardo
dated 8 Feb. 1818 and concerned
with details of the Finance Account
for the previous year has also been
omitted as of too little interest in

the absence of Ricardo's side of
the discussion (MS in British
Museum, Add. 27,836, fol. 90).
[4] An appreciation of the character
and influence of Sharp, as 'much
more than the diner-out and the
town-wit', is given by John Morley
in 'The Life of James Mill', *Fort-
nightly Review*, 1 April 1882, pp.
496–8.
[5] Quoted by permission from Mrs
Eustace Hills' MS book mentioned
below.

early years of this correspondence, in which his name constantly recurs.

The papers of Richard Sharp are in the possession of the Hon. Mrs Eustace Hills (Nina L. Kay-Shuttleworth), who in 1933 on the basis of them wrote a biography of Richard Sharp, which has remained unpublished. She has made available Ricardo's letter and has also kindly lent the MS of her book.

Sir John Sinclair (1754–1835), the first President of the Board of Agriculture on its foundation, was responsible for the *Statistical Account of Scotland* and wrote a large number of books and pamphlets on finance and many other subjects. In his letters to him Ricardo accedes to requests for his opinion on proposals or publications by Sinclair, but is evidently unwilling to be drawn into prolonged discussion.

The five letters from Ricardo were included in *The Correspondence of the Rt. Hon. Sir John Sinclair, Bart.*, 2 vols., London, Coburn and Bentley, 1831, published in Sinclair's lifetime. There must have been some further letters; one of them evidently comes between Sinclair's letters to Ricardo of 19 and 29 Oct. 1814, and a sentence from a later one is quoted by Sinclair's biographer: ' "I am favourable to a system of banking in this country similar to that which prevails in Scotland"—Letter from David Ricardo, Esq., 25th March, 1823.'[1] The papers of Sir John Sinclair, however, have not been found. His great-grandson, Sir Archibald Sinclair, M.P., has caused a search to be made at Thurso Castle, Caithness, the family seat, without result. John Rae, when he was preparing his *Life of Adam Smith*, 1895, presumably attempted to trace these papers, in connection with a letter to Sinclair from Adam Smith of which he says that it 'is no longer extant' (p. 344).

Thomas Tooke (1774–1858), the economist, was a Russia merchant, being partner of Stephen Thornton, Brothers and Co. He gave evidence to the Committees of 1819 on the Resumption of Cash Payments, and was called by Ricardo as a witness before

[1] *Memoirs of the Life and Works of Sir John Sinclair*, by his son, the Rev. John Sinclair, 1837, vol. II, p. 307, n.

the Agricultural Committee of 1821, in which connection two of his letters to Ricardo arose. He was, with Ricardo, one of the founders of the Political Economy Club in 1821. Although he is famous as the author of the *History of Prices*, in Ricardo's lifetime he only published a first essay, the *Thoughts and Details on the High and Low Prices of the Last Thirty Years*, 1823.

Tooke's letters are in the Ricardo Papers. Enquiries were made in 1932 of Tooke's great-grandsons, Mr F. G. Padwick and Mr J. C. Padwick; but no letters of Ricardo could be found.

EDWARD WAKEFIELD (1774–1854), father of Edward Gibbon Wakefield and author of *An Account of Ireland, Statistical and Political* (1812), was a long-standing friend of Mill and Place, and was employed by Ricardo as his land agent. There is a considerable number of his letters from 1815 to 1823 in the Ricardo Papers concerning exclusively the purchase and management of Ricardo's estates. Of these, four letters have been included in the present correspondence because they deal with the acquisition of a seat in Parliament.

In the case of other correspondents whose interchange with Ricardo was limited to one letter, a brief biographical note is given with the letter or (as in the case of Étienne Dumont, below, p. 18, of John Whishaw, p. 66 and of Lord Grenville, VII, 220) where the name is first mentioned.

### IV. *The Letters in the Present Edition*

As has been said in section I, these four volumes comprise the letters to and from those persons with whom Ricardo corresponded on subjects of economic or political interest. But once a correspondent has been included, all the extant letters are given, even though some of them may be only of a personal or business character.[1]

The order in which the letters are arranged is that in which they were written or received by Ricardo. This occasionally diverges

---

[1] Exceptions to this rule have been noted above under Bentham, Grenfell and Wakefield.

from the order of the dates written at the head of each letter, such anomalies arising whenever letters cross in the post or are received after delay. An extreme example is letter 510 from Maria Edgeworth, which, having been written on 9 July 1822, just before Ricardo left for his continental tour, was received by him only on his return in December, and is therefore placed *after* a letter of November of the same year.

To the heading of each letter there is attached a footnote which gives:

(*a*)  the address on the cover whenever this is extant,

(*b*)  the location of the original MS, if available,

(*c*)  a reference to any previous publication of the letter.

It will be noticed, with regard to (*a*), that the address is more often given in the case of letters previous to Ricardo's entry into Parliament in 1819 than in subsequent ones. The reason for this disparity is that, since a lower postage was charged on letters of a single sheet,[1] there was a general tendency to write the address on the back of the letter itself, instead of using a separate sheet as cover. In the later period, however, as a member of Parliament, Ricardo had the privilege of 'franking' letters and also of receiving them free of postage; there was accordingly no longer any objection to separate covers for the address, and these were liable to be destroyed.

(A person entitled to frank letters had to write the address in his own handwriting, adding the date, with the day and the month spelt out in full, and his signature. A facsimile of this type of letter, franked by Ricardo, will be found at the end of Volume IX. This can be compared with the earlier specimen, before he was in Parliament, which is given at the end of Volume VII.)

Letters here published for the first time are recognizable by the absence of reference to previous publication. Besides, in the Contents and in the Index of Correspondents in each volume such new letters are denoted by an asterisk. In the case of letters which are only partly new, however, the sole indication of this is

---

[1] The postage had to be paid by the recipient, which incidentally helps to explain the occasional tone of apology by a writer for any unusual frequency in his letters.

in the note to the heading of each letter: this applies to letters to Say which appear for the first time in the original English; to letters from Say given for the first time in their original version; to letters to Maria Edgeworth of which only extracts have previously been published; and to variants in drafts hitherto unpublished which are appended in notes to the letters to which they refer.

The heading of each letter gives references to the letter to which it is a 'reply' and to the one by which it is 'answered', where these exist. The link thus described may cover anything from mere acknowledgement to full discussion of the earlier letter. When a letter is labelled as being the reply to another one, no attempt is made to explain, in footnotes, allusions to events, persons or books which can be clarified by reference to the other letter.

Since the letters are dated by the day of the month, while references in the text of the letters are usually to the day of the week, calendars have been provided in each volume for the respective years (except for 1810, 1812 and 1813 where the number of letters is small).

In nearly every case it has been possible to establish the text on the original MS.[1] Letters previously published have been printed from a copy of the earlier edition, corrected by collation with the MS; but no specific mention has been made of any errors in those editions, except in dates, that have been rectified.

In a number of cases it has been necessary to correct or to complete the date as written on the letter (the most common mistakes being in the year, which are apt to occur soon after its beginning). In such instances what seemed to be the correct date has been supplied in square brackets and the grounds for the inference, unless obvious, have been given in footnotes. Where the date at the head of a letter is given in square brackets without any explanation this invariably means that the date was omitted in the MS.

Most alterations in the MS have been described in the editor's footnotes, and this has been done more fully in the case of

[1] In the few cases where the original MS has not been available, this can be inferred from the relevant footnotes.

Ricardo's own letters.  As in previous volumes, the spelling (even when eccentric), punctuation and abbreviations of the original MS have been retained, except for '&', M$^r$, M$^{rs}$ and D$^r$ which have been printed as 'and', Mr., Mrs. and Dr.

Ricardo's letters are usually written on quarto-size note-paper and in the later years this is often gilt-edged.  After 1814, when he acquired a coat-of-arms, they are fastened with wax impressed

with one or other of his two seals (here redrawn in the size of the originals from wax impressions on his letters), more frequently the small one with his initials surmounted by the bird crest, and only occasionally the larger one with his full coat-of-arms.

# CALENDARS for 1811, 1814 and 1815

## 1811

|  | JAN. | FEB. | MAR. | APRIL | MAY | JUNE |
|---|---|---|---|---|---|---|
| S | – 6 13 20 27 | – 3 10 17 24 | – 3 10 17 24 31 | – 7 14 21 28 | – 5 12 19 26 | – 2 9 16 23 30 |
| M | – 7 14 21 28 | – 4 11 18 25 | – 4 11 18 25 – | 1 8 15 22 29 | – 6 13 20 27 | – 3 10 17 24 – |
| Tu | 1 8 15 22 29 | – 5 12 19 26 | – 5 12 19 26 – | 2 9 16 23 30 | – 7 14 21 28 | – 4 11 18 25 – |
| W | 2 9 16 23 30 | – 6 13 20 27 | – 6 13 20 27 – | 3 10 17 24 – | 1 8 15 22 29 | – 5 12 19 26 – |
| Th | 3 10 17 24 31 | – 7 14 21 28 | – 7 14 21 28 – | 4 11 18 25 – | 2 9 16 23 30 | – 6 13 20 27 – |
| F | 4 11 18 25 – | 1 8 15 22 – | 1 8 15 22 29 – | 5 12 19 26 – | 3 10 17 24 31 | – 7 14 21 28 – |
| S | 5 12 19 26 – | 2 9 16 23 – | 2 9 16 23 30 – | 6 13 20 27 – | 4 11 18 25 – | 1 8 15 22 29 – |

|  | JULY | AUG. | SEPT. | OCT. | NOV. | DEC. |
|---|---|---|---|---|---|---|
| S | – 7 14 21 28 | – 4 11 18 25 | 1 8 15 22 29 | – 6 13 20 27 | – 3 10 17 24 | 1 8 15 22 29 |
| M | 1 8 15 22 29 | – 5 12 19 26 | 2 9 16 23 30 | – 7 14 21 28 | – 4 11 18 25 | 2 9 16 23 30 |
| Tu | 2 9 16 23 30 | – 6 13 20 27 | 3 10 17 24 – | 1 8 15 22 29 | – 5 12 19 26 | 3 10 17 24 31 |
| W | 3 10 17 24 31 | – 7 14 21 28 | 4 11 18 25 – | 2 9 16 23 30 | – 6 13 20 27 | 4 11 18 25 – |
| Th | 4 11 18 25 – | 1 8 15 22 29 | 5 12 19 26 – | 3 10 17 24 31 | – 7 14 21 28 | 5 12 19 26 – |
| F | 5 12 19 26 – | 2 9 16 23 30 | 6 13 20 27 – | 4 11 18 25 – | 1 8 15 22 29 | 6 13 20 27 – |
| S | 6 13 20 27 – | 3 10 17 24 31 | 7 14 21 28 – | 5 12 19 26 – | 2 9 16 23 30 | 7 14 21 28 – |

## 1814

|  | JAN. | FEB. | MAR. | APRIL | MAY | JUNE |
|---|---|---|---|---|---|---|
| S | – 2 9 16 23 30 | – 6 13 20 27 | – 6 13 20 27 | – 3 10 17 24 | 1 8 15 22 29 | – 5 12 19 26 |
| M | – 3 10 17 24 31 | – 7 14 21 28 | – 7 14 21 28 | – 4 11 18 25 | 2 9 16 23 30 | – 6 13 20 27 |
| Tu | – 4 11 18 25 – | 1 8 15 22 – | 1 8 15 22 29 | – 5 12 19 26 | 3 10 17 24 31 | – 7 14 21 28 |
| W | – 5 12 19 26 – | 2 9 16 23 – | 2 9 16 23 30 | – 6 13 20 27 | 4 11 18 25 – | 1 8 15 22 29 |
| Th | – 6 13 20 27 – | 3 10 17 24 – | 3 10 17 24 31 | – 7 14 21 28 | 5 12 19 26 – | 2 9 16 23 30 |
| F | – 7 14 21 28 – | 4 11 18 25 – | 4 11 18 25 – | 1 8 15 22 29 | 6 13 20 27 – | 3 10 17 24 – |
| S | 1 8 15 22 29 – | 5 12 19 26 – | 5 12 19 26 – | 2 9 16 23 30 | 7 14 21 28 – | 4 11 18 25 – |

|  | JULY | AUG. | SEPT. | OCT. | NOV. | DEC. |
|---|---|---|---|---|---|---|
| S | – 3 10 17 24 31 | – 7 14 21 28 | – 4 11 18 25 | – 2 9 16 23 30 | – 6 13 20 27 | – 4 11 18 25 |
| M | – 4 11 18 25 – | 1 8 15 22 29 | – 5 12 19 26 | – 3 10 17 24 31 | – 7 14 21 28 | – 5 12 19 26 |
| Tu | – 5 12 19 26 – | 2 9 16 23 30 | – 6 13 20 27 | – 4 11 18 25 – | 1 8 15 22 29 | – 6 13 20 27 |
| W | – 6 13 20 27 – | 3 10 17 24 31 | – 7 14 21 28 | – 5 12 19 26 – | 2 9 16 23 30 | – 7 14 21 28 |
| Th | – 7 14 21 28 – | 4 11 18 25 – | 1 8 15 22 29 | – 6 13 20 27 – | 3 10 17 24 – | 1 8 15 22 29 |
| F | 1 8 15 22 29 – | 5 12 19 26 – | 2 9 16 23 30 | – 7 14 21 28 – | 4 11 18 25 – | 2 9 16 23 30 |
| S | 2 9 16 23 30 – | 6 13 20 27 – | 3 10 17 24 – | 1 8 15 22 29 – | 5 12 19 26 – | 3 10 17 24 31 |

## 1815

|  | JAN. | FEB. | MAR. | APRIL | MAY | JUNE |
|---|---|---|---|---|---|---|
| S | 1 8 15 22 29 | – 5 12 19 26 | – 5 12 19 26 | – 2 9 16 23 30 | – 7 14 21 28 | – 4 11 18 25 |
| M | 2 9 16 23 30 | – 6 13 20 27 | – 6 13 20 27 | – 3 10 17 24 – | 1 8 15 22 29 | – 5 12 19 26 |
| Tu | 3 10 17 24 31 | – 7 14 21 28 | – 7 14 21 28 | – 4 11 18 25 – | 2 9 16 23 30 | – 6 13 20 27 |
| W | 4 11 18 25 – | 1 8 15 22 – | 1 8 15 22 29 | – 5 12 19 26 – | 3 10 17 24 31 | – 7 14 21 28 |
| Th | 5 12 19 26 – | 2 9 16 23 – | 2 9 16 23 30 | – 6 13 20 27 – | 4 11 18 25 – | 1 8 15 22 29 |
| F | 6 13 20 27 – | 3 10 17 24 – | 3 10 17 24 31 | – 7 14 21 28 – | 5 12 19 26 – | 2 9 16 23 30 |
| S | 7 14 21 28 – | 4 11 18 25 – | 4 11 18 25 – | 1 8 15 22 29 | – 6 13 20 27 – | 3 10 17 24 – |

|  | JULY | AUG. | SEPT. | OCT. | NOV. | DEC. |
|---|---|---|---|---|---|---|
| S | – 2 9 16 23 30 | – 6 13 20 27 | – 3 10 17 24 | 1 8 15 22 29 | – 5 12 19 26 | – 3 10 17 24 31 |
| M | – 3 10 17 24 31 | – 7 14 21 28 | – 4 11 18 25 | 2 9 16 23 30 | – 6 13 20 27 | – 4 11 18 25 |
| Tu | – 4 11 18 25 – | 1 8 15 22 29 | – 5 12 19 26 | 3 10 17 24 31 | – 7 14 21 28 | – 5 12 19 26 – |
| W | – 5 12 19 26 – | 2 9 16 23 30 | – 6 13 20 27 | 4 11 18 25 – | 1 8 15 22 29 | – 6 13 20 27 – |
| Th | – 6 13 20 27 – | 3 10 17 24 31 | – 7 14 21 28 | 5 12 19 26 – | 2 9 16 23 30 | – 7 14 21 28 |
| F | – 7 14 21 28 – | 4 11 18 25 – | 1 8 15 22 29 | 6 13 20 27 – | 3 10 17 24 – | 1 8 15 22 29 – |
| S | 1 8 15 22 29 – | 5 12 19 26 – | 2 9 16 23 30 | 7 14 21 28 – | 4 11 18 25 – | 2 9 16 23 30 – |

# ABBREVIATIONS

| | |
|---|---|
| *R.P.* | Ricardo Papers (consisting of letters received by Ricardo, and other of his papers, in the possession of Mr Frank Ricardo). |
| Mill-Ricardo papers | The letters and papers of Ricardo that belonged to James Mill, and which passed into the possession of the Cairnes family and Mr C. K. Mill. |
| 'at Albury' | Papers in the possession of Mr Robert Malthus, of The Cottage, Albury, Surrey. |

The following abbreviations are used by Malthus, Mill and Bentham, respectively, in their letters:

E.I. Coll., for East India College, Haileybury.
E.I. House, for East India House, London.
Q.S.P., for Queen Square Place, Westminster.

*56 Upper Brook Street
Grosvenor Square
Ricardo's London House, 1812-1823*

## 1. RICARDO TO HORNER[1]

Sir

In your observations, in the House of Commons, on the 5 Feb. 1810 present high price of gold,[2] you stated that you did not agree with those who attributed the excess of the market above the mint price, wholly, and solely, to the superabundance of the paper circulation. In your view of the subject, you said, a part of that excess might be caused by the peculiar state of our commerce, owing to the hostile decrees of the enemy, which rendered it necessary for this country to pay bullion for many of the commodities which she imported, such as corn, naval stores &c[a]. You also thought that an excess of the market above the mint price of gold, would be produced, and had been produced, by the demand for gold both at home and abroad, and from that demand not being supplied in the usual manner from the mines in South America.

On this subject, Sir, I beg leave to differ from you and further to trouble you with my reasons for so doing, not doubting that though I may not be so fortunate as to convince you by my arguments, you will pardon me for the observations which I take the liberty of offering.

It appears then to me, that no point can be more satisfactorily established, than that the excess of the market above

---

[1] MS (as printed in the text) in the possession of Lady Langman. Also a draft, containing small variants and corrections, in *R.P.* —The draft is printed in *Minor Papers*, pp. 37–42.

[2] On 1 Feb. 1810, moving for various accounts with a view to an enquiry by a Select Committee 'into the causes of the present high price of bullion, and the consequent effect upon the value of the paper currency' (*Hansard*, XV, 269 ff.). The Bullion Committee was appointed on 19 February.

5 Feb. 1810 the mint price of gold bullion, is, at present, wholly, and solely, owing to the too abundant quantity of paper circulation. There are in my opinion but three causes which can, at any time, produce an excess of price such as we are now speaking of.

First, The debasement of the coins, or rather of that coin which is the principal measure of value.

Secondly, A proportion in the relative value of gold to silver in the market, greater than in their relative value in the coins.

Thirdly, A superabundance of paper circulation. By superabundance I mean that quantity of paper money which could not by any means be kept in circulation if it were immediately exchangeable for specie on demand.

I might add here a fourth cause[1]. The severity of the law against the exportation of gold coins, but from experience we know that this law is so easily evaded, that it is considered by all writers on political economy, as operating in a very small degree on the price of gold bullion.

It will be readily acknowledged that the debasement of the coins is not now the cause of the excess of the market above the mint price of gold.[2] Our gold coin, which is the principal measure of value, being at this moment of its standard weight and actually not received at the Bank unless each guinea weighs 5 dwt 8 gr$^s$—the lowest weight at which guineas are current by law.

The second cause is limited in its effects under any and every circumstance, to the superior value which gold may bear to silver in the market over and above its proportionate value in the coins. The relative value of gold and silver, in the market, was stated by you, and I believe correctly, as $15\frac{1}{2}$

---

[1] In draft, 'reason'.
[2] In draft this replaces 'The first of    these causes is not now operating; this will be readily acknowledged.'

to 1. Their relative value in the coins is $15\frac{9}{124}$ to 1. Thus then an ounce of gold, which is coined into £3. 17. $10\frac{1}{2}$ of gold coin, is worth, according to the mint regulations, $15\frac{9}{124}$ ounces of silver, because that weight of silver is also coined into £3. 17. $10\frac{1}{2}$ of silver coin. But if £3. 17. $10\frac{1}{2}$ in gold coin, or an ounce of gold, will sell in the market for more than $15\frac{9}{124}$ ounces of silver;—if it be, as it now is, of equal value with $15\frac{1}{2}$ ounces of silver, or as much silver coin as $15\frac{1}{2}$ oz are coined into, viz 80 shillings, then it will no longer be worth only £3. 17. $10\frac{1}{2}$ but £4[1].—Accordingly the alteration in the relative value of gold and silver, which it is acknowledged by me[2] has of late considerably increased,[3] cannot[4] have produced any excess of the market above the mint price of gold of more than $2/1\frac{1}{2}$ or between 2 and 3 pc[t]. This cause, however, has in my opinion, produced no effect whatever, because in the present state of things silver cannot be considered as the standard measure of value, and therefore neither gold bullion, silver bullion, nor any commodity whatever is rated in the silver but in the gold coin.

My reasons for forming this conclusion are as follows. Whilst the relative value of gold and silver is under 15 to 1 gold will necessarily be the standard measure of value, because no one would then send $15\frac{9}{124}$ ounces of silver to the mint to be coined into £3. 17. $10\frac{1}{2}$, when he could sell that quantity of silver in the market for more than £3. 17. $10\frac{1}{2}$ in gold coin; and this he could do by the supposition that less than 15 ounces of silver would sell for[5] an ounce of gold.

But if the relative value of gold to silver be more in the

---

[1] Draft has here in addition 'because $15\frac{1}{2}$ oz. of silver are coined into 80 shillings'.
[2] Above, III, 67, n. 1.
[3] Last eleven words are ins. in draft.

[4] Draft has here in addition 'at the present moment,'.
[5] In draft, 'sell for' is written above 'purchase'.

5 Feb. 1810 market than the mint proportions of $15\frac{9}{124}$ to 1, no gold would then be sent to the mint to be coined, because the possessor of an ounce of gold would not send it to the mint to be coined into £3. 17. $10\frac{1}{2}$ of gold coin, whilst he could sell it, which he could do in such case, for more than £3. 17. $10\frac{1}{2}$ of silver coin. Not only would not gold be carried to the mint to be coined, but the illicit trader would melt the gold coin and sell it as bullion for more than its nominal value in the silver coin; he would as I have already stated obtain for it 80 shillings in silver coin, a profit of 2 to 3 pc.[1] Thus then gold would disappear from circulation and silver[2] become the standard measure of value. This would be the case *now* if the coinage of silver were allowed at the mint, but it is prohibited, while that of gold is freely permitted.[3]

How can silver become the measure[4] of value whilst this law continues in force? The quantity of silver in circulation is barely sufficient or rather is insufficient for small payments and is now bought at a prem.ᵐ of 7 pc.[5] Were the relative value of gold to silver to become as 1 to 30 in the market, gold would still be the measure of value. It would be in vain that the possessor of the 30 ounces of silver should know that he once could have discharged a debt of £3. 17. $10\frac{1}{2}$ by getting $15\frac{9}{124}$ ounces[6] of silver coined at the mint into that sum of silver coin,—to discharge that debt now he would have no other means, if coins only were in circulation,[7] but selling his 30 oz of silver[8] for 1 oz of gold, and procuring

---

[1] 'on every ounce melted' is del. here in draft.
[2] In draft, 'silver coin'.
[3] This argument is embodied in *High Price of Bullion*, ed. 3, above, III, 68.
[4] In draft, 'the standard measure'.

[5] This sentence is ins. in draft.
[6] In draft, '15 ounces'; superscribed in another hand (? Mill's): 'mistake— $\frac{9}{120}$ EB'.
[7] Last six words are ins. in draft.
[8] Draft has here in addition 'at the market value, that is to say,'.

*that* to be coined into £3. 17. 10½, or at once obtain for it that sum of gold coin.

The effects which may be produced by the third cause, namely, the superabundance of paper circulation, are too obvious to be disputed, and indeed have been admitted by you.

Having laid down these principles, I shall now proceed, Sir, in endeavoring to prove that the other causes which you assign for an excess of the market above the mint price of gold, are insufficient and could in no case produce such an effect.

I will for a moment allow, what in point of fact cannot I think ever be the case, that the hostile decrees of the enemy, might reduce our trade to that state, which should render it necessary for us to pay for all our imports with bullion, yet I should contend that that is not an adequate cause[1] for a rise in the money price of gold bullion. Its *value* would no doubt be increased, and it is from not distinguishing between an increase in the *value* of gold, and an increase in its *money price*, that much of the error of our reasoning is derived. If corn were to become scarce from large exportations, not only its value, but[2] its money price would be affected, because in comparing it with money we are in fact comparing it with another commodity; and when we export money or bullion[3], in the same manner, on comparing it with corn, its corn price would be affected, but its money price could not alter.[4] In neither case would a bushel of corn be worth more than a bushel of corn, or an ounce of gold whether in bullion or in coin,[5] more than an ounce of gold. The *price* of *gold*, whatever the demand might be, could never, whilst it was measured by *gold coin*, or bank

[1] In draft, 'reason'.
[2] Draft does not contain 'not only its value, but'.
[3] 'or bullion' is ins. in draft.
[4] Last six words (with 'would' in place of 'could') and the full stop are ins. in draft.
[5] Last six words are not in draft.

notes which were an obligation to pay gold coin, and were of equal value with it, be more than £3. 17. 10½.

If the price of gold were estimated in *silver* indeed, the price might rise to £4, £5, or £10- an ounce, but silver I think I have already proved is not the standard in which the value of gold is estimated;—But if it were;—as an ounce of gold is only worth 15½ oz of silver, and 15½ oz of silver is precisely equivalent, or is coined into 80 shillings, an ounce of gold could now only then[1] be worth and sell for £4.

Those then who maintain that silver is the measure of value, cannot prove that any demand for gold which may have taken place, from whatever cause it may have proceeded, could have raised its price above £4 p$^r$ oz. All above that price must, on their own principles, be called a depreciation in the value of Bank notes. It therefore follows that if Bank notes be the representatives of gold coin, they are depreciated 15 pc$^t$. If they are the representatives of silver coin, then an ounce of gold selling as it now does for £4. 10, sells for an amount of notes which represent 17½ oz of silver, whereas in the bullion market it is allowed that it can only be exchanged for 15½ oz. Fifteen and a half ounces of silver bullion are therefore of equal value with an engagement of the Bank to pay to *bearer* seventeen ounces and a half.[2]

On the same grounds, I think, I could successfully shew, that no increase or decrease in the supply of the American mines could produce any variation in the money value of gold bullion.

Whilst gold continues the standard measure of value, it might be possible, either that an increased demand for silver, or a deficient supply, might raise the money price of silver

---

[1] Draft reads 'could only then'. In final copy 'could now only' was first written; 'then' was ins.

[2] The last two paragraphs are reproduced in *High Price of Bullion*, ed. 3, above, III, 84–5.

to 5/6, to 6/-, to 8/- nay even to an equal or greater price than 5 Feb. 1810 an ounce of gold. This effect would be produced by an alteration in the relative value of gold and silver, but no scarcity of *gold*, nor any demand for it, however great, could raise *its price*, tho' it might raise its value, because it is itself the medium in which its price is estimated.[1]

Mr. Marryat, I believe, contended that the unfavorable exchange was the cause of the high price of gold bullion.[2] He mistook, I apprehend, the cause for the effect, as I have elsewhere attempted to shew.[3] He observed too that a guinea was worth in Hamburgh 26 or 28/- shillings; but if we should therefore suppose that a guinea would sell there for as much silver as is contained in 26 or 28 shillings we should be very much deceived. The silver for which a guinea will now sell at Hamburgh would, if sent to our mint, coin into 21/6 or perhaps a penny or two pence more, and that it will fetch so much is owing to an alteration in the relative value of the two metals. It is nevertheless true that that same quantity of silver will at Hamburgh purchase a bill payable in London in Bank notes for 26 or 28 shillings. Can there be a more satisfactory proof of the depreciation of our circulating medium?[4]

I have the honor to be<br>
Sir<br>
Your most obed. and humble Serv<sup>t</sup>

New Grove Mile-end
5<sup>th</sup> feb<sup>y</sup> 1810.

DAVID RICARDO

F. Horner Esq<sup>r</sup>

---

[1] Cp. the same argument in *High Price of Bullion*, ed. 3, above, III, 60.
[2] Speech of Joseph Marryat, on Horner's motion, 1 Feb. 1810 (*Hansard*, XV, 275).

[3] Above, III, 75, n. 1, and cp. *ib*. 64, n. 1.
[4] The substance of this paragraph, and the actual wording of the last two sentences, are reproduced in *High Price of Bullion*, ed. 3, above, III, 80–1.

## 2. RICARDO TO HORNER[1]

6 Feb. 1810　　As gold is the standard of currency in England, and silver in all other countries, there can be no fixed par of exchange between England and those countries, it being subject to all the variations which may take place in the relative value of gold and silver. Thus if 33 schillings 8 grotes of Hamburgh currency be equal in value to a pound sterling or $\frac{20}{21}$ of a guinea, when silver is at 5/4 p$^r$ ounce, (and which it was when Mr. Eliason declared in his evidence before the house of Commons that 33.8 was the par with Hamburgh[2]) they can no longer be so when silver falls to 5/2, or 5/- p$^r$ oz, because a pound sterling in gold being then worth more silver is also worth more of Hamburgh currency.

To discover the real par, therefore, we must ascertain what the relative proportion between gold and silver was when the par was 33.8, and what its relative value at the time we wish to calculate it. Thus in 1797 the price of gold was £3. 17. 10$\frac{1}{2}$, and of silver 5/4 p$^r$ oz, so that an ounce of gold was of equal value with 14.6 oz of silver; and in 1798 gold was £3. 17. 10$\frac{1}{2}$, and silver 5s $\frac{1}{2}$d p$^r$ oz, so that an ounce of gold was then worth 15.44 oz of silver.

If £1- ster$^g$ at par be worth 14.6 of silver, then at 15.44 it will be at 6 pc$^t$ prem$^m$, and 6 pc$^t$ prem$^m$ on 33.8 is 2 schillings, so that the par when gold is to silver as 15.44 to 1 will be 35 schillings 8 grotes.

In 1798 Mr. Mushet in his tables states the exchange at 38.2 and observes that it was 13 pc. in favor of England but

[1] MS in the possession of Lady Langman (Papers of Francis Horner).
[2] See evidence of Daniel Eliason in 'Reports from the Committee of Secrecy on the Outstanding Demands of the Bank; and on the Restriction of Payments in Cash', 1797 (*Reports from Committees of the House of Commons*, vol. XI, p. 159).

according to my view of it, it was then only 7 pc$^t$ in favor of 6 Feb. 1810 England.[1] Indeed I doubt whether it was nearly so much. In the year 1797 there was much difference of opinion about the par of exchange with Hamburgh, Mr. Eliason stated it at 33.8, and Mr. Boyd I think above 35.[2]—If 35 be taken as the standard or par in 1797, then in 1798, 37 would be the par and consequently 38.2 only 3 pc$^t$ in favour of England. Lord King observes that probably the real par is rather below 35,[3] so that I think Mr. Mushet has attached too much weight to Mr. Eliason's evidence on this disputed point.

The above calculation may perhaps be more easily made by stating as follows

$$\text{As } 14.6 : 33.8 :: 15.44 : 35.7\tfrac{3}{10}$$
And if 35 be the par of 1797
$$\text{As } 14.6 : 35 :: 15.44 : 37$$

The par, being 33.8 when gold was in the proportion of 14.6 more valuable than silver, will be when gold is to silver

| | | | |
|---|---|---|---|
| as 1 to $14\tfrac{1}{2}$ – – – – | 33.5 nearly |
| $14\tfrac{3}{4}$ – – – – | 34.– |
| 15 – – – – | 34.7 |
| $15\tfrac{1}{4}$ – – – – | 35.2 |
| $15\tfrac{1}{2}$ – – – – | 35.9 |

[1] *An Enquiry into the Effects produced on the National Currency, and Rates of Exchange, by the Bank Restriction Bill...*, by Robert Mushet, of His Majesty's Mint, London, Baldwin, 1810, Appendix. In 2nd ed., 1810, Mushet's estimate for 1798 is reduced to 5·7 per cent. in favour of England.
[2] In his evidence before the Lords' Committee on the Restriction of Cash Payments, 1797, Walter Boyd gives the par of exchange as '34 Schillings 3 Grotes Banco' (*Journals of the House of Lords,* vol. XLI, p. 221).
[3] *Thoughts on the Restriction of Payments in Specie at the Banks of England and Ireland,* London, Cadell and Davies, n.d. [1803], p. 89. In the 'second edition enlarged', published under the title *Thoughts on the Effects of the Bank Restriction, ibid.,* 1804, the statement is slightly altered ('about 35', p. 151).

6 Feb. 1810　But if the par were in 1797, 35, when gold was to silver as 1 to 14.6, then when gold is to silver

$$
\begin{aligned}
\text{as 1 to } 14\tfrac{1}{2} \text{ the par will be } & 34.9 \text{ nearly} \\
14\tfrac{3}{4} \; - \; - \; - \; - \; & 35.4 \\
15 \; - \; - \; - \; - \; & 35.11 \\
15\tfrac{1}{4} \; - \; - \; - \; - \; & 36.6 \\
15\tfrac{1}{2} \; - \; - \; - \; - \; & 37.2
\end{aligned}
$$

DAVID RICARDO

6ᵗʰ feb 1810

### 3. RICARDO TO SIR PHILIP FRANCIS[1]

New Grove Mile-end
24ᵗʰ April 1810

Sir

24 April 1810　　In compliance with your request, when I had the honour of seeing you, I will endeavor to repeat in writing, as nearly as possible, the substance of the observations, which I made in defence of the passage in my pamphlet, on which you have animadverted in the second edition of your work.[2] Your dissent from my conclusions is expressed in the following words

"Supposing any given quantity of paper (and no more) to be necessary for the uses of circulation, and that any issue beyond that quantity would be superfluous, then the consequence seems to be, that, in proportion as the Bank issued

---

[1] MS (a copy or draft in Ricardo's handwriting) in *R.P.*—Headed 'To *Sir Philip Francis*' in Osman Ricardo's handwriting.

Sir Philip Francis (1740–1818) is the reputed author of *Junius*; the 'Franciscan' theory of the

authorship however was not advanced till 1816.

[2] *Reflections on the Abundance of Paper in Circulation, and the Scarcity of Specie*, by Sir Philip Francis, K.B., 2nd ed., London, Ridgway, 1810.

more of *their* paper, the country banks must issue less, because so much less, on the whole, would be wanted."[1]

To which I answer, that if the quantity of paper necessary
for the uses of circulation were a given quantity, and would
not admit of increase, the truth of the above proposition
could not be successfully controverted, but, as the circulation, under the present circumstances of the restriction on
the Bank-payments in specie, admits of an indefinite increase, the issues of the Bank of England will be the cause
of a proportionate increase in the issues of the country-banks.

Let us suppose, that the whole amount of the paper currency in England, in circulation, is, at any one moment
twenty millions, and that that sum is fully adequate to all
the purposes of circulation;—that of these 20 millions,
5 millions, are exclusively current in London and consist of
Bank of England notes; and that the Bank, without any
alteration in the state of commerce or of credit, increase the
amount of their notes one million.

The circulation of the London district being increased
one fifth, from 5 to 6 millions, whilst that of the country
continued as before,—the prices of commodities would be
considerably raised in London, at the same time that they
continue stationary in the country. Commodities would
therefore be sent from the country to be sold in London, and
this would continue till the usual level between London and
country prices were again restored, and the additional

---

[1] p. 60. The passage continues:
'I should be much obliged to
David Ricardo, as I am already
on other accounts, if he would
explain this matter by its process,
in a plain popular way, without
resorting to metaphysics; and
also on what evidence he states
it, as a matter of fact, or why he
believes it to be *probable*, that any
increase in the issue of Bank paper
*enables the country banks to add
more than four times that amount
of their own.* [*High Price of Bullion*,
above, III, 86–7 and cp. n. 1.] All
this, he would be able to explain,
if it be true, by a short paragraph
in the MORNING CHRONICLE.'

24 April 1810 million had been divided between London and the country, in the same proportion as the 20 millions had been originally divided.

This would be the operation if the country Banks did not increase the amount of their notes; but the conductors of those establishments are sufficiently alive to their interests readily to avail themselves of any opportunity which might offer of increasing the issue of their notes, provided they had a reasonable probability of being able to continue them in circulation. This opportunity would now be afforded them. The London currency having been increased and the prices of goods raised in the London markets, the country banks would be enabled to add to the country currency till the same effect had been produced on the prices of commodities in the country. The amount necessary for such purpose would be precisely a fifth of the country currency, or three millions, that having been the proportion in which the currency of London had been increased. The country currency would for a short time[1] be relatively deficient but could not continue so, and must therefore be raised to its usual proportion to the London currency, either by participating in the million which the Bank of England had added to the general circulation[2], or by increasing the amount of the country bank notes. The bank of England then by increasing the amount of their notes one million, would enable the country banks to increase theirs three millions, so that four millions would be added to, and absorbed in the general circulation of England.

If the country banks commenced this operation by adding to the amount of their notes, whilst the amount of those of the Bank of England remained stationary, they could not

[1] 'for a short time' is ins.
[2] Replaces 'either by decreasing the amount of Bank of England notes'.

maintain them in circulation. Their notes would be exchanged for Bank of England notes till they were reduced to their former amount. The steps by which this would be effected are these. There would be a rise in the prices of commodities in the country only; which would therefore be sent from London to the country to be sold for country bank notes in the dearer market; the country bank notes would be exchanged, as by law they may be, for bank of England notes, as these would be wanted to purchase again in the cheaper market, and this would continue whilst there existed any profitable difference in the prices of commodities in the two markets. By these means the country bank notes would speedily be reduced to their former amount. 24 April 1810

I hope Sir I have been so fortunate as to make myself understood by you;—if I have not, I shall be happy to give you any further explanation of my meaning. If you see occasion still to differ from me, I shall be glad to have your reasons for so doing; but if, as I hope, you should agree with me in the principle here stated, I shall be gratified by the communication.

[On the reverse side of the sheet, in Osman Ricardo's hand-writing:
'The signature of this letter to Sir Philip Francis was cut off to give to Mr Edwards of Ross who wished to have my Father's signature. O.R. Oct: 26th 1846'.]

## 4. MILL TO RICARDO[1]

*[Answered by 5]*

My dear Sir

I send you the first part of the papers I took occasion to mention to you.[2] You can read this, while I am reading the remainder. What I send you is about a third part of the whole. 25 Dec. 1810

[1] Addressed: 'David Ricardo Esq.' —not passed through the post. MS in *R.P.*

[2] The MS of Dumont's translation of Bentham's *Alarm (Sur les prix)*; see above, III, 269 ff.

25 Dec. 1810   —The whole will interest you, unfinished as is the state in which you will find it—but I do not think it will do for publication. In some respects it is too elementary—in others too abstruse—the premises and conclusions are not placed in the most lucid order, and the views are not always correct. —In fact they are loose papers of the author, not put in order, on a subject which he ceased to study before he had probed it to the bottom.—

I shall thank you to jot down your remarks—and to make them pretty minute. Because as my opinion will be followed by the translator in regard to the propriety of publishing, I shall be glad to have my opinion fortified by yours.

I long to see your pamphlet[1] in its *tout-ensemble*. Take care they dont neglect to print a table of contents—as they did in the first Edition of Mushets.[2]

Dear Sir<br>Yours truly

Dec.ʳ 25ᵗʰ 1810
Newington Green

J. MILL

## 5. RICARDO TO MILL[3]

[*Reply to 4—Answered by 6*]

My dear Sir

1 Jan. 1811    I have read rather more than half of the MS which you sent to me with which I have been very much pleased. As far as I am able to judge it contains some very able and just views of the subject on which it treats, which I should be sorry should be wholly lost to the public; but at the same

[1] *Reply to Bosanquet.*
[2] Mushet's *Enquiry into the Effects produced on the National Currency and Rates of Exchange by the Bank Restriction Bill*, 1810. The table of contents was added in the 2nd ed., 1810.

[3] Addressed: 'J. Mill Esqʳ.—Not passed through the post. Docketed by Mill: 'Mr. Ricardo / Janʸ 1811 / On $\frac{\text{Bentham}}{\text{Dumonts}}$ Money papers'.
MS in Mill-Ricardo papers.

time I am of opinion that it contains some radical defects
which will prevent it, as a whole, from effecting much good
without considerable alterations. In giving my opinion I
hope you will consider me as feeling all becoming diffidence
when it is opposed by so ingenious and profound an author,
but every man must judge with the portion of understanding
which is allotted to him. First, then, the author does not
appear to have been aware how effectually a paper circulation
is, in the sound state of a currency, kept within due bounds
by the value of the precious metals;—on the contrary he
argues as if he thought it admitted of indefinite increase till
at last it would become so enormous as to produce some
great public catastrophe. This view is not warranted by any
experience of the past, nor does any just examination of the
science render such an extension of a paper circulation whilst
convertible into specie either probable or possible. From
my knowledge of your sentiments I have not the slightest
doubt of your full acquiescence in this opinion. Secondly,
the author has not taken any notice, as far as I have read, of
the effects which would follow from an unrestrained issue
of paper on our foreign relations; an effect highly important
to be considered. Thirdly; Much of his argument is built on
the assumption that an increase of the circulating medium
though attended with the effect of depreciating the value of
the currency, is also attended, (provided it be introduced
through commercial channels,) with an increase of capital
and commodities, and is so far beneficial;—he has supposed
that money calls goods into existence which but for that
money would not have been produced.—This opinion is
advanced in many parts of his work, and was to me of great
difficulty, as he had not advanced any reasons for enter-
taining it. At length however just before the place where
I have left off I found a section or chapter devoted to that

1 Jan. 1811 purpose,[1] and after giving it my most serious attention I confess I should come to quite an opposite conclusion. As paper money is generally introduced for commercial purposes he is of opinion that it is almost always attended with the advantages which he had before ascribed to the proper introduction of metallic money. As much of the revenue of a country consists in a fixed money rent he supposes an unwillingness in those who receive it to save or rather to expend it on those objects which shall cause a future increase of revenue. Now as all the money introduced by commercial means would be so expended he considers the same beneficial effects would follow as if those with monied incomes had thus beneficially employed their rents and annuities.

The increase of money in my opinion can have no other effect than raising the prices of commodities. By such means some members of the community are enriched at the expence of others; there is a mere transfer of property, but no creation. Whether those who are enriched will employ their additional income more economically or more advantageously than those who before possessed it, must be matter of speculation only. My opinion however is that by no class are greater savings made than by those who are in possession of fixed monied rents and annuities. As far as they have come under my observation, and I have seen a good deal of monied men, they are amongst the most accumulating of the community.

There appears to me only one way in which any addition would be made to the Capital of a country in consequence of an addition of money; it would be this. Till the wages of labour had found their new level with the altered value of money,—the situation of the labourer would be relatively worse; he would produce more relatively to that which he consumed, or rather he would be obliged to consume less.

[1] Cp. Note 34 on Bentham's Livre II; above, III, 318.

The manufacturer would be enabled to employ more labourers as he would receive an additional price[1] for his commodities; he might therefore add to his real capital till the rise in the wages of labour placed him in his proper sphere. In this interval some trifling addition would have been made to the Capital of the community.—

Fourthly the author supposes that the issues of Bankers are and may be regulated by the proportion of their deposits, —but this is clearly an erroneous opinion. A banker may issue 300,000 on a deposit of 100,000 perhaps safely; but it does not therefore follow that with a deposit of a million he might safely issue 3 millions.

To what I have already observed relatively to the effects of an increase of money,—I may add that the importation of money by commercial means would not only not be attended with an increase of commodities, but with an actual diminution. Money or the metal from which money is made could not be imported unless from the increased production of the mines, the value of that metal had generally fallen in the world which would force an increased use for it. Now in the state of money gold (or silver) is not productive to us nor does it augment our riches,—but to obtain this unproductive commodity we should in return export commodities which may be considered as really effective capital. Not only would individuals be injured by the greater abundance of gold but all countries excepting that which possessed the mine, as they would all contribute by their labour to produce those commodities with which money must necessarily be purchased by them.—

These are a few of the principles which have struck me as radically wrong in the work which I have perused,—it contains however much that is excellent and I should be

[1] In MS 'prices'.

1 Jan. 1811  sorry if we should lose what is good because some error may
be mixed with it.

I do not know whether you are in a hurry to have the
whole or part returned to you, I have unfortunately been
much engaged of an evening lately and shall be for some
days to come. I staid at home yesterday morning and employed myself exclusively in considering the passages to
which I have alluded. I shall finish it in a few days, perhaps
a week, if you can spare it so long, but if you can not let me
know and I will return it immediately. I have marked with
a pencil in the margin by a number, those passages which
do not appear clear to me or from which I dissent and have
made some short remarks upon them on a paper which I
had before me. You will I fear be tired with this long unin-
teresting scroll, I therefore hasten to relieve you from any
further fatigue attending its perusal. I hope you will write
me a line informing me on what day in the next week you
can make it convenient to take your mutton with me. I hope
you will not quit me again before day light.

Y<sup>rs</sup> truly<br>
DAVID RICARDO

1 Jan<sup>y</sup> 1811.


6. MILL TO RICARDO<sup>1</sup>
[Reply to 5]

My dear Sir

4 Jan. 1811      I saw Mr. Dumont<sup>2</sup> yesterday and explained to him the
observations which you and I had made upon the work. He
seemed averse to the idea of giving it up, and appeared disposed to work upon it in any way, that it could be rendered
fit for the public. Without being familiar with the subject, his

<sup>1</sup> MS in R.P.                        of Geneva, disciple, editor and
<sup>2</sup> Étienne Dumont (1759-1829)    French translator of Bentham.

mind is well qualified to reason upon the principles. I told him that I had shewed it to you, and as I thought there might be use in making you and him acquainted, I said that I thought the best thing would be for you and him to converse together on the subject, for that you would have read the papers much more attentively than I had, and that the points of the subject were more minutely present to your mind than to mine. He answered that he should like very much to be acquainted with you. As I was sure he was an acquaintance whom both Mrs. Ricardo and you would like— for he is not only a man of uncommon intellectual acquirements, but consummately well bred, and of great knowledge of the world, having lived with all the greatest people in France, in England, and in Russia—and with all an extremely pleasant, unaffected man; I said that I thought the best plan would be for him to dine with you—He expressed great pleasure at the idea—only the distance. I said I knew you could give him a bed and if he would walk to your Counting House in Throgmorton Street I would join him there, and we would contrive to get ourselves conveyed from thence. To this he readily assented.

—All this, however, provided only it is perfectly agreeable and convenient to you. If otherwise the thing is in such a state that it can without the smallest awkwardness be dropt. If you would like, however, to see him—and if you shall have done with reading the papers, what objection have you to invite him for Friday? He is anxious to have his mind decided about the subject as soon as possible. I am only afraid of the inconvenience of the bed, at present when you have your large family at home. But as you have a bed for him (for you have offered one to me) I can come home, if there is the least inconvenience in disposing of me, or you may stow me away in any hole you can find.

4 Jan. 1811   Now as you see I have used no ceremony with you in this matter—I only beg you will have no hesitation in saying immediately and plainly whether the arrangement is agreeable to you or not. If it is agreeable I think you should send immediately (for fear of his being engaged) a note to Dumont (19 Hay Market) to invite him to a Family dinner, and to a conversation of ourselves three on the subject of his papers. He is a man who requires no ceremony; and who will see you have not invited him to a party, because a party would destroy the purpose for which we meet.

I am my dear Sir—ever most truly
Yours
J. MILL

Newington Green
4 Jan.ʸ 1811


## 7. RICARDO TO DUMONT[1]

Dear Sir

6 Jan. 1811   My friend Mr. Mill has offered me a pleasure which I cannot but eagerly embrace, an introduction to your acquaintance. He dines with me on friday next[2] and has given me hopes that you will be willing to accompany him. I write these few lines to assure you that I shall feel highly honoured with your visit, and promise myself much pleasure in the discussion of some of the points of the ingenious MS which I have been reading.[3]

We have beds both for you and Mr. Mill; and I hope you will be in no hurry to quit me on Saturday. If you kindly

---

[1] Addressed: '—Dumont Esq.ʳᵉ/ Nº 19/Haymarket'. Seal, 'PAR' (Priscilla Ann Ricardo) surmounted by the 'Cornish chough' (the crest of the Wilkinsons, later adopted by Ricardo).

MS in Bibliothèque Publique et Universitaire de Genève, Ms. Dumont, 33, III, fols. 287–8.— [*Revue d'Hist. éc.*, 1940, p. 259.]
[2] 11 January.
[3] See above, p. 13, n. 2.

consent to my wishes will you have the goodness to meet 6 Jan. 1811
Mr. Mill at my office N⁰ 16 Throgmorton Street at $\frac{1}{2}$ past 3 on
friday, from whence we will perform our journey together.
I remain Dear Sir
                    Your obed$^t$ and obliged Serv$^t$
                                        DAVID RICARDO
New Grove Mile End
    6$^{th}$ Jan? 1811


## 8. MALTHUS TO RICARDO[1]

*[Answered by 9]*

                                        East India College Hertford
Dear Sir,                                June 16$^{th}$ 1811.

One of my principal reasons for taking the liberty of 16 June 1811
introducing myself to you, next to the pleasure of making
your acquaintance, was, that as we are *mainly* on the same
side of the question, we might supersede the necessity of a
long controversy in print respecting the points in which we
differ, by an amicable discussion in private. I have certainly
been for some time of opinion that many of the modern writers
in political economy in their zeal to correct the absurd notions
of the mercantile classes about the balance of trade have overlooked the real differences that exist between the precious
metals and other commodities, from the circumstance of their
having been adopted as a medium of exchange; and I have
intended to take some opportunity of expressing this opinion
in print. But if you in any degree prefer it, I will state this
opinion without a specific reference to your name, though if
I do mention it, it will undoubtedly be with that respect and
approbation which the talents and information which you
have shewn on this subject so richly merit. Having entered

[1] **Addressed:** 'David Ricardo Esqr / 16 Throckmorton Street / London'.
**MS. in** *R.P.*

upon the question, my sole view in prosecuting it is to arrive at, and circulate the truth, and I had rather make any concessions to the other side, than defend any position which does not appear to me to accord with the just principles of political economy.

After the most mature reflection on all that you have written and said on this subject, I am still obliged to retain my opinion that the manner in which you have used the term redundancy[1] conveys an incorrect impression of the fact; and that the term is by no means allowable merely because bullion may be the most advantageous commodity to export. At the very time that this export takes place there may be other commodities in the country really redundant, that is selling at prices which do not yield average profits; and yet if from having already exported many of these commodities, or from any other cause, they do not bear a higher price, or only one or two percent higher in the foreign country, I imagine that from the greater expence of exporting bulky commodities, and the greater danger of lowering the foreign market, the preference would be given to bullion although in reference to the mass of commodities it might have exactly the same value in both countries, and there is of course no comparative redundancy. In this case it goes merely because something must go to pay the debt, and other commodities not being at the time in sufficient demand to pay the proper profits even with the assistance of the premium received on the bill, the medium of exchange is resorted to which is always in such demand as not to occasion a greater loss than the price of transport and perhaps coinage.

Generally also, I cannot but be still of opinion that it must be the interest of different nations, occasionally to make use of their medium of exchange for foreign payments; and that

[1] In *High Price of Bullion*; see, e.g., III, 61.

it is much more natural and probable that an average level of the precious metals should be maintained, by a principle always ready to act in the correction of temporary fluctuations, than that no such temporary fluctuations should ever exist. On these and some other topics, I should like much to hear your opinions when we have next the pleasure of meeting. In the mean time, in reference to the general question, can you give me any information respecting the state of the computed exchange with those countries from which we have lately imported bullion Jamaica for instance. I cannot help thinking that with some of these countries the computed exchange must be unfavourable owing to our depreciated currency; but if a clear instance of this kind could be produced, it would shew at once what a large part of our unfavourable exchanges is nominal. I hope you will be able before long to pay us a visit in Hertfordshire. Would it be convenient to you on saturday or sunday next.—perhaps Horner might be able to meet you. I shall leave home for some little time the middle of the following week. Believe me with sincere respects

Your obed<sup>t</sup> serv<sup>t</sup>

T. Rob<sup>T</sup> Malthus

16 June 1811

## 9. RICARDO TO MALTHUS[1]

*[Reply to 8.—Answered by 10]*

Dear Sir

I lose no time in answering your obliging letter and endeavoring as far as lies in my power to remove the very

18 June 1811

---

[1] Addressed: 'The Rev<sup>d</sup> T. R Malthus/East India College/Hertford.'
MS at Albury (as printed in the text); also a draft, dated in pencil 'June 17' and apparently written before receiving Malthus's letter of 16 June, in *R.P.* (the main variants are given in footnotes).— *Letters to Malthus*, VI.

18 June 1811 few objections which prevent us from being precisely of the
same opinion on the subject of money, and the laws which
regulate its value in the countries which have constant commercial intercourse with each other. I have no view in this
discussion but that which you have avowed, the circulation
of truth; if therefore I should fail to convince you, and you
should express your opinions in print it is immaterial to me
whether you mention my name or not. I trust you will do
that which shall most fully tend to establish the just principles of the science.[1]

There does not appear to me to be any substantial difference between bullion[2] and any other commodity, as far as
regards the regulation of its value, and the laws which determine its exportation or importation. It is true that bullion,
besides being a commodity useful in the arts, has been
adopted universally as a measure of value, and a medium of
exchange;[3] but it has not on that account been taken out of
the list of commodities. A new use has been found for a particular article, consequently there has been an increased
demand for it, and an augmented supply. This new use has
made every man a dealer in bullion, he buys it to sell it
again, and the general competition of all these dealers will
as surely, and as strictly, regulate its value in every country,
as the competition of the same or other dealers will regulate
the value of all other commodities. I have your sanction[4] for

---

[1] In place of this paragraph the
draft reads: 'As we are so nearly
agreed on the principles which
regulate the value of money in the
countries which have constant
commercial intercourse with each
other, I am desirous that we
should endeavor, by amicable
discussion in private, to remove
the few objections which prevent

us from being precisely of the
same opinion.'
[2] Draft reads 'money (or bullion)'.
[3] Draft does not contain 'and a
medium of exchange;'.
[4] In the review (by Malthus) of
Ricardo and others on bullion,
*Edinburgh Review*, Feb. 1811,
p. 352.

calling every purchaser of commodities a dealer in bullion, and though in the language of commercial men the sellers of money are in all cases called purchasers, it is not on that account less true that they are sellers of one commodity and purchasers of another. The nature of corn was not changed by the discovery that a new use might be made of it by fermentation and distillation[1]; and if we should hereafter discover that it might be used for a hundred other purposes contributing to the comforts and enjoyments of mankind, the demand for it would increase, and its price would[2] in the first instance be considerably augmented, but this would be the only change it would undergo;—it would continue to be imported and exported by the same rules as every other commodity. I have no doubt that on this point we should not differ; it remains therefore for you to shew why the new uses to which gold has been applied in consequence of its being adopted as the money of the world should exempt it from the general law of competition,[3] and why it should not certainly and invariably (invariably only as that term is applied to other commodities) seek the most advantageous market.

It is probable that the word "redundancy" has not been happily chosen by me to express the impression made on my mind of the cause of an unfavourable balance of trade[4], but on looking over the article in the Review[5] I find that you use it precisely in the sense in which I wish to convey my mean-

---

[1] Draft reads: 'The nature of corn was not changed, nor the laws which regulated its export and import by the discovery that spirituous liquors could be obtained from it by fermentation and distillation'.
[2] Draft 'might possibly be' in place of 'would'.

[3] The draft has here a full stop and does not contain the remainder of the paragraph.
[4] Draft 'to express my impression of the fact'.
[5] *Edinburgh Review*, Feb. 1811, pp. 342–3.

18 June 1811 ing; for you admit that a relatively redundant currency may be and frequently is a cause of an unfavourable balance of trade but you contend that it is not the only cause. Now I, so understanding the word, contend that it is the invariable cause. This relative redundancy may be produced as well by a diminution of goods as by an actual increase of money, (or which is the same thing by an increased economy in the use of it) in one country; or by an increased quantity of goods, or by a diminished amount of money in another. In either of these cases a redundancy of money is produced as effectually as if the mines had become more productive. I do not deny that temporary fluctuations do occur in the value of the precious metals;—on the contrary I maintain that these fluctuations never cease, but I attribute them all to one cause, namely; a redundancy of currency produced in one of the ways above mentioned, and not to the demand for particular commodities. These demands are in my opinion regulated by the relative state of the currency,—they are not causes but effects.[1] You appear to me not sufficiently to consider the circumstances which induce one country to contract a

[1] Draft, in place of the last five sentences (from 'Now I', etc.), reads: 'Now my opinion is that it is the relative redundancy of currency which is the only cause; —this relative redundancy may be produced by some alteration either here or abroad in the absolute quantity of goods which may make the amount of money which before circulated those goods relatively redundant,—or it may be produced by the actual increase of money in one country, or the diminution of it in another. I do not deny that temporary fluctuations do occur in the value of the precious metals, on the contrary I maintain that their value never ceases fluctuating but I attribute it to one or other of the causes just mentioned, and as not at all arising in ordinary times from the debts which one country has contracted to another. Your observation is just concerning the extra expences attending the exportation of bulky commodities,—but in all these discussions we must suppose these expences to make part of the price of the commodity,—our comparison is made on the prices at which the importer could afford to sell them, and those prices necessarily include expences of every sort.'

debt to another. In all the cases you bring forward you always 18 June 1811 suppose the debt already contracted, forgetting that I uniformly contend that it is the relative state of the currency which is the motive to the contract itself. The corn, I say, will not be bought unless money be relatively redundant; you answer me by supposing it already bought and the question to be only concerning the payment. A merchant will not contract a debt for corn to a foreign country unless he is fully convinced that he shall obtain for that corn more money than he contracts to pay for it, and if the commerce of the two countries were limited to these transactions it would as satisfactorily prove to me that money was redundant in one country as that corn was redundant in the other. It would prove too that nothing but money was redundant. If indeed sugar were exported by some other merchant the debt for corn would be paid without the exportation of money and I should say that sugar was the redundant commodity;[1] and the exportation of sugar the more redundant commodity, by diminishing the aggregate amount of commodities would raise the value of money, so that in a short time money would, if corn continued to be imported and sugar exported no longer be redundant even as compared with corn. Your observation is just concerning the extra expences attending the exportation of bulky commodities,—but in all these discussions we must suppose these expences to make part of the

[1] From here, where it has a full stop, the draft reads: 'But it may be said "money was relatively redundant in England because the merchant importing the corn was willing to export it";—true; but the exportation of sugar the more redundant commodity raises the value of money by diminishing the amount of commodities, ['And if the value of sugar in the importing country is as much higher, as the value of corn exceeds' is del. here] and the exportation of money does not take place because it is cheaper than one commodity only in the foreign country, but because it is cheaper than all [replaces 'it is the cheapest exportable commodity'].' This ends the sheet of the draft; the remainder is wanting.

18 June 1811 price of the commodity;—our comparison is made on the prices at which the importer could afford to sell them and those prices necessarily include expences of every sort.

I do not think that the knowledge of the computed exchange of Jamaica would throw any light on the subject in dispute, I will however endeavor to learn every particular concerning it and hope to be able on saturday next to pay you a visit in Hertfordshire when we will further discuss these seeming difficulties.

I am Dear Sir with great respect,<br>
Y$^r$ obed$^t$ Serv$^t$<br>
DAVID RICARDO

Throgmorton Street 18$^{th}$ June 1811.

10. MALTHUS TO RICARDO[1]<br>
[Reply to 9]

East India College
June 20$^{th}$ 1811.

Dear Sir,

20 June 1811     I shall be most happy to see you on saturday.[2] On account of the arrival of a sister in Town sooner than I expected, I am obliged to go to London tomorrow, but I shall be back on saturday by five o'clock when I hope to have the pleasure of meeting you. Should any thing happen to prevent your coming, pray have the goodness to write me a line by the twopenny post directed to Bedford Coffee House, Southhampton Row Russel Square. In that case, which I hope however will not happen, perhaps you could arrange a breakfast with Mr. Sharpe[3] on saturday morning and let me know on friday evening.

I confess I cannot yet conceive that redundancy of currency

---

[1] Addressed: 'David Ricardo Esqr. / 16 Throgmorton Street. / London'.—MS in R.P.    [2] 22 June.    [3] Richard Sharp.

is the sole motive for contracting a debt, but we will discuss 20 June 1811
this point when we meet.

I am dear Sir

Sincerely Yours

T Rob<sup>T</sup> Malthus.

## 11. MALTHUS TO RICARDO[1]

Bedford Coffee House
Russel Square June 21, 1811

Dear Sir,

I have just received your obliging note.[2] As Mrs. Malthus  21 June 1811
cannot return till sunday or monday, and as there is a better
chance of getting Mr. Sharpe at your house than mine, perhaps I had better accept your kind offer. I will therefore
have the pleasure of breakfasting with you tomorrow, but it
will be out of my power to stay dinner. I hope you will be
able to persuade Mr. Sharpe to be of the party.

I am dear Sir

Sincerely Yours

T Rob<sup>T</sup> Malthus

## 12. RICARDO TO [MALTHUS][3]

[*Fragment*]

New Grove  Mile end
23<sup>d</sup> June 1811

Dear Sir

After giving the subject which you yesterday men-  23 June 1811
tioned due consideration, I cannot agree with you in opinion

---

[1] Addressed: 'David Ricardo
Esqr / 16 Throgmorton Street. /
London'; not passed through
the post.
    MS in *R.P.*
[2] Ricardo's note is wanting.

[3] MS (in Ricardo's handwriting)
in *R.P.* This is an incomplete
draft of a letter which may not
have been sent: only the contents
suggest that it was intended for
Malthus.

23 June 1811 that the exchange will not accurately express the degree of depreciation which the currency may have experienced.

I think your statement was this, The currency has been depreciated 2 pc.$^t$ or in other words goods have experienced a rise of 2 pc.$^t$, but it will not necessarily follow that the exchange shall be depressed 2 pc.$^t$ only, because as this rise of goods will be common to home goods as well as to foreign goods the exchange will probably be affected as much as 4 pc.$^t$. To me however it appears that no rise in the price of goods arising from a depreciation in the currency would occasion any alteration either in the amount of commodities or the real prices, at which they would be imported or exported, until the exchange reached that limit at which it would pay the expences attending the exportation

[The bottom of the sheet is cut off; what follows is written on the reverse side.]

The currency has been augmented 2 pc.$^t$ consequently the prices of all commodities, more or less, both inland and foreign would rise 2 pc.$^t$. The encouragement to the importation of goods, and the discouragement to exportation would be speedily counteracted by the demand for bills which would raise the price of them, or in other words lower the foreign exchange, 2 pc.$^t$. The trade would then go on as before but would be estimated in a medium depreciated 2 pc.$^t$. The real prices of commodities would be, to foreigners, unaltered. If the exchange fell 5 or 7 pc.$^t$ in consequence of further depreciation metallic money would go as long as we had any to send, after which the trade would be restored to its accustomed level, and exports would precisely balance

[The remainder is wanting.]

## 13. MALTHUS TO RICARDO[1]

E I Coll. July 7th
1811

Dear Sir,

I am just returned from the bustle of Cambridge,[2] and   7 July 1811
hasten to say that I hope I shall very soon be able to thank
you in person for your obliging letter.[3]

I expect to be in Town tomorrow and have written to
Mr. Sharpe to say that I would breakfast with him on
tuesday.[4] I hope you will be able to join us, if he is dis-
engaged, as I fear my stay in Town will be short, and I may
not be able to find an afternoon that is not preoccupied.

I am dear Sir
Sincerely Yours
T R MALTHUS

## 14. RICARDO TO [MALTHUS][5]
### [A Note on the Jamaica Exchange]

The Par of Exchange with Jamaica is stated to be £140 –   July 1811
currency for £100. The dollar is current in Jamaica for 6/8
currency consequently 420 dollars are also equal to £100 –
sterling. But that this is not the true par is obvious, a dollar

---

[1] Addressed: 'David Ricardo
Esqr / 16. Throgmorton Street /
London'.
MS in R.P.
[2] Several days of festivities had
followed the installation of the
Duke of Gloucester as Chancellor
of the University on 29 June
1811. (See C. H. Cooper, *Annals
of Cambridge*, vol. IV, pp. 497–8.)
[3] Possibly letter 12.
[4] 9 July.
[5] MS (in Ricardo's handwriting)

in R.P.; not dated, signed or
addressed. Paper watermarked
1806.
  This appears to be a draft of
the 'account of the Jamaica Exchange', sent by Ricardo to Malthus, probably just before their
meeting of 9 July, and discussed
by Malthus in the next letter.
Malthus made use of the information which it contains in his second
article on bullion in the *Edinburgh
Review*, Aug. 1811, pp. 453–4.

July 1811 being worth and containing only as much pure silver as $4/3\frac{3}{4}$ sterling;—420 dollars therefore are only of equal value with £90. 11. – sterling in silver, or to the same quantity of gold if the market and [mint][1] prices of gold agree. 463.72 dollars or £154. 11. 6 currency are the true par of £100 – sterling in silver,—but if gold be considered as the standard of English currency whilst silver is legal tender to any amount in Jamaica the par of exchange must vary with every alteration in the relative value of the precious metals and now that gold is 16 times the value of silver the par must be £164. 2 – in Jamaica currency or 492.34 dollars. The price of a bill in Jamaica now is from 5 to $2\frac{1}{2}$ pc$^t$ prem$^m$ on 140 their estimated par, supposing it 5 pc$^t$ the price of a bill is £147 more than £17 – under the true par, or rather less than $10\frac{1}{2}$ pc$^t$ in favor of Jamaica. At the same time Jamaica finds it advantageous to export Dollars to England the exchange being only nominally in her favor, but really unfavourable to the amount of the expences attending the exportation of money. £147 – Jamaica currency the price for a bill, or which is the same thing 441 dollars each weighing 17 dw$^t$ 8 grains* will at the present price of dollars in England sell for £113 – sterling making dollars a more advantageous remittance than a bill by 13 pc$^t$, from which however must be deducted all the expences attending the exportation of the dollars. In considering the value of gold 16 times that of silver, the price of dollars being 5/11 p$^r$ oz and standard silver 6/1 pr oz, gold must be £4. 17. – p$^r$ oz. This is actually its value if the price of doubloons which are now £4. 13. 6 p$^r$ oz be taken as the standard, but it is probable that the price of standard gold

[*] This is the mint weight of the dollar, but it is probable that the actual weight of the current dollar may be under this standard.

[1] Omitted in MS.

which has not lately been quoted is rather below this price. July 1811
It would appear then that the computed exchange with
Jamaica is 10½ pc! unfavourable to England, that the real
exchange is really 13 pc! in favour of England, and that
these two added together will be within 3 or 4 pc! of[1] the
depreciation of the currency of England reckoning the price
of standard gold at £4. 17. –.[2]

### 15. MALTHUS TO RICARDO[3]
*[Answered by 16]*

East India Coll. Hertford
July 14ᵗʰ 1811
Dear Sir

In the eagerness of our discussion when I had the 14 July 1811
pleasure of seeing you, I forgot to thank you for the account
of the Jamaica Exchange. An export of bullion under a
favourable computed exchange appears to me as strong a
proof as one can well have of a depreciated paper currency
in the country to which the bullion is exported; but in the
present case as a nominal premium is still given for an English
bill, the evidence would be more striking if it could be shewn
that a greater premium was given formerly, when little or no
bullion was exported. Perhaps you may have an opportunity
of ascertaining what was the premium in 1808, and what has
been the progress of its fall.

With regard to the points of difference, between us, though
perhaps we have approximated a little in our late conversations, I think, it seems, that we are not likely entirely to agree.

---

[1] Replaces 'between 3 or 4 pc!
of', which in its turn replaced
'about equal to'.
[2] 'and which diffᶜᵉ may be accounted for by a deficiency in the

actual weight of the dollar' is del.
here.
[3] Addressed: 'David Ricardo
Esqr / 16 Throgmorton Street /
London'.—MS in *R.P.*

I have only to add that in the use of the term redundant as applied to currency, I have been, as far as I recollect, always consistent. I have always applied it to such a state of things as tends to produce a comparative rise of prices, generally, without a tendency to lower the prices of any commodities; and never to a state of things where a rise in the prices of one set of commodities is necessarily accompanied by a fall in the price of others, as in the case of a scarcity of corn or of any necessary articles; and I still think that these two states of things which lead to two such different consequences ought to be differently designated.

If you have leisure I wish to recommend to your attention the 18 chapter[1] of the 2$^{nd}$ book of Sir James Steuarts Political Economy. Though I by no means agree with him in his general conclusions in that chapter; yet I think you will see there, what I mean by a comparative rise of prices not occasioned by a comparative redundancy of currency.

Hume, Smith, Huskisson and all the most respectable writers on these subjects have uniformly considered an unfavourable real exchange as tending strongly to correct itself before it arrives at the expence of transporting the precious metals; and I cannot help most decidedly agreeing with them. I do not see otherwise what would be the encouragement to the exportation of a greater quantity of manufactures during a war. But no such encouragement would be given if, as you say, the variations in the rate of exchange always represent corresponding variations in the values of the currencies.

We expect our house to be full with Mrs. Malthus's family for the next week, after which I shall go into Lincolnshire for

---

[1] Entitled 'Methods of lowering the Price of Manufactures in order to make them vendible in foreign Markets.'

about ten days.[1] On my return I hope we shall have the 14 July 1811
pleasure of seeing you at Hertford. I am dear Sir

Sincerely Yours

in great haste        T R MALTHUS

## 16. RICARDO TO MALTHUS[2]

[*Reply to* 15.—*Answered by* 17]

Dear Sir

I have been so much engaged since I had the pleasure 17 July 1811
of receiving your letter that I have not had an opportunity
of answering it till this evening.

The information which you are desirous of obtaining respecting the premium on bills in Jamaica from the year 1808
to the present period, I will endeavor to procure, but, as
these transactions all take place in Jamaica, and as the merchants here are frequently not acquainted with the prices at
which the bills remitted to them are negociated, I am not sure
that I shall be successful.

I very much regret that there is so little probability of our
finally agreeing on the subject which has lately engaged our
attention. The definition which you give of the word redundant, as applied to the currency, is not satisfactory to me.
Though it should be allowed that the rise in the price of one
commodity, in the case of a scarcity of corn, should be

[1] This and later visits of Malthus to Lincolnshire (below, VII, 193, VIII, 226 and cp. VIII, 349) were no doubt in connection with the living of Walesby, Lincs., to which he had been presented by Henry Dalton, his father's cousin, in 1803, and which he held 'as a non-resident incumbent for the rest of his life, leaving the parish in charge of a succession of curates.' (See J. M.

Keynes, 'Robert Malthus' in *Essays in Biography*, reprint of May 1933, p. 113.)
[2] Addressed: 'Rev⁴ T. R. Malthus /E. I. Coll:/Hertford'; franked by Richard Sharp 'July eighteen 1811'.
    MS. at Albury (as printed in the text); also a draft, incomplete and undated, in *R.P.* (the main variants are given in footnotes).—*Letters to Malthus*, VII.

17 July 1811  accompanied with a fall in the prices of all others, why should
a redundancy of currency be impossible under such circumstances? The currency must, I apprehend, be considered as
a whole and as such must be compared with the whole of the
commodities which it circulates. If then it be in a greater
proportion to commodities after than before the scarce
harvest, whilst no such alteration has taken place in the proportions between money and commodities abroad, it appears
to me that no expression can more correctly describe such a
state of things than a "relative redundancy of currency".
Under these circumstances not only money but every other
commodity would become comparatively cheap as compared
with corn, and would therefore be exported in return for the
corn which would be in demand in this country. By relative
redundance then I mean, relative cheapness, and the exportation of the commodity I deem, in all ordinary cases, the proof
of such cheapness. Indeed from one who allows that the
amount of money employed in any country is regulated by
its value, and might, therefore, be comparatively redundant
though it consisted only of a million, or deficient though it
amounted to 100 millions, I should not have expected any
difference of opinion on the comparative cheapness of money
being the only satisfactory proof of its redundance.[1] If how-

[1] In place of the first part of this paragraph the draft reads: 'I very much fear that we shall not finally agree on the point which we have lately discussed. I am not satisfied with your definition of the word redundant as applied to the currency, because as the prices of commodities are at all times varying from different causes it might happen that a very decided addition to the currency of England (and to that of England only) might be accompanied with a fall in the price of some few commodities, and yet, I think, you would not hesitate to admit that under such circumstances there would be a real redundancy of currency. I cannot help thinking that a redundant currency may be called that which from any causes whatever is increased in relative proportion to the commodities which it circulates, (whether it be really increased or diminished in amount)

ever I thought that the difference between us was as to the correct use of a word, I should immediately yield the point in dispute, but I am persuaded that we do not agree in the principle. You are of opinion that a bad harvest will raise the price of corn, but will lower in some degree the prices of other commodities. Whether it would or would not do so is not material; but if your opinion is correct then I say there would be no exportation of money because money would not be the cheapest exportable commodity. If before the deficient harvest money was at the same value in any two countries, that is to say all their exportable commodities without exception were at the same prices in both, then, according to your view of the question, after the scarcity the prices of all commodities would fall in the country where such scarcity occurred. Whilst then the prices were unequal in the two countries commodities only would be exported in exchange for corn, and there would be no question between us, because we differ as to the cause of the exportation of money.[1]

whilst no such alteration in the relative amount of money and commodities had taken place in other countries. The exportation of money is, in my opinion the proof of its comparative abundance. I should not think it incorrect to say that if France had only $\frac{3}{4}$ of an average crop of wheat, and England had only $\frac{1}{2}$ an average crop, and in consequence wheat bore a better price in England than in France, that wheat was exported from France to England because it was comparatively redundant. If however I should be wrong in so using the term as applied to wheat I can have no doubt that it would be correct as applied to money, because the amount of money employed in any country is regulated by its value and might therefore be comparatively redundant though it consisted only of a million, or deficient though its amount exceeded 100 millions.'

[1] In place of the last three sentences the draft reads: 'Whether it would or would not do so, is not material to my argument; I will therefore for the present admit that it would. If then, before the bad harvest, the prices of commodities were precisely equal in any two countries, after it, such prices must be lower in the country having the bad harvest than in the other, and consequently commodities will be exported in exchange for corn imported. I ask you to explain on what principle

17 July 1811 You have indeed said that there may be a glut of commodities in the foreign market.[1] What! a glut of commodities with a dearer price! impossible,—these two circumstances are incompatible. If the price of any commodity had been £20 in both countries and in consequence of the bad harvest it had been lowered to £15 in one of them, there could not be a glut of that commodity in the other country till it had there also fallen to £15.[2] Not only must the price of one commodity fall in the foreign market, but the prices of all (because you suppose them all to have fallen in England) before money could be exported in exchange for corn, and then I would allow that money would be exported, but even then it would be so only because it was more cheap on the whole, as compared with commodities, in the exporting country, and this I contend is the proof of its relative redundance.[3]

You maintain that money is rendered cheap by a bad harvest as compared with corn only, but with all other commodities it is dearer than before,—and then what appears to me very inconsistent you insist[4] that this commodity thus

money can be exported whilst goods can be more advantageously employed to procure the corn.'
[1] In *Edinburgh Review*, Feb. 1811, p. 345, quoted above, III, 101.
[2] Draft reads 'to £15, or nearly to £15.'
[3] In place of this sentence the draft reads: 'The fact of money being exported is admitted by both, we differ as to the cause. I say that its exportation is not the necessary consequence of the bad harvest; because that money is rendered cheap though frequently accompanying a bad harvest is not a necessary result.—Money then if exported is so because it is

rendered not only cheap, but cheaper than any other exportable commodity, and this I contend is the proof of its relative redundancy.'
[4] From here to the end of the paragraph the draft reads: 'that this commodity which when comparatively cheaper we would not part with nor would the foreign country accept of it, now that is rendered dearer will have a tendency to leave us, whilst too there are commodities which have undergone quite an opposite change, which from being dearer have become cheaper. This is a mode of reasoning which I in vain endeavor to reconcile.'

rendered scarce and dear will be exported, though before it had increased in value, it had no tendency to leave us, whilst too there are commodities which have undergone an opposite change, which from being dearer have become cheaper, and which will nevertheless be obstinately retained by us. This is a mode of reasoning which I cannot reconcile.

With respect to the other point, namely, that the exchange accurately measures the depreciation of the currency, I cannot but humbly retain that opinion notwithstanding the high authorities against[1] me. I do not mean to contend that a convulsed state of the exchange, such as would be caused by a subsidy granted to a foreign power, would accurately measure the value of the currency, because a demand for bills arising from such a cause would not be in consequence of the natural commerce of the country. Such a demand would therefore have the effect of forcing the exports of commodities by means of the bounty which the exchange would afford. After the subsidy was paid the exchange would again accurately express the value of the currency. The same effects would follow, as in the case of a subsidy, from the foreign expenditure of Government. These have a natural tendency to create an unfavourable exchange, yet if the demand for bills is regular it is surprising how this bounty on exportation will be reduced by the competition amongst the exporters of commodities. I am of opinion that in the ordinary course of affairs, if from any of the circumstances so often mentioned, there should be a slight alteration in the value of the currencies of any two countries it will speedily be communicated to the exchange and if such a state of things should permanently continue the exchange has no tendency to correct itself. The fact however appears to be that there is no degree

[1] The sheet of the draft ends at this point; the remainder of it is wanting.

17 July 1811  of permanence in the proportions between the currencies and
the commodities of nations,—they are subject to constant
fluctuations always approaching an absolute level but never
really finding it. I hope I have not wearied you with the defence which I have endeavored to make for the opinions
which I have imbibed. I assure you that I am not obstinately
attached to any system but am ready to relinquish any views
I may have taken as soon as I am satisfied that they are incorrect. I shall not fail attentively to consider the chapters in
Sir J. Steùart's work which you have mentioned. I hope
before the summer is over to pay you a visit at Hertford.

I am Dear Sir
Yours very sincerely
DAVID RICARDO

New Grove  Mile end
17<sup>th</sup> July 1811

### 17. MALTHUS TO RICARDO[1]

[*Reply to 16*]

E I. Coll. Hertford
July 26<sup>th</sup> 1811

Dear Sir,

26 July 1811       I am just returned from Lincolnshire and find your letter
of the 21<sup>st</sup>[2] for which I am much obliged to you. The account
of the Jamaica bills is very curious and satisfactory. I suppose
it would be difficult to ascertain whether, when they bore a
premium of 20 per cent and above, frequent remittances were
made in bullion. If not, the remittances in bullion which are
said to have been lately made from Jamaica at the premium
of only five per cent, and in the actual state of the comparative
prices of gold and silver, appear to me to afford so incon-

[1] Addressed: 'David Ricardo
Esqr / 16 Throgmorton Street /
London'.

MS in *R.P.*
[2] This letter of Ricardo is wanting.

testible a proof of our unfavourable exchanges being chiefly 26 July 1811 nominal, that the most prejudiced merchant could hardly resist it. I should not wonder if it were to be found that the real exchange had been actually in our favour even with some parts of the continent during that part of 1810 when the nominal exchanges were less unfavourable.

If I should write again in the review, I will certainly mention your plan with the approbation which I think it deserves.[1]

In meditating on the subject of your letter of the 17$^{th}$ during my journey into Lincolnshire I think I seized more fully than I had hitherto done your view of the subject. Allowing as you now do that in the foreign expenditure of government, and the payment of a subsidy, bullion will be used in a greater proportion than other commodities on account of its being the currency of the commercial world and universally acceptable, I should allow that in all other cases, (at least if the contract made for goods were immediately fulfilled) bullion would be set in motion from its comparative redundancy according to your definition of redundancy: but I still think that to express what you mean the term cheapness would be more correct, and to convey the cause of the motion of the precious metals in the commercial intercourse of nations most intelligibly to the reader it would be still better to use the expression comparative cheapness of commodities abroad, than comparative cheapness of currency at home—particularly in all those cases where the variations have originated in the supplies of the commodities, and not in the supplies of the currencies.

The reason why I think the term cheapness of currency more correct than redundancy of currency may be explained

---

[1] The ingot plan, which Ricardo had outlined in the Appendix to ed. 4 of the *High Price of Bullion*, was praised by Malthus in the *Edinburgh Review*, Aug. 1811, p. 470. Cp. below, p. 47.

26 July 1811 by the following case which I have no[1] doubt sometimes happens. In a general scarcity of corn a rich nation which can afford to give very high prices on such occasions purchases corn of a poor nation, although the comparative deficiency of corn may be greater in the poor nation than in the rich, and consequently it would be quite i[ncorre]ct[2] to say that the corn was exported o[n account] of [a] comparative redundancy. In my opi[nion] currency is more wanted for *use* in a scarcity of corn than at other times; and according to our accustomed notions, one can hardly call a commodity redundant which is more wanted than usual; but still in reference to the mass of commodities currency is cheap, or rather as I should say home commodities are dear, and bullion goes in search of the cheaper commodities abroad.

You have misunderstood me in one of your letter[3] of the 17th; but I have been interrupted, and find I have not time to explain the matter and finish what I had to say; so I must defer it till I have the pleasure of seeing you here, which I hope will be soon, as I am now likely to be stationary for some time, and shall be happy to see you the first day that suits you, after the beginning of next week. I shall probably not be in Town soon, so pray send me Mr. Thorntons pamphlet.[4] Perhaps you could send it by the 3 o'clock Hertford coach tomorrow. I am impatient to see it. I beg my respects to Mrs. Ricardo and am dear Sir

very sincerely Yours

T R. MALTHUS

I congratulate you on the rise of omnium.[5]

[1] Written 'do' in MS.
[2] MS torn here and below.
[3] The word 'letter' begins a new page, hence the slip in construction.
[4] *Substance of Two Speeches of Henry Thornton, Esq. in the De-* bate in the House of Commons on the Report of the Bullion Committee, on the 7th and 14th of May, 1811, London, Hatchard, 1811. Advertised in *The Times* of 24 July.
[5] See below, p. 49, n. 1.

## 18. RICARDO TO PERCEVAL[1]

[*Answered by* 19]

New Grove   Mile end
27th July 1811

Sir

During the late discussions in Parliament on the subject   27 July 1811
of the Paper currency, you distinctly admitted that a reduction in the amount of Bank notes would increase their
value, and would therefore lower the price of bullion, but
you thought that such a reduction could not be effected
without impairing our resources, cramping our trade, and
distressing our commerce.[2] It appears, then, that you acknowledge the truth of the principles advanced by the
Bullion Committee but hesitate as to the expediency of the
remedy which they have recommended. I will not trouble
you, Sir, with my opinions on this subject; they are already
before the public; but beg leave to suggest, for your consideration a measure, which, if adopted, I cannot help thinking would greatly tranquilise the public mind respecting the
further depreciation of Bank notes. This measure appears to
me to be in strict accordance with those principles to the
truth of which you have given your sanction. Let the Bank

---

[1] MS (a copy in Ricardo's handwriting) in *R.P.*
  Spencer Perceval was Prime
Minister and Chancellor of the
Exchequer from 1809 till 1812,
when he was assassinated.—Early
in 1810 Ricardo had sent him
a copy of his *High Price of
Bullion*, which was acknowledged
by the following letter, dated
'Downing Street 5th February
1810' and signed by Thomas
Brooksbank: 'I am directed by
Mr. Perceval to acquaint you that
he has received your Letter to
him of the 2nd Instant, and to return you his best thanks for the
Book which accompanied it.' (MS
in *R.P.*)
[2] 'He did not differ from those
gentlemen who maintained, as an
abstract proposition, that a diminution of Bank paper would have
a tendency to diminish the balance of exchange; it would produce that effect; but it would be
at the expence of the most dreadful calamities to the country.'
(Perceval's speech in the House of
Commons on the Report of the
Bullion Committee, 8 May 1811.
*Hansard*, XIX, 1071–2.)

27 July 1811  be obliged to sell gold bullion, for their own notes, to any purchaser that shall apply for a quantity not less than 5 ounces, at the rate of £4.. 15 p$^r$ oz for standard bullion, and whatever the bullion so delivered by the Bank may arise from, whether from foreign coin, or from light guineas, let it be freely exportable at the will of the purchaser.

An enactment to this effect would secure the public against any depreciation of the currency beyond that to which it has already reached. The Bank would be at full liberty, at their leisure, and after the most mature consideration, to adopt such other means as might be necessary, when no danger should appear even to the most timid, gradually to reduce the amount of their paper within such limits, as should raise it to the actual value of the standard of the coin. If such a regulation were to take place much of the alarm which at present exists, and which cannot fail to increase, would subside; and though we should have to deplore that the denomination of the coin, had *in effect*, for a time at least, been raised from £3. 17. 10½ to £4.. 15 yet we should feel confidence as to the future, and should no longer be justly apprehensive that we were about to tread the same ruinous course that had involved the finances of other countries in irretrievable distress and difficulties. Neither could it in any way be considered as a hardship on the Bank, to subject it to such a regulation. Before the restriction they were actually obliged to sell gold to the public at £3. 17. 10½ p$^r$ [oz.]$^1$, because at that rate they were obliged to furnish gold coin in exchange for their notes, and yet with the controul which their issues had on the price of gold, no practical inconvenience was suffered by them excepting in the year 1797, a period of great alarm, which occasioned a demand for gold for local purposes only, the exchange at the time being greatly

$^1$ Omitted in MS.

in favour of England. Whilst the Bank have the power of limiting their issues of paper, they have the power of counteracting any tendency to a rise in the price of gold, whatever the demand for that article may be, either on the continent of Europe, or in any other part of the world.

If, Sir, you should deem it necessary, at the expiration of the bill which has just received the Royal assent,[1] to make Bank notes a legal tender, a provision to the effect which I have suggested, would I am confident deprive such a measure of almost all its terrors, as it would give the public complete security against the further depreciation of Bank notes; without which they would have too much reason to fear, from their observations on the past, that the paper currency would continue progressively to sink in value. It is not necessary to point out the effects which will follow from such a conviction on all future leases and contracts.

I hope, Sir, you will pardon the liberty I am taking in addressing you on this subject, and I trust you will be assured that if my opinions are erroneous, they are at least the honest convictions of my mind, as I have no other interest in the correction of our present monetary system than that of all the other annuitants and Stock holders in the Kingdom.

I have the honour to be

Sir

Your obed$^t$ and humble Serv$^t$

DAVID RICARDO

The Right Honb$^{le}$ Spencer Perceval

---

[1] Lord Stanhope's Act, which in substance though not in name made bank-notes legal tender, was to remain in force during one year.

## 19. PERCEVAL (BY ROSENHAGEN) TO RICARDO[1]

[*Reply to* 18]

Downing Street
Sir, 2nd August 1811.

2 Aug. 1811    I am desired by Mr. Perceval to acknowledge the receipt of your letter to him of the 27th of last month, proposing for his consideration a regulation by which the Bank of England should be obliged to furnish Standard Gold Bullion in exchange for its notes, at the rate of £4..15. per ounce.

Mr. Perceval directs me to observe, in reply, that you must be aware that, during the recess of Parliament, the plan you have proposed could not be adopted; nor can you, he apprehends, be surprized that, taking a view so very different from your own, of the present state of our currency and of the causes to which it is to be ascribed, he should not be disposed to adopt the remedies which appear to you to be desirable.

I have the honour to be,
Sir,
Your very obedient humble Servant
A: ROSENHAGEN
David Ricardo Esq.re

## 20. RICARDO TO BENTHAM[2]

Dear Sir                                    Mile end 13th Aug 1811

13 Aug. 1811    I beg you to accept my thanks for your kind communication. I should have been most happy to have passed a few weeks in your neighbourhood, as besides the pleasure of

[1] Addressed: 'David Ricardo Esqre / New Grove / Mile-end.' MS in *R.P.*
A. Rosenhagen was Private Secretary to the Chancellor of the Exchequer.

[2] Docketed by Bentham: '1811, Aug 14, Ricardo (David) Mile End to J.B. Q.S.P. [Queen Square Place] declines the house at Bletchingley.' Bentham and Mill spent the late summer and

Mr. Mill's society it would have afforded me the opportunity 13 Aug. 1811 which I have long desired of procuring the gratification of your acquaintance, but there are obstacles in the way of my wishes which cannot be surmounted. My family is large, and for Mrs. Ricardo's comfort it would be necessary to have the whole of it with us. She would not be happy if one child were absent. At the present time this would be unattainable unless we were to withdraw the greatest part of our children from school, to which they have, after a long vacation but just returned. I regret that I have been the occasion of so much trouble to you. I trust that on your return to London, to compensate me for my present disappointment, you will give me your company at Mile end,—a pleasure which Mr. Mill has often flattered me with and to which your obliging letter appears to have given me a new claim.

I am Dear Sir with great esteem<br>
Your obed<sup>t</sup>. Serv<sup>t</sup>,<br>
DAVID RICARDO

J. Bentham, Esq<sup>r</sup>


## 21. MALTHUS TO RICARDO[1]

Dear Sir,
E I College August 14<sup>th</sup> 1811

 I have been in hopes of hearing from you to say when 14 Aug. 1811 I might have the pleasure of seeing you at the College; and I write a line now in haste to ask whether it will be convenient to you to come on saturday next, as I am about the Review,[2] and should like to consult you on some points. I fear that

the autumn of this year at Barrow Green, a short way from Bletchingley, in Surrey.
MS in British Museum, Add. 33,544, fol. 549.—*Letters to Trower*, I.

[1] Addressed: 'David Ricardo Esqr / 16. Throgmorton Street / London.'—MS in *R.P.*
[2] *Edinburgh Review*, Aug. 1811, Art. X, 'Pamphlets on the Bullion Question.'

14 Aug. 1811 Mr. Sharpe is not in Town, or should be most happy to see him with you. I must send off the review early next week. It will be quite of a general nature, and will have nothing to do with our controversy which appears to me to be too nice a question for the generality of readers to be interested about. Have the goodness to write a line by return of post to say whether I may expect the pleasure of seeing you.

I am dear Sir<br>
very sincerely Yours<br>
T Rob<sup>T</sup> MALTHUS.

We dine at five.


## 22. MILL TO RICARDO[1]

[Answered by 23]

Barrow Green House<br>
Godstone—Surry  22 Sept<sup>r</sup> 1811

My dear Sir

22 Sept. 1811     First and foremost this letter is intended to operate as a memento to both of us, that neither is dead. But in the next place it has another purpose which you will learn by and bye.

In pursuance of the first purpose, you are to learn that here we are all, extremely well, enjoying much this delightful weather, and very much your friends. The first thing of a newspaper which is looked at every morning is the price of Omnium; which has behaved itself so well since we came here, that we are in pretty good humour with it. I know not that any of us has been more deeply interested in its operations than Mr. Bentham, who was in real distress about you at one time; and it required all I could say about your steadiness and knowledge of what you was about, to give him

---

[1] Addressed: 'David Ricardo Esq. / Stock Exchange / London'. MS in *R.P.*

comfort.[1] He has renewed and solemnly confirmed his promise 22 Sept. 1811 to visit you as soon as the weather gets good in spring.

Well—in return for all this information, this very valuable information, we shall want something said about certain persons at Mile End. I do not wish to hear that any harm has befallen them. Some persons, in my place, might say, they wished them all manner of good; that they deserve much; that they are very amiable; that they think of me and behave to me better than I deserve; and so forth. But as for me, I hate flattery. Besides, I have not forgot a certain trimming I was treated with. No, no—Praise, indeed! Deserve, or not deserve—Am I obliged to praise wherever people deserve it? People who scold me? I know better things. However, as I said before, I should like to hear a little about them; if they are mending their manners or so; as for example, if Miss Ricardo is getting rid of her sulky, bad temper. There is a family of Ricardos, too, at Islington,[2] whom I hate very much—if you can tell me that any mischief has befallen them, it will be highly satisfactory.

Now after the first and foremost thing, comes the second and the last; and that is Bullionism. You are to know that before coming down here, Mr. Bentham, hearing that there were opinions of his on the bullion subject, which some friends of his could not digest, had formed a project, that certain dialogues should be held on the subject here, between the parties capable of taking a part in them. As I was looked to, to be the principal spokesman on these occasions, and as I found the discourse was apt, in conversation, to run pretty wide, I thought of setting down upon paper a condensed

[1] The Omnium, or Scrip, of the loan of £12,000,000 contracted by Ricardo and others on 20 May 1811 had gradually fallen, reaching 2¼ per cent. discount in July; it had now recovered and on 20 September stood at par.

[2] Ricardo's father, with his unmarried children.

22 Sept. 1811   view of the argument, both as a recapitulating instrument, and as a sort of standard of reference, to keep our conversations to the point by. I began, at odd times, to put my thoughts together for this purpose, and continued writing, by fits and starts, till the thing has grown into considerable size.—It has been pretty successful in producing convictions here; and as I know you would like to read it, and I had an opportunity of sending it to London, I have sent it for your perusal.[1] To tell me what you think of it, after you have read it, will be an additional topic for the letter I expect from you.

It is at Mr. Benthams house Queen Square Place Westminster addressed to you, and I am afraid you will be under the necessity of sending for it.—I have read the Ed. Rev. Bullion article.[2] You will easily guess what I think of it.

The paper I send you, you will find drawn up, as if it were a review. It was done so in consequence of some jesting that had passed in our conversations.

I hope you will write your remarks as you go along—and what are not fit for a letter I shall see when I come to town. The paper itself you may also keep by you till then, if you think it worthy of house room.

I am very truly,

My Dear Sir

Your friend and ser.[t]

J. MILL

We shall not be in town earlier than the middle of next month—after which it will not be long before I see you.

I have forgot your Throgmorton Street N.[o] so direct to you at the Stock Exchange.

Address to me as per date, 1.[st] page

---

[1] Mill's paper on bullion has not been found.

[2] Malthus's article in the *Edinburgh Review*, Aug. 1811, Art. X.

## 23. RICARDO TO MILL[1]

*[Reply to 22.—Answered by 24]*

[London, 26 Sept. 1811]

My dear Sir

At the very moment that you are using the most delicate and refined flattery, you declare that you are no flatterer. What was it which gave so much pleasure to the inhabitants of New Grove, in the letter which I received from you on tuesday, but the ingenuity with which you had contrived to make us all feel comfortable with ourselves? Even my sulky tempered girl suffered her features to relax into a smile,—she participated in the self-satisfaction of her father in being thought of so kindly, in the company too in which you are now passing your time. Whenever I perceive that such complacent feelings are excited, I am sure there has been flattery in the case, and equally sure that it has been administered by an able hand. Mr. Mill not given to flatter! look at the note to the last page of the MS which you have just sent to me,—how is Mr. Ricardo there spoken of? If you do not feel yourself under any obligation to give praise where it is deserved, you certainly have no scruples in bestowing it where it is not merited. I thank you however for your letter, and was truly glad to learn that you were all well, and had been employing your time in a way so conformable to my wishes. It was but the day before that we had been speaking of you, speculating on the time when you would come home, —which I am sorry to find is yet so distant. Mrs. Mill and the children will, I hope, have laid in a good stock of health and spirits during the delightful weather which has just passed, to enable them to encounter the less enlivening season

26 Sept. 1811

[1] Addressed: 'J. Mill Esq[r] / Barrow Green House / Godstone / Surry'. London postmark, 26 Sept. 1811.—MS in Mill-Ricardo papers.

26 Sept. 1811 which is fast approaching. For Mr. Bentham's and your kind solicitude, about the price of Omnium, I am really grateful. It is still very rickety, but my apprehensions of any very serious fall have considerably abated. You estimated at a false value my steadiness and knowledge of its nature. These qualities, even if I possessed them are of very little avail in managing so ungovernable a commodity as Omnium, but there is one security which I always take on these occasions, and which I consider by far the most important.—I play for small stakes, and therefore if I am a loser, I have little to regret.

You have given me much satisfaction by informing me that you have obtained a solemn renewal of Mr. Bentham's engagement to favor me with his company in the spring. I hope it will not now be necessary to defer it till that period, and that he will be of the same opinion when I communicate to you that I am going to live in town, and shall not be more than a mile distant from him. Mrs. Ricardo has lately, on account of the increasing age of our girls and to be nearer to their masters, expressed a wish to go to town:—this wish every hour acquired new force and in a short time became absolutely irresistible. Search was made after a house, and as ill-fortune would have it, one was found, to be disposed of, in Upper Brook Street    Grosvenor Square,—the very thing to suit us,—brimfull of every convenience, and containing precisely the number of rooms which our large family required. There was however one obstacle to its purchase, and that a most serious one, the price was enormous, and I would not listen to it. Difficulties however only stimulate the brave and when familiarly contemplated, at every view, appear less formidable. I soon found that my opposition abated in the same ratio as the wishes of those about me increased, and in a few days I was completely vanquished.

In short the house is mine. In addition to some other regrets which I shall feel at leaving Mile end will be that of going somewhat more distant from you,—but then I say to myself that it is to town, and to walk from town is never so bad, though rather more distant, as[1] to walk across dangerous cross roads,—besides I shall have a spare bed which I shall hope I may often prevail on you and Mrs. Mill to occupy.[2]

A truce however to my affairs. I shall leave no room for the remarks which I mean to make on your MS. Well then I like it very much,—it assails our adversaries in most of their strongholds and contains the most close reasoning of any thing that has appeared on our side of the question. I shall not rest till you publish it.

We have so often compared our opinions on this subject that it was not probable that I should find any thing material from which to dissent. There are some trifling points re-garding the extent of the admissions of our adversaries;— the idea which they affix to the word depreciation;—the effect produced on prices by the augmentation of circulating medium modified as it necessarily must be by enlarged or diminished bargains on credit or for promissory notes and bills of exchange &c.ª &c.ª which I will submit to your atten-tion when we meet. I doubt too whether at a time when there is no alarm, either of internal convulsions, or of foreign invasion, the notes of a Bank notoriously insolvent would not circulate at par, provided they were less in quantity than the level of circulation required, and the Government con-tinued to receive them in payment of the taxes. I am much inclined to believe that the notes of a Bank where they were

[1] In MS 'at'.
[2] Ricardo moved from New Grove, Mile End to 56, Upper Brook Street, Grosvenor Square, in the spring of 1812.

26 Sept. 1811 received by Government have never been in any country depreciated from any other cause but from an excess of quantity. I should have been glad if you had shewn the extreme folly of Lord Stanhope's observation, that it is only in times of barbarism that gold can be required as the standard of currency,[1]—and the total impossibility of regulating the value of a paper currency without some standard of reference. The increased price of commodities is frequently ascribed not to any, fall in the value of paper, but to the increased number of purchasers caused by the augmented wealth of the country. Taxation is supposed to be another cause. On these points you might give us much useful instruction;—it is a part of the subject which has been much neglected and your work will not be complete if you are silent on it.

You have no where defined the word value. It has a very different meaning from the word price and yet I think you have often used th[ese word]s[2] as synonymous. You say Page 27. "The value of the precious metals throughout the globe is uniform",—or rather "the only difference which can exist is the difference constituted by the expence of carriage." I should have agreed with you if you had said "price" instead of "value". If a bill on London for £100 will sell in Hamburgh for £98 or as much of the money of Hamburgh as is equal to the bullion in £98 of our's then I should say that the price of bullion differed 2 pct in the two countries. But when we speak of the value of bullion we mean

---

[1] 'To believe gold necessary to a circulating medium was an idea only fit for Hottentots. To think a circulating medium of gold necessary was only shewing that we were just at the commencement of civilisation, or rather on the verge of barbarism.' (Lord Stanhope's speech on his own Resolutions respecting a Circulating Medium, 16 July 1811, *Hansard*, XX, 982.)

[2] Covered by seal.

a very different thing—we mean, I apprehend, to measure it by some other commodity,—corn, coffee, hardware or any amongst the thousands of commodities which may be exported. Estimated in either of these commodities money or bullion may differ in value in any two countries, not only all the expences attending its exportation, but also all the expences attending the importation of the commodity to be given in exchange for it. Thus if the expence of sending money to the East Indies amounted to 5 pc⸀, and the expence of sending Muslins from the East Indies to London amounted to 10 pc⸀, before money can be exported from England for the purpose of procuring Muslins in return, its value estimated in that commodity must be at least 15 pc⸀ higher in the East Indies than in England. You 'seem to have been aware of some difficulty in this part of the subject because you observe Page 34 that the consumers pay these expences. Undoubtedly they do but in the first instance they are advanced by the exporter and constitute part of the price of the commodity, and certainly do though it is not immediately apparent determine the exportation of bullion. I think you will agree with me that Bullion will be exported if its price in one country differs any thing more than the expences attending its exportation from its price in the other,—but that when its price does so differ we may be quite certain that its value estimated in some commodity differs considerably more than these expences.

I have the same objection to the follow⸀ passage Page 45. "If it be asked at what limit the importation of corn stops, we answer, at the very limit when the value of gold and silver in the country in question rises above its value in other countries." It appears to me that the circumstance here stated would prevent the exportation of gold and silver but it would not limit the importation of corn,—England might

26 Sept. 1811 have a thousand things which were cheaper than corn and which she might therefore be disposed to give in exchange for it. You observe that the *demand* for corn is unlimited. It is clear that you attach a different meaning to the word demand to what I do. I should not call the mere desire of possessing a thing a demand for it, such desires are undoubtedly unlimited,—but by demand I should understand a desire to possess with the power of purchasing. If so demand is limited.—There are one or two other points which I shall discuss with you when we meet.—I think you must by this time be sufficiently weary of me. On this subject I have no discretion. If you have leisure I should be glad to hear from you again.—

I have not seen but a small part of the Ricardos of Islington, —those whom I have seen entertain sentiments for you no way differing from those which you feel towards them, so take care of yourself. Consider how they unite when attacked. All the Mills in the world would not be a match for them when fairly roused.

Y<sup>rs</sup> most truly

DAVID RICARDO

NB. On looking again at the passage Page 45 I am sure we should agree if the word *value* was more confined in its use for example "at the very limit when the value of gold and silver in the country in question, *estimated in corn*, rises above its value in other countries."

## 24. MILL TO RICARDO[1]
[*Reply to 23*]

Barrow Green House
Godstone—Surry Oct.[r] 15th 1811

My dear Sir

As I foresee that there will be certain points to clear up   15 Oct. 1811
between us when we meet, I have thought that such of them
as it appeared to me that I could, without overloading you
with too many words, clear up beforehand, it might be as
well to have removed out of the way.

As to the things which I have not done and which you
say you wish I had done, these I shall leave till another time.

There are two things to which you object, 1. the having
talked of "the *value* of the precious metals" without having
defined the word value; and 2. the having said that the
importation of corn stops at the point where the value of
gold and silver rises above its value in other countries.

1. By the value of the precious metals in any country I
mean uniformly their value as compared with the *commodities*
of the country. And when I say that the precious metals are
of an equal value in all countries, I mean that they are of an
equal value in respect to commodities, account being taken
of the expence of transmitting the commodities from one to
another of the places which are the subject of comparison.
Thus, for example, every body would say that the precious
metals are of an uniform value all over Great Britain; yet
there are places in Great Britain where a family can live at
one half of the expence at which it can live in some other
places, the difference being constituted entirely by the expence of the carriage of the commodities which form the
grand articles of expenditure.—By the *price* of the precious

[1] Addressed: 'David Ricardo Esq. / 16 Throgmorton Street / London'.
MS in *R.P.*

15 Oct. 1811 metals, I mean the quantity of the currency of any nation, which happens to be given for a definite weight of them.

2. To your next objection I cannot answer so clearly, because I do not recollect so distinctly my own doctrine. You say that the rising of the value of gold and silver above the level of other countries would not stop the importation of corn, because there might be other articles still to give in exchange for corn, which articles might be cheaper. But, if I recollect right, it appears certainly enough by the very argument, that this is precisely the circumstance which could not exist; that gold and silver could not rise above the level of other countries by the purchase of corn, while there was any thing cheaper to give for the corn. My recollection of the argument is already extremely indistinct, as I did not attend to it so much as to fix it in any degree in my memory; and to recall it I must re-invent the whole chain of thought. But I beg you to look into the argument with this view, and see if the matter be not as I now suppose. If it be not, it appears to me just now that it may certainly be proved, that there could be no such cheapness of commodities, in the case of the rise in the value of the bullion which is supposed.

As to the use of the word *demand*, I follow Dr. Smith's rule, which is to call it *effectual demand*, as often as it means the *will* to purchase combined with the *power*.[1] In a year of great scarcity a nation may be said to have a demand for its usual quantity of corn; though it may be unable to purchase, by a considerable proportion, so large a quantity.

So much for your objections. None of them, I think, even in your opinion impair the conclusiveness of the argument. The only question for us is—whether the argument, being conclusive, has any thing in its mode of being put, which is more likely to silence our adversaries, and convince those

[1] *Wealth of Nations*, Bk. I, ch. vi; Cannan's ed., vol. I, p. 58.

who are not our adversaries, than the mode in which it has been put by any other body. I should not be easily persuaded, to take all the trouble about it that would be necessary to fit it for the press. What I mean is, that I should not do so, unless I thought that considerable good was to be done by it. By the bye, if you have any body at hand, on whose knowledge of the subject one could place reliance, you might offer them a reading of it, Sharpe, for instance, or Malthus,[1] without saying whose it is—that by their opinion we might help to shape our own.

I know not what to say about your removal to the West end of the town. I like not to live there myself. I hope you mean not to set forward in the career of fashionable life; which is a source of misery not of happiness even to those who pursue it; which is gone into by one half of its votaries to escape from *ennui*, by another half in the wretched contest of who shall appear to be richest, to have most to spend; and some are dragged into it from mere listlessness and indolence, from an unwillingness to take the trouble of resisting the torrent. One consequence of such a course of life, which in your case I should tremble to think of, is so general as to be almost unavoidable, that the children are brought up with minds thoroughly incapable of happiness, without resources in themselves, and totally dependent on the accidents which govern the sort of life to which they have been habituated. This however is preaching—and I hate preaching, which was never more useless than it is on the present occasion—As for its impertinence, preachers have a title to be impertinent. If I were in a pulpit you would love me the better, the worse I should tell you that I thought of you. Moreover, in regard to the training of children to the best chance of happiness, as I have much attended to it, I hold myself a little entitled to

[1] See letter 25.

15 Oct. 1811 speak, and yours are children who deserve attention to be bestowed upon them, and will repay it.

We shall not be in town till the very end of the month. If any thing occurs to you in the mean time to say to me, let me know it. Mrs. Mill, (who begs her best respects, along with mine, to Mrs. Ricardo &.c. &.c. &.c.) and the little ones are in thriving condition—and I am my dear Sir with much esteem and regard

Yours faithfully<br>J. MILL

I forgot to tell Mr. Bentham I was writing to you, and he is gone to bed

## 25. RICARDO TO MALTHUS[1]

[Answered by 26]

Dear Sir

17 Oct. 1811    I hoped long ere this to have had the pleasure of seeing you in London. I am anxious for an opportunity of introducing Mrs. Malthus and Mrs. Ricardo to each other, and I shall certainly claim the half promise which Mrs. Malthus made me on that subject when I experienced your hospitality at Hertford. We have few engagements, and have a bed always at your disposal so that I shall hope on your very first visit to London you will favour me by occupying it.

A friend[2] of mine has been writing on the subject of bullion.—I take the liberty of sending you the MS. If you could look over it and give me your opinion of it you will much oblige me. He would be induced to prepare it for the press, if he thought that the mode in which the argument is put is more likely to silence our adversaries and convince those

[1] MS at Albury.—*Letters to Malthus*, VIII.    [2] Mill; see above, p. 59.

who are not our adversaries than the mode in which it has 17 Oct. 1811
been put by any other person.

Should you be so engaged that you cannot devote your attention to it at the present time, use no ceremony with me, but return the MS by the coach directed to me at No. 16 Throgmorton Street.

With best respects to Mrs. Malthus I am
Dear Sir
Your's very truly
DAVID RICARDO

Stock Exch^ge
17^th Oct^r 1811

## 26. MALTHUS TO RICARDO[1]

*[Reply to 25.—Answered by 27]*

E I Coll. Hertford
*[ca.* 20 October 1811]

Dear Sir,

I have not been in Town since I had the pleasure of 20 Oct. 1811
seeing you at Hertford, or I should certainly have called upon you; and the first time that Mrs. Malthus accompanies me, she will be very happy to be introduced to Mrs. Ricardo.

I am a good deal engaged at present and have therefore only been able to look over your friends pamphlet in a cursory manner. As far as I can judge from such a reading I cannot say that I think it upon the whole very good either in point of style or matter. The style appears to me to be rather heavy and laboured, too much abounding in repetitions; and with a pretension to accuracy and precision which it does not fulfill. From the introduction I concluded that I should find very accurate definitions of the words money value currency

---

[1] Addressed: 'D. Ricardo Esqr / 16 Throgmorton Street / London.'—not passed through the post; probably enclosed in a parcel with Mill's MSS.
MS in *R.P.*

and exchange; but I did not observe any explanations of these terms calculated to give greater precision to the discussion.

With regard to the matter; though some of it is very good, and the arguments occasionally well stated, yet it appears to me to be by no means unmixed with error. A great deal of labour and time is used to prove that the value of gold is not higher in this country than on the continent; but the only supposition that can at all account for the present phenomena, independently of excessive issues, is an increased value of gold on the continent and not a greater value here, than abroad. The arguments of the author therefore on this point appear to me to be misdirected.

On the subject of the level of the precious metals all over the world, I cannot by any means agree with him, in the mode in which he has stated it; and on many minor points he does not appear to me to be right. I should not therefore upon the whole expect that it will silence many adversaries, and I had rather see something more from your own pen the effect of which I have no doubt would be considerably greater.

I will not however absolutely promise to be brought over to all your opinions even by your own good style and clear statements. For the more I have reflected on the subject of our late conversations the more I feel convinced that it is positively incorrect to state redundancy or cheapness of currency in any sense in which these terms can be fairly understood, as the sole cause of the variations of the exchange, and I feel myself compelled after the most careful and (as far as I can judge) the most impartial consideration of the subject to retain my opinion that the precious metals move for other purposes than to restore the level of currency.

I should like much to have a little more conversation with you on the subject. Can you pay us another visit soon. We

shall always be most happy to see you at Hertford and if 20 Oct. 1811
Mrs. Ricardo should feel inclined to a short country excursion
Mrs. M will feel great pleasure in seeing her at the College.

I am dear Sir sincerely Y<sup>rs</sup>

T R MALTHUS

27. RICARDO TO MALTHUS[1]

[Reply to 26]

Throgmorton Street<br>22<sup>d</sup> Oct.<sup>r</sup> 1811

Dear Sir

    I am exceedingly obliged to you for the trouble which 22 Oct. 1811
you have taken in looking over the papers which I sent you,
and for the remarks which you have made upon them.
Notwithstanding your flattering encouragement I think I
shall not have sufficient confidence again to address the public;—the object which I had in view is completely attained,
—the public attention has been awakened, and the discussion
is now in the most able hands. I regret, however, that you
cannot bring yourself to subscribe to my doctrine respecting
the exchange being influenced by no other causes but by the
relation which the amount of currency bears to the uses for
which it is required in the different nations of the earth. This
may proceed from your interpreting my proposition somewhat too rigidly. I wish to prove that if nations truly understood their own interest they would never export money
from one country to another but on account of comparative
redundancy. I assume indeed that nations in their commercial transactions are so alive to their advantage and profit,
particularly in the present improved state of the division of

[1] Addressed: 'The Rev<sup>d</sup> T. R
Malthus/East India College/Hert-
ford'.

MS at Albury; an identical
copy, not in Ricardo's handwriting, in R.P.—Letters to Malthus, IX.

22 Oct. 1811 employments and abundance of Capital, that in point of fact money never does move but when it is advantageous both to the country which sends and the country that receives that it should do so. The first point to be considered is, what is the interest of countries in the case supposed? The second what is their practise? Now it is obvious that I need not be greatly solicitous about this latter point; it is sufficient for my purpose if I can clearly demonstrate that the interest of the public is as I have stated it. It would be no answer to me to say that men were ignorant of the best and cheapest mode of conducting their business and paying their debts, because that is a question of fact not of science, and might be urged against almost every proposition in Political Economy. It rests with you therefore to prove that a case can exist where it may become the *interest* of a nation to pay a debt by the transmission of money rather than in any other mode, when money is not the cheapest exportable commodity,—when money (taking into account all expences which may attend the exportation of different commodities as well as money) will not purchase more goods abroad than it will at home. You appear to me to have repeatedly admitted that it is the relative prices of commodities which regulates their exportation. Is it not then as certain that money will go to that country where the major part of goods are cheap, as that goods will go to any other country where the major part are dear. I say the major part because if the cheapness of one half of the exportable commodities be balanced by the dearness of the other half, in both countries, it is obvious that the commerce of such countries will be confined to the exchange of goods only. When you say that money will go abroad to pay a debt or a subsidy, or to buy corn, although it be not superabundant, but at the same time admit that [it][1]

[1] MS torn here and below.

will speedily return and be exchanged for goods, you appear 22 Oct 1811 [to me] to concede all for which I contend, namely, that it would be the *interest* of both countries, when money is not superabundant in the one owing the debt, that the expence of exporting the money should be spared, because it will be followed by another useless expence—sending it back again.

If in any country there exists a dearness of importable commodities and no corresponding cheapness of exportable commodities money in such country is above its natural level and must infallibly be exported in payment of the dear commodities,—but what does this state of things indicate but an excess of currency, and it may surely be correctly said that money is exported to restore the level not to destroy it: I ought to apologize for again troubling you with my opinions, but you have drawn me into it. I shall be happy to renew our conversation on these disputed points as soon as you can make it convenient to visit us in London, and I trust it will not be long before Mrs. Malthus and you will favour us with your company. On some future day I shall have great pleasure in again visiting you at Hertford.

I am Dear Sir<br>Your's very truly<br>DAVID RICARDO

## 28. MALTHUS TO RICARDO[1]

My dear Sir, E I Coll Decem<sup>r</sup> 3<sup>rd</sup> 1811

    I am quite vexed to be obliged to say that the Pro- 3 Dec. 1811 fessor's bed which I expected to have obtained for you on saturday is engaged. You know I believe that we have only

---

[1] Addressed:'David Ricardo Esqr/16. Throgmorton Street/London'. MS in *R.P.*

3 Dec. 1811 two in our own house. I had engaged Mr. Hamilton's[1] bed, before I went to Town for either Horner or Sharp, and when I saw you I expected to be able to get another; but I could not speak, as I told you, with certainty, and it now turns out, that I was right not to be too confident. The Inn is too far off to allow of its being proposed at this time of the year.

I hope this disappointment will not be the occasion of any long delay of a visit from you. Can you come on the saturday following?[2] I think Mr. Sharp[3] may be persuaded to accompany you; and if you will then have the goodness to bring the remarks which you alluded to on the last Edinburgh Review,[4] I shall have great pleasure in hearing them, and, we can have a fair and full discussion of the whole subject. One reason indeed that makes me regret rather less my present disappointment than I otherwise should do, is, that I find from Mr. Whishaw[5] that it is the intention of the party to return on sunday morning, which if we asked any body to meet them on saturday, would allow little or no time for the discussion of such a point as that which we wish to [decide.][6]

I hope you will be able to come on saturday s'ennight.

I am my dear Sir<br>
very sincerely Yours<br>
T Rob<sup>t</sup> Malthus

---

[1] Professor Alexander Hamilton.
[2] 14 December.
[3] First written 'Sharpe', then corrected.
[4] Malthus's article on bullion in the August number; see above, p. 47, n. 2. Ricardo's remarks have not been found.
[5] John Whishaw (1764–1840), of Lincoln's Inn, one of the Commissioners of Audit, and a prominent figure in Whig society. He had been a contemporary of Malthus at Cambridge. (See 'A Memoir of Whishaw' by W. P. Courtney, in *The 'Pope' of Holland House, Selections from the Correspondence of John Whishaw and his friends*, ed. by Lady Seymour, London, 1906, pp. 19–37; a book which is largely made up of Whishaw's letters to the Smiths of Easton Grey.)
[6] Covered by seal.

## 29. RICARDO TO TIERNEY[1]

*[Answered by 30]*

New Grove Mile end
11ᵗʰ Decʳ 1811.

Sir

I am encouraged by my friend Mr. Sharp, to submit to    11 Dec. 1811
your consideration some remarks on the means which might
be advantageously adopted, first, to[2] arrest the progress of
the depreciation of our currency, and secondly to restore it
to its standard value.

The first of these objects appears to me, in the circumstances in which we are placed, to be the most pressing and
perhaps the most important. Depreciation cannot be effectually checked by any other means than by depriving the Bank
of the power which they at present possess of adding in-
definitely to the amount of their notes. This might be done
in a direct manner, by limiting the amount beyond which
their paper should not be issued; but it has been plausibly
urged against such a measure that occasions may arise in
which sound policy may require a temporary augmentation
of bank paper, and to deprive the Bank of the power of
increasing their notes at such periods might[3] be the cause of
considerable distress and difficulty to the mercantile classes.

This argument does not appear to me to have as much
weight as those who advance it imagine. The objection however may be obviated by the measure which I beg leave to
recommend; it is simply to oblige the Bank to sell gold
bullion to any purchaser of not less than 50, 100, or 200

---

[1] MS (a copy in Ricardo's handwriting) in *R.P.*
   George Tierney (1761–1830),
the Whig leader, who had been a
member of the Bullion Committee.
Both plans outlined by Ricardo
in this letter were adopted by
Parliament in 1819; see above,
V, 364 ff.
[2] 'remedy' is del. here.
[3] 'occasion' is del. here.

11 Dec. 1811 ounces at a fixed price somewhere about the present market price,—such regulation to continue for six months.

This would secure the public against any further depreciation of Bank notes, as the Bank would be obliged for their own safety to keep the amount of their circulation within the present limits whilst commerce and credit continued in its present state, to prevent such a rise in the price of bullion as would make it profitable to individuals to purchase it of them for exportation;—and if a greater circulation were required from the operation either of increased commerce, or of embarrassed credit, the bank might augment their issues without producing any effect whatever on the price of bullion, and consequently without exposing the Bank to any inconvenience, or depriving the merchants of that increased accomodation, which might be essential to their operations.

If no further measures were taken to approximate the currency to our ancient standard, the adoption of the one here recommended would alone give complete security as to the future:—the depreciation of our currency would be effectually checked, and the bank deprived of the alarming power which they at present possess, of diminishing, at their pleasure, the value of the monied property of every man in the kingdom. It would afford leisure too for the consideration of such further measures as might be necessary, without pledging Parliament to any particular course of proceeding. And if it should be thought expedient to make bank notes a legal tender, the knowledge which the public would have that though already depreciated more than 20 pc.ᵗ, the depreciation of Bank notes would go no further, and that their value would no longer depend on the caprice or false theory of Bank Directors, would deprive that measure of all the alarm which without such security it is so much calculated to produce.

To accomplish the second object, namely, to restore the 11 Dec. 1811 currency gradually to its mint value, I should recommend that at the expiration of six months, the bank should be obliged to sell gold bullion at $6^d$ or $9^d$ $p^r$ oz less than the price now to be fixed, this regulation to continue for one month only. At the end of that period they should again lower the price $6^d$ or $9^d$ $p^r$ oz for the next month, and so on for every succeeding month till the price was reduced to £3. 17. $10\frac{1}{2}$. This reduction would be as gradual as the most timid would think necessary, as if the price of bullion were to fall $6^d$ $p^r$ month, nearly 4 years would elapse before the currency would be raised to its standard value; and if it were to fall $9^d$ $p^r$ month it would not be effected in less than 3 years. When this desireable object should be attained it would be of little comparative importance to the public, whether the Bank were allowed to continue to supply the whole circulation, as they now do, with their notes, or whether they should be compelled to pay in specie. It is not money but money's worth that the holders of notes require, and it can be of little consequence to any reasonable man whether he goes to market with 20 guineas or £21 in notes, provided he can purchase precisely as much with one as with the other. If the public were secured against depreciation by possessing the power of exchanging their notes for bullion at the mint value of gold, I should prefer a circulation, such as ours, consisting wholly of paper, to any other, even as a permanent measure, as being more economical and possessing other obvious advantages.

It need not be observed that the whole of the above plan proceeds on the supposition that the Bank have uncontrouled power of regulating the rise or fall in the price of gold bullion, a point which was most satisfactorily proved during the late discusion on the report of the Bullion Committee.

11 Dec. 1811   Before I conclude I think it right to mention that I took
the liberty of recommending to the Chancellor of the Exchequer the measure which I have stated in the first part of
this letter, as one which might be advantageously adopted
to prevent alarm if Bank notes were to be made a legal
tender. He politely declined to follow my suggestions.[1] I
have now only to apologize for having so long intruded on
your attention and have the honour to be

Sir

Your obed<sup>t</sup> and very humble Ser<sup>t</sup>

Your obed$^t$ and very humble Ser$^t$

DAVID RICARDO

Right Honb$^{le}$ George Tierney.


[The following is written on another sheet.]

In my letter to Mr. Tierney it was my intention to have
added the following passage, but on consideration there
appeared to be some objections to this part of the plan, the
consideration of which would have led me to a longer discussion than was consistent with the object which I had in
view.


There is yet a part of the plan to be mentioned, which
though by no means essential to it, might possibly be
adopted with advantage. It cannot be supposed that the
Bank would willingly do any thing which might be hurtful
either to public or to private credit. Whatever my opinion
of their mistakes may be no one can be more persuaded than
I am of the general integrity of their motives. If however
from a mistaken view of the subject they should diminish
the circulation too rapidly they might raise its value in a ratio
which might involve individuals in much perplexity and

---

[1] See letters 18 and 19.

distress. As well therefore as possessing a security against   11 Dec. 1811
an undue increase of Bank notes for particular periods, it
would be desirable that the Public should also be secured
against a too rapid diminution of their amount. This object
might be most fully attained by enacting that the Bank
should be obliged to buy gold bullion (not less than a fixed
quantity) during the whole period of the reduction of their
notes, at a price not less than 2/- p$^r$ oz under the price at
which they were then selling. When they sold gold bullion
at £4. 17. p$^r$ oz, they should be obliged to buy at £4..15. –.
When they sold at £4. 15– they should buy at £4. 13.
Thus would complete security be obtained for a reduction
of the currency without any danger of the reduction being
made but by means just as gradual as Parliament should
think expedient.

### 30. TIERNEY TO RICARDO[1]
*[Reply to 29]*

Sir,

By the favor of Mr. Sharp I was this morning honor'd   12 Dec. 1811
with your letter. I am extremely obliged by the communication of your suggestions for remedying in some degree
the evils attendant on the present state of our circulation, and
will give to them all the attention they deserve. I shall
probably soon have an opportunity of seeing our Friend
Sharp, and will beg of him to convey to you what may occur
to my mind on the subject in question.

I have the honor to be
Sir
Y$^r$ obliged and obed$^t$ Serv$^t$
GEORGE TIERNEY

Grafton Street
Dec$^r$ 12$^{th}$ 1811

[1] MS in *R.P.*

## 31. MALTHUS TO RICARDO[1]

My dear Sir,                                    E I Coll. Decem$^r$ 12$^{th}$ 1811

12 Dec. 1811     You will probably know before this that Mr. Sharp cannot, unfortunately, come to us on saturday. We rely however upon the pleasure of seeing you. I am sorry you will not come to dinner; but if you really prefer dining before you leave Town, we must content ourselves with expecting you at tea.

I hope to have a Mr. Smyth[2] a friend of mine from Cambridge who is Professor of Modern History there, and has occasionally attended to subjects of Political Economy, to meet you.

I beg my best respects to Mrs. Ricardo, and am

My dear Sir

very sincerely Yours

T Rob$^t$ Malthus


## 32. RICARDO TO MALTHUS[3]

[*Answered by* 33]

New Grove  Mile end

My dear Sir                                    22$^d$ Dec$^r$ 1811.

22 Dec. 1811     I write to you, in the first place to remind you that Mrs. Ricardo and I fully depend on having the pleasure of Mrs. Malthus' and your company at Mile end in the next month, when we hope that our endeavors to make your visit com-

---

[1] Addressed: 'D. Ricardo Esqr. / 16 Throgmorton Street/London'. MS in *R.P.*

[2] William Smyth (1765–1849).

[3] Addressed: 'To The Rev$^d$ T. R Malthus / East India College / Hertford'.

MS at Albury (as printed in the text); also a draft of the same date, complete with cover, in *R.P.* (the main variants are given below in footnotes).—*Letters to Malthus*, X.

fortable, will induce you to make a long stay with us. In the second place, I am desirous of correcting some of the errors in the papers[1] which I left with you and which I have been enabled to discover,[2] as I have many others, by the ingenious arguments with which you have opposed my conclusions. In my endeavors to trace the effects of a subsidy in forcing the exportation of commodities, I stated, if I recollect rightly that it would occasion, first, a demand for bills; secondly, an exportation of all those commodities the prices of which already differed so much, in the two countries, as to require only the trifling stimulus which the first fall in the exchange would afford; thirdly, a real alteration in the relative state of prices, viz a rise in the exporting and a fall in the importing country,—in a degree too to counterbalance the advantage from the unfavourable exchange; and lastly, a further fall of the exchange and a consequent exportation of an additional quantity of goods and then of money till the subsidy were paid. It appears, then, that if the subsidy were small it would be wholly paid by the exportation of commodities, as the fall in the exchange would be sufficient to encourage *their* exportation, but not sufficient to encourage the exportation of money. If the exportation of money were in the same proportion as the exportation of commodities, that is to say, supposing the commodities of a country to be equal to 100, and its money equal to 2, then if not less than one fiftieth of the exports in payment of the subsidy consisted of money, prices would after such payment be the same as before in both countries, and although the exchange must have fallen to that limit at which the exportation of money became profitable, it would immediately have a tendency to recover, and would

[1] See above, p. 66.
[2] In the draft the remainder of this sentence reads: 'by the objections which you offered to my theory, in the conversations which we lately had at your house.'

22 Dec. 1811 shortly rise to par; but it is precisely because less than this proportion of money will be exported that the exchange will continue permanently unfavourable and will have no tendency to rise, more than it will have to fall.

I believe you admit, that in the case of an augmentation of 2 pc.<sup>t</sup> to our currency, altho' it were wholly metallic, the prices of commodities would rise in this country 2 pc.<sup>t</sup> above their former level, and that such rise being confined to this country alone it would check exportation and encourage importation; the consequence of which would be a demand for bills and a fall in the exchange. This rise of prices and fall of the exchange, proceeding from what you do not object to call a redundant currency, would not be temporary but permanent, unless it were corrected by a reduction of the amount of the currency here, or by some change in the relative amount of the currencies of other countries.

That these would be the effects of a direct augmentation of currency, I believe, you, with very few qualifications admit. Now as a bad harvest or the vote of a subsidy tend to produce the very same effects, namely, a relative state of high prices at home, accompanied by an unfavourable exchange they admit only of the same cure,—and [1] as in the case of an augmentation of currency the exchange would have no tendency to rise, neither would it in the case of a subsidy the unfavourable exchange being in both instances produced by a redundant currency, or in more popular language by a relative state of prices which renders the exportation of money most profitable. I have uniformly maintained that the money of the world is distributed amongst the different countries according to their commerce and payments, and that if in any

[1] In the draft the remainder of this sentence reads: 'as in the first case the exchange would have no tendency to rise, neither would it in the second.'

country it should from any cause happen to exceed that proportion, the excess would infallibly be exported to be
divided amongst the other countries. I have, however,
always supposed that my readers would understand me to
mean that this would be strictly the fact only if money could
be exported free from all expence. If the expences of exporting money to France be 3 pc$^t$, to Vienna 5 pc$^t$, to Russia
6 pc$^t$, and to the East Indies 8 pc$^t$, the currency of England
may exceed its natural level as compared with those countries
by 3, 5, 6 and 8 pc$^t$ respectively, and consequently the
exchange may permanently continue depressed in those
proportions. If an excess of currency once occurs, an unfavourable exchange must continue till some alteration in
the relative amount of currency. The circumstances which
may occasion such an alteration are numerous, and are fully
detailed in the papers which I left with you. To the precise
agreement between the effects of an augmented currency and
the effects of a subsidy[1] I most particularly request your
attention, as on such agreement depends the whole success of
the argument which I am advancing in favour of my opinion
that an unfavourable exchange has no tendency to correct
itself.

It may be urged that the relative state of high prices at
home occasioned by an augmentation of currency is the
natural effect of such a cause,[2] but that this is not the case in
a subsidy; that the exportation of commodities in payment
of a subsidy is forced and that it will produce a glut in the
foreign market, but that after the subsidy is paid and the
necessity for exportation shall cease prices will rise in the
foreign market to their former rate.[3] This however will not

---

[1] Draft has in addition 'voted to a foreign power'.
[2] Draft reads 'is their natural

state' in place of the last eight words.
[3] Draft reads 'former level.'

22 Dec. 1811 be true. Commodities may rise in a trifling degree abroad but cannot regain their former rate unless the exchange should also rise to par, but this it can never do whilst the demand for bills do not exceed the supply. Now as the prices[1] of foreign commodities in the home market which could not have been[2] supplied in the usual abundance during the operation of the subsidy when we had a large balance to pay, would fall, and would be in greater[3] demand from the moment that our commodities would be received in exchange,[4] the exportation of our goods would be balanced by the importation of foreign goods and the sellers of bills would neither exceed nor fall short of the purchasers. These are the substance of the amendments which I wish to make to my paper, which is now so faulty that I shall be glad to have it returned to me. Have the goodness to bring it with you when you come to town.

I am my dear Sir

Y<sup>rs</sup> with great esteem

DAVID RICARDO

### 33. MALTHUS TO RICARDO[5]

[Reply to 32]

Weston House Guildford
Jan<sup>y</sup> 1<sup>st</sup> [1812].[6]

My dear Sir,

1 Jan. 1812    I write from Surrey which will account for my not answering your obliging letter before.

---

[1] In draft the last three lines read: 'but cannot regain their former level whilst the exchange continues depressed, and this it would do whilst the purchasers of bills did not exceed in amount the sellers; and this would not take place because the prices', etc.

[2] Draft reads 'which were not'.

[3] Draft does not contain 'greater'.

[4] Draft reads 'in exchange for them; thus'.

[5] Addressed: 'D. Ricardo Esqr / 16 Throgmorton Street/London'. MS. in R.P.

[6] In MS '1811'; post-mark, 1812.

I was sorry to find before I set out that on account of some 1 Jan. 1812 expected communications from the Directors relative to the late troubles in the College,[1] it would be necessary for the Professors to meet a week before the termination of the vacation, which I fear will entirely prevent our paying you and Mrs. Ricardo a visit at Mile End in our way thro Town from Surrey. I hope however that we shall be able to indemnify ourselves early in the Spring. I will endeavour to see you myself if I can about the 14$^{\text{th}}$. We may either breakfast at Mr. Sharpe's, or at some Coffee house in the neighbourhood of the Change; and I will then bring your papers. I shall be obliged to return to the College the same day.

I most entirely approve of the first part of the paper you were so good as to leave with me; but notwithstanding your last explanation I am still of opinion that the exchange has a strong tendency to recover itself. In the case we were considering, it is true that our goods abroad would fall, but the foreign goods which we were in the habit of importing would remain at the same price, and it is not possible to conceive that the usual competition for bills to pay for these commodities, should not prodigiously slacken, when the means of payment were clogged with an unfavourable exchange of 3 per cent.

You desire my particular attention to the resemblance between the effects of what I allow to be a redundancy of currency, and the granting of a subsidy or the purchase of large quantities of corn in a scarcity. I do attend, but cannot

---

[1] 'Some tumult has recently taken place among the students at the East India College, at Hertford, which rendered it necessary for several of the Directors to go down on Tuesday; when tranquility was promptly restored among those misguided youths. The insubordination was noticed on the 4th inst. when the Masters reprobated the practice of firing off pistols, etc. on the anniversary of Guy Faux.' (*The Times*, 18 Nov. 1811.)

1 Jan. 1812 see the strong resemblance you speak of. In the one case there is a strong tendency to an immediate importation of commodities and exportation of bullion; and in the other case the immediate tendency is to an exportation of commodities. And even after the first effect is over, when there may be some apparent resemblance, yet upon a nearer view it fails. In the case of a real redundancy of currency all commodities are affected, and are rendered dearer at home and comparatively cheaper abroad; whereas in the other cases the prices of particular commodities alone, are affected, which I hold to be a most important difference.

If bullion only goes abroad to restore the level of currency, of course a compression of the paper at home would have the same effect, but suppose in a subsidy of 4 millions, 2 millions remained yet unpaid after the exchange had fallen to the price of the transport of the precious metals, would you not by compressing the currency instead of sending the bullion, force out commodities in order to pay the remaining debt which ought not naturally to have gone, to the obvious inconvenience of both nations.

I write in great haste and in the midst of company, so you must make allowance for errors.

Very sincerely Yours<br>T R Malthus

## 34. RICARDO TO HORNER[1]

My dear Sir

4 Jan. 1812     The paragraph in the Morning Chronicle concerning the rise in the exchange with the Continent,[2] excited my

---

[1] MS in the possession of Lady Langman.
[2] 'A very unexpected alteration took place on Tuesday in the exchange, between this metropolis and the north of Europe. The

attention as well as yours, and I immediately referred to Wetenhall's list[1] to see if the statement was correct.

It appears, by that list, that the exchange with Paris has, within a short period, risen 5 pc.<sup>t</sup>, and that of Hamburgh, in a still shorter, 10 pc.<sup>t</sup> The exchange with Russia is not noted, and I have not been able to day to obtain any information regarding it. I should however apprehend, that the rise could not have been occasioned by any recent operations of the Russian Government upon their paper currency, because, in that case, the rise would have been confined to the Russian exchange only, whereas, in the present instance, the exchange with Hamburgh and with Paris are equally affected.

The exchange in my opinion is, even in these turbulent times, rarely operated upon but by two causes: one, and that by far the most common is an alteration, or an apprehended alteration, in the relative prices of commodities in the two countries between which the exchange is estimated, and is in most cases to be traced to some augmentation or diminution in the amount of the currency of one of them. The other is an increased or diminished difficulty and expence, (or the anticipation of such) attending the transmission of money. The exchange with the continent has, I believe, for a length of time, not only been unfavourable to this country to the amount of the depreciation of our currency but considerably more, as much more probably as 10 to 15 pc.<sup>t</sup> This real difference in the *price* of money, (for the exchange expresses nothing more than the relative price, and not the relative value of money) as well as the real difference in the[2]

rise in favour of this country is nearly 10 per cent. We understand numerous and large remittances have been received from Russia by the Anholt Mail.' (*Morning Chronicle*, Thursday, 2 Jan. 1812.)

[1] *The Course of Exchange*, published every Tuesday and Friday by James Wetenhall.
[2] 'relative' is del. here.

price of sugar or coffee, may be attributed to the difficulties which our enemy has interposed in the way of exportation. If then these difficulties should diminish, or should be expected to diminish, from the pacific disposition of one or more of the continental Powers the relative price of money as well as of all other commodities would be raised in England,—or in other words, the exchange would become less unfavourable to England by the whole amount of the diminished risk and expence attending the exportation of money. Whether in the present instance the exchange has been affected by such a cause, or by any other circumstance attending the present violent and unnatural state of commerce, I am not competent to judge.

With respect to the observation in the Chronicle "that large remittances had been received from Russia by the Anholt mail" the writer cannot mean that money has been actually transmitted,—the exchange even now would not pay the charges of such transmission. He means nothing more than that bills to a large amount have been negociated at an improved exchange. Wherever there is a remitter there must be a drawer of a bill;—wherever there is a seller there must be a buyer. It would be as correct therefore to say that by the last Anholt mail many bills had been drawn, as that many bills had been remitted[1]. Nothing can be called a bonâ fide remittance but goods or money,—bills of exchange transfer a debt but never pay it.

I am happy that so many good heads are employed on the subject of the depreciation of our currency, and watching the symptoms which attend it. If no other good should result I trust that the further progress of depreciation will be arrested and that the public will receive so much correct information as will in all future times prevent the recurrence

---

[1] Replaces 'transmitted'.

of so alarming an evil. I shall read Lord Lauderdale's tract[1]  4 Jan. 1812
with much interest.

I am sorry that my information is so scanty.

Believe me most truly Your's
DAVID RICARDO

New Grove  Mile end
  4<sup>th</sup> Jan.<sup>y</sup> 1812.

I am informed by a respectable broker that the exchange
with Hamburgh is not really so high as quoted by 2 pc<sup>t</sup>,—
that in fact there are two prices for bills depending on the
credit of the parties,—that in the present interrupted state
of trade this difference is greater than was ever before known.
This will account for a portion of the rise.

F. Horner Esq<sup>re</sup>


35. MALTHUS TO RICARDO[2]

E I. Coll. Feb.<sup>y</sup> 23. 1812.

My dear Sir,

I have been so much engaged since my return to the  23 Feb. 1812
College that I have not been able to think of a visit to Town.
Mrs. Malthus and I, however, have not forgot Mrs. Ricardo's
kind invitation, and have always intended to fulfil our promise the very first opportunity. We have some idea that we
may be able to leave home for a day or two the latter end of
this week, and I write to know whether that time will suit
you and Mrs. Ricardo for our proposed visit. If you are
moving, or preparing for it, or if from any other cause the
time I have mentioned or the following friday, should not
be convenient, don't make the slightest ceremony of saying

---

[1] *The Depreciation of the Paper Currency of Great Britain Proved*, by the Earl of Lauderdale, London, Longman, 1812.

[2] Addressed: 'D. Ricardo Esqr. / 16. Throgmorton Street / London'. MS in *R.P.*

so, as I have no doubt we shall be in Town for some days, later in the spring, and can then take the opportunity of paying our respects to Mrs. Ricardo in Brooke Street, where I suppose you will be settled by april or May.[1]

I should like to see again the paper which you were so good as to read at Mr. Sharpe's,[2] and indeed to look over the other once more.[3] I think however that I have seized pretty clearly your view of the subject; but after the fullest consideration that I can give it, I cannot quite agree with you. It really appears that a desire to simplify, which has often led away the most scientific men, has induced you to ascribe to one cause phenomena that properly belong to two, and not to give sufficient weight to the facts which (to me at least) appear to make against your doctrine. I confess I am still of opinion that these facts are not all satisfactorily explicable upon your principles; and I never look over the tables of exchange without being more and more confirmed in the truth of what I stated in my first review,[4] that "though the effects of a redundancy of currency upon the exchange are *sure*, they are slow compared with the effects of those mercantile or politi[cal][5] transactions, not connected with the question of currency and while the former of these causes is proceeding with a steady and generally uniform pace, the more rapid movements of the latter are opposing aggravating or modifying their operations in various ways, and producing all those complex and seemingly inconsistent appearances which are to be found in the computed exchange".

There is one part of the question between us which can only (it appears to me) be determined by experience. You

---

[1] Cp. above, p. 53, n. 2.
[2] Presumably on 14 January; see above, p. 77.
[3] Cp. above, pp. 66, n. 4 and 73.
[4] The review of Ricardo and others on bullion, *Edinburgh Review*, Feb. 1811, p. 360.
[5] MS torn; the review, as published, does not contain 'or political'.

think that in the payment of a subsidy more commodities will go in proportion than bullion. I think, that if it be considerable, more bullion would go than had before been used to circulate the commodities sent. The decision of the point must depend upon whether it has been found in practice that a stimulus within the expence of the transport of the precious, (or only for so short a time at that price, as to carry over a less than the usual proportion of the metals) is *sufficient* to pay a debt of 3 or 4 millions; or insufficient. If insufficient, then it is clear that more bullion would go in proportion than commodities; because no commodity that requires a greater stimulus than bullion could be sent while bullion was to be had at the mint price.

The alarm which the Bank is known to feel on occasion of granting a subsidy appears to me to shew unquestionably which way experience has decided. With regard to the state of the exchange being a correct exponent of the relative value of different currencies,—surely such a position is inconsistent with the idea of a stimulus to exportation being given by an unfavourable exchange, a stimulus the effects of which you have yourself calculated upon as the chief reason why a subsidy would be paid with little or no necessity for the transport of the precious metals. I believe I made a little mistake in my letter from Surrey[1] but I still think that the exchange has a tendency to recover itself. The very stimulus we are now speaking of is a proof.

Very sincerely Yours,<br>T R Malthus

[1] Letter 33.

## 36. RICARDO TO MALTHUS[1]

*[Fragment]*

Summer
1812 or 1813

[...] by assuring you that I was not going to weary you with a repetition of my hundred times told tale, and I am ashamed to see that I have filled four sides with nothing else. There are some other points on which I shall make some remarks when I have the pleasure of seeing you. If you should come to town will you do me the favor to call at the Stock Exch^ge, unless my house should not be much out of your way. I recommend your calling there because I am just about deserting Brook Street for some time. Mrs. Ricardo and all the family are going to Ramsgate to morrow morning, and she will not consent to let me remain at home by myself, so that when I am in London I shall be chiefly with my brother[2] at Bow;—now and then I shall pass a night at home. My business is so uncertain that I cannot at all foresee what portion of the next two or 3 months I shall be able to spend at the sea side. It is probable that I shall be so much in town that I shall be found by you at the Stock Exch^ge. —Be so good as to make my compliments to Mrs. Malthus and believe me

Your's most truly

DAVID RICARDO

[1] Only the last half-sheet of this letter is preserved. Addressed on back: 'The Rev^d T. R Malthus'; not sealed and not passed through the post; was perhaps enclosed in a parcel with a MS of Malthus. The date must be 1812 or 1813 (after Ricardo's moving to Brook Street, and before his taking Gat-comb Park); in both those years the Ricardos went to Ramsgate in the summer. The paper is water-marked '1807' and is identical with that of letter 38.

MS at Albury.—*Letters to Malthus*, p. 105 (not numbered).

[2] Moses Ricardo.

## 37. RICARDO TO MALTHUS[1]

London 29th Aug[t] 1812

My dear Sir

I intend leaving town this evening for Ramsgate, where 29 Aug. 1812
I think I shall stay about a fortnight, so that I cannot accept
your kind invitation for saturday next; but I hope it will not
be long before I bend my steps towards your hospitable roof.
—If on saturday the 19th of Sept[r] you should be quite dis-
engaged, and it should be every way convenient to you and
Mrs. Malthus I shall be glad to take tea with you on the
evening of that day. I shall be obliged to quit you on the
monday morning. I hope I need not say that I shall be exceedingly sorry if I put you to the least inconvenience, and
that it will be equally agreeable to me to visit you on any
saturday after the 19th if I am not engaged to go to Ramsgate.

Perhaps you will be so good as to write a few lines
directed to the Stock Exch[ge] a few days previously to the 19th
as I shall certainly be in town at that time. I am obliged to
you for the interest you take in the price of Om[m],—it
appears to be in a very thriving condition.[2] Mr. Goldsmid[3]
informs me that at the period of the improvement in the
exch[ge] about Xmas last there were no importations, as far as
he knows, of gold from France. A small quantity was imported from Lisbon. I have consulted Wetenhall's list and
the following appear to be the variations in the exch[ge] and
the price of gold about Christmas last.

---

[1] Addressed: 'The Rev[d] T. R
Malthus / East India College /
Hertford'.
    MS at Albury.—*Letters to Mal-
thus*, XI.
[2] The Omnium, or Scrip, of the
Loan of £22,500,000 for England,
Ireland and the East India Com-

pany, which had been contracted
by Ricardo and others on 12 June
1812, was now at 6 premium.
[3] Aaron Asher Goldsmid or Isaac
Lyon Goldsmid, partners in the
house of Mocatta and Goldsmid,
bullion brokers to the Bank of
England.

29 Aug. 1812

| | Exch$^{ge}$ with Hamb$^{h}$ | Doubloons | Portg$^{e}$ gold |
|---|---|---|---|
| **1811** | | | |
| Nov. 29 | 24 | £4. 15. – p$^{r}$ oz. | |
| Dec$^{r}$ 3 | 24. 6 | | £4. 18. 6 |
| 6 | 24. 6 | 4. 14. 6 | 4. 18. 6 |
| 13 | 25 – | 4. 15. 6 | |
| 20 | 25. – | | 4. 19. – |
| 31 | 27. 6 | | |
| **1812** | | | |
| Jan.$^{y}$ 3 | 27. 6 | 4. 14 – | 4. 18. 6 |
| 31 | 27. 6 | | 4. 18. 6 |
| feb. 21 | 28 | | 4. 17 |
| March 20 | 29. – | | 4. 15. 6 |
| 31 | 29. 4 | 4. 14. 6 | 4. 13. 6 |
| April 21 | 29. 4 | 4. 17. 6 | 4. 17. 6 |
| June 5 | 28. 6 | | 4. 18. 6 |
| July 31 | 28. 9 | 4. 19. – | 5. – – |
| Aug 28 | 28. 9 | 5. – – | |

The price of dollars yesterday was 6/3½ p$^{r}$ oz higher by one penny than any price ever yet quoted, I should think that a very trifling rise more will send the tokens out of circulation. We will speak on our old subject when we meet.[1] I am now in great haste and must therefore conclude. Pray make my kind compliments to Mrs. Malthus and believe me

My dear Sir

Y$^{rs}$ very truly

DAVID RICARDO[2]

---

[1] 'We quite agree that taxation will re' is del. here.

[2] Malthus writes at the end in pencil 'Was any bullion imported from Hamburgh in March.'

## 38. RICARDO TO MALTHUS[1]

London 17 Dec.ʳ 1812

My dear Sir

I have written to Mr. Thornton[2] to request him to meet  17 Dec. 1812
you at dinner, at my house, on any day most convenient to
him, after saturday, and before thursday, but I have not had
his answer in time for this day's post. I will send you a line
at the King of Clubs.[3] I shall only ask Mr. Sharp to meet us.

Will you not stay with us whilst you are in Town? I assure you it would be quite convenient, and it would afford
me great pleasure. If Mrs. Malthus accompany you it will be
still more agreeable, and I am desired by Mrs. Ricardo to add
her solicitations to my own.

On many points connected with our old question we are
I believe agreed,—though there is yet some difference between us. I have not lately given it so much consideration as
you have,—and I always regret that I do not put down in
writing, for I have a very treacherous memory the chief
points of difference that occur in our discussions. I cannot
help thinking that there is no unfavourable exchange which
may not be corrected by a diminution in the amount of thè
currency, and I consider this to afford a proof that the currency must be redundant for a time at least. Whilst the exchange is unfavourable it is always accompanied though not

---

[1] Addressed: 'To / The Revᵈ
T. R. Malthus / East India College /
Hertford'.
MS at Albury.—*Letters to Malthus*, XII.
[2] Henry Thornton (1760–1815),
M.P. for Southwark, one of the
authors of the Bullion Report.
[3] A small society, chiefly of
Whig politicians, which met
monthly for dinner from 1798 to

1823. Malthus had been elected
a member on 4 April 1812 and
Ricardo was elected on 7 June
1817. Sharp, Mackintosh and
Whishaw were among the found-
ers. (See *The Clubs of London*,
1828, vol. II, pp. 159–201; and
W. P. Courtney, 'The King of
Clubs', in *The 'Pope' of Holland
House*, 1906, pp. 333–40.)

17 Dec. 1812 always caused by an excess of currency. With best respects to Mrs. Malthus

I am My dear Sir
Your's most truly
DAVID RICARDO

If you will occupy our room be so good as to write me a line, and again let me say that by complying with my request you will give me great pleasure.

As I was about leaving the city I rec⁴ Mr. Thornton's answer he is engaged on wednesday and thursday, and has fixed on monday for our meeting but he wishes us to meet at his house as there is to be a debate in the House of Lords on the Bullion question¹ and he is not sure that his presence may not be necessary in the Commons. I will settle this point with him and if you do not hear from me I shall expect you at my house on monday, if you do not agree to come on saturday even᷽

39. RICARDO TO MALTHUS²

Stock Exchᵍᵉ
25ᵗʰ Febʸ 1813
My dear Sir

25 Feb. 1813    I have just time, after a very busy day, to tell you that I will endeavor to get Mr. Mushet to meet you at my house at breakfast on sunday morning. At any rate I shall expect you, and if Mushet is engaged, I shall be able to tell you whether he will meet us on monday or tuesday in the City. He is exceedingly obliging, and would I am sure not mind trouble, if he could contribute to throw light on the subject

¹ The Lords' debate, however, took place on Friday, 18 December, when the Gold Coin Bill (for continuing Lord Stanhope's Act of the previous year) was passed.

² Addressed: 'The Rev⁴ T. R Malthus / East India College / Hertford'; postmark, 1813. MS at Albury.—*Letters to Malthus*, I, where it is misdated 1810.

of exchanges, yet I think he will not be inclined to publish any thing under his own name as he gave great offence to the higher powers on a former occasion.[1]

You have clearly stated the point of difference now between us;—I think we never so well understood each other before. There are some causes which operate on the exchange which are in their nature of transitory duration,—there are others which have a more permanent character.

If we agree that a change of taste in one country for the commodities of the other,—and the transmission of a subsidy[—]will produce certain effects on the exchange, the only question between us is as to their duration. I am of opinion that they will operate for a very considerable time, and that in fact recourse is not had to bullion but as a last resort.

I cannot believe that you give a correct account of your habits of application, any more than you did of your memory when I last saw you. From all my observations I should have been led to the very opposite conclusions from those which you have formed and I believe most of your friends would be of my opinion. When you have once fairly begun I expect that you will advance at a giant's pace.

I beg you to remember me kindly to Mrs. Malthus.

I am my dear Sir

Your's very truly

DAVID RICARDO

[1] By his pamphlet of 1810; see above, p. 9, n. 1.

## 40. RICARDO TO MALTHUS[1]

Stock Exch<sup>ge</sup>
22 March 1813

My dear Sir

　　Mrs. Ricardo is expecting Mrs. Malthus to accompany her on friday next to Knyvett's concert, and will I am sure be very much disappointed at the information which I am to give her that she will not be able to accompany you to town. I will not however quite give up all hopes of seeing her.—

You must positively not think of leaving us before tuesday. I have engaged several of your friends to meet you at dinner on monday, and I not only advance my own claims but those of Mr. Wishaw, Mr. Sharp, Mr. Tennant[2] and Mr. Dumont.

I have been making enquiries concerning a bullion merchant. I find that the trade is mostly carried on by a class of people not particularly scrupulous in their modes of getting money, and I am told that they would not be very communicative, particularly on the subject of their *exports*. There are however some well informed merchants who know a great deal of the trade without themselves being actively engaged in it, to whom I hope I shall be able to introduce you.

I do not admit that if you were to double the medium of exchange it would fall to half its former value, not even if you were also to double the quantity of metal which was the standard of such medium. The consumption would increase in consequence of its diminished value, and the fall of its value would be regulated precisely by the same law, as the fall in the value of indigo, sugar or coffee.

---

[1] MS at Albury.—*Letters to Malthus*, II, where it is misdated 1810.

[2] Smithson Tennant (1761–1815), who was appointed Professor of Chemistry at Cambridge this year; he was a member of the Council of the Geological Society.

Mr. Mushet will dine with us on sunday. What do you  22 March 1813
think of Mr. Vansittart's financial talents?[1]

$Y^{rs}$ very truly

DAVID RICARDO


## 41. RICARDO TO MALTHUS[2]

Stock Exch$^{ge}$

24 M$^{ch}$ 1813

My dear Sir—

I have left you quite free for friday, but I regret that  24 March 1813
your engagements will not conveniently allow you to come
to us on that day. We shall expect you on saturday morning.
I hope Mrs. Malthus' visit will not be deferred longer than
the next meeting of the King of Clubs.

It appears to me that you ascribe the difference in the
variations of price, which would probably be the effect of
doubling the quantity of Coffee, Sugar, and Indigo, on one
hand; or of doubling the quantity of the precious metals on
the other, to a wrong cause. Coffee, sugar and Indigo are
commodities for which, although there would be an increased use, if they were to sink much in value, still as they
are not applicable to a great variety of new purposes, the
demand would necessarily be limited; not so with gold and
silver. These metals exist in a degree of scarcity, and are
applicable to a great variety of *new* uses;—the fall of their
price, in consequence of augmented quantity, would always
be checked, not only by an increased demand for those purposes to which they had before been applied, but to the want

---

[1] Nicholas Vansittart, who had
succeeded Perceval as Chancellor
of the Exchequer, had introduced
a New Plan of Finance in the
House of Commons on 3 March
1813; cp. above, IV, 158 ff.

[2] Addressed: 'To / The Rev$^d$ T R
Malthus / East India College /
Hertford'; postmark, 1813.
MS at Albury.—*Letters to Mal-
thus*, III, where it is misdated 1810.

24 March 1813 of them for entirely new employments. If they were in sufficient abundance we might even make our tea kettles and saucepans of them. It is to this essential difference between these commodities, and not to the circumstance of one of them being employed as a circulating medium, that I should attribute the different effects which would follow from the augmentation of their quantity. In any point of view however I do not see how it bears materially on the question between us, namely whether the precious metals are frequently resorted to for the payment of debts between countries when no disturbance has taken place in the amount or proportion of the currency.—

I wonder as you do that the stocks have not felt the effects of Mr. Vansittart's vigorous system. The delay which has taken place in creating new stock; the good news from abroad; and above all the want of reflection in the mass of stockholders may be considered as the cause.

Ever truly Yours<br>
DAVID RICARDO

## 42. RICARDO TO MALTHUS[1]

London 10 Aug. 1813

My dear Sir

10 Aug. 1813     On my return to London after a short excursion to Tunbridge Wells I found your obliging letter.[2] The information which it contains respecting the distinction between the town of Berkhamstead and the village Berkhamstead,[3] has again made me wish to get over the remaining obstacles to my possessing the house with which I was so

---

[1] Addressed: 'To / The Rev<sup>d</sup> T R Malthus / East India College / Hertford'; postmark, 1813. MS at Albury.—*Letters to Mal-*

*thus*, IV, where it is misdated 1810.
[2] Malthus's letter is wanting.
[3] Great Berkhamstead and Little Berkhamstead, in Hertfordshire.

much pleased,—particularly as I have seen nothing in my
short tour, which I undertook chiefly for the purpose of
looking after a house, likely to suit me. I have had a civil
letter from Mr. Talbot, he wishes Mrs. Ricardo to see his
house as he thinks he could suggest a mode of increasing
the number of chambers at a moderate expence. I have of
course answered his letter.

I am sorry that I must decline your kind invitation for
Saturday next, but I have made an engagement which will
preclude me from accepting it.—

On further reflection I am confirmed in the opinion which
I gave with regard to the effect of opening new markets or
extending the old. I most readily allow that since the war,
not only the nominal but the real value of our exports and
imports has increased,—but I do not see how this admission
will favour the view which you take of this subject.

England may have extended its carrying trade with the
Capital of other countries. Instead of exporting sugar and
coffee direct from Guadaloupe and Martinique to the continent of Europe the planters in those colonies may first export them to England, and from England to the continent.
In this case the list of our exports and imports will be swelled
without any increase of British Capital. The taste for some
foreign commodity may have increased in England at the
expence of the consumption of some home commodity. This
would again swell the value of our exports and imports but
does not prove a general increase of profits nor any material
growth of prosperity.

I am of opinion that the increased value of commodities is
always the effect of an increase either in the quantity of the
circulating medium or in its power, by the improvements in
economy in its use,—and is never the cause. It is the
diminished value, I mean nominal value, of commodities

10 Aug. 1813  which is the great cause of the increased production of the mines,—but the increased nominal value of commodities can never call money into circulation. It is certainly an effect and not a cause. I am writing in a noisy place,—you must therefore excuse all blunders. I must offer the same apology for my two half sheets. I did not like to copy the first half over again. With best compliments to Mrs. Malthus

I remain

Y<sup>rs</sup> very sincerely

DAVID RICARDO

43. RICARDO TO MALTHUS[1]

Stock Exch<sup>ge</sup>

My dear Sir                                      17 Aug 1813

17 Aug. 1813       I believe I must not think of Mr. Talbot's house, but I cannot deny myself the pleasure of accepting your kind invitation for saturday next—I will be with you at the usual hour.

That we have experienced a great increase of wealth and prosperity since the commencement of the war, I am amongst the foremost to believe; but it is not certain that such increase must have been attended by increased profits, or rather an increased rate of profits, for that is the question between us. I have little doubt however that for a long period, during the interval you mention,[2] there has been an increased rate of profits, but it has been accompanied with such decided improvements of agriculture both here and abroad,—for the French revolution was exceedingly favorable to the increased production of food, that it is perfectly reconcileable

---

[1] Addressed: 'To / The Rev<sup>d</sup>    MS at Albury.—*Letters to Mal-*
T R Malthus / East India College /   *thus*, V, where it is misdated 1810.
Hertford'; postmark, 1813.        [2] Probably 1793 to 1813: cp.
                                  above, II, 282 and below, p. 168.

to my theory. My conclusion is that there has been a rapid increase of Capital which has been prevented from shewing itself in a low rate of interest by new facilities in the production of food.—

I quite agree, that an increased value of particular commodities occasioned by demand has a tendency to occasion an increased circulation, but always in consequence of the cheapness of some other commodities. It is therefore their cheapness which is the immediate cause of the introduction of additional money.

I have not been home since I rec⁴ your letter,[1] I will look at the passage you refer me to in Adam Smith, and will consider of the other matters in your letter, so as to be prepared to give you my theory when we meet.

The facts you have extracted from Wetenhall's tables are curious and are hardly reconcileable to any theory. I attribute many of them to the state of confusion into which Europe has been plunged by the extent, and nature of the war,—and it would be quite impossible to reason correctly from them without calculating what the state was of the real as well as the computed exchange during the periods referred to. Pray make my best respects to Mrs. Malthus and believe me

Truly Yours<br>DAVID RICARDO

[1] Malthus's letter is wanting.

## 44. RICARDO TO TROWER[1]

Upper Brook Street  8ᵗʰ Novʳ 1813

Dear Trower

After reading the Pamphlet[2] which you were so kind as to send me, I fully intended calling on you, to thank you for the pleasure and information which I had received from it,—but I am so circumstanced at present that I am seldom at this part of the town at an hour when I am likely to meet you. Even yesterday,[3]—a day generally at my disposal, I was obliged to leave home immediately after breakfast, and I did not return till this evening. In about a fortnight my family will return from Ramsgate when I shall live more like a rational being. I shall then hope to see you both at your house and at mine.

I have read the letters written by you and Laicus (for the first time) with very great interest. All that can be said on the subject has, I think, been ably said on both sides. My opinion coincided with yours before I read your letters and it is now very much strengthened by the facts and reasoning which you have brought forward. I quite rejoice that your time is so usefully employed.

Yʳˢ very truly

DAVID RICARDO

---

[1] MS at University College, London.—*Letters to Trower*, II.
[2] *Christianity in India.—Letters between Laicus and An East India Proprietor as they appeared in the Times Newspaper in the months of August, September and October, 1813*, London, Rivington, n.d., 102 pp. In Trower's copy (now in the possession of Dr Bonar) 'Hutches Trower Esq.' is written on the title-page after 'An East India Proprietor'; the Editors of the *Letters to Trower* assign to him, on the basis of his family papers, both the authorship of the 'East India Proprietor's' letters and the editorship of the pamphlet as a whole. In these letters he deprecates attempts at the conversion of the Hindoos, which he considers impossible as well as inexpedient.
[3] A Sunday.

## 45. RICARDO TO MALTHUS[1]

My dear Sir

London 30$^{th}$ Dec$^r$ 1813.

I have been amusing myself for one or two evenings in calculating the exchanges, price of gold, &c,—at Amsterdam, and I enclose the result of my labours. I have every reason to believe that my calculations are correct,—though I am somewhat puzzled at the profit which there appears to be on the importation of gold from Amsterdam, if the prices there be quoted correct. If the difference were the other way we might ascribe it to the money of Holland not being so good as it ought to be by the mint regulations, but in the present instance, for guilders as good as they are coined gold can be bought 9$\frac{1}{2}$ pc$^t$ cheaper than in London. I am told that Gold which cannot be exported has sunk considerably in price altho' gold that may be exported keeps its price. I fully expect that foreign gold will be lower.

We have had a continuance of foggy weather ever since monday—we are obliged to burn candles during the day, and at night it is with the greatest difficulty we can find our way to our homes. I hope you are more fortunate and breathe a clearer atmosphere.

We shall expect you in Brook Street on your next visit to London. Have the goodness to write to me the day before you come. With best wishes to Mrs. Malthus I am Dear Sir

Yours very truly

DAVID RICARDO

30 Dec. 1813

[1] MS at Albury.—*Letters to Malthus*, XIII.

| 1 | 2 | 3 | 4 | 5 | 6 | 7 | Rea |
|---|---|---|---|---|---|---|---|
| Price of Gold at Amsterdam $P^m$ on ƒ355 $p^r$ marc | Value of a marc in Current Guilders | Corresponding price of an oz of stand$^d$ gold in London* | Corresponding price of an oz of stand$^d$ silver in London | Value of an oz of stand$^d$ gold in Flemish current Shillings | Value of an oz. of standard gold in Flemish Banco Shill$^{gs}$ †Agio 3 pc$^t$ | Real par of Exch$^{ge}$ in Flemish Current Shill$^{gs}$ $p^r$ £ ster$^g$ in gold. | Rea Ex Flem Shill ster Ag |
| | | | Pence | | | | |
| Par ƒ355 | ƒ355 | | 68.00 | 137 | 133 | 35.20 | |
| 1 p.c. P$^m$ | 358.55 | | 67.32 | 138.4 | 134.3 | 35.55 | |
| 2 | 362.10 | | 66.67 | 139.8 | 135.7 | 35.90 | |
| 3 | 365.65 | | 66.02 | 141.3 | 137.2 | 36.25 | |
| 4 | 369.20 | | 65.38 | 142.5 | 138.6 | 36.61 | |
| 5 | 372.75 | | 64.76 | 143.9 | 139.8 | 36.95 | |
| 6 | 376.30 | | 64.15 | 145.3 | 141.1 | 37.31 | |
| 7 | 379.85 | | 63.55 | 146.6 | 142.5 | 37.66 | |
| 8 | 383.40 | | 62.96 | 148 | 143.9 | 38.01 | |
| 9 | 386.95 | | 62.39 | 149.3 | 145.3 | 38.36 | |
| | 389.37 | £3. 17. 10½ | 62 | 150.3 | 146.0 | 38.61 | |
| 10 | 390.50 | 3. 18. 1 | | 150.7 | 146.3 | 38.71 | |
| 11 | 394.05 | 3. 18. 10 | | 152.1 | 147.6 | 39.06 | |
| 12 | 397.60 | 3. 19. 6½ | | 153.5 | 149.0 | 39.62 | |
| 13 | 401.15 | 4. -. 3 | | 154.8 | 150.3 | 39.77 | |
| 14 | 404.70 | 4. - 11½ | | 156.2 | 151.7 | 40.12 | |
| 15 | 408.25 | 4. 1. 8 | | 157.5 | 152.9 | 40.48 | |
| 16 | 411.80 | 4. 2. 4½ | | 158.9 | 154.3 | 40.83 | |
| 17 | 415.35 | 4. 3. ½ | | 160.3 | 155.6 | 41.18 | |
| 18 | 418.90 | 4. 3. 9 | | 161.7 | 157.0 | 41.54 | |
| 19 | 422.45 | 4. 4. 5½ | | 163.1 | 158.3 | 41.89 | |
| 20 | 426. | 4. 5. 2 | | 164.5 | 159.6 | 42.24 | |
| 21 | 429.55 | 4. 5. 10½ | | 165.8 | 161.0 | 42.59 | |

* When the price of gold in Holland is above 10 pc$^t$ P$^m$ and the mint in England is open the public silver will be the standard in London consequently its market and mint prices will agre and gold will be above the mint price. When under 10 pc$^t$ silver will be above the mint pri and gold will be below the standard.

When the price of gold in Holland was above 9 pc$^t$ p$^m$ the english £ ster$^g$ would be estimat in silver and therefore the par of exchange would invariably continue 38.61 currency; and 37. Banco if the agio were 3 pc$^t$

† The agio is variable but is supposed to be constant in this table for the purpose of calculatio

| 9 | 10 | 11 | 12 |
|---|---|---|---|
| hen the e of gold London Bank otes is p⁫ oz. | The bullion Par must be multiplied by | Price of standard silver in London in Bank notes p⁫ oz. | Par of exch^ge with Amsterdam in Banco (Agio 3 pc⁫) |
| 4. - | ·973 | 5/2 | 37.48 |
| 4. 1 | ·961 | 5/3 | 36.88 |
| 4. 2 | ·949 | 5/4 | 36.30 |
| 4. 3 | ·938 | 5/5 | 35.75 |
| 4. 4 | ·927 | 5/6 | 35.21 |
| 4. 5 | ·916 | 5/7 | 34.68 |
| 4. 6 | ·905 | 5/8 | 34.17 |
| 4. 7 | ·895 | 5/9 | 33.67 |
| 4. 8 | ·885 | 5/10 | 33.19 |
| 4. 9 | ·875 | 5/11 | 32.72 |
| 4. 10 | ·865 | 6/- | 32.27 |
| 4. 11 | ·856 | 6/1 | 31.84 |
| 4. 13 | ·838 | 6/2 | 31.42 |
| 4. 15 | ·820 | 6/3 | 30.98 |
| 4. 17 | ·803 | 6/4 | 30.58 |
| 4. 19 | ·786 | 6/5 | 30.17 |
| 5. - | ·779 | 6/6 | 29.79 |
| 5. 2 | ·764 | 6/7 | 29.41 |
| 5. 4 | ·749 | 6/8 | 29.04 |
| 5. 6 | ·735 | 6/9 | 28.69 |
| 5. 8 | ·721 | 6/10 | 28.33 |
| 5. 10 | ·708 | 6/11 | 27.99 |
| | | 7/- | 27.66 |
| | | 7/1 | 27.32 |
| | | 7/2 | 27.02 |
| | | 7/3 | 26.71 |
| | | 7/4 | 26.40 |
| | | 7/5 | 26.11 |
| | | 7/6 | 25.82 |

marc weight = 3798 ains troy. marc is divided into 20 assen. 200 assen pure silver in a ilder. Gold and silver sold by the marc Holland perfectly e.

British standard } Gold—11 fine 1 alloy Silver 11. 2 fine 18 dwts. alloy

Columns 11 and 12 will shew on inspection whether silver be passing from London to Amsterdam, or from Amsterdam to London. Suppose the price of silver in London to be 6/7 and the exch^ge with Amsterdam 28/- Against 6/7 in Col. 11, the par of exch^ge is 29/41 in Col. 12 consequently being at 28 it is unfavorable to Amsterdam and silver can be exported from Amsterdam to London with a profit of 5 pc⁫ If under the same circumstances the exch^ge had been 31 silver could have been exported to Amsterdam with a profit of 5 pc⁫

Col. 8, 9 and 10 will shew from which country gold may be profitably exported. Suppose the price of gold in Amsterdam to be 16 pc⁫ p^m, the agio 3 pc⁫, the exch^ge with London 31 and the price of gold in London £5. 10; from which country would gold be exported and with what profit?

Against 16 pc⁫ in Col. 1, the par of exch^ge in Col. 8 is 39.64 and against £5. 10 the price of gold in London in Col. 9, the multiplier .708 stands in Col. 10. 39.64 multiplied by .708 gives 28.06 as the par for Bank notes, therefore when the exch^ge is at 31 it is unfavorable to Holland and gold may be imported from thence with a profit of 10½ pc⁫ nearly. Or thus[.] An oz of standard gold when the marc could be bought at 16 pc⁫ p^m at Amsterdam would cost 154.3 flemish Shillings Banco when the agio was 3 pc⁫, which reduced into English money at 31 shillings per £ sterling will give £4. 19. 6¾, but it will sell in London for £5. 10 which is a profit of 10½ pc⁫ nearly.

## 46. RICARDO TO MALTHUS[1]

My dear Sir                       London 1 Jan.ʸ 1814

1 Jan. 1814      Having finished a table for the Hamburgh exchanges, similar to that which I have already sent you for Holland, I thought you might like to have a copy of it. In this as well as in the other the result is not quite satisfactory, for example; at the present time I believe the exch.ᵍᵉ with Hamburgh is quoted 28/ and the price of dollars 6/11½. By the table it appears that with [such][2] a price of dollars, the exch.ᵍᵉ at par would be 25/; consequently it is now unfavorable to Hamburgh 12 p.cᵗ—which appears to me to be excessively high. In fact, under the present circumstances, there can be no intercourse with Hamburgh, and the quotation must be only nominal.

Mrs. Ricardo and I leave London to-morrow early for Bradford,[3]—from thence we intend going to Gatcomb[4] and expect to be in town again on thursday. I hope we shall soon see you. With best wishes to Mrs. Malthus I am

My dear Sir
Yours very truly
DAVID RICARDO

[1] Addressed: 'To / The Revᵈ T. R. Malthus / East India College / Hertford'.
   MS at Albury.—*Letters to Malthus*, XIV.
[2] MS torn.
[3] In Wiltshire. The visit was no doubt in connection with the marriage of Ricardo's daughter Henrietta to Thomas Clutterbuck, of Bradford Leigh, which took place on 17 Feb. 1814.
[4] Gatcomb Park, which he purchased later this year.

| Price of a ducat or 53 grains of fine gold in marks Banco | Price of an oz of standard gold in flemish Shillings Banco | Par of Exchᵍᵉ with London in flemish shillings Banco pʳ £ sterᵍ of gold | Corresponding price of an oz of standard silver in London in Pence | Corresponding price of an oz of standard gold in London in £ &cᵃ | When the price of gold in London in Bank notes is pʳ oz | The bullion par of exchᵍᵉ must be multiplied by | When the price of dollars in London is pʳ oz (s. d) | The par of exchᵍᵉ in silver is |
|---|---|---|---|---|---|---|---|---|
| 5.39 | 119.33 | 30.60 | 70.97 | | £4 | .973 | 4. 11½ | 35.08 |
| 5.45 | 120.66 | 30.94 | 70.19 | | 4. 1 | .961 | 5. 1 | 34.22 |
| 5.51 | 121.99 | 31.28 | 69.43 | | 4. 2 | .949 | 5. 2½ | 33.39 |
| 5.57 | 123.32 | 31.63 | 68.68 | | 4. 3 | .938 | 5. 4 | 32.61 |
| 5.63 | 124.65 | 31.97 | 67.95 | | 4. 4 | .927 | 5. 5½ | 31.87 |
| 5.69 | 125.98 | 32.33 | 67.23 | | 4. 5 | .916 | 5. 7 | 31.15 |
| 5.75 | 127.31 | 32.68 | 66.53 | | 4. 6 | .905 | 5. 8½ | 30.47 |
| 5.81 | 128.64 | 33.03 | 65.84 | | 4. 7 | .895 | 5. 10 | 29.82 |
| 5.87 | 129.96 | 33.37 | 65.17 | | 4. 8 | .885 | 5. 11½ | 29.19 |
| 5.93 | 131.29 | 33.72 | 64.51 | | 4. 9 | .875 | 6. 1 | 28.59 |
| 5.99 | 132.62 | 34.07 | 63.86 | | 4. 10 | .865 | 6. 2½ | 28.02 |
| 6.05 | 133.95 | 34.42 | 63.23 | | 4. 11 | .856 | 6. 4 | 27.46 |
| 6.11 | 135.28 | 34.76 | 62.61 | | 4. 13 | .838 | 6. 5½ | 26.93 |
| 6.17 | 136.61 | 35.08 | 62. – | 3.893 | 4. 15 | .820 | 6. 7 | 26.42 |
| 6.23 | 137.92 | 35.42 | | 3.931 | 4. 17 | .803 | 6. 8½ | 25.93 |
| 6.29 | 139.25 | 35.76 | | 3.968 | 4. 19 | .796 | 6. 10 | 25.46 |
| 6.35 | 140.57 | 36.11 | | 4.005 | 5 | .779 | 6. 11½ | 25 |
| 6.41 | 141.89 | 36.45 | | 4.043 | 5. 2 | .764 | 7. 1 | 24.55 |
| 6.47 | 143.21 | 36.79 | | 4.081 | 5. 4 | .749 | 7. 2 | 24.13 |
| 6.53 | 144.54 | 37.14 | | 4.119 | 5. 6 | .735 | | |
| 6.59 | 145.86 | 37.48 | | 4.157 | 5. 8 | .721 | | |
| 6.65 | 147.19 | 37.83 | | 4.195 | 5. 10. – | .708 | | |
| 6.71 | 148.51 | 38.18 | | 4.233 | | | | |
| 6.77 | 149.84 | 38.52 | | 4.270 | | | | |
| 6.83 | 151.17 | 38.87 | | 4.308 | | | | |
| 6.89 | 152.50 | 39.22 | | 4.346 | | | | |

When dollars are 4/11½, standard is 2¼ Pence more
When 6/1   3 Pence more
When 7/-   3½ Pence more

N.B. 3 marks are equal to 8 flemish shillings Banco

## 47. TROWER TO RICARDO[1]
[*Answered by* 48]

33. Harley Street.—
Mar. 2. 1814—

Dear Ricardo—

2 March 1814    As I am unwilling to deprive Mr. Mill of the pleasure of seeing your very interesting papers on the profits of Capital[2] I return them to you with many thanks; and shall really be glad to see them again when you can spare them—as I should like to pursue some reflections they have suggested.—In the meantime I send you some Notes I have made in considering your view of the subject; but I beg to assure you, that I submit them with great diffidence, and more with the desire of ascertaining whether I rightly understand you, than with the expectation, that they will be found correct.[3] Should I be in error I shall be much obliged to you to point out *where it is*; as it frequently happens, that the detection of a single error will lead to the discovery of a mass of misconception—

Yrs ever very truly—

HUTCHES TROWER.

I need not say that the Notes I send you are quite in the rough as that circumstance will be sufficiently evident to you—Have you Malthus's reply to you.[4]

[1] Addressed: 'To/David Ricardo Esqr / Upper Brook Street / Grosvenor Sqre—'.    Not passed through the Post.
MS in *R.P.*

[2] Probably an early draft of the *Essay on Profits*, published in 1815.
[3] Trower's Notes are wanting.
[4] Malthus's reply is wanting.

## 48. RICARDO TO TROWER[1]
[*Reply to* 47]

Upper Brook Street
8ᵗʰ March 1814.

Dear Trower

I called at your house yesterday; I wished to tell you 8 March 1814
that though well disposed to enter into the defence of my
opinions, I was now so much occupied by business, that I
could not devote the necessary time to it. Not having found
you at home I must tell you so by "these present". At the
same time I must observe that what I feared, I believe, has
happened. To one not aware of the whole difference between
Mr. Malthus and me, the papers you read were not clear, and
I think you have not entirely made out the subject in dispute.

Without entering further into the question I will endeavor
to state the question itself. When Capital increases in a
country, and the means of employing Capital already exists,
or increases, in the same proportion, the rate of interest and
of profits will not fall.

Interest rises only when the means of employment for
Capital bears a greater proportion than before to the Capital
itself, and falls when the Capital bears a greater proportion
to the arena, as Mr. Malthus has called it, for its employment.[2]
On these points I believe we are all agreed, but I contend that
the arena for the employment of new[3] Capital cannot increase
in any country in the same or greater proportion than the

---

[1] Addressed: 'Hutches Trower
Esqʳ/ 33 Harley Street'.
    MS at University College, London.—*Letters to Trower*, III.
[2] The phrase appears first in
Malthus's *Additions to the Fourth
and Former Editions of An Essay
on the Principle of Population*,
1817, p. 111: 'This country, from
the extent of its lands, and its rich
colonial possessions, has a large
*arena* for the employment of an
increasing capital'; see also above,
II, 293. Malthus had presumably
used the expression in an earlier
paper in this controversy.
[3] 'new' is ins.

8 March 1814 Capital itself,* unless there be improvements in husbandry,— or new facilities be offered for the introduction of food from foreign countries;—that in short it is the profits of the farmer which regulate the profits of all other trades,—and as the profits of the farmer must necessarily decrease with every augmentation of Capital employed on the land, provided no improvements be at the same time made in husbandry, all other profits must diminish and therefore the rate of interest must fall. To this proposition Mr. Malthus does not agree. He thinks that the arena for the employment of Capital may increase, and consequently profits and interest may rise, altho' there should be no new facilities, either by importation, or improved tillage, for the production of food;—that the profits of the farmer no more regulate the profits of other trades, than the profits of other trades regulate the profits of the farmer, and consequently if new markets are discovered, in which we can obtain a greater quantity of foreign commodities in exchange for our commodities, than before the discovery of such markets, profits will increase and interest will rise.

In such a state of things the rate of interest would rise as well as the profits of the farmer, he thinks even if more Capital were employed on the land. Do you understand?

Nothing, I say, can increase the profits permanently on trade, with the same or an increased Capital, but a really cheaper mode of obtaining food. A cheaper mode of obtaining food will undoubtedly increase profits says Mr. Malthus but there are many other circumstances which

* the following to be inserted: unless Capital be withdrawn from the land[1]

[1] To this footnote of Ricardo Trower adds in pencil: 'because the employment of capital depends upon the existence of capital.'

may also increase profits with an increase of Capital. The 8 March 1814
discovery of a new market where there will be a great
demand for our manufactures is one.

Believe me

Y.$^{rs}$ very faithfully

DAVID RICARDO

I have written this in great haste after devoting the
necessary time to my accounts. You must excuse the scrawl,
and corrections.

## 49. MILL TO RICARDO[1]

My dear Sir

I find on conversing with one or two persons, and 18 April 1814
particularly Mr. Bentham, that the impression conveyed by
the late paragraph of Mr. C. Johnstone, is, that you received
a civil letter from him, and did not answer it; and Mr.
Bentham said, that if he had known nothing of the two parties
he should have condemned you, from what appeared on the
face of the publication, and therefore it was his opinion that
you should by a statement of all the facts set the matter right
with the public.—I have thought it right to let you know
that this is likely to be the common impression, and to add
that I, too, now think, explanation may not be useless.

I would merely say, that in consequence of Mr. Cochrane
Johnstones publication in the newspapers, I had thought it
necessary to state, that on return home from a short absence
I had found the following letter—inserting it—that in conse-
quence I answered by the following, inserting it—that Mr. C.
Johnstone returned the following—that in consequence an

---

[1] Addressed: 'David Ricardo Esq. / Upper Brook Street / Grosvenor
Square'. Postmark, 18 April 1814.—MS in *R.P.*

18 April 1814 interview took place—and you may state the leading circumstances of the interview, or not, only if you do, paying particular attention to the mode of saying it.

Ever my Dear Sir   Yours &.c.

J. MILL

Queen Square
Monday Morning [18 April 1814]

[This letter refers to an incident in the investigation of the famous fraud on the Stock Exchange which was carried out on 21 Feb. 1814 by staging the arrival from France of a courier dressed as a staff officer and bringing the news of a great victory. The Omnium immediately rose 5½ points, only to fall back as soon as the hoax was exposed; in the meantime large profits had been made by, amongst others, Lord Cochrane, the radical member for Westminster, and his uncle A. Cochrane Johnstone (who had been the neighbour and tenant of Bentham at Queen Square Place; see Bentham's *Works*, vol. x. p. 449). Ricardo, as a member of the Stock Exchange Committee for the Protection of Property against Fraud, was active in pressing forward the detection and later the prosecution of the conspirators (as it appears from the MS Minutes of the Stock Exchange Committee for General Purposes). While the investigation was in progress, Johnstone wrote to the Chairman of the Stock Exchange that one Macrae was willing to disclose the circumstances of the fraud for a reward of £10,000; his letter was considered at a meeting (reported in the *Morning Chronicle* of 14 April) when it was remarked that Macrae had not been induced to come forward till after the arrest, which had recently been effected, of Beranger, the chief actor in the fraud. Johnstone replied, in a letter to the *Chronicle*, pointing out that so far back as the 30 March he had written to 'Mr. David Ricardo of Upper Brook-Street' a letter (of which he enclosed a copy) asking to be received in order to give some information 'which, if followed up with vigour by the Stock Exchange, may probably lead to the detection of those concerned in the late fraud'; the next day he communicated to Ricardo that the information could be obtained from Macrae; 'from that period I have never been favoured with any communication from Mr Ricardo.' These two letters of Johnstone were printed in the *Morning Chronicle* of 15 April 1814, and they form the 'paragraph' mentioned by Mill; no reply from Ricardo appeared.

At the trial before Lord Ellenborough, in June 1814, Lord Cochrane,

A. Cochrane Johnstone and others were found guilty and severely  18 April 1814
sentenced. The conviction of Lord Cochrane was attributed by the
Radicals to political vindictiveness, but a widely held opinion was that
expressed by Joseph Hume in a letter to him in 1852: 'I knew at the
time the alleged offence was committed, Mr. Cochrane Johnstone, and
my conviction at the time was, and still is, that you were the dupe of
his cupidity, and suffered from his act. With David Ricardo, who was
the prosecutor on the part of the Stock Exchange on that occasion,
I have often conversed on the subject.' (See *The Autobiography of a
Seaman*, by the Earl of Dundonald [*i.e.* Lord Cochrane], London, 1860,
vol. II, p. 389; in a footnote the author mistakes Ricardo for the
solicitor of the Stock Exchange.)]


## 50. RICARDO TO MALTHUS[1]

[*Answered by* 51]

London 26 June 1814

My dear Sir

 I yesterday received your letter[2] dated from Bangor,  26 June 1814
and was very glad to learn that you had had a pleasant
journey, and had taken up your abode in a beautiful situation.
I hope you may meet with as few obstructions to your comfort as in any case fall to the lot of travellers.

 I do not recollect the precise spot of the Penryn Arms,
I think I was at an Inn close to the water side.—I suppose it
is your intention to make Bangor your head quarters, and
not Carnarvon, as you projected when you left London.—
I expect that your eye will be quite weary of the bare mountains of Wales and you will hail with pleasure the more
fruitful country of England.

 Another year I hope I shall better understand your wishes
respecting y[r] taking a share in the Loan. In making the sale
for you which I have done I have by no means prevented

---

[1] Addressed: 'The Rev[d] T. R     MS at Albury.—*Letters to Mal-*
Malthus / Penryn Arms / Bangor /     *thus*, XV.
North Wales'.                         [2] Malthus's letter is wanting.

26 June 1814 you from having an interest in the success of the Om$^{m}$ during the year, for I can without the least trouble repurchase your £1000; and if the price do not vary before I hear from you, at a profit of $1\frac{3}{4}$ pc$^{t}$, it being now only $3\frac{1}{4}$ p$^{m}$—[1]

If you are so inclined you will write accordingly. If I do not hear from you I shall not do any thing.

I cannot partake of your doubts respecting the effects of restrictions on the importation of corn, in tending to lower the rate of interest. The rise of the price or rather the value[2] of corn without any augmentation of capital must necessarily diminish the demand for other things even if the prices of those commodities did not rise with the price of corn, which they would (tho' slowly) certainly do. With the same Capital there would be less production, and less demand. Demand has no other limits but the want of power of paying for the commodities demanded. Every thing which tends to diminish production tends to diminish this power. The rate of profits and of interest must depend on the proportion of production to the consumption necessary to such production,—this again essentially depends upon the cheapness of provisions, which is after all, whatever intervals we may be willing to allow, the great regulator of the wages of labour.

Nothing can tend more effectually to diminish the demand abroad for our manufactures than to refuse to import corn and all other commodities which we had usually taken in exchange for such manufactures. If we rigorously refused to import any foreign commodity whatever I firmly believe that we should soon cease to export any commodity, even if we made gold an exception to the general rule. Our money

[1] The Omnium, or Scrip, of the Loan of £24,000,000 contracted by Ricardo and others on 13 June 1814 was quoted on the day of the contract at 5 per cent. premium, when Ricardo apparently sold Malthus's share.

[2] 'or rather the value' is ins.

would stand at a higher level than in other countries but  26 June 1814
there are limits beyond which it could not go. All trade is at
last a trade of barter[1] and no nation will long buy unless it can
also sell,—nor will it long sell if it will not also buy. If by
adopting such policy a country were to enhance the value of
the raw materials which it consumed, of which corn is the
principal, it would thereby lower the rate of interest. If
otherwise it might be deprived of many luxuries and many
comforts, or might enjoy them in less abundance, but the
rate of interest would not fall.

This is a repetition you will say of the old story, and I
might have spared you the trouble of reading at 200 miles
distance what I had so often stated to you as my opinion
before, but you have set me off, and must now abide the
consequences.

I never was more convinced of any proposition in Polit:
Economy than that restrictions on importation of corn in an
importing country[2] have a tendency to lower profits.
Remember me kindly to Mrs. Malthus

Y.[rs] very truly

DAVID RICARDO


### 51. MALTHUS TO RICARDO[3]

*[Reply to 50.—Answered by 53]*

Bangor July 6th 1814.

My dear Sir,

I am in so large and agreeable a family party, and there  6 July 1814
are so many delightful excursions to be made from Bangor
that I do not expect to be very soon tired of the mountains,

[1] The phrase is Malthus's (*Observations on...the Corn Laws*,
1814, p. 24).
[2] Last six words are ins.

[3] Addressed: 'D. Ricardo Esqr /
Stock Exchange / London'.
MS in *R.P.*

6 July 1814 particularly as we do not absolutely live in the midst of them, but only see them at such a respectful distance, as to make them lose all their terrors, and shew only their beauties. We were some of us going to Conway today, which I have not yet seen, but were prevented by the rain, which has once or twice interrupted us, though upon the whole the weather has been tolerable.

I think as I am at such a distance I will not begin dealing afresh in the loan, and increasing your trouble, but be satisfied with what has been done, which is certainly a very fair per centage, and I am much obliged to you for it. I am rather surprised however that omnium should fall. I can't help thinking that it must rise before the end of the year.[1]

You have not yet removed my doubts on the effects of Restrictions upon the *profits* of *stock* and *interest* of money, although of their general effect to impoverish a country and to diminish its foreign trade, I feel no doubt. But high profits and interest are more frequently, you will allow, the concomitants of poverty than of abundance. You observe that in the case supposed, there would be less production and less demand with the *same* capital; but surely there would be *much less capital*. There would be a smaller quantity both of corn, and of all other commodities, and every monied accumulation would command less labour and less produce. The question then seems to be whether production or demand would decrease the fastest? and as in my opinion the dearness of labour would have more effect in diminishing capital than in diminishing revenue, particularly rents, I do not see why the usual effects of a diminution of capital should not take place.

I can by no means agree with you in thinking that every

---

[1] The Omnium which was now at 3¾ per cent. premium fell at the end of 1814 to 1¼ discount.

thing which diminishes produce, tends to diminish the power of paying for the commodities wanted, or as you intimate, to diminish the effective demand. If this were true, why do profits rise at the commencement of a war when stock is destroyed? or why do not profits invariably increase with the increase of capital, as *produce* unquestionably does. But you must mean that it is the *rate* of production, not the absolute quantity of produce which determines profits. But even this rate of production, or more definitely speaking, the proportion of production to the consumption necessary to such production, seems to be determined by the quantity of accumulated capital compared with the demand for the products of capital, and not by the mere difficulty and expence of procuring corn. If it [is][1] necessary to employ a hundred days labour instead of fifty, in order to produce a certain quantity of corn, there seems to be no reason whatever that the person who possesses an accumulation sufficient to make the necessary advances should have a less remuneration for his capital. The effects of a great difficulty in procuring corn would in my opinion be, a diminution of capital, a diminution of produce, and a diminution in the *real* wages of labour, or their price in corn; but not a diminution of profits; although unquestionably low profits might accompany a great difficulty of procuring corn, if at the same time that this difficulty existed there was a great abundance of capital. In short all will in my opinion depend upon the state of capital compared with the demand for it. This will be the prime mover, and it is this which will determine the profits which a capital employed in agriculture shall yield, whether the land be naturally rich or naturally poor, much worked or little worked.

The demand for capital depends, not upon the abundance

[1] Covered by seal.

6 July 1814  of *present* produce, but upon the demand for the future products of capital, or the power of producing something by
means of capital which shall be more in demand than the
produce actually employed. And in this question that great
element of effective demand,—the desire to consume in
those who possess revenue, must always have great influence.
I think you overlook it too much.

Kind regards to Mrs. R.

Ever truly Yours

T R MALTHUS


### 52. RICARDO TO BENTHAM AND MILL[1]

15 July 1814       Mr. D. Ricardo is very much obliged, both to Mr.
Bentham and Mr. Mill, for the perusal of the MS. on the
subject of the proposed school.[2] He will be happy to give his
assistance, as far as a subscription in money will promote the
object desired.[3]

Upper Brook Street
    15 July 1814

[1] Docketed by Bentham: '1814
July 15 Chrestomathia D. Ri-
cardo to J. B. and Mill Promises
subscription to Chrestomathia'.
    MS at University College,
London, Bentham Papers, Case
No. 165.

[2] *Chrestomathia*, a collection of
papers first published in 1816,
reprinted in Bentham's *Works*, ed.
Bowring, vol. VIII; it contains
the plan of the 'Chrestomathic
School' which was to apply
Lancaster's system of education
'to the higher branches of learn-
ing, for the use of the middling
and higher ranks in life.'

[3] In May 1816, when a committee was formed to organize
the Chrestomathic Day School,
Ricardo became one of its members, with Mill, Place, Owen and
others, and attended their meetings regularly. He subscribed
£300 and collected £900 from
the following among his friends
on the Stock Exchange each of
whom subscribed £50: F. N.
Duboulay, George Basevi, John
Spicer, Jacob Ricardo, Francis
Ricardo, Ralph Ricardo, James
Steers, John Hodges, Will^m
Hodges, L. A. de la Chaumette,
V. A. Mieville, Robert Podmore,

## 53. RICARDO TO MALTHUS[1]
*[Reply to 51.—Answered by 54]*

Gatcomb Park, near Minchin Hampton
Gloucestershire 25ᵗʰ July 1814

My dear Sir

I am writing to you from Gatcomb, where I arrived 25 July 1814
with Sylla[2] as my companion yesterday afternoon. To enable
me to quit London at the time I did I was obliged to bestow
an unusual degree of attention to business of all sorts,—and
though I had written a letter to you in answer to your last
before I left Brook Street I was so dissatisfied with it that I
could not resolve to send it.—I shall I fear succeed no better
now, but you shall have it whatever it may be, as if I defer
writing any longer you may have quitted Bangor before my
letter arrives there.

It appears to me that you have changed the proposition on
which we first appeared to differ. The proposition advanced
by you, if I recollect right, was that restrictions on the importation of corn would not lower the rate of profits and
interest,—but now you add or rather your argument leads
to that conclusion, "if the consequence of such restriction be
a great reduction of Capital." So amended I should not
object to the proposition,—but I think it material that
causes should be kept distinct, and their due effects ascribed

Robert Podmore Junr., Charles
Podmore, William Hammond
Junr., Thomas Brown, David
Walters, Richᵈ Smaler. When the
project was abandoned in 1821,
the money was returned to the
subscribers. (See the Minute Book
and other MSS in British Museum
Newspaper Library, Place Collection of Newspaper Cuttings,
vol. 60, 'Chrestomathic School',
Nos. 9, 10, 13.)

[1] Addressed: 'To / The Revᵈ T R
Malthus / Penryn Arms / Bangor /
North Wales', redirected 'E.I.
College / Hayleybury / Hertford',
and marked '*Miss!* to *Aylesbury*'.
    MS at Albury.—*Letters to Mal-
thus*, XVI.
[2] Priscilla, the second daughter
of Ricardo.

25 July 1814 to each. Restrictions on the trade of corn, if capital suffers no diminution, will occasion a fall in the rate of profits and interest. A reduction of capital independently of restrictions on importation of corn will have a tendency to raise profits and interest,—but there is no necessary connection between these two operating causes, as they may at the same time be acting together or entirely in opposite directions.

Effective demand, it appears to me, cannot augment or long continue stationary with a diminishing capital; and your question why if this were true profits rise at the commencement of a war? does not I think bear any connection with the argument, because profits will augment under a diminution of capital and produce, if demand tho' diminished does not diminish so rapidly as Capital and produce. For the opposite[1] reason profits will diminish when Capital and produce increase. This is totally independent of the rate of production, and often, I think, may counteract the effects which usually follow, and in the long run will almost[2] always follow, from increasing or diminishing capital.—

You say that "the proportion of production to the consumption necessary to such production, seems to be determined by the quantity of accumulated capital compared with the demand for the products of capital, and not by the mere difficulty and expence of procuring corn." It appears to me that the difficulty and expence of procuring corn will necessarily regulate the demand for the products of capital, for the demand must essentially depend on the price at which they can be afforded, and the prices of all commodities must increase if the price of corn be increased.—The capitalist "who may find it necessary to employ a hundred days labour instead of fifty in order to produce a certain quantity of corn" cannot retain the same share for himself unless the labourers

[1] Replaces 'same'.　　　　　[2] 'almost' is ins.

who are employed for a hundred days will be satisfied with  25 July 1814
the same quantity of corn for their subsistence that the
labourers employed for fifty had before. If you suppose the
price of corn doubled, the capital to be employed estimated
in money will probably be also nearly doubled,—or at any
rate will be greatly augmented and if his monied income is
to arise from the sale of the corn which remains to him after
defraying the charges of production how is it possible to
conceive that the rate of his profits will not be diminished?
I hope you continue to enjoy yourself amidst the wild
scenery with which you are encompassed.—The weather
here is delightful and I am as happy as I can be separated
from the whole family, (except Sylla) and surrounded by
upholsterers, carpenters, &ᵃ. I do not expect Mrs. Ricardo
in less than a fortnight,—she is unwilling to bring the children here till the whole house is perfectly arranged. Kind
regards to Mrs. Malthus.

Yᵗˢ very truly

DAVID RICARDO

I believe that in this sweet place I shall not sigh after the
Stock Exchᵍᵉ and its enjoyments.

54. MALTHUS TO RICARDO[1]

[*Reply to* 53.—*Answered by* 55]

My dear Sir,                         E I Coll August 5ᵗʰ 1814

Your letter reached me here the day before yesterday,  5 Aug. 1814
after being missent to Aylesbury from Bangor. I was in
Town almost immediately after my return from Wales, and
called in Brook Street with the hope of seeing you before

[1] Addressed: 'D. Ricardo Esqr / Gatcomb Park / Minchin Hampton /
Gloucestershire.'—MS in *R.P.*

5 Aug. 1814 you left Town. Mrs. Ricardo, whom I had the pleasure of finding at home told me of your expedition with Sylla; and I was very glad to hear from her, and to find it confirmed in your letter that your retirement quite answers to you. Indeed I always thought that you would be able to employ yourself agreeably in the country, and would not often regret the bustle and stimulus of the Stock Exchange. By the by I found on calling at Hoares that you had paid in 50£ to my account.[1] I am much indebted to you for the trouble you have taken for me, and indeed almost feel as if you had presented me with 50£, as I fear it was taken from what would otherwise have been your own. I am surprised that omnium should have fallen so, and can't help thinking that it will rise before the end of the year, though I will not venture to become an active speculator on the subject. The fall in the price of gold and the rise of the exchanges seem to be going on notwithstanding the increase of Bank of England notes. I think it however not improbable that the whole circulation may have diminished in spite of this issue, owing to the alarm among the Country banks. The present state of things tends to confirm me more and more in my old notions.

With regard to our present question, I am not aware that I have in any degree changed the proposition; because I do not say that restrictions upon the importation of foreign corn will raise profits, *if* they are attended with a diminution of capital. But I say that they *must necessarily* be attended with a diminution of capital, and *therefore* that they must tend to *raise* rather than *lower* profits. You seem to think that there is no necessary connection between restrictions upon importation, and a reduction of capital. I think on the contrary that there is an absolutely necessary connection, and that it is

---

[1] The profit on £1000 Omnium sold at 5 per cent. premium: see above, p. 108.

precisely owing to this connection that profits do not fall. If the capitalist in the Cotton or Woollen manufacture be obliged to pay more for the labour which he employs, owing to restrictions upon importation, he will not be able to work up the same quantity of goods with his capital; the goods will in consequence rise in price, and his profits, from the general scarcity of capital, will be increased.

You say yourself most justly that profits will augment under a diminution of capital and produce, *if demand tho'* *diminished* does not diminish *so rapidly* as capital and produce; but this is exactly what happens in all cases of diminution of capital, and shews that what you say in another place cannot be quite correct namely, "that effective demand cannot augment or long continue stationary with a diminishing capital." The whole amount of demand will from advanced prices diminish of course, but the *proportion* of *demand* to the *supply* which is always the main point in question, as determining prices and profits, may continue to increase as it does in all countries the capital of which is retrograde. In such countries the effective demand compared with the supply is permanently great, and the profits of stock very high. If the nominal price of corn be doubled, and the nominal amount of capital employed, be not quite doubled which you seem to allow might be the case, instead of saying "how is it possible to conceive that the rate of profits will not be diminished" I should say how is it possible to conceive that it should not be increased? In no case of production, is the produce exactly of the same nature as the capital advanced. Consequently we can never properly refer to a material rate of produce, independent of demand, and of the abundance or scarcity of capital. The more I reflect on the subject, the more firmly I feel convinced, that it is the state of capital, or the general profits of stock and interest of money, which deter-

5 Aug. 1814 mines the particular profit upon the land; and that it is not the particular profits or rate of produce upon the land which determines the general profits of stock and the interest of money. A slight fall in the real[1] price of labour, which according to general principles ought to take place on any diminution of capital, or what comes to the same thing, a rise in the price of produce without a *proportionate* rise of labour, a most natural and frequent occurrence, will allow of great variations in the rate of produce[2] on land, and easily make up for some increase of difficulty in procuring corn.

The question we are at present discussing involves some very fundamental points in political Economy, and I wish we could settle it satisfactorily.

My objection to taxes upon necessaries compared with taxes on luxuries and income taxes on the higher classes of society, is, that they must diminish capital and produce, though I dont think they would diminish profits and interest.

Remember me kindly to your fair companion.

Ever truly Yours

T R Malthus

## 55. RICARDO TO MALTHUS[3]
[*Reply to* 54.—*Answered by* 56]

My dear Sir                         Gatcomb Park 11ᵗʰ Augᵗ 1814

11 Aug. 1814     I received your letter last sunday, and in the evening of that day Mrs. Ricardo and the rest of my family arrived here. I have been shewing them all the beauties of this place, and my time has been pretty well engrossed by them

---

[1] Replaces 'relative'.
[2] 'the rate of produce' replaces 'the rate of profit to be made'.
[3] Addressed: 'To / The Revᵈ

T. R Malthus / East India College / Hertford'.
        MS at Albury.—*Letters to Malthus*, XVII.

these three last days.—I have always regretted that I did not
sooner know your wish of being a subscriber to the last loan.
In the list for the next I will not fail to ask you what sum you
would like to be interested in. The fall in Om$^m$ is I believe to
be attributed to our continued expences, and the expectation
of another loan before the payments on the present are completed.—The present state of the Exch$^{ges}$ seem to indicate a
real fall in the value of foreign currencies;—It cannot be
attributed to any change of taste for particular commodities,
or any other caprice. I expected that Peace would lower the
value of foreign currency, but I confess not in the degree
which has taken place.[1] It leaves the question between us
undecided, namely whether the exchange is not operated
upon solely by the relative preponderance of currency.
Peace has rendered the currency of the continent much more
efficacious to the business to be done.

With regard to our present question, we differ as to effects
which must *necessarily* follow from restrictions on the importation of foreign corn. I do not think that a diminution
of Capital is a *necessary*, but a probable effect. We agree as to
the consequences which will attend a diminution of capital,
but I should say that a real diminution of capital will diminish
the work to be done, and consequently will affect the wages
of labour, and the demand for food. In the case supposed,
restrictions on importation of corn, encouragement is given
to the further cultivation of our own land,—but *if* accompanied by a diminution of capital a discouragement is also
given to the cultivation of the land, and whether profits rise
or fall must in my opinion depend upon the degree of these
contrary operating causes.—It is true that the Woollen or

---

[1] Since the Peace of Paris (30
April 1814) the price of gold had
fallen from 105/- per ounce to
84/- and the Paris exchange from
19.30 to 23.40.

11 Aug. 1814 Cotton manufacturer will not be able to work up the same quantity of goods with the same capital if he is obliged to pay more for the labour which he employs, but his profits will depend on the price at which his goods when manufactured will sell. If every person is determined to live on his revenue or income, without infringing on his capital, the rise of his goods will not be in the same proportion as the rise of labour, and consequently his percentage of profit will be diminished if he values his capital, which he must do, in money at the increased value to which all goods would rise in consequence of the rise of the wages of labour.—In such case I should say that the effective demand had diminished, because the same quantity of commodities could not be annually consumed. If the same quantity of commodities continued to be consumed then it must be evident that it would be at the expence of capital. In such case capital would diminish faster than demand, which would tend to keep up profits.—But how long will [people]¹ continue to indulge in luxuries at the expence of a continual diminution of capital?—It is the road to ruin, and though frequently persisted in by a few individuals, it is not often found to be the folly of nations. On the contrary if any causes interrupt the progress of nations, if restrictions on their trade, or expensive wars tend to diminish their capital,—at such times more economy is practised, and as Adam Smith has observed the profusion of goverments is counteracted by the frugality of individuals. If so I cannot be incorrect in saying that though for a short period capital and produce may diminish faster than demand,—yet in the long run effective demand cannot augment or continue stationary with a diminishing capital. You say, what I did not before understand you to admit, "that the whole amount of demand will

¹ MS torn.

from advanced prices diminish of course, but the proportion of demand to supply, which is always the main point in question, as determining prices and profits, may continue to increase, *as it does in all countries the capital of which is retrograde"* but I do not agree even to this explanation,—and it appears to me to be at variance with an opinion which I have often heard you express, viz. The temptation to save from revenue to augment capital is always in proportion to the rate of profits, and if from accumulation of capital profits and interest should fall very low indeed, at that point accumulation would nearly stop, because it would be almost without an object.—In this opinion I most cordially agree and I cannot help thinking that it is at variance with the above sentence which I have quoted from your letter. I maintain, as I think you have done, that consumption as compared with production is always greatest where Capital is most accumulated. Diminish the capital of England one half, and you will undoubtedly augment profits, but it will not be in consequence of a greater proportion of demand but of a greater proportion of production, demand as compared with production could hardly fail to diminish. Individuals do not estimate their profits by the material production, but nations invariably do. If we had precisely the same amount of commodities of all descriptions in the year 1815 that we now have in 1814 as a nation we should be no richer, but if money had sunk in value they would be represented by a greater quantity of money, and individuals would be apt to *think* themselves richer.—I shall be in town either next week or the week after. I wish you would return here with me. We would discuss these important points in our shady groves. With kind regards to Mrs. Malthus

I am Y$^{rs}$ truly,

DAVID RICARDO

## 56. MALTHUS TO RICARDO[1]
[*Reply to* 55.—*Answered by* 58]

My dear Sir,                                    E I Coll August 19<sup>th</sup> 1814

19 Aug. 1814    I have delayed writing longer than I intended; and now write in a great hurry that I may not miss you in Town. It would give me great pleasure to pay you a visit at Gattcomb, but it is quite out of my power at present and I fear will remain so for a considerable time. Should your business in Town leave you an idle interval of a day or two, while waiting for any particular event or period, you know we shall be most happy to see you at Haileybury for as long a time as you can spare. This state of the omnium is a strange and sad business, and I fear will be a serious loss to you.[2] I am truly sensible of your kind offer about a future loan, and if you are sure it would not be inconvenient should like to have about £5000.

The alteration that has taken place in the price of bullion and the exchanges is certainly greater than one could have expected, and proves in my opinion that a greater part of the difference between gold and bank notes, arose from the dearness of gold, than we were aware of. I always thought that much of it was so occasioned, but not so much as it has turned out. The stoppage of the great drains of Spain and the Continental armies I was prepared to expect would produce a considerable effect, and to these causes are added at present our great exports 3 or 4 months ago, and perhaps some approach to a restoration of confidence in the commercial transactions of Europe. Probably also there may be an influx of the

---

[1] Addressed: 'D. Ricardo Esqr. / 56. Upper Brook Street / London'. MS in *R.P.*

[2] The Omnium had now fallen to 1 per cent. discount.

precious metals, from the great efforts which government 19 Aug. 1814 has made within the last five years to obtain them.

I always meant to say that the actual quantity of demand would diminish from an increased difficulty of obtaining corn, as it does in all cases of scarcity; but that the proportion of demand to supply would increase, which seems to be almost as invariable a consequence. I still think that high profits have a strong *tendency* to produce saving; but when I speak of a retrograde capital, it is absolutely making the supposition that this tendency has not its probable effect; and such cases unquestionably occur in fact. There are countries where the interest of money is 12 per cent, and yet the capital is not increasing. In these countries however the demand for produce compared with the supply is very great, and is in truth the reason of the high profits.

I can by no means agree with you in thinking that if the capital of this country were diminished one half "demand as compared with production would diminish". Precisely the reverse would I think take place. You do not certainly take sufficiently into your consideration the natural desires of man, which are after all the foundation of all demand. When corn is scarce there is a greater demand for corn than for labour, for produce, than for population.

Remember me kindly to Mrs. Ricardo

Ever truly Yours

T R MALTHUS

## 57. MILL TO RICARDO[1]

My dear Sir

Having no little desire to be much acquainted with your history, and what pleasures Gatcomb affords, I know no way likely to procure me that gratification but giving you the history of myself, since we parted—which I hope will entitle me to make a demand for yours.

We left London on the day, or near the day (I forget which) we originally intended, and arrived here without any memorable accident. I would describe the road, as travellers are wont, but for two objections which have weighed with me. One is, that you probably know every inch of it, better than I do, and in the next place, you have read a hundred descriptions of it already, or may do, whenever you please. The wonders of Bagshot heath, over which it so happened that I had never passed before, were the spectacle that principally struck me. I know not by what tenure it is held, nor to whom it belongs. It appeared to me, that it is not the natural barrenness of it which has kept it in its present state. Its vicinity to the capital is the remarkable circumstance.

We arrived at Ford Abbey in two days travelling (no miraculous dispatch), having treated ourselves with a bed at Salisbury, and another look at its beautiful cathedral. We found the house empty, that is to say, with only the gardener and an old woman in it. Mr. Bentham and I, carrying my little boy along with us, came down before the rest of our party, on purpose to meet with the proprietor, with whom certain things were to be settled upon the spot, which could not be settled any where else. The Proprietor aforesaid was expected to have been here before us, but did not come till

[1] Addressed: 'David Ricardo Esq. / Gatcomb Park / Minching Hampton / Gloucester Shire'.—MS in *R.P.*

the evening of the day after. And now I will tell you what
sort of a place the house is. But in the first place, I mean to
anticipate an objection. There is a certain young lady, now
called Miss Ricardo (how long she may be called so, God
only knows) who, if she were to read this letter, would say—
And what is that house to us? and where is the mighty
pleasure in receiving a description of a house? Let me, then,
humbly suggest, that I promised no more than a history of
myself during the last six weeks; and a description of this
house is part of that history. And in the next place a man
deserves indulgence when he has given the best of what he
has. And how should I have here any thing better than an
old house to describe? It is an irregular pile of building, of
large extent, which originally belonged to a cargo of monks,
and still retains a large share of its monkish appearance, the
inside however made into rooms, which have comforts and
some of them no little magnificence, for the taste of people
of a more mundane description than monks. It is one of the
places which travellers come to see; and we have many
visitors. I was afraid they would be a nuisance; but I find it
less than I expected. It stands upon the river Axe, at the very
bottom of a tolerably pretty valley, surrounded with hills of
the Devonshire breed, of gentle ascent and moderate altitude,
and rather too much than too little covered with wood. There
is cloisters in the house, a piece of very beautiful Gothic
architecture, which acts as a long wide passage in summer,
in winter receives green house plants, and acts as a green
house and passage; there is also in it an ancient Gothic hall,
which looks like a church; there is an apartment called the
saloon, built by Inigo Jones, on express purpose to receive
some beautiful tapestry which still adorns its walls, and of
this room the dimensions are 50 feet by 25, with correspondent
height; there is a very handsome dining room and drawing

28 Aug. 1814 room; there are two very comfortable rooms called the library and little drawing room, which are the ordinary family rooms; there is a suite of apartments, consisting of a bed room, dressing rooms, and two ante-rooms, all elegant, if antique rather than modern splendour may be called elegant; and the rest consists, as far as inhabited, of tolerable bed rooms, and the other necessary appendages. I must not forget, that there is also a chapel, for which the family some time ago kept a chaplain, which is kept in good repair, and which serves as burial place to the family.—Enough of the house, which I should not have begun with, had I thought it would keep me so long. The grounds about are far from ugly—but not much has lately been done to improve them by art. There is a deer park, containing 140 head of deer, of which we have already killed a few.

Now for the proprietor, who is a curiosity, though of a different sort, as great as his house. The Manor of Ford Abbey is worth to him about £2000 a year, he possesses another estate in this country of about £1500 a year, and another of £1500 a year in Wales. He is notwithstanding very poor, though he has [no][1] wife and no child. He has a mistress, however, who came down with him—and with him and his fair one, Mr. Bentham and I spent a week. It is not easy to describe him. What is called the best English education had been bestowed on him. He was at one of the best of the schools and at Oxford, the reasonable time, and is said, by the clergyman here who was at school with him, to have been a good scholar at school; but excepting a scrap of Latin which proceeded from him now and then, and of which he seemed to know the meaning, it would be difficult to find a mind more thoroughly vacant, and more wonderfully feeble —to his servants and dependents, full of caprice and un-

[1] MS torn.

steadiness—and without real tyranny but rather good nature 28 Aug. 1814
in his heart, producing the effects of tyranny on those around
him. His lady, in whom I expected to find the over-done
airs and pretensions of half-breeding, guided by a mixture
of jealousy and pride, was a simple, country girl, whom he
had picked up in the neighbourhood, bashful and awkward,
but not without beauty.—So much for Ford Abbey, and its
owner. We had Mr. Horner here for two days, as he passed
on the circuit.[1] Mr. Hume[2] is here now, having come from a
watering place, he was at on the coast—and with the exception of General Bentham[3] and family, who were here for a
day or two, before setting out for France, we have had no
visitors, and nothing to do, but study.—I hope you will
allow that this is not only a long letter, but filled with important matter—therefore I hope a due return will make its
appearance from you. We find that you have sent back the
papers of Mr. Bentham, on school &.c.[4]—and the remarks
which you promised to write down, we beg you will send
to us by coach as soon as possible, as Mr. B. wishes to see
them before sending the papers to Brougham.

I have hardly left room to send compliments. I must
include you all in one precious assemblage. When you send
me the account of yourselves, send me also some account of
those of our friends who are left behind. Forget not what is
occupying your own studious liesure. (Ford Abbey Chard
Somerset is sufficient direction) Bath and Bristol Coaches to
Exeter in plenty for the parcel, if your remarks on the M.S.
amount to more than a letter.

Believe yours most truly
J. MILL

[1] See Francis Horner's account of this visit in his *Memoirs and Correspondence*, London, 1843, vol. II, pp. 178–80.

[2] See below, p. 138, n.

[3] Sir Samuel Bentham, Jeremy's brother.

[4] See letter 52.

## 58. RICARDO TO MALTHUS[1]

*[Reply to 56.—Answered by 59]*

Gatcomb Park<br>
Minchin Hampton<br>
30th Aug. 1814

My dear Sir

30 Aug. 1814    I left London on the 19th, the day before your letter arrived there, having dispatched all my business in 4 days. The appearance of the Om[m2] was not sufficiently inviting to induce me to protract my stay longer than was absolutely necessary. David[3] who is come to pass his holidays with us brought me your letter;—I regret that I shall not see you for some time, as you cannot come here, and I shall not have it in my power at present to visit Hailybury. I expected to have a great deal of leisure time in the country, but as yet I have not had any. Walking and riding with my family, and friends who have visited us, have entirely occupied me;— besides which the only room in my house which is not finished is the library, owing to the tedious time which they have taken to fix my bookcases.—

I think if we could talk together we should not very much differ on the question which has lately engaged us, our principal difference is about the permanence of the effects.—It will often happen that the scarcity of a commodity, or the increasing demand for it will for a time increase profits, but it is not therefore correct to say that where profits are high they are so because the demand for produce is great compared with the supply. There are many other causes which will occasion profits to be permanently high. There may be

---

[1] Addressed: 'To / The Rev[d] T. R Malthus / East India College / Hertford'.
   MS at Albury.—*Letters to Malthus*, XVIII.

[2] The Omnium had now fallen to 2 per cent. discount.

[3] Ricardo's second son, then at school at Charterhouse.

two countries in one of which from bad government and the consequent insecurity of property,—or from the little disposition to saving in the people, profits may be permanently high and interest at 12 pc${}^t$, whilst in the other where these causes do not operate, profits may be permanently low and interest at 5 pc${}^t$ It would surely be incorrect to say that the cause of the high profits was the greater proportion of[1] demand for produce, when in both countries, the supply would be, or might be, precisely equal to the demand, and no more. In America profits are higher than in England and yet I can have no doubt that the proportion of supply to demand is greater in the former country. I think it must necessarily be so in all countries which are most rapidly increasing in riches, for from whence do riches come but from production preponderating over consumption.—Profits are sometimes high when corn is scarce and dear, but this arises from the stimulus which the high price gives to industry. If the population could immediately accomodate itself to the scanty supply no such effects would follow; and in fact they only continue till time has gradually equalized them.

I sometimes suspect that we do not attach the same meaning to the word demand. If corn rises in price, you perhaps attribute it to a greater demand,—I should call it a greater competition. The demand cannot I think be said to increase if the quantity consumed be diminished, altho much more money may be required to purchase the smaller than the larger quantity. If it were to be asked what the demand was for Port wine in England in the years 1813 and 1814, and it were to be answered that in the first year she had imported 5000 pipes and in the next 4500 should we not all agree that the demand was greater in 1813, yet it might be true that double the quantity of money was paid for the 4500 pipes.

[1] 'greater proportion of' is ins.

30 Aug. 1814   Have you read the report of the Lord Committee on
the corn question?¹ It discloses some important facts, but
how ignorant the persons giving evidence appear to be of
the subject as a matter of science. The Editor's remarks too
are very unworthy of his paper.²

When next you write to me you will oblige me by telling
me where you had your low gig built. I think such a one
would suit me here. Did you not consider it as more favorable to the horse in going up hill, but to his disadvantage in
going down. With best complim$^{ts}$ to Mrs. Malthus

I am Y$^{rs}$ truly

DAVID RICARDO


## 59. MALTHUS TO RICARDO³

*[Reply to 58.—Answered by 60]*

My dear Sir,                                    E I Coll Sep$^r$ 11. 1814

11 Sept. 1814   I dont wonder that you find your time much engaged in
walking and riding about your beautiful place, and in the
general pleasures and cares of a Country gentleman, particularly at first, when the change from your London life
must be so striking. Perhaps another year you will find a
little more leisure; but I have no idea of your finding too
much, or of your being tired of your retirement.

¹ 'First and Second Reports from
The Lords Committees appointed
to enquire into the state of the
Growth, Commerce, and Consumption of Grain, and all Laws
relating thereto', 25 July 1814
(*Parliamentary Papers,*. 1814–15,
vol. v).
² This seems to refer to the
editorial comments in one of the
newspapers which had been publishing extracts from the report
and evidence. There is nothing
that could be called 'Editor's
remarks' either in the official
folio edition of the Reports or in
the 8vo reprint by Ridgway, 1814.
³ Addressed: 'D. Ricardo Esqr. /
Gatcomb Park / Minchin Hampton / Gloucestershire'.
MS in *R.P.*

I had my chair made at a Mr. Bookers at Edmonton. The plan upon which it is constructed is certainly very favourable to the horse in going up hill, or through very heavy roads. There is in short comparatively little draft. But then the horse carries a greater weight, which though it does not I think push him much forward in going down hill, may perhaps incline him more to fall, and certainly fatigues him more comparatively in smooth and good roads. I have driven however my mare ten years without a fall, and when it does happen, as I have experienced with other horses, the lowness of the carriage and the length of the shafts prevent any evil consequences from it.

I agree with you in thinking that we should not probably differ much on our present subject of discussion, if we could talk it well over. I think you would allow that when capital is scanty compared with the means of employing it, from whatever cause arising, whether from insecurity of property, or extravagant habits, profits will be high not only temporarily but permanently. And I cannot help being of opinion that these high profits always indicate a comparative excess of demand above supply, even though the demand and supply should *appear* to be precisely equal. Effectual demand consists of two elements the *power* and the *will* to purchase. The power to purchase may perhaps be represented correctly by the produce of the country whether small or great; but the will to purchase will always be the greatest, the smaller is the produce compared with the population, and the more scantily the wants of the society are supplied. When capital is abundant it is not easy to find new objects sufficiently in demand. When capital is scarce nothing is more easy. In a country abundant in capital the value of the whole produce cannot increase with rapidity from the insufficiency of demand. In a country with little comparative capital the value of the yearly produce

11 Sept. 1814 may very rapidly increase from the greatness of demand. In short I by no means think that the power to purchase necessarily involves a proportionate will to purchase; and I cannot agree with Mr. Mill in an ingenious position which he lays down in his answer to Mr. Spence, that in reference to a nation, supply can never exceed demand.[1] A nation must certainly have the power of purchasing all that it produces, but I can easily conceive it not to have the will: and if we were to grow next year half as much corn again as usual, a great part of it would be wasted, and the same would be true if all commodities of all kinds were increased one half. It would be impossible that they should yield the expence of production. You have never I think taken sufficiently into consideration the wants and tastes of mankind. It is not merely the proportion of commodities to each other but their proportion to the wants and tastes of mankind that determines prices.

I have been reading the Lord's Report on the Corn Laws. It contains as you observe some very curious information. The evidence is a little suspicious, though it is a good deal such as I expected from Theory.

Mrs. M's regards to Mrs. Ricardo

Ever Yours,

T R MALTHUS.

---

[1] James Mill, *Commerce Defended, An Answer to the Arguments by which Mr. Spence, Mr. Cobbett, and Others, have Attempted to* *Prove that Commerce is Not a Source of National Wealth*, London, Baldwin, 1808, p. 83.

## 60. RICARDO TO MALTHUS[1]

[*Reply to 59.—Answered by 62*]

Gatcomb Park 16 Sep.<sup>r</sup> 1814

My dear Sir

I am obliged to you for the information which you have 16 Sept. 1814
given me concerning your chair. I believe as the season is so
far advanced I shall defer building one till next spring.

I agree with you that when capital is scanty compared with
the means of employing it, from whatever cause arising,
profits will be high. Whether temporarily or permanently
must of course depend upon whether the cause be temporary
or permanent. It is however very important to ascertain
what the causes are which make capital scanty compared with
the means of employing it,—and how far when ascertained
they may be considered temporary or permanent.

It is in this enquiry that I am led to believe that the state
of the cultivation of the land is almost the only great permanent cause. There are other circumstances which are
attended with temporary effects of more or less duration,
and frequently operate partially on particular trades. The
state of production from the land compared with the means
necessary to make it produce operates on all, and is alone
lasting in its effects.—

We agree too that effectual demand consists of two elements, the *power* and the *will* to purchase, but I think the will
is very seldom wanting where the power exists,—for the
desire of accumulation will occasion demand just as effectually as a desire to consume, it will only change the objects on
which the demand will exercise itself. If you think that with
an increase of capital men will become indifferent both to

[1] Addressed: 'To / The Rev.<sup>d</sup>     MS at Albury.—*Letters to Mal-*
T. R Malthus / East India College /     *thus*, XIX.
Hertford'.

16 Sept. 1814 consumption and accumulation, then you are correct in opposing Mr. Mill's idea, that in reference to a nation, supply can never exceed demand,—but does not an increase of capital beget an increased inclination for luxuries of all description, and tho' it appears natural that the desire of accumulation should decrease with an increase of capital, and diminished profits, it appears equally probable that consumption will increase in the same ratio. Exchanges will be as active as ever the objects only will be altered. If demand *appears* more active, where capital is scarce, it is only because the *power* to purchase is comparatively greater. Wherever capital is scanty the necessaries of life are cheap, if the country is commonly fertile;—and as capital and population increase[1] the necessaries of life rise in price, and thus is the power of purchasing, though really greater, comparatively less. In a country with little comparative capital the value of the yearly produce may very rapidly increase, and if it be said to be in consequence of the greatness of demand, I should contend that in such country the demand would not be limited, in the same degree, by a want of power,—as in a country abounding in capital; and merely because provisions would not rise in the same proportion in the two countries. —If half as much corn again as usual were produced next year, a great part of it would undoubtedly be wasted, and the same might be said of any commodities which we might be ingenious enough to name,—but the real question is this; If money should retain the same value next year, would any man (if he had it) want the will to spend half as much again as he now does,—and if he did want the will, would he feel no inclination to add the increase of his revenue to his capital, and employ it as such. In short I consider the wants and tastes of mankind as unlimited. We all wish to add to our

---

[1] Replaces 'as capital increases'.

enjoyments or to our power. Consumption adds to our 16 Sept. 1814 enjoyments,—accumulation to our power, and they equally promote demand.

Mrs. Ricardo and I are going this morning to Cheltenham, which is 18 miles distant from us,—we shall return to-morrow. Mr. Smith whom I met at your house lives about 9 miles from here.[1] He and Mrs. Smith have been very kind and attentive to us. I suspect that I am much indebted to him for the notice which has been taken of us by our neighbours. Mr. Tennant was at his house for a short time and did me the favor to call, but I was unfortunately from home, and being obliged to go to London I did not pay my visit to Mr. Smith till he was gone.

I hope you recollect that we are not quite 28 miles from Bath. You and Mrs. Malthus might I think give us the pleasure of your company for a few days during your Christmas vacation and might at the same time visit your friends.[2] But as you have seen them so lately you would give us great pleasure if you would give us the whole of your time. Mrs. Ricardo who is standing by me has made me express myself in a more than usually bungling manner. She unites with me in kind regards to Mrs. Malthus

Y.ʳˢ very sincerely

DAVID RICARDO

[1] Thomas Smith whom Ricardo had met at Haileybury early in May of this year 1814 (see *The 'Pope' of Holland House*, p. 56, and for a notice of the Smiths, pp. 6–9). He was a barrister, but being unable to practise owing to an impediment of speech, he led the life of a country gentleman at Easton Grey, his residence near Malmesbury; he and his wife (Elizabeth Chandler) were Unitarians and they became intimate with the Ricardos, as is apparent from their unpublished letters to Ricardo, which are in *R.P.* He died in 1822.

[2] The Eckersalls, Mrs Malthus's family, who lived at Bath.

## 61. MILL TO RICARDO

My dear Sir                    Ford Abbey Sept.$^r$ 30$^{th}$ 1814

30 Sept. 1814    After reading this letter you will be left inquiring what could be the motive in writing it. At least this, I think, is very likely to be the case, for I have wonderfully little which is worth your hearing, to write about. However, there is one part of your letter,[2] namely your kind invitation to visit you at Gatcomb Park, which indisputably requires an answer at some time; and no time seems more proper than the present. —Oh! very well—a good come off—here's a very satisfactory reason for writing to you, already—which I am very thankful for, because I was unwilling it should appear I had written, only because I had a pleasure in corresponding with you. That would have affected your vanity too sensibly— set you up too much.

Now as to this same visit, the only thing I can pronounce about it with certainty is, that I have a great desire to pay it. The duration of my stay here of course does not altogether depend upon myself. I hold myself engaged to remain with Mr. Bentham, who will soon have no body with him, except myself and appendages, and who would not stay a day alone, as long as he finds it agreeable to remain. The present intention is not to return to London much before Xtmass, but whether the pleasure of remaining here will not be exhausted a good deal before that time, I hold very doubtful. As for prevailing upon Mr. Bentham, unless there were something particular creating a motive sufficiently strong to overcome the reluctance he has always felt to visit among strangers, the case, I suspect, is hopeless; though he was much gratified

[1] Addressed: 'David Ricardo      MS in *R.P.*
Esq. / Gatcomb Park / Mincing    [2] Ricardo's letter is wanting.
Hampton / Gloucester Shire'.

with the terms in which you pressed the invitation in your 30 Sept. 1814
letter. The scheme, however, which is in my head, is this. To
return from this place by Bath wants not much, all things
considered, of being the best mode of getting home. When at
Bath, it is scarcely 20 miles out of the way, to come round by
your Seat, at which I should contentedly abide for some days.
The mischief is, that I cannot come without all my incumbrances, consisting of a wife, and five brats, and a maid. I
am not afraid that we should be a nuisance in any other
respect than that of house-room. We need, no less than four
beds, but should be very well contented with two rooms. The
quantity, unless you are well provided indeed, considering
the numbers you draw to yourself, is very large—as to
*quality*, you will give us credit I hope, for having no choice.
Though the chance of accomplishing this scheme is not very
great, for there are too many circumstances which may interfere with it, yet I shall be glad to hear from you upon the
subject; and have only one thing to beg, but that I do beg
very sincerely; that you will not allow your complaisance to
impose upon you the smallest inconvenience; which would
be without any adequate object, as so very soon after the time
I could see you at Gatcomb, I shall see you all in London,
and could only have the new satisfaction of seeing your new
situation.

I am highly gratified to learn from you that you are all,
after experience, so highly satisfied with the place. One
thing only I hope; which is, that its pleasures and business,
and the pleasures of those who resort to it, will not condemn
you to live, as you complain of it, without opening a book.
There will be so many reasons for reproaching you, if you
continue in that track, that I will not enter upon them, at the
fag end of my letter, but reserve them till I see whether they
are wanted. I shall address myself to the ambition of Mrs.

30 Sept. 1814 Ricardo, who has a husband that could so much distinguish himself, if his modesty, or his neglect of distinction would only allow him. That he might be of great use to a favourite science, and to a most important department of practical politics, which altogether depend upon that science, ought to be sufficient motive with him, to improve every hour and every moment, nay to place himself in that situation in which his tongue, as well as his pen might be of use.

I should like now, to address myself to the ladies, if I could find something very smart to say. As for Mrs. Ricardo, I shall get a rap on the knuckles from her, unless I take care what I am about. I am very ambitious too of ingratiating myself. But what to talk to her about, as all her occupations, and all her enjoyments at this same Gatcomb, are unknown to me, deuce take me if I know! If she were that generous lady, I have always taken her for, she would take up her own pen, and describe to me every thing—that she would—or write part, and make those two tall, hau— young ladies, one *sui juris* (at least I believe so) t'other not, club their shares. What an honour, and what a delight it would be, to receive a letter from three *such* hands!

It is not at all unlikely that Mr. Hume, who has resided with us here for some weeks, and leaves us on wednesday next for Cheltenham, will pay you a visit as he passes. I have given him an invitation to call upon you—and you will find him a good-humoured clever man. He is hot upon the study of political economy—but with some little propensity to go wrong.[1]

Most truly yours

J. MILL

[1] Joseph Hume (1777–1855) whose friendship with Mill dated from their school days at Montrose Academy; having made a considerable fortune in India, as army surgeon and paymaster, he was returned to Parliament in 1812 for Weymouth as a Tory and in 1818 for Aberdeen as a Reformer.

## 62. MALTHUS TO RICARDO[1]
[*Reply to 60.—Answered by 64*]

E. I. Coll. Oct. 9th 1814.

My dear Sir,

We are very much obliged to you and Mrs. Ricardo for 9 Oct. 1814 your kind invitation to Gatcomb Park at our Xmas vacation, but I fear it will not be in our power to accept it. If we go from home we can hardly avoid going into Surrey; but we have latterly come to the resolution not to make distant excursions more than once a year, and I believe therefore we shall confine ourselves to Hayleybury and London. Our best chance of seeing Gatcomb and particularly of seeing it in beauty will be during some summer vacation in our way to or from our friends near Bath. Perhaps next summer we may be in that part of the world, and it will be a great additional pleasure, in our excursion, to be able to pay you a visit.

I do not write so soon after receiving your letter as I should perhaps feel inclined, for fear of occupying too much of your time, as well as my own. But I think that a letter now and then on these subjects will do us no harm, and perhaps may be the means of settling some important points relating to the metaphysics of Political Economy.

You seem to think that the state of production from the land, compared with the means necessary to make it produce, is almost the sole cause which regulates the profits of stock,

---

[1] Addressed: 'D. Ricardo Esqr. / Gatcomb Park / Minchin Hampton / Glocestershire'.
MS in the Goldsmiths' Library of the University of London; it was purchased for them in March 1907 by Professor Foxwell from Messrs. Sotheran.—Published in *Economic Journal*, June 1907, pp. 273–6. In a note Professor Foxwell there suggested that this letter may have been the one given by Ricardo to Mrs. Smith of Easton Grey for her collection of autographs (see pp. 164–5 and 169 below); this is the more plausible inasmuch as Mrs. Smith's collection was 'sold and dispersed at her death in 1859' (*The 'Pope' of Holland House*, p. 8).

9 Oct. 1814 and the means of advantageously employing capital. After
what I have written on the subject of food and population I
can hardly be supposed not to allow a very great effect to so
very great a cause. But unless it could be shewn that no improvements were ever to take place either in agriculture or
manufactures, and that upon a rise in the price of raw produce,
new leases would be immediately granted, new taxes levied,
and that the price of labour and of every other commodity
both foreign and domestic would rise without delay exactly
in proportion, the doctrine is evidently not correct in practice.
And as these contemporaneous effects are in my opinion not
only improbable but impossible, it would be quite useless to
lay much stress upon it even as a theoretical groundwork. It
appears to me that nearly all which can be safely advanced
respecting the dependence of profits on the state of the land
is, that the facility of acquiring food, and particularly the
possession of a great quantity of good land is the main cause
of high profits, and of a rapid increase of capital population
and demand, and that the difficulty of acquiring food is the
main cause of low profits, and the ultimate check to the indefinite extension of capital population and demand. But
that in the interval between the two extremes, considerable
variations may take place; and that practically no country
was ever in such a state as not to admit of increase of profits
on the land, for a period of some duration, from the advanced
price of raw produce.

The Profits of stock, or the means of employing capital
advantageously may be said to be accurately equal to the
price of produce, *minus* the expence of production. And consequently whenever the price of produce keeps a head of the
price of production the profits of stock must rise. And this
has unquestionably been the case on the land in this country
during the last 20 years. It is not the *quantity* of produce

compared with the expence of production that determines profits, (which I think is your proposition) but the exchangeable value or money price of that produce, compared with the money expence of production. And the exchangeable value of produce is not of course always proportioned to its quantity. In poor countries of rich land the profits of stock are in general not nearly so high as they ought to be according to your theory; and in rich countries of middling land and of an increasing commerce, they are often much higher. In stating the cause of high profits you seem to me to consider almost exclusively the expence of production, without attending sufficiently to the price of produce, and greatly to underrate the wants and tastes of mankind in affecting prices, and consequently in affecting the means of profitably em[ploying][1] capital.

What is it I would ask that enables the foreign merchant to sell the tea sugar and tobacco which he imports at a higher price than the manufactures which he has sent out in exchange for them. Solely their being better suited to the wants and tastes of society. There is no greater power to purchase them, but there is a greater will. And the *final cause* of the wealth which the country derives from these commodities, and of the means of profitably employing capital in their importation, is the existence of a taste for them. It is in considering merely of the proportions of commodities to one another, and not of their proportions to the wants and tastes of mankind that the error of Mr. Mill, in my opinion, consists.

I cannot by any means agree with you in your observation that "the desire of accumulation will occasion demand just as *effectually* as a desire to consume["] and that "consumption and accumulation equally promote demand." I confess in-

[1] MS torn.

9 Oct. 1814 deed that I know no other cause for the fall of profits which I believe you will allow generally takes place from accumulation than that the price of produce falls compared with the expence of production, or in other words that the *effective* demand is diminished. For this is how I understand the term effective demand, and this I think is the interpretation of it given by Adam Smith.[1] And according to this interpretation, that is upon the supposition that a greater effective demand means a greater excess of the price of produce above the expence of production, you would surely allow that the effective demand would always be greatest when the quantity of capital was comparatively the smallest, or the profits of stock highest.

The true question relative to Mr. Mill's proposition is not whether a man would like to spend half as much again; but whether you can furnish to persons of the same incomes a great additional quantity of commodities without lowering their price so much compared with the price of production as to destroy the effective demand for such a supply, and consequently to check its continuance to the same extent.

The principal difficulties on the present question appear to me to arise from the very different effects of an increase, or diminution of capital on the land, and in manufactures and commerce; particularly with regard to price, occasioned by the different nature of the instruments employed, one set naturally growing worse, and the other generally growing better. But I have no room for more, so adieu.

Ever truly Yours,<br>T. R. MALTHUS

[1] Cp. above, p. 58.

## 63. SINCLAIR TO RICARDO[1]

Dear Sir,

I have now quitted my former residence at Edinburgh, 19 Oct. 1814 and have settled with my family at Ham Common, where I hope to enjoy leisure enough to complete some laborious literary undertakings, in particular, "*A Code of Agriculture*,"[2] —"*A Code of Health*" in a form more compressed than the one already published;[3]—and "*A Code of Finance*".[4]

Since my arrival here, I feel much disappointed, in regard to the state of our public credit, the price of Stocks, &c; and should be glad to have a conversation with you, and some other intelligent members of the Stock Exchange upon that subject. If you could form a party to discuss these particulars, I would come to town on purpose any day next week, and we might dine together at the British Coffeehouse, The Clarendon Hotel,—the London Tavern, or any other convenient place.—I leave the whole arrangement to you.

I remain, Dear Sir,
Your very obedient Servant—
JOHN SINCLAIR

Ham Common—
near Richmond
Surrey.
19th October 1814.

[1] MS in *R.P.*—Ricardo's reply is wanting, but its tenour can be inferred from letter 65.
[2] *The Code of Agriculture, including Observations on Gardens, Orchards, Woods, and Plantations,* London, 1817.
[3] *The Code of Health and Longevity; or a Concise View of the Principles calculated for the Preservation of Health, and the Attainment of Long Life...,* 4 vols., London, 1807; 3rd ed., in 1 vol., London, 1816.
[4] This was never written; cp. *Correspondence of Sir John Sinclair,* London, 1831, vol. II, p. 38 ff. of the Appendix.

## 64. RICARDO TO MALTHUS[1]

*[Reply to 62.—Answered by 67]*

My dear Sir                                    Gatcomb Park 23ᵈ Octʳ 1814

23 Oct. 1814    On the day that you were writing your last letter to me
I was travelling to London with Mrs. Ricardo, where my
business detained me a little more than a week. On my
return your letter was delivered to me. I am sorry that you
cannot make it convenient to pay us a visit at Christmas; I
shall however depend on your not allowing any common
occurrence to prevent you and Mrs. Malthus from favoring
us with your company during your next summer vacation.

I hope you will not repent having set me the example of
using a larger sized paper. If you are tired with my long
letter you only will be to blame for it.

It does not appear to me that we very materially differ in
our ideas of the effects of the facility, or difficulty, of procuring food, on the profits of Stock. You say "that I seem
to think that the state of production from the land, compared with the means necessary to make it produce, is almost
the sole cause which regulates the profit of stock, and the
means of advantageously employing capital." This is a
correct statement of my opinion, and not as you have said in
another part of your letter, and which essentially differs from
it, "that it is the *quantity* of produce compared with the expence of production, that determines profits." You, instead
of allowing the facility of obtaining food to be almost the
sole cause of high profits, think it may be safely said to be
the main cause, and also a difficulty of acquiring food the
main cause of low profits. There appears to me to be very

[1] Addressed: 'To / The Revᵈ     MS at Albury.—*Letters to Mal-*
T. R Malthus / East India College /     *thus,* XX.
Hertford'.

little difference in these statements. You infer that my doctrine is not correct because improvements may take place in agriculture or manufactures,—because new leases may not be granted precisely at the time of the rise in the price of raw produce,—and because the price of labour may not rise without delay in the same proportion. But improvements in agriculture, or in machinery, which shall facilitate or augment production, will, according to my proposition, increase profits, because "it will augment production compared with the means necessary to that production." The same may be said of the wages of labour not rising in the same proportion as the price of produce. As for old leases affecting the question you will observe that in calculating the profits made by agriculture we must estimate leases at the value which they bear at the time of the calculation, and not at the value agreed upon at an antecedent period. If the question were concerning the profits of a manufactory; a distiller's, for example, we should calculate such profits according to the then value of barley, altho' a few individual distillers might have been so fortunate as to purchase their barley when it was 25 pc.ᵗ cheaper. These points then are expressly allowed for in my proposition and are by no means at variance with it. You add to your statement ["]that in the interval between the two extremes (of high profits and low profits caused by facility or difficulty of procuring food) considerable variations may take place; and that practically no country was ever in such a state as not to admit of increase of profits on the land for a period of some duration, from the advanced price of raw produce." I agree that variations will take place, because the means of obtaining produce are not always equally expensive,—and if they should be, the produce itself may become more valuable, and in either case profits will vary. But even during these temporary variations, the great cause namely the accumulation of capital may be paving the way for permanently diminished profits. It appears to me important to ascertain what the causes are which may occasion a rise in the price of raw produce, because the effects of a rise, on profits, may be diametrically opposite. A rise in the price of raw produce may be occasioned by a gradual accumulation of capital which by creating new demands for labour may give a stimulus to population and consequently promote the cultivation or improvement of inferior lands,—but this will not cause profits to rise but to fall, because not only will the rate of wages rise, but more labourers will be employed without affording a proportional return of raw produce. The whole value of the wages paid will be greater compared with the whole value of the raw produce obtained. A rise of raw produce may proceed from one or more bad seasons, which will undoubtedly increase profits, because the price of produce would rise considerably more than in the proportion of the deficient quantity, and would therefore be much a head of the price of production. An advanced price of raw produce may also proceed from a fall in the value of currency, which would raise the price of produce, for a time, more than it would wages, and would therefore raise profits. Both these you will allow are temporary causes, no way affecting the principle itself, but merely disturbing it in its progress. Restrictions on importation of raw produce may cause a rise in its price, which will be permanent or temporary according as the bad policy which dictated the restrictive law may be permanent or temporary. In the first instance profits will be raised, but they will ultimately fall below their former level.[1] From what I have said it will appear that I am of opinion that a

---

[1] Cp. above, I, 161 ff. for a similar discussion of the different effects of four causes of the rise in the price of raw produce.

permanent rise in the rate of profits on land is never preceded by a rise but by a fall in the price of raw produce, and tho' profits may be raised by a rise of the price of produce they will generally[1] ultimately settle at a rate lower than that from which they started. The converse of this as it regards low prices of produce I hold to be equally true. I should be glad to have your sentiments on this point. There may be other causes of high price which do not at present occur to me.

I allow that no country ever was or ever can be in such a situation as not to admit of increase of profits on the land, because there is no country which is not liable to lose or waste part of its capital, there is no country which is not liable to bad seasons,—to depreciated currency—to a real fall in the value of the precious metals, and to other accidents which will, some permanently, and some temporarily, raise profits. You observe that in rich countries profits are often much higher, and in poor countries much lower than according to my theory, to which I reply that profits are very much reduced in the poor country by enormous wages;— the wages themselves may be considered as part of the profits of stock,—and are frequently the foundation of new capital. In rich countries wages are low, too low for the comforts of the labourers;—too large a portion of the gross produce is retained by the owner of stock, and is reckoned as profit.

I am not aware that I have under-rated the effect of the wants and tastes of mankind on profits,—they frequently occasion large profits on particular commodities for short periods,—but they do not I think often[2] operate on general profits because they do not often influence the growth of

---

[1] 'generally' is ins.

[2] 'often' is ins. here and nine words below.

23 Oct. 1814 raw produce. Adam Smith in Book 5 Chap 1 Page 134 con-
cisely expresses what appears to me correct, of the effects of
demand on the prices of commodities.[1] I go much further
than you in ascribing effects to the wants and tastes of mankind,—I believe them to be unlimited. Give men but the
means of purchasing and their wants are insatiable. Mr. Mill's
theory is built on this assumption. It does not attempt to say
what the proportions will be to one another, of the commodities which will be produced in consequence of the
accumulation of capital, but presumes that those commodities only will be produced which will be suited to the
wants and tastes of mankind, because none other will be
demanded.

The very term accumulation of capital supposes a power
somewhere to employ more labour,—it supposes the total
income of the society to be increased and therefore to create
a demand for more food and more commodities. You ask
"whether we can furnish to persons of the same incomes a
great additional quantity of commodities without lowering
their price so much compared with the price of production as
to destroy the effective demand for such a supply, and consequently to check its continuance to the same extent." We
answer this is not our case, we are speaking of larger incomes not of the same incomes[2], and instead of anticipating
a fall in the price of commodities we should expect a rise,
because the fall of profits which generally follows accumula-

---

[1] 'The increase of demand, besides, though in the beginning it
may sometimes raise the price of
goods, never fails to lower it in the
long run. It encourages production, and thereby increases the
competition of the producers, who,
in order to undersell one another,
have recourse to new divisions of
labour and new improvements of
art, which might never otherwise
have been thought of.' Ricardo's
page reference applies to any ed.
of the *Wealth of Nations* from the
3rd to the 9th (1784–1799), vol. III;
in Cannan's ed., vol. II, p. 239.
[2] 'the same incomes' replaces
'less'.

tion is in consequence of the increase in the price of pro- 23 Oct. 1814 duction, compared with the price of produce; although they would both undoubtedly rise. You appear to think,—indeed you say "that you know no other cause for the fall of profits which generally takes place from accumulation than that the price of produce falls compared with the expence of production, or in other words that the *effective* demand is diminished" and by what follows you seem to infer that commodities will not only be relatively lower but really lower, and this is in fact the foundation of our difference with regard to the theory of Mr. Mill.—

You will by this time feel that you have enough if not too much.

Y<sup>rs</sup> truly<br>DAVID RICARDO

65. SINCLAIR TO RICARDO[1]<br>[Answered by 66]

Dear Sir,

So you have given up the Stock Exchange, and taken 29 Oct. 1814 to farming.—When joined to literary pursuits, the plan will answer, but otherwise, an active and intelligent mind finds a vacuum.

It would be obliging in you send me a list of those persons on the Stock Exchange, with whom it would be most advisable to consult on Financial subjects; and as you probably know them, letters of introduction to them.—As, in that case, the packet may be large, it may be addressed to me, under the cover of S. R. Lushington Esq<sup>r</sup>. M.P. Treasury Chambers, London, by whom it will be carefully forwarded.

---

[1] Addressed: 'David Ricardo Esqr / Gatcomb Park / Minchin Hampton / Gloucestershire'.—MS in *R.P.*

29 Oct. 1814    When you come to London, I shall be glad to give any
information you may wish for, on the subject of agriculture,
the doctrines of which are now so much simplified, that in a
few months you may acquire all the information necessary
to become a good farmer.—

I remain—<br>
Dear Sir—<br>
Your very obt Servt<br>
JOHN SINCLAIR

Ham-Common.—
  near Richmond.—
    Surrey.—
29<sup>th</sup> October 1814

David Ricardo Esqr.—
  &c    &c    &c

## 66. RICARDO TO SINCLAIR[1]

### [*Reply to 65*]

Gatcomb Park, Minchin-Hampton, 31st October 1814.

Dear Sir,

31 Oct. 1814    I have not quite given up the Stock Exchange; but for
a few months in the year, I mean to enjoy the calm repose
of a country life.

Though I have a few acres of land in hand, I am not yet
become a farmer. I leave the management of them wholly
to others, and hardly take sufficient interest in what is going
on, to make it probable that I shall ever be conversant with
agricultural subjects.

The Stock Exchange is chiefly attended by persons who
are unremittingly attentive to their business, and are well
acquainted with its details; but there are very few in number

[1] *Correspondence of Sir John Sinclair*, vol. I, p. 371; *Letters to Trower*,
IV.

who have much knowledge of political economy, and con- 31 Oct. 1814
sequently they pay little attention to finance, as a subject of
science. They consider more, the immediate effect of passing
events, rather than their distant consequences. Amongst the
most enlightened, I should name Mr. —— ——, Mr. ——
——, Mr. —— ——, and Mr. —— ——¹; but I cannot
answer that they will be able to afford time, or feel sufficient
zeal, to engage in financial discussions. I am going to write
to my brother, Ralph Ricardo, who is a member of the Stock
Exchange, and I will request him to mention your wish to
the above gentlemen, so that they will be prepared for any
application you may make to them. I am, Dear Sir, your
obedient and humble servant,

DAVID RICARDO.

## 67. MALTHUS TO RICARDO²
[*Reply to 64.—Answered by* 70]

E I Coll. Nov 23. 1814
My dear Sir,

I hope we shall be able some summer to pay you a visit 23 Nov. 1814
at Gatcomb, but I am a little afraid that our vacation will be
earlier in general than the commencement of your residence
in the country, and that our chief intercourse must be while
you are in Town.

You need not be afraid of my being tired of reading your
letters, though I may have some apprehensions about the
time required to answer them. In fact these subjects lead to so
many interesting points of discussion that it is difficult to

¹ The *Correspondence* omits the
names 'to prevent invidious com-
parisons.' The list below, VII, 14,
no doubt includes some of those
who were mentioned here.

² Addressed: 'D. Ricardo Esqr /
Gatcomb Park. / Minchin Hamp-
ton'.
MS in *R.P.*

23 Nov. 1814 comprize what one wishes to say even in a long letter. I had rather have you here to criticize what I could better develop at greater length.

I have never that I recollect doubted or denied the general *tendency* of the accumulation of capital upon the land to diminish profits. But the acknowledgment of this obvious truth appears to me to be very different from the general position that the state of the land *regulates* profits.

Nothing can be more certain, for instance, than that the state of the land is the main cause of high wages, or the most scanty wages, according as it is fertile and abundant, or comparatively poor and scarce. But still it would be most incorrect to say that the state of the land *regulates* wages; because there are numerous instances where land is fertile and abundant, and yet wages are very low and the population stationary or retrograde. The reason of this is, that tho' fertile land and a great plenty of it are the main cause of high wages of labour, yet they are not the sole or regulating cause, and without the accumulation of capital, which may be prevented by extravagant habits or a bad government[,] are inefficient to produce such high wages. In the same manner though the state of the land,—whether it is fresh and fertile, or comparatively at its utmost stretch of exertion, be the main cause of high profits, and of the final fall and almost ultimate extinction of profits, yet as the state of the land is by no means the sole cause which determines profits, but as they are powerfully influenced by the varying demands for produce occasioned by the prosperous or adverse state of commerce and manufactures, and the constant tendency to a fall in the wages of labour, it neither accords with theory or experience to call the state of the land the *regulator* of general profits. It is of course by no means enough to say that from the state of production from the land, compared with the means necessary to make it produce, you can infer with certainty the state of general profits; as this is merely saying what every body knows, that all profits must *cæteris paribus* be on a level. But the question is whether agriculture always takes the lead in the determination? and I should certainly say that it did not. When a new foreign commerce is opened, and new objects greatly in demand are brought into the market, the profits of such commerce must be higher than usual; and you allow that in this case capital may be taken from the land. But to allow this is at once to allow that the profits of foreign commerce determine in this case the profits on the land and that whichever is the highest will take the lead of the other.

Without however supposing capital to be taken from the land, the throwing of new objects of desire into the market will increase the value of the whole mass of commodities in the country, estimated either in money, or in corn and labour, and there will in consequence be a greater value of commodities to be exchanged for the raw produce. This increase in the value of raw produce must raise the profits of farming for a period of some duration; and it is in fact during these periods (with the exception of the first start as in America) that capital is most rapidly accumulated upon the land and the greatest improvements are made. With regard to the actual duration of such a period, it must of course depend upon various circumstances, particularly upon the extent and duration of the commerce, and the continued improvements made in manufacturing machinery. And without meaning to deny that a foreign commerce however prosperous is more easily saturated with capital than a large extent of fresh land. Yet both theory and experience shew that a period of comparatively high profits, (for 20 years perhaps), may take place contemporaneously in agriculture manufactures and foreign

23 Nov. 1814 commerce, after a period of comparatively low profits. These periods I consider are of great importance to nations, and not to be undervalued, because as the progress of population and capital cannot be absolutely unlimited, the further you proceed the nearer you must approach to the limit. *Permanent* high profits cannot take place but under the greatest national misfortunes—a premature but permanent and effective check to accumulation or a great and irrecoverable loss of capital, and I entirely agree with you that they would be accompanied with low instead of high prices, at least with regard to agricultural products.

It is of great importance as you justly observe to ascertain the causes which may occasion a rise in the price of raw produce, and in enumerating them I cannot help thinking that you have too much overlooked those natural and necessary,—not accidental causes, which in every rich and populous country make a bushel of corn command a much greater quantity of manufactured and foreign produce, and generally of labour, than in a poor, country; and which owing to circumstances which counterbalance the principle you lay down, diminish rather than increase in rich and highly cultivated countries, the proportion of the whole population employed upon the land. My conclusion therefore on the whole is this, that tho I should allow without the least hesitation and quite as a matter of course, the *tendency* of an accumulation of capital on the land as well as in every other employment, to lower profits, yet I should say that this tendency was at times so counterbalanced by other causes naturally accompanying the progress of improvement, that a period when the profits on land were 8 per cent, might often be followed by a period of 20 years perhaps, when they were 10 or 12 per cent, and this, without the removal of capital from the land but while the progress of cultivation was going on[1] and during these periods the state of manufactures and commerce would regulate the profits on land. The diminution of wages is a more directly necessary consequence of a difficulty in obtaining food, than the diminution of profits, as wages are the great regulator of the progress of population.

I cannot agree with you in thinking that the wants and tastes of mankind do not essentially influence general profits and the growth of raw produce. Taking man, as he is, and not supposing him to accumulate without motive, I believe that these tastes and wants as contradistinguished from the desire of mere necessaries, are, in these climates, and in the state of property derived from the feudal system, the cause of perhaps one third more raw produce, and 2 thirds more manufactured and foreign produce than we should have had without such tastes and wants.

Accumulation of *produce* is not accumulation of *capital*, unless what is accumulated is worth more than it cost, and if you were at once to employ all our soldiers sailors and menial servants in productive labour, the price of produce would fall more than ten per cent, and the encouragement to employ the same quantity of capital would cease.

I think I am right in what I said about the *same incomes*. In fact unless the commodities produced are new and more desirable, or cheaper, the producers will certainly be left to consume what they have produced them selves. Others will neither have the power nor the will to consume more. When I say I know no other cause &c: I mean to include of course a rise of produce accompanied by a still greater rise in the price of production; but I am of opinion that a positive fall of price is a very common effect of the employment of more capital, and will always take place when produce is increased by the employment of an unusual quantity of capital, before

[1] The remainder of the sentence is ins.

23 Nov. 1814 the wants and tastes of mankind and their power of purchasing have been increased in proportion. No more room

Ever truly Y<sup>rs</sup>

T R MALTHUS

## 68. MILL TO RICARDO[1]

My dear Sir                                    Ford Abbey Nov.<sup>r</sup> 24<sup>th</sup> 1814

24 Nov. 1814    Your kind letter[2] gave me a great deal of pleasure. In
truth it is not easy to avoid being pleased at finding that one
stands pretty high in the opinion of those whom one loves
and esteems. But I will come to the business part of this
letter before I say one word more about any thing else.—
Mons. Say, the author of the excellent book with which you
are well acquainted, entitled *Economie Politique*, is in this
island. It would be a thousand pities that you and he should
not see one another. I have therefore been endeavouring to
plan a meeting between you. He is known to a friend of
mine.[3] But at present he is in Scotland, gone to see Dugald
Stuart and the other philosophers of that region. I have
written, however, to my friend, to endeavour to prevail
upon him when he returns (that will be the beginning of next
month) to pay you a visit at Gatcomb Park.[4] I am persuaded

[1] Addressed: 'David Ricardo Esq. / Gatcomb Park / Mincing Hampton / Gloucester Shire'. MS in *R.P.*
[2] Ricardo's letter is wanting.
[3] Francis Place.
[4] Mill had written to Place on the same day (24 November) suggesting that Say should be 'prevailed upon to pay Mr. Ricardo a visit (though at the distance of Gloucester shire) as the man the most profoundly versant both in the theory and practice of political economy'. He added 'But I have another treat for him, and, if he be a man whose [? with a] passion for science, the highest treat he can meet with in this country—and that is a sight of Mr. Bentham who is by far undoubtedly the first philosopher in existence. If he will pay Mr. Ricardo a visit—who will treat him like a lord—I shall be able I think to prevail upon Mr. R. to accompany him hither where Mr. Bentham will be glad or rather extremely de-

the meeting with a man so eminent in your favourite science 24 Nov. 1814
would be highly agreeable to you; and if he has half the love
for political economy which the author of his book must of
necessity have, he must be delighted to have had an opportunity of conversing with you. But this is not the whole of the
project. There is something in it also for myself. On men-
tioning to Mr. Bentham my project of bringing together you
and Mons. Say, he started an idea which is perfection itself.
If you can prevail upon M. Say, said he, to go to Mr. Ricardos,
perhaps we may prevail upon both Mr. Ricardo and Mr. Say
to come here. I am persuaded *you* will not think much of the
journey. It is little more than 50 miles hither from Bath; and
if Mr. Say should here leave you to go to London, the Bath
and Exeter Stage passes at a few miles distance every day,
so that you can return any way that you chuse. It would be
a high treat to me to see you here, and to see you along with
Say. To him I have no doubt it will be an object to meet with
Mr. Bentham; and I am sure you will be gratified to be made
acquainted with him. Both he and I have set our hearts upon
the project, and will be much disappointed, if it should not
succeed.[1]

sirous to see them both, and where
they may stay one or two, or as
many days as they please.' (MS
in British Museum, Add. 35,152,
fol. 110; quoted by Halévy, *La
Formation du Radicalisme philosophique*, 1901, vol. II, p. 349.)
[1] Ricardo's reply is quoted in a
letter of Mill to Place, dated Ford
Abbey, 4 Dec. 1814: 'I have a
letter from Mr. Ricardo, which
begins—"My Dear Sir—The
meeting which you have projected between M. Say and myself
cannot but be delightful to me.
I should like much to have the
opinions of so eminent a man on

several points which I consider as
yet unsettled. I hope your friend
will be able to prevail on him to
visit me at Gatcomb—I will do
every thing I can to make it
agreeable to him." He also
further promises he will accompany him here. I write therefore
at present to enable you to assure
M. Say that both Mr. Bentham
and Mr. Ricardo are extremely
desirous of having an opportunity
of seeing him and will be highly
delighted to receive him in their
houses—to beg also that you will
use all your endeavors to prevail
upon him to come and prepare

24 Nov. 1814 As for your kind importunity to make a circuit by you on our return home, the resolution is taken to remain here as long, I suppose, as you mean to stay at Gatcomb Park. We shall be here till after Xtmass, that is, till the first week in January at the earliest. It follows that I must postpone the gratification of my curiosity till another season.

Mr. Hume came to your gate with the intention of paying you a visit—but was informed at the Lodge that you and Mrs. Ricardo had that morning set off for London—and therefore he did not call. Gatcomb Park he wrote to me, is a large, elegant, modern built house, standing in a hollow, like Cricket Lodge, the seat of Lord Bridport, in this neighbourhood; I have therefore, a very exact idea of your situation. He gives a formidable idea of the steepness of your roads. I understand, he says, that Gatcomb estate is a very good purchase. I am very glad to hear it. I shall, however, be very well pleased when I hear that you have less of it in your own farming hand. You will but lose money by that. I have some friends who have so much pleasure in losing money by farming, that it would be a pity to blame them for a little extravagance on a favourite mistress; but as you have no such concupiscence, it is loss without a return to you.

When you was in London, did you hear any political economy news, that was worth the repeating? What says the bullion market? It seems to be intimated pretty distinctly by the ministers, that the Bank restriction is to be continued. Is any body meditating any thing to excite the attention of the public to the subject, and make, or at least try to make them think as they ought? What is to be done in regard to the corn-importing law? Will the prohibition gentry push their

Mr. Godwin to join his influence to yours.' (MS copy in British Museum, Add. 35,152, fol. 117; see William Godwin's letter of 7 Oct. 1814 introducing Say to Place, *ib.*, fol. 95.) On the visit to Ford Abbey, see below, p. 161.

project anew, and if they do, will they succeed? What is 24 Nov. 1814
Mr. Malthus doing with his notes on Adam Smith? I see
Buchannans book is out.[1] Have you seen any thing of it?
    I know not that I shall have any thing to say to the ladies
this time—because they will have nothing to say to me.
Oh they are modest—they don't like to shew themselves.
As if ladies like them were ever afraid of shewing every thing
that is about them to the men. Oh, no—I see how it is. They
do not think poor me worth the shewing any thing to. The
mischief of it is, too, that I do not see any means I have to
make them repent of their sauciness. In revenge, I would
avoid liking them, if I could. Adieu—Believe me

Yours truly

J. MILL

[1] *Wealth of Nations*, 'With
Notes, and an additional Volume,
by David Buchanan', 4 vols.,
Edinburgh, Oliphant, 1814. On
his own projected edition of the
*Wealth of Nations* Malthus had
written to Francis Horner on
10 Nov. 1813: 'I have lately seen
the advertisement of the new
Edition of Adam Smith. It is to
be sure precisely upon the same
plan as that which I had projected,
and if it is done tolerably well
the author must anticipate me in
some points. Under these circumstances I am not sure whether
it may not be necessary for me
to change my plan and to publish
only a volume of essays instead
of a new edition of Smith. I
suppose I had better however
wait to see what sort of work it
is, before I finally make my determination. The circumstance on
the whole is rather unfortunate.'
This change of plan was confirmed
a year later, as it appears from a

letter of Whishaw to Horner,
dated Lincoln's Inn, 28 Oct. 1814:
'Malthus is very well, and was
here a few days ago. He seems
to have relinquished his plan of
editing Adam Smith (in consequence of being forestalled by
Buchanan); and seems disposed
to publish a volume or two of
essays on distinct branches of
political economy.' (MSS in the
possession of Lady Langman.)
It is curious that as late as in
January 1815 Ricardo still expected that Malthus would publish
his Notes; see below, p. 169.
Malthus's Notes were never published and the MS has not been
found. The Inverarity MS in the
Marshall Library at Cambridge
(which Dr Bonar, in *Economic
Journal*, 1929, p. 210, has supposed to contain these Notes) is
merely a series of questions on
the *Wealth of Nations* set by
Malthus to his pupils at Haileybury.—A letter from Malthus

## 69. PLACE TO RICARDO[1]

Charing Cross London
Dec. 7. 1814.

Sir

7 Dec. 1814     Yesterday I received a letter[2] from my excellent friend Mr. Mill dated Ford Abbey Dec. 4$^{th}$ in which he informed me of your desire to see Mr. Say at Gatcomb. I have since seen Mr. Say who has consented to leave London on Saturday by the Stage at 4 P.M. and I have thought proper to apprise you of this circumstance lest the cross post from Ford Abbey should not be in time.

Mons. Say is rather an elderly man of a plain appearance he possesses much simplicity of character, and the ease of a well bred gentleman. May I request that you will examine the xiii chapter of the first vol. of his work a copy of which he will of course leave with you, and give Mr. Mill your opinion thereon—and further that you will have the goodness to request Mr. Mill to let me have a line by Mons. Say on that subject—to me much of it appears useless and might be expunged without detriment to the work.[3]

I have the honor to be

Sir Your Ob$^t$ S$^t$

FRANCIS PLACE.

dated 3 Sept. 1812 on the proposed edition, which was 'to consist of foot notes where only short remarks were required, with an additional volume of longer notes and dissertations,—to be finished in about two years', is given in *The Publishing Firm of Cadell and Davies, Select Correspondence and Accounts, 1793–1836*, ed. by T. Besterman, Oxford, 1938, p. 163–4. (I owe this reference to Professor Jacob Viner.)

[1] MS (a copy in Place's handwriting) in British Museum, Add. 35,152, fol. 118b.
[2] See above, p. 157, n. 1,
[3] *Traité d'Économie politique*, 2nd ed., Paris, 1814, Livre I$^{er}$, ch. XIII, 'Des produits immatériels, ou des valeurs qui sont consommées au moment de leur production'. Place, it appears, intended to translate the *Traité*, but his project was not realised; see, on the first English translation, by Prinsep, below, VIII, 315, n. 2.

## 70. RICARDO TO MALTHUS[1]

*[Reply to 67.—Answered by 72]*

My dear Sir

Gatcomb Park 18 Dec.ʳ 1814

Since I rec.ᵈ your last letter I have been unexpectedly called from home, besides having had friends staying with me, which have prevented me from writing sooner. I have been twice to Bath and once to Cheltenham, and have also been as far as Devonshire to the old Abbey which Mr. Bentham at present inhabits. I accompanied Mons.ʳ Say the author of Economie Politique on a visit to him and Mr. Mill, —and had it not been for the incessant rain, we should have had a very pleasant excursion.[2]

Mons.ʳ Say came to me here from London at the request of Mr. Mill who wished us to be acquainted with each other. He intends seeing you before he quits this country. He does not appear to me to be ready in conversation on the subject on which he has very ably written,—and indeed in his book there are many points which I think are very far from being satisfactorily established,—yet he is an unaffected agreeable man, and I found him an instructive companion.

---

[1] Addressed: 'To / The Revᵈ T. R Malthus/East India College/ Hertford'.
MS at Albury.—*Letters to Malthus*, XXI.

[2] 'Ricardo and Say came here yesterday at dinner unexpected; whether they go, however, or no, tomorrow, as was originally intended, I know not. Both very intelligent and pleasant men, and both seem highly pleased.' (Bentham to Koe, from Ford Abbey, 15 Dec. 1814; in *Works*, ed. by Bowring, 1843, vol. x, p. 484.) Say's impressions are recorded in a letter of Place to Mill, 15 Jan. 1815: 'He spoke with rapture of you all, Mr. Bentham's Philosophy, and, as Mr. Say expressed it, "his heart full of benevolence in every thing" made his eyes sparkle as he pronounced the words.—You and Mr. Ricardo are, he says, profound economists, from both of you, he says, he has learnt much that will be useful'. (MS in British Museum, Add. 35,152, fol. 128; quoted by Halévy, *La Formation du Radicalisme philosophique*, 1901, vol. ii, p. 349.)

18 Dec. 1814    We intend to be in London in the middle of Jan.ʸ and have little doubt that we shall return here quite time enough to receive a visit from Mrs. Malthus and you next summer vacation, so I trust you will not project an excursion to any other quarter.

I perceive that we are not nearly agreed on the subject which we have been lately discussing. I have been endeavoring to get you to admit that the profits on stock employed in Manufactures and commerce are seldom permanently[1] lowered or raised by any other cause than by the cheapness or dearness of necessaries, or of those objects on which the wages of labour are expended. Accumulation of capital has a tendency to lower profits. Why? because every accumulation is attended with increased difficulty in obtaining food, unless it is accompanied with improvements in agriculture; in which case it has no tendency to diminish profits. If there were no increased difficulty, profits would never fall, because there are no other limits to the profitable production of manufactures but the rise of wages. If with every accumulation of capital we could tack a piece of fresh fertile land to our Island, profits would never fall.[2] I admit at the same time that commerce, or machinery, may produce an abundance and cheapness of commodities, and if they affect the prices of those commodities on which the wages of labour are expended they will so far raise profits;—but then it will be true that less capital will be employed on the land, for the wages paid for labour form a part of that capital.

A diminution of the proportion of[3] produce, in consequence of the accumulation of capital, does not fall wholly on the owner of stock, but is shared with him by the labourers.

---

[1] 'permanently' is ins.          [3] 'the proportion of' is ins.
[2] Cp. *Essay on Profits*, above, IV, 18.

The whole amount of wages paid will be greater, but the 18 Dec. 1814
portion paid to each man, will in all probability, be somewhat diminished.—

I do not recollect ever having allowed that an extension of
foreign commerce will take capital from the land, unless we
were an exporting country as far as regards corn, in which
case my proposition would be true, namely That the
rate of¹ profits can never permanently rise unless capital be
withdrawn from the land. I am not sanguine about the
principle, if true, being of any use; but that is another consideration;—its utility has nothing to do with its truth, and
it is the latter only which I am at present anxious to establish.

I cannot agree with you when you say that "without
supposing capital to be taken from the land the throwing of
new objects of desire into the market will increase the value
of the whole mass of commodities in the country, estimated
either in money, or in corn and labour,"—and it is because
I think that there will not be a greater value of commodities
to be exchanged for the raw produce, or for money that I
conclude no increased profits will any where be made. If the
mass of commodities be increased we diminish their exchangeable value as compared with those things whose
quantity is not augmented. If we double the quantity, or
rather double the facility of making, stockings, we diminish
their value one half, as compared with *all* other commodities. If we do the same with regard to hats and shoes,
we restore the accustomed relations between stockings, hats,
and shoes, but not with respect to other things. It is here I
think, that our difference rests and I hope soon to hear all that
you have to advance in favor of your view of the question.

Mr. Say, in the new edition of his book, Page 99 Vol. 1,
supports, I think, very a[bly]² the doctrine that demand is

¹ 'the rate of' is ins.        ² MS torn here and below.

18 Dec. 1814 regulated by production.[1] Dema[nd is] always an exchange of one commodity for another. The shoemaker when he exchanges his shoes for bread has an effective demand for bread, as well as the baker has an effective demand for shoes, —and although it is clear that the shoemaker's demand for bread must be limited by his wants, yet whilst he has shoes to offer in exchange he will have an effective demand for other things,—and if his shoes are not in demand it shews that he has not been governed by the just principles of trade, and that he has not used his capital and his labour in the manufacture of the commodity required by the society,—more caution will enable him to correct his error in his future production. Accumulation necessarily increases production and as necessarily increases consumption. Accumulation of *produce* if properly selected *may* always be accumulation of *capital*, and it cannot fail to be worth more than it cost, estimated in corn or labour,—and this I think would be true although all our soldiers, sailors, and menial servants were employed in productive labour.—It appears to me that the consideration of money value may be the foundation of our difference on this point.—

I must leave room for a request which I hope you will not refuse. I dined a little while ago at Mr. Smith's whom I first met at your house. Mrs. Smith told me that she had a collection of the hand writing of a great number of men who had distinguished themselves by their writings, and she wished

---

[1] 'De manière ou d'autre, soit qu'on dépense improductivement une épargne, soit qu'on la dépense productivement, elle est toujours dépensée et consommée; et ceci détruit une opinion bien fausse, quoique bien généralement répandue, c'est que l'épargne nuit à la consommation. Toute épargne, pourvu qu'elle soit replacée, ne diminue en rien la consommation, et, au contraire, elle donne lieu à une consommation qui se reproduit et se renouvelle à perpétuité, tandis qu'une consommation improductive ne se répète pas.' (*Traité d'Économie politique*, 2nd ed., 1814.)

that I would give her a letter of yours to add to her collec- tion. Knowing that I had many which would not discredit you, I assented; but after I came home I thought I had no right to do it without your consent,—which I hope you will not refuse. I should be sorry to disappoint her, and should really cut a poor figure in making my apologies if I did, yet as my opinion, that I should not do it without your consent, is confirmed by Mrs. Ricardo, I must falter out my excuses if you are inexorable.[1]

With kind regards to Mrs. Malthus I am

Ever Yours truly

DAVID RICARDO

## 71. RICARDO TO SAY[2]

Gatcomb Park Minchinhampton
24th Decr 1814

Dear Sir

The plan for the currency of France which you have sent me to look over[3] differs in no very essential point from that which I recommended for our Bank of England,[4] excepting that you propose Government to be the issuers, and to derive the advantages from the substitution of paper for metallic money.

In all countries, I should think, there exists a repugnance to entrust to Government the power of issuing paper money,

---

[1] See above p. 139, n. 1.
[2] Addressed: 'J. B. Say Esqr / 21 Nassau Street/Middlesex Hospital/ London'.
MS in the possession of M. Raoul-Duval.
[3] Say had been commissioned by the French Government to study economic conditions in England and bring back such informa- tion as might find useful applica- tion in France. (See 'Notice sur J.-B Say', in his Œuvres diverses, p. xi.) The currency plan may have been part of his report, which was not published.
[4] The ingot plan, outlined in the Appendix (1811) to the High Price of Bullion.

24 Dec. 1814 and when we consider that perhaps in no instance they have not abused such a power, it is not wonderful that such fears are prevalent. I am however so fully persuaded that the value of a currency depends on its quantity, and if your plan is adhered to there is such security against the quantity becoming excessive, that I cannot doubt of its success. My only doubt is whether Government will under all temptations rigidly abide by its own rules.

In justice the public ought to derive the benefits which result from the substitution of a paper for a more valuable currency, but it has hitherto been given to a company of Bankers or merchants because they were more under the controul of authority and could not with impunity use so formidable an engine to the injury of the public. At no time has the theory of money been so well understood as at present, and if the practice is conformable to it every thing respecting paper money will go on well.

In the last paragraph you have noticed a danger against which there can be no complete guard. It is a danger inherent in the Banking system and even a circulation of metallic money, only, is not wholly exempt from it.

I am sorry that you are obliged to leave this country so soon. I hoped to have had the pleasure of seeing you in London before your departure.

I hope you will have the satisfaction of witnessing the abolition of all those laws which so materially interfere with the prosperity of nations, the evils of which your writings have so ably disclosed.

With best wishes for your happiness
I am Dear Sir
Your obed.̲ humble Servant
DAVID RICARDO

## 72. MALTHUS TO RICARDO[1]
*[Reply to 70.—Answered by 73]*

E I Coll Decemb<sup>r</sup> 29<sup>th</sup> 1814

My dear Sir,

I am very busy just at present writing an "Inquiry into   29 Dec. 1814
the nature and origin of rent, and the Laws by which it is
governed"[2] and can only afford therefore to take a common
sheet of paper. I have some thoughts of publishing it if I
can, before the meeting of Parliament, together with a third
edition of my observations on the Corn Laws, which has
been some time out of print.[3] I once intended to accompany
them, with an Inquiry into the causes which affect the exchange, and the prices of the precious metals, (a part of which
you saw formerly) preparatory to the discussion relating to
the Bank; but I think now I shall defer the latter and publish
what relates to Corn first.

We should explain what we mean by *permanently*. Of
course I never mean to say that the high price of raw produce
compared with the price of production, occasioned, (in my
opinion) by a prosperous commerce, can be really *permanent*.
It is the nature of all such means of employing capital to
become less and less advantageous. And all that I contend for
is that a period of some duration may occur (20 years for
instance) when the profits of commerce will take the lead, and
regulate the profits of agriculture.

You do I confess a good deal surprise me when you say
that cannot agree with me in thinking that foreign com-

[1] Addressed: 'D. Ricardo Esqr. /
Gatcomb Park / Minchinhampton / Glocestershire.'
MS in *R.P.*
[2] See below, p. 172, n. 2.
[3] *Observations on the Effects of the
Corn Laws, and of a Rise or Fall*
*in the Price of Corn on the Agri-
culture and General Wealth of the
Country*, London, Johnson, 1814
(2nd ed., *ib.* 1814). A third
edition was published by Murray
early in February 1815.

29 Dec. 1814 merce increases the value of the whole mass of commodities. I have certainly always thought that in the exchange of the tin of Cornwall for the deals of Norway, both countries had the value of the whole mass of their commodities decidedly increased; and this increase of value has always appeared to me to be the consequence of all profitable exchanges both external and internal.

You say that profits depend entirely upon the low price of Corn? What was the reason that from 1720 to 1750 the interest of money and the profits of stock fell very considerably and were very low at the same time that the price of corn was gradually becoming cheaper; while from 1793 to 1812 the interest of money and the profits of stock were high, at the same time that the price of corn was becoming peculiarly dear.

I do not think that a prosperous commerce would have an effect very essentially different from a great foreign demand for our raw produce. But supposing a great foreign demand for our raw produce, would not the profits of capital employed in agriculture be increased, although certainly more rather than less capital would be employed upon the land. The instruments of production compared with the price of produce would be cheaper, but it could not with any propriety be said that capital was withdrawn from the land.

I had remarked the passage you mention in Mr. Says work, and think it well done, though I cannot quite agree with him. I think the source of his error is, that he does not properly distinguish between the necessaries of life and other commodities,—the former create their own demand the latter not.

I quite agree with you that a piece of fertile land added to the country upon every increase of capital would prevent the fall of profits, but more in my opinion from its increasing the demand for manufactures by increasing the number of people than by its preventing the rise of wages, an effect which it would probably not have. You are welcome to use one of my letters as you propose. Kind regards. 29 Dec. 1814

Ever truly Yours<br>T R MALTHUS

## 73. RICARDO TO MALTHUS[1]
### [*Reply to* 72]

Gatcomb Park. 13 Jan.<sup>y</sup> 1815

My dear Sir—

I am pleased to learn that you are busy writing with a view to immediate publication. The public pay a most flattering attention to any thing from your pen, and you are not fulfilling your duty to society, if you do not avail yourself of this disposition to endeavor to remove the cloud of ignorance and prejudice, which every where exists on the subjects which have particularly engaged your time and reflection. I hope your notes on Adam Smith[2] are in great forwardness, and that they will soon follow the smaller publications which you are now preparing. I expect that they will not only be very useful in giving correct notions to the public, but also in calling the attention of those, who are well informed in the science of political economy, to many points which have hitherto escaped their consideration. 13 Jan. 1815

I cannot help thinking that Lord Lauderdale was mistaken, (and I believe you hold the same opinion as him) in supposing[3] the farmer to lie under any particular disadvantage from not having the monopoly of the home market, whilst so many other trades were enjoying that benefit. You will

[1] Addressed: 'To / The Rev<sup>d</sup> T R Malthus / East India College / Hertford'.
MS at Albury.—*Letters to Malthus*, XXII.

[2] See above, p. 159, n. 1.
[3] In *A Letter on the Corn Laws*, London (for Constable, Edinburgh), 1814, pp. 8–9.

13 Jan. 1815 agree that the monopoly of the home market is eventually of no great advantage to the trade on which it is conferred. It is true that it raises the price of the commodity by shutting out foreign competition but this is equally injurious to all consumers, and presses no more on the farmer than on other trades. If monopolies tend to raise the price of labour, the inconvenience must be suffered by all who employ labour, and will therefore not be particularly injurious to the farmer or landlord. If all the monopolies of the home market were immediately abolished, there would be at least as much disposition to import corn;—if so they do not interfere with the natural course of the corn trade. Lord Lauderdale with his opinion of the effect of monopolies is I think quite consistent in recommending a duty on the importation of corn.

I thought you maintained, that the high or low profits on commerce were totally independent of the amount of capital which might be employed on the land; consequently that high profits might continue as long as commerce was prosperous, whether that was for 20 or for 100 years. I now understand you to say, that the profits of commerce may take the lead, and may regulate the profits of agriculture for a period of some duration, possibly for 20 years.

I have always allowed that under certain circumstances profits on agriculture might be diverted from their regular course for short periods, so that we only appear to differ with respect to the duration of such profits; instead of 20 years I should limit it to about 4 or 5.

If with the same labour we could obtain double the quantity [of]¹ tin from the mines in Cornwall, after prices had found the[ir l]evel, would the value of the whole mass of commodities be increased in England? Should we obtain the same quantity of deals from Norway in exchange for a

¹ MS torn.

given quantity of tin as we now do? Although the mass of commodities both in the markets of Norway and in those of England would increase by the greater abundance of tin, or of some other commodity, if the labour employed in procuring tin were diverted to other objects, yet the estimated value of all their commodities, in corn, money, or any article but tin, would, it appears to me, continue unaltered. It is sufficient that deals can be purchased cheaper in Norway than elsewhere to determine a portion of foreign trade to that quarter, although it should yield no more profits than those of other trades.

On the supposition which you have made of a great foreign demand for our raw produce, there can be no question that more capital would be employed on the land, and I think profits would fall. Such a demand cannot exist in the present situation of the world. Raw produce is always imported into the relatively rich country, and never exported from it, but on occasions of dearth or famine. I have no doubt that if the free importation of corn is allowed into this country, inasmuch as it will direct foreign capital to foreign land, it will tend to lower foreign profits, and if all the earth were cultivated, *with equal skill,* up to the same standard, the rate of profits would be every where the same, though the superior industry and ingenuity of particular countries might secure to them a greater abundance of other commodities.

I leave Glocestershire on the 20<sup>th</sup>. Mrs. Ricardo with part of the family will stay a week or two after me. I shall hope to see you in Brook Street very soon after my arrival in London. Your club[1] meets I think on the 28<sup>th</sup>—pray take a bed at our house. Kind regards to Mrs. Malthus

Truly Y<sup>rs</sup>

DAVID RICARDO

[1] The King of Clubs.

## 74. RICARDO TO MALTHUS[1]
[*Answered by* 75]

[London, 6 Feb. 1815]

My dear Sir

6 Feb. 1815    I have now read with very great attention your essay on
the rise and progress of rent,[2] with a view of selecting every
passage which might afford us subject for future discussion.
It is no praise to say that all the leading principles in it meet
with my perfect assent, and that I consider it as containing
many original views, which are not only important as connected with rent, but with many other difficult points, such
as taxation &c.ᵃ &c.ᵃ.

I cannot however help regretting that you did not consider separately the relations of rent, with the profits of
Stock, and the wages of labour. By treating of the joint
effect of the two latter on rent, you have, I think, not made
the subject so clear as it might have been made.

There are some parts of the essay with which I cannot
agree. One of these is the effects of improvements, whether
in the practice of Agriculture, or in the implements of husbandry, on rent. They appear to me in their immediate
effects to be beneficial to the farmer only, and not to the
landlord. All the augmented produce obtained, or the saving
in obtaining the same quantity of produce, is I think wholly
to the advantage of the farmer, and that the landlord only
benefits remotely from it, as it may encourage accumulation,
and the cultivation of poorer lands.—

---

[1] Addressed: 'To / The Revᵈ
T. R Malthus / East India College /
Hertford'. Dated by Malthus
in pencil 'Febr. 1815'; London
postmark, 6 Feb. 1815.
MS at Albury.—*Letters to Malthus*, XXIII.

[2] *An Inquiry into the Nature and
Progress of Rent, and the Principles
by which it is Regulated*, London,
Murray [another issue, Murray
and Johnson], 1815.

I think too that rents are in no case a creation of wealth, 6 Feb. 1815
they are always a part of the wealth already created, and are
enjoyed necessarily, but not on that account less beneficially
to the public interest, at the expence of the profits of stock.[1]
Viewing rents in this light it follows that I must withdraw
the concession which I was inclined to make[2] when you first
started the question "whether in importing corn at a cheaper
price than we could grow it the whole difference of price was
saved, or whether some abatement should not be made from
the advantage for the loss of rent?", as I now decidely think
that the whole difference of price would be gained without
any deduction whatever. The arguments then of those who
contend for a free trade in corn remain in their original full
force, as rents are always withdrawn from the profits of stock.

I will try if I have a little leisure to put my thoughts on this
subject on paper, and shall attempt to shew that the effects of
a tax and of rent are very different as far as regards importation. It may be economical to grow corn if its price is
raised merely by taxation, as by importing it a part of the tax
would be wholly lost to the country [impor]ting.[3] No such
consideration should influence us w[ith regar]d to rent being
lost.—

I diff[er to]o, as you know, as to the effects of taxati[on] on
the growth of produce. You appear to me not quite consistent in admitting as you unequivocally do that the last
portion of land cultivated, yields nothing more than the
profits of stock,—no rent, and yet to maintain that taxes on
necessaries or on raw produce fall on the landlord and not
on the consumer.[4]

I hope you found Mrs. Malthus quite well, and that your

---

[1] 'stock' replaces 'trade'.
[2] Not mentioned before in this correspondence.
[3] MS torn here and below.
[4] *An Inquiry into the Nature...of Rent*, pp. 52–3.

6 Feb. 1815 little boy is recovered from the accident he lately met with. Mrs. R and the rest of my family arrived safe in London on friday last.

I have paid Wetenhall £2. 8 – for two year's lists, but it has since occurred to me that I paid him, and you paid me, for one year, and therefore that only one year can be due to him. If so let me know that I may get back £1. 4 –

Ever Y$^{rs}$

DAVID RICARDO

## 75. MALTHUS TO RICARDO[1]

[*Reply to* 74.—*Answered by* 76]

E I Coll Feb$^y$ 12. 1815

My dear Sir,

12 Feb. 1815     I am much obliged to you for the attention you have paid to my Essay, and shall be very happy to discuss with you the points on which we differ. Could not you pay us a visit at the College for a day or two? We shall be most happy to see you whenever you can come. Will nex friday or saturday suit you?

If I had treated the subject as you propose, I think I should have been too much detained by the question of profits, about which we differ, and which certainly deserves a separate discussion. I am rather surprised that you do not think that improvements in the practice of agriculture and in the implements of husbandry affect rents. While they are confined to a few and during the current leases, the advantage of them must of course go to the farmers. But afterwards they appear to me to affect rents almost exclusively. This has been remarkably the case in Scotland.

Rents are undoubtedly a part of the wealth already created,

[1] Addressed: 'David Ricardo Esqr / Upper Brook Street / Grosvenor Square.'—MS in *R.P.*

but they are not on that account less a creation. A man hires an instrument of me for 20 years, from the use of which with the assistance of his capital he makes fair and ample profits. But at the end of the 20 years my instrument is worth double what it was before. Is not this a creation of value which would not have taken place, if the same capital had been employed in commerce or manufactures? It is true that during the time of his lease the farmer enjoyed the benefit of this additional value of the instrument in the shape of profits; but if these high profits were to continue to the farmer after the time of his lease, they would be *property*, and totally of a different nature and character from the profits of those trades where the competition is free. Many of the Scotch farmers during the latter part of their long leases some few years ago, made I dare say above thirty per cent; but surely this could not be considered as the natural profits of stock, and when the machines were returned to their owners very much increased in value, it could hardly be said to be at the expence of the general profits of stock, which could not be much influenced by these particular instances confined to particular spots. Profits naturally find a level, and when the benefits of a particular employment of capital continue much greater than usual, either monopoly or rent must be concerned.

I shall like much to see your written opinions on the influence of taxation upon cultivation. You say very justly that it sometimes tends to clear up these matters, to put money out of the question. Upon this plan I would ask whether a man who was going to take some poor land into cultivation, might not be at once deterred from it, if for every six quarters of corn which he raised from it he was obliged to pay one for the support of the state. If the land were very poor the remainder might not be sufficient to support the labourers upon it, or pay the expences of cultivation.

12 Feb. 1815  With regard to the tax *being thrown off on* the Landlord I did not certainly express myself as I meant. I intended to alter it before I left Town but forgot it. It is now corrected. I think however there are often cases where taxes are thrown off on the landlord, and I meant to say that those which had not already been thrown off on the consumer would then be thrown off on the landlord.

I find that I paid for two years of Wettenhalls lists, last February. I think there can be only one due now.

I hope Mrs. Ricardo is quite well. Mrs. M desires to be kindly remembered.

truly Yours<br>T R MALTHUS

What do you say to the Appendix?[1] I fear the *Rents* is too abstruse.


### 76. RICARDO TO MALTHUS[2]
[*Reply to* 75]

London 13<sup>th</sup> feb 1815

My dear Sir

13 Feb. 1815  I shall accept your kind invitation and intend being with you on saturday evening at the usual time. We can then talk over the points on which we differ.—I will bring with me the papers on which I have been busy since you left London, and in which my objections are more fully stated than can be done in the compass of a letter.[3]

---

[1] Malthus's *The Grounds of an Opinion on the Policy of Restricting the Importation of Foreign Corn; intended as an Appendix to 'Observations on the Corn Laws'*, London, Murray and Johnson, 1815.
[2] Addressed: 'To / The Rev<sup>d</sup>

T R Malthus/East India College/ Hertford'.
MS at Albury.—*Letters to Malthus*, XXIV where it is misdated '10 Feb. 1815'.
[3] The MS of *Essay on Profits*, which was published a few days later (*ca.* 24 February).

In the case of the Scotch farmers who made such large profits on their capital during the latter part of their leases, they appear to me to have been enjoying rent, arising not from improvements in agriculture, but from poorer land being taken into cultivation. If their leases had expired sooner, rent would have been increased long before on those farms. It would be desirable to know what the rent on those farms was when the lease was originally granted, or rather what proportion it bore to the capital then employed, and what the proportion of rent is to the capital now employed.

The effects of monopoly cannot I think be felt till no more land can be advantageously cultivated. You have yourself said, and I very much admire the passage,[1] that the last portion of capital employed on the land yields only the common profits of stock, and does not afford any rent. If so corn like every thing else is regulated in its price by the cost of production, and every other portion of capital employed on the land is reduced to the same level of profits only because no more capital can be employed with more advantage, and all which it any where yields more is rent and not profit.—

I have read the Appendix also with great attention and cannot help thinking that you have quite thrown off the character of impartiality to which in the observations[2] I thought you fairly entitled. You are avowedly for restrictions on importation; of that I do not complain. It is not easy to estimate justly the dangers to which we may be exposed.— Those who are for an open trade in corn may underrate them, and it is possible that you may overrate them. It is a most difficult point to calculate these dangers at their fair value,— but in an economical view, altho' you have here and there

[1] *An Inquiry into the Nature...of Rent*, p. 3, note; the passage is quoted above, **IV**, 37–8.

[2] *Observations on the Effects of the Corn Laws*, 1814 (3rd ed., 1815).

13 Feb. 1815 allowed that we might be benefited by importing cheap, rather than by growing dear—you point out many inconveniences which we should suffer from the loss of agricultural capital, and from other causes; which would make it appear as if even economically you thought we ought[1] to import corn,—such is the approbation with which you quote from Adam Smith of the benefits of agriculture over commerce in increasing production, and which I cannot help thinking is at variance with all your general doctrines.[2]—

Your observations on the advantages, (and therefore on the injustice to other classes) which the stockholder would reap from a low price of corn are I think very correct,—but I do not think these objections should stand in the way of the general good. They the stockholders have at different periods suffered much, and if the sinking fund be now appropriated to other services another striking injustice will be added to the long list. I meant to write only a few lines, and have filled a long letter.—Kind regards to Mrs. Malthus

Y$^r$ very truly

DAVID RICARDO

## 77. RICARDO TO MALTHUS[3]

[*Answered by* 78]

London 9$^{th}$ March 1815

My dear Sir

9 March 1815     My acquaintance lies so little amongst political economists that I have very few opportunities of knowing whether, what you consider as my peculiar opinions, have any sup-

---

[1] Should be 'ought not', as the sense requires.
[2] Cp. above, IV, 37.
[3] Addressed: 'To / The Rev$^d$

T. R Malthus/ East India College/ Hertford'.
MS at Albury.—*Letters to Malthus*, XXV.

porters, or indeed whether they are read or attended to.[1] As 9 March 1815 for my own judgement on the subject, it is perhaps too partial to merit attention, but after my best efforts not to be biassed in favor of my own opinions I continue to think them correct.

I would indeed rather modify what I have said concerning the stationary state of the prices of commodities, under all variations of the price of corn, either from wealth on the one hand, or the importation from foreign countries, or improvements in agriculture, on the other. I made no allowance for the altered[2] value of the raw material in all manufactured goods; they would I think be subject to a variation in price not on account of increased or diminished wages, but on account of the rise or fall in the price of the raw produce which enters into their composition and which in some commodities cannot be inconsiderable.[3]

It is a matter of mortification to me that my execution has been so faulty,—I was too much in a hurry, and have not made my meaning intelligible even to those who are familiar with such subjects, much less to those who skim over these matters.

Since I have seen you I recᵈ a note from Mr. Edwᵈ West who is the author writing under the title of a fellow of University College,[4]—he speaks in favor of my opinions, of course; because they are very similar to his own.—I have read his book with attention and I find that his views agree

---

[1] Ricardo's *Essay on the Influence of a Low Price of Corn on the Profits of Stock* had been published about 24 Feb. 1815.

[2] 'altered' is ins.

[3] See *Essay on Profits*, above, IV, 20; and cp. *Principles*, I, 117. Ricardo in this letter adopts the opinion of West (see p. 38 of West's *Essay* referred to in the next note).

[4] *An Essay on the Application of Capital to Land, with Observations shewing the Impolicy of any Great Restriction of the Importation of Corn, and that the Bounty of 1688 did not lower the Price of it*, 'By a Fellow of University College, Oxford', London, Underwood, 1815. Cp. Ricardo's statement, written on his copy of this tract, above, IV, 6.

9 March 1815  very much with my own. He is a barrister,—a young man and appears very fond of the study of political economy. Mr. Brougham has, I think he said, promised to introduce him to you.—

Mr. Jacob has handled both him and me rather roughly,— but he will not condescend to argue with us.[1] I shall be very easy if he is the most formidable opponent that is to attack me, for he seems totally ignorant of the scientific part of the subject.

The opposition to the bill is more formidable than I expected, but they appear so determined in the House of Commons that I suppose it will finally pass. I regret that the people should have proceeded to acts of riot and outrage.[2] I am too much a friend to good order to wish to succeed through such means, besides that I am persuaded that they hurt rather than promote the object which they and I have in view.

I wish you could have dined with me on saturday. I expect Mr. Phillips[3] and Mr. Dumont,—it would be a very agreeable surprise to me if you should join our party. Perhaps you may be inclined to come to London and will take a bed in Brook Street. Do if you can; but do not think it necessary to write on purpose if you cannot.—I shall fully depend on your staying with us when you come to the next club.[4]

---

[1] William Jacob, *A Letter to Samuel Whitbread, Esq. M.P. being a Sequel to Considerations on Protection required by British Agriculture; to which are added Remarks on the Publications of A Fellow of University College, Oxford; of Mr. Ricardo, and Mr. Torrens*, London, Johnson, 1815.
[2] The riots in London on 6, 7 and 8 March against the proposed Corn Law prohibiting importation till the price of wheat rose to 80s. a quarter. The Bill was finally passed in the House of Commons on 10 March.
[3] Probably William Phillips (1773–1828), the Quaker bookseller and geologist, one of the original members of the Geological Society.
[4] The King of Clubs.

Sir F. Burdett[1] and some others think that the high price   9 March 1815
of our corn is owing to enormous taxation, and that it ought
not, nor cannot fall, without oppression to the landholders
till our debt is diminished. If I could convince myself that
any part of the price of corn was owing to taxation I should
be in favour of a protecting duty to that amount. But if he
were right, the high price would not be accompanied by high
rents and by the cultivation of inferior lands. These I consider as unequivocal marks of the high price being caused by
wealth and a scarcity of fertile land. Indeed my theory leads
me to think that no taxes but those directly on the land, or on
its produce, would raise the price of corn and even such
taxes would have no effect if all exportable commodities were
taxed in the same degree, for a tax on exportable commodities
in a country which imports corn does not act very differently
from a duty on the importation of corn. Kind regards to
Mrs. Malthus

Ever Y[rs]

DAVID RICARDO

78. MALTHUS TO RICARDO[2]

*[Reply to 77]*

E I Coll March [10th][3] 1815
My dear Sir,

I should like much to join your party tomorrow, but it   10 March 1815
is out of my power. I am not sure whether I shall be in Town

---

[1] Sir Francis Burdett (1770–
1844), Radical M.P. for Westminster. His views on Taxation
and the Corn Bill were expressed
in his speech in the House of
Commons on 10 March 1815
(*Hansard*, XXX, 97–102).
[2] Addressed: 'D. Ricardo Esqr /

Upper Brook Street / Grosvenor
Square'.
   MS in *R.P.*
[3] In MS '9th'; undoubtedly a
slip, Ricardo's party of Saturday
the 11th being referred to as of
'tomorrow'. London postmark,
11 March.

10 March 1815 at the next club, and whether if I am, Mrs. Malthus will be with me. If circumstances allow of it, I shall be very happy to be with you in Brook Street.

Not having been in Town I have seen no Political Economists, and cannot therefore say anything about the reception of your pamphlet.[1] The only person at all conversant with the subject, that I have heard speak of it, is Sir James Mackintosh whom I saw just before I left Town. He thought it rather difficult, and not sufficiently practical, to assist him in forming a parliamentary opinion or argument; but said that he should certainly study it if he was going to give lectures on the subject. The doctrines, he thought, wanted a more full development. From having talked with you so frequently on the subject, I made the same mistake with regard to your pamphlet, as I did with regard to my own on *Rents*, and fancied that things which were familiar to me would be readily intelligible to other people. I now see my error in both cases. Considering the short time you were employed about it, the essay has great merit; but it might certainly have been improved by more time and attention.

I have been intending to add a few notes to the Grounds for another edition,[2] but have been so much engaged since I returned from Town that I have not yet begun.

I confess I think that the kind of calculation which I mentioned to you in Town,[3] shews in what manner profits on land may rise decidedly, from the alteration in the relative value of corn, and therefore shews that general profits may be determined by the general supply of stock compared with the means of employing it, and not merely by the stock employed on the land. Nor can I yet satisfy myself either from theory or experience that profits depend solely on the

[1] *Essay on Profits.*          [3] See below, p. 186–7.
[2] Cp. below, p. 201.

price of corn. I am struck by your persevering conviction, 10 March 1815
but I cannot see the subject in the same light; and it appears
to me that experience is clearly against it.

The Post is here, and I have only time to say that tho I
think the country will feel considerable inconveniences, from
a great fall in the price of corn, yet I should be sorry to see
the measure carried in spite of such a crowd of petitions.
The mob of course should not be regarded; but a neglect of
such numerous petitions may in many respects be a bad
precedent.[1] Mrs. M desires to be remembered

Ever truly Yours<br>T R MALTHUS.

When can you come and see us again.

## 79. TROWER TO RICARDO[2]

Unsted Wood—Godalming<br>March 10—[1815]³

Dear Ricardo

Many thanks for your Essay,[4] which I have been reading 10 March 1815
with very great interest. I highly approve of the view you
take of the subject and concur in the objections you make to
some of Malthus' arguments.—He seems to me to labor hard
to prove, what is self evident, but which if admitted, will not
bear him out in his conclusions. No doubt the higher the
price the farmer obtains for his produce the greater is the

---

[1] According to Lord Grey, 'the greatest number of petitions had been presented, that had ever, perhaps, been known in the history of parliament, the petitioners uniformly stating that the measure would have the effect of preventing a cheap supply of food to the labouring classes' (*Hansard*, XXX 127).

[2] Addressed: 'To/David Ricardo Esqr/Upper Grosvenor Street/ Grosvenor Square'.
MS in *R.P.*
³ Omitted in MS. Postmark illegible; paper watermarked 1814. The contents leave no doubt as to the year.
[4] *Essay on Profits.*

10 March 1815 encouragement to encrease that produce, but where is this argument to stop, has it no limits; and may not the same reasoning be applied with equal propriety to manufactures? The *reason of the thing* is unquestionably against him, but still I admit, that the necessities of the present case require some *moderate, temporary,* measure to prevent any sudden and great shock to the farmers, and to *let them down easily.* That they cannot go on long at the present rents and prices I believe, but then they should look to their *landlords* and not to the *public* for relief. This is the natural remedy, and which is even now in a course of operation.

What you say on the subject of rent is very important and interesting, and your table very ingenious. With respect to the question, whether the surplus arising from improved agriculture and diminished wages, belongs to *rent* or *profit,* I confess it appears to me, that it cannot be asserted to belong positively to either. If the average profits of the farmer should be on a level with the profits of capital otherwise employed at the time the surplus arises, in that case I think it would fall into the rent, but should the farmers profit be below the general average then I think it would be added to those profits, and under other circumstances it might be divided between rent and profit.—The columns of our paper are filled with the disgraceful and dangerous [procee]dings of your London Mobs,[1] against which I am very indignant— Odi profanum vulgus—and if I were to consider this question with the eye of a *moralist,* rather than that of a *statesman,* I should strenuously recommend that employment of the public industry which leads to the peaceful pursuits of agriculture, in which

> With silent course that *no loud storms* annoy
> Glides the smooth current of domestic joy.[2]

[1] See above, p. 180, n. 2.    [2] Goldsmith's *Traveller,* 433.

We shall be in town in the course of a fortnight when 10 March 1815 I shall hope to have the pleasure of seeing you. Mrs. Trower unites with me in best compliments to Mrs. R. and family and I remain

Yrs very sincerely<br>HUTCHES TROWER

## 80. MALTHUS TO RICARDO[1]

[Answered by 81]

My dear Sir,

E I Coll March 12. 1815.

Have you seen Mr. Torren's publication.[2] It is ably 12 March 1815 written, tho I think there are some important errors in it, And as it likely to be generally read, I believe I must say something about them.

Pray think once more on the effect of a rise in the relative price of corn, upon the whole surplus derived from land already in cultivation. It appears to me I confess, as clear as possible that it must be increased. The expences estimated in Corn will be less, owing to the power of purchasing with a less quantity of corn, the same quantity of fixed capital, and of the circulating capital of tea sugar cloaths &c: for the labourers; and consequently more clear surplus will remain in the shape of rent and profits together, (no matter which) for home demand. Pray tell me whether any objection to this strikes you.[3]

[1] Addressed: 'D. Ricardo Esqr / Upper Brook Street / Grosvenor Square'.—MS in *R.P.*
[2] R. Torrens, *An Essay on the External Corn Trade; containing an Inquiry into the General Principles of that Important Branch of Traffic; an Examination of the Exceptions to which these Principles are liable; and a Comparative Statement of the Effects which Restrictions on Importation and Free Intercourse, are calculated to produce upon Subsistence, Agriculture, Commerce, and Revenue*, London, Hatchard, 1815.
[3] See note at the end of this letter.

12 March 1815   Have you Lord Lauderdales pamphlet[1] which I once left with you. I want to read it once again. There are some appearances of rents not having risen so much as one should have expected from theory. I believe they have not risen much more than in the proportion to the fall in the value of currency. Poor lands might be cultivated from the improvements in agriculture. If you have got Lord Lauderdale, I wish you could sent it tomorrow or next day by the coach which goes from the George and Blue Boar Holbourn about half past two o'clock.

I believe I shall write some notes to my *Grounds*,[2] and make some remarks on Mr. Torren's publication. I had thoughts also of saying something of yours. Do you wish it or not? I will do just as you like.

Let me know as soon as you can, your opinion on the effects of a rise in the relative value of corn, upon rents and profits united.

In great haste.

Ever truly Yours

T Rob[T] Malthus

I quite agree with you that Mr. Jacob has scientific knowledge on the subject.[3]

[The problem referred to in the second paragraph of the above letter was first submitted by Malthus to Ricardo in conversation (cp. above p. 182). The initial position was therefore never fully stated in their correspondence. The following letter, hitherto unpublished, fills the gap.

MALTHUS TO HORNER[4]

E I Coll March 14th 1815

My dear Horner,

Will you have the goodness to allow me to ask you a question

[1] See above, p. 169, n. 3.
[2] Cp. below, p. 201.
[3] No doubt Malthus meant to say (as Ricardo had said, p. 180) the contrary.

[4] Addressed: 'F. Horner Esq.[r] M.P. / Lincoln's Inn. / London.' MS in the possession of Lady Langman.

in political economy, on which I should very much like to have your 14 March 1815
opinion.

On the supposition which is generally allowed, that in a rich and progressive country, corn naturally rises compared with manufactured and foreign commodities, will it not follow that, as the real capital of the farmer which is advanced does not consist merely in raw produce, but in ploughs waggons threshing machines &c: and in the tea sugar clothes &c: &c: used by his labourers, if with a less quantity of raw produce he can purchase the same quantity of these commodities, a greater quantity of raw produce will remain for the farmer and landlord, and afford a greater surplus from the land for the maintainance and encouragement of the manufacturing and mercantile classes.

The Economists calculate that one third of the raw produce obtained by the farmer is advanced to the steril classes. On this supposition let the produce of an acre be represented by 8 of which $\frac{1}{4}$ goes to the landlord, and $\frac{3}{4}$ are received by the farmer, that is, 2 go to the landlord, and 6 to the farmer, out of which latter sum the farmer expends one third or 2 in the commodities above mentioned. The farmer therefore retains 4 for his raw produce-expenditure, and profits; that is, he retains the value of the half of the gross produce.

Let us now suppose the price of corn to double, while the price of manufactured and foreign commodities rises only one fourth. The whole produce will then be represented by 16 of which $\frac{1}{4}$, as before, or 4, go to the land and only $2\frac{1}{2}$ instead of 4 go to the expenditure in manufactured and foreign commodities; the consequence of which will be, that $9\frac{1}{2}$ out of 16 will remain to the farmer instead of 4 out of 8, that is about $\frac{3}{5}$ instead of $\frac{1}{2}$. Out of this increased produce the farmer will either receive proportionably in[creased][1] profits, or will divide them with the l[andlord] and thus a rise in the price of [corn] appears to increase the productiveness of all the capital previously employed on the land.

This proposition appears to me to involve consequences so very important with regard to home demand, that I should like much to know whether you see any error in the premises or conclusion.

The fault of Mr Ricardo's table[2] which is curious, is that the advances of the farmer instead of being calculated in corn, should be calculated either in the actual materials of which the capital consists,

[1] MS torn: the missing words are supplied in pencil (? by Leonard Horner).

[2] In *Essay on Profits*, above, IV, 17.

14 March 1815   or in money which is the best representative of a variety of com-modities. The view I have taken of the subject would greatly alter his conclusions.

I was much pleased with your speech the other night on the Bank Restriction. I can quite go with you. I remain firm in my opinion as to the Policy of some Restrictions[1], but tho I would not yield to the mob, I should be disposed to yeild to the prodigious weight of Petitions, and let the people have their way. What an enterprise of Bonaparte.[2]

Ever truly Yours

T R Malthus]

## 81. RICARDO TO MALTHUS[3]

*[Reply to 80.—Answered by 82]*

Upper Brook Street

14 March 1815

My dear Sir

14 March 1815   I have read Mr. Torrens' pamphlet, and think it, on the whole a very able performance. I differ with him in most of his views in Chap 2 Part 2,—with many of the $3^d$ Chap, and with a few in the remainder of the work. I am glad to hear that you are going to make some observations on it.— I think he is an adversary worthy of your pen, and the friends of truth cannot fail to profit by the discussion.

With regard to any remarks on my opinions, you must be governed by your own discretion. If those opinions are wrong I should like to see them refuted, but thinking as I do that they are in all essential points founded on correct principles, I ask for no mercy.—I do not care how severely they are attacked,—there is nothing you could say of them which would hurt me, if what you said did not express contempt, and that I know you do not feel for me. Act therefore to-

---

[1] On the importation of corn.
[2] Cp. below, p. 194, n. 2.
[3] Addressed: 'To / The Rev⁴ T R Malthus / East India College / Hertford'.—MS at Albury.— *Letters to Malthus*, XXVI.

wards me as if I were a perfect stranger, and notice me or not as you think best.

I cannot hesitate in agreeing with you that if from a rise in the relative value of corn less is paid for fixed capital and wages,—more of the produce must remain for the landlord and farmer together,—this is indeed self evident, but is really not the matter in dispute between us, and I cannot help thinking that you overlook some of the circumstances most important connected with the question. My opinion is that corn can only permanently rise in its exchangeable value when the real expences of its production increase. If 5000 quarters of gross produce cost 2500 quarters for the expences of wages &c$^a$, and 10000 quarters cost double or 5000 quarters, the exchangeable value of corn would be the same, but if the 10000 quarters cost 5500 quarters for the expences of wages &c$^a$ then the price would rise 10 pc$^t$ because such would be the amount of the increased expences. A rise of the price of corn and a fall in the corn price of labour is in my opinion incompatible, unless it be owing to something in the currency and it is not necessary to enquire here what effects that would produce. Observe that I do not question that each individual labourer may receive a less corn price of labour because I believe that would be the case, but I question whether the whole corn amount of wages &c$^a$ paid for the cultivation of the land can be diminished with an increase of the exchangeable value of corn. If no more labourers were employed and the price of corn rose your proposition could not be disputed, but the cause of the rise of the price of corn is solely on account of the increased expence of production.

I have lost Lord Lauderdale's pamphlet or rather it has been taken from my office. If I can get another, it sh[all]$^1$

---

$^1$ MS torn here and below.

14 March 1815 accompany this. The improvement in agri[culture] I believe have had more effect in ke[eping] down r[ents] than we have ever imagined. On my theory they fully account for rents being no higher; on yours they would tell the other way.

I meant to reproach you when I saw you [for] speaking of Mr. Jacob's pamphlet with so much [praise] as you did when Mr. Basevi[1] asked your opinion of it,—I am glad that you allow he is very deficient in scientific knowledge.—

You will see by what I have said that a rise in the price of corn is always in my opinion accompanied by a less material surplus produce, but it may be of equal value as compared with other things. Of this produce the landlord gets so large a share that in spite of the rise of produce the situation of the farmer is constantly getting worse.

Y<sup>r</sup> very truly

DAVID RICARDO

## 82. MALTHUS TO RICARDO[2]
### [Reply to 81.—Answered by 83]

My dear Sir,                          E I Coll March 15. 1815

15 March 1815    You may rely upon it that if I make any remarks upon your publication, they will written in that spirit of respect and friendship which I shall always feel for you; but to say the truth I have been so much interrupted lately, that I do not know when I shall have time to do what I intend.

In what you have said in answer to my statement, I think you have omitted a most important consideration. You seem to forget what I think you had formerly allowed, that it is only the last 500000 quarters of corn that have been added to

---

¹ George Basevi, sen.; see below, VII, 10, n. 1.
² Addressed: 'D. Ricardo Esqr. /

Upper Brook Street. / Grosvenor Square.'
MS in *R.P.*

the mass, which require for their production a greater quan- 15 March 1815
tity of capital. You distinctly allow that if no more labour and
capital be employed, the productive power of that labour and
capital, or the surplus of rents and profits, will increase, owing
to an increase in the relative price of corn. Consequently
when a rise in the price of corn takes place from an increasing
population, or restrictions upon importation, all the capital
previously employed upon the land will become more productive, and it is only the new capital that will be less so;
that is you will have the capital which produces the previous
ten millions of quarters of wheat, yield a greater material
surplus, while it is only the last additions to the mass which
require more labour. And even these last additions will require no more labour in proportion to the value of the produce than the last 500000 quarters of the ten millions did
before the rise of price. Under these circumstances it is quite
clear to me that a rise in the relative value of corn, will
occasion the whole mass of corn to be raised at a less corn-
expenditure; and consequently will leave a larger surplus for
the maintenance and encouragement of the mercantile and
manufacturing classes. This, if true, is a most important
principle and deserves to be thoroughly considered.

Observe, that, if poor land be brought under cultivation
merely by the fall of profits as in your table,[1] this effect of
course will not follow, and in this case indeed corn will not
necessarily rise, although there will be a rise of rents. But if
poor land be brought under cultivation by a rise of prices as
has been the case during the last 20 years, it appears to me
that the whole capital on the land must have become more
and more productive. This seems to be confirmed by the
circumstance of a much smaller proportion of the population
being employed on the land than formerly. Pray tell me where

[1] Above, IV, 17.

15 March 1815  you think I am wrong. The conclusion half startles me. If
I am right it will establish the effect of the high price of
corn on home demand. I am much obliged to you for Lord
Lauderdale. Mrs. Malthus desires to be remembered to
Mrs. Ricardo.

Ever truly Yours<br>T R MALTHUS

## 83. RICARDO TO MALTHUS[1]
[*Reply to* 82.—*Answered by* 84]

My dear Sir
London 17 M<sup>ch</sup> 1815

17 March 1815      If your statement was correct this extravagant consequence would follow from it, that in proportion as population increased and worse land was brought under cultivation,
the proportion of produce to the corn expences of procuring
it would increase. If we now had 20 millions of quarters
with an expence of 5 millions of quarters, we should when
we expended 10 millions of quarters obtain more than 40,
notwithstanding that in the latter period many more than
double the quantity of hands were employed in cultivation,
in consequence of the poorer quality[2] of the land. If this be
true the principle of population is false, because the more you
increase the people the greater surplus of abundance will
appear. Your statement is however very ingenious, and
carries a great deal of plausibility with it; but I think you err
in supposing it possible that the proportion of the whole corn
expenditure, to the produce obtained, can fall, with an increase of the price of corn. The two are incompatible,—
either the whole corn expences of production will be in-

[1] Addressed: 'To / The Rev<sup>d</sup>        MS at Albury.—*Letters to Mal-*
T. R Malthus / East India College /     *thus,* XXVII.
Hertford'.                              [2] Replaces 'quantity'.

creased or not. If they be the price of corn will rise,—but if they be not I can see no reason for a rise in the price of corn. I admit that it is only the last portion of capital employed on the land which will be attended with an increased corn expence, but unless it renders the whole produce together at an increased expence the price of produce will not rise.

Suppose the produce of the country 10 millions of quarters, with the price at £4 p$^r$ quarter, the number of labourers employed 2½ millions, each receiving 2 quarters of corn annually as wages. Suppose too that the population increases, and 5 millions of quarters more are required, but that it can not be obtained with less labour than that of 2 millions of men. If we suppose the price to increase in proportion to the number of men employed, it will rise to £4. 16, because to raise 10 millions of quarters an average of 3 millions of men would be now required instead of 2½ millions. Suppose now each man to consume one quarter annually for food, and to exchange the remainder for other necessaries, 14 bushels will be sufficient wages for him; the expenditure of corn for wages will then be for 15 millions of produce 7,875,000 quarters and for 10 millions 5,250,000. Before it was only 5 millions, consequently the proportion of surplus produce has diminished.

In making this calculation I have very much favored your view of the question, because the price of corn would not I think rise in proportion to the greater number of men employed but to the greater amount of wages paid,—it would not therefore rise to £4. 16. but to £4. 4 because as 5 : 5¼ :: £4 : £4. 4. – but, if the price was only £4. 4 – more corn would be required by the labourer than 14 bushels that calculation being founded on a greater exchangeable value of corn.—

It appears too that your statement if true does not account

17 March 1815 for the less proportion of the population now emp[loyed on]¹ the land, because you always suppose more men to [be emplo]yed but at less corn wages.—It can never happen I [think] that profits can fall, and encourage the cultivation of poor [land in] the manner assumed in my table, without a rise in the price of corn. It is by the rise of the price of corn that all other profits are regulated to agricultural profits. If the price of corn remained low money wages would not rise and general profits could not fall.

If it be true that capital has become more and more productive on the land, it can I think only be accounted for on the supposition that great improvements have taken place in agriculture, and that wages have been kept moderate by the improvements in those manufactures which supply the poor with the necessaries on which a part of their wages are expended.—

What a dreadful change in our political horizon has occurred within a few days.²—Will it be possible to remain at peace if Bonaparte establishes himself as sovereign of France? The prospect is very gloomy. Mrs. Ricardo unites with me in kind regards to Mrs. Malthus

Ever Yʳˢ

DAVID RICARDO

## 84. MALTHUS TO RICARDO³
*[Reply to 83.—Answered by 85]*

My dear Sir,                          E I Coll. March 19. [1815]⁴

19 March 1815     Your letter almost entirely confirms me in my position. If in order to controvert it⁵ it is necessary to suppose that the

¹ MS torn here and below.          Upper Brook Street / Grosvenor
² Napoleon, returned from Elba,    Square'.
was now marching across France;        MS in *R.P.*
on 10 March he entered Lyons.      ⁴ Omitted in MS. Postmark, 1815.
³ Addressed: 'D. Ricardo Esqr /    ⁵ 'it' is del. in MS.

same ten millions of quarters which formerly required 2½ 19 March 1815
millions of men, should on account of a greater demand for
such corn, require for their production 3 millions, it may be
considered as established; because no good reason can possibly
be given for an increased number of men being required to
produce precisely the same quantity of corn from precisely
the same land.

Nor is it correct to reason from such assumptions as you
have made, which dont at all approach towards the facts.

What would be the real process. Not such a jump as from
ten millions to fifteen; but from ten millions to ten millions
and a half; and I maintain that if half a million more quarters
of corn were wanting either from the natural increase of
population, or from restrictions upon importation, that the
effect would be first a rise of price, which rise of price would
increase the productiveness of all the capital previously employed, and awarding only 14 bushels instead of two quarters
to the precisely the same number of men would leave a
greater portion of the ten millions of quarters for the maintenance and encouragement of the manufacturing classes. In
the mean time this increased cheapness in the instruments of
production would occasion more poor land to be brought
under cultivation, and more men to be employed upon the
land; but still so as to leave a larger surplus for the manufacturing and mercantile classes, as it is impossible to suppose
that the increased corn expences upon the new land should
equal the diminished corn expences upon the old land.

The natural price of corn depends entirely upon the price
of the last additions, and it does not matter whether with
regard to the old land, a capital yields 50 per cent (rent and
profit together) or 20 per cent. In either case the price of corn
on such land has nothing to do with the cost of production.

I am not alarmed at what you say about the principle of

19 March 1815 population; as I can easily conceive that the addition of another labourer on the land would not pay his expences, although not more than $\frac{1}{4}$ of the population were employed upon the land. No pressure can destroy rents. This you know is what I have always maintained.

My present proposition however is certainly very important, and I wish it to have a full discussion. I write in the greatest haste.

Let me hear from you again.

Ever truly Yours<br>T R M.

We expect Whishaw and Smyth saturday. I shall not be in Town at the Club.

I cant look over my letter

## 85. RICARDO TO MALTHUS[1]

[*Reply to* 84.—*Answered by* 86]

My dear Sir London 21 March 1815

21 March 1815   On no subject that we have been lately discussing have we so materially differed as on the one now occupying our attention. Your position, if established, would, I think, overturn both your theory of rent and population, for I understand you to maintain that the higher the price of corn rises, in consequence of more men being employed on the poorer land, the greater will be, not only the surplus produce after paying the labourers, but the ratio of that surplus produce to the whole capital employed on the land. If this be true there is no check to the increase of population, and food can be increased in a ratio exceeding that at which mankind in-

[1] Addressed: 'To / The Rev⁴    MS at Albury.—*Letters to Mal-* T R Malthus / East India College / *thus*, XXVIII. Hertford'.

crease. Your statement requires that with every additional labourer not only an equal increase[1] but a greater increase of surplus produce should be obtained. More labourers may then be employed without limit, and rent and profit together must not only increase, but increase in a geometrical progression. I am sure I am correct in thus stating your proposition, because if as you say the whole corn expense of production p$^r$ quarter will be diminished with every rise of price, the surplus must increase in a geometrical ratio with the capital employed. If you meant only that the surplus produce would increase with every accumulation of capital on the land, though in a diminishing ratio to the capital employed on the land, that is not only advanced, but strenuously maintained as the groundwork of my theory, and is the basis also on which my table is formed. You have misapprehended a passage in my last letter. I certainly never said, nor ever thought, that any good reason could be given for an increased number of men being required to produce precisely the same quantity of corn from precisely the same land. What I said was that if at one period the number of labourers required to produce 10 millions of quarters of corn was $2\frac{1}{2}$ millions of men, and at another, in consequence of increased demand, 15 millions of quarters could not be produced with a portion of worse land at a less cost of labour[2] than that of $4\frac{1}{2}$ millions, at this latter period a production of 10 millions would require 3 millions of men, because 15 is to $4\frac{1}{2}$, as 10 to 3. And if we supposed the price of corn under such circumstances to increase in the proportion of $2\frac{1}{2}$ to 3, a supposition much more favorable to your view of the question than we should be obliged to concede, yet that it would not support the conclusions to which you arrive but on the con-

[1] 'increase' here and 'increase of' four words below are ins.

[2] The last twelve words replace 'with less labour'.

trary would prove my theory to be the correct one. If the calculation had been made, as you think would have been more correct, on an increase from 10 millions to 10½ millions, the result would have been the same, but we should be puzzled with the decimals or fractions which must be employed on such a supposition.—

I agree with you "that the natural price of corn depends entirely upon the price of the last additions and it does not matter whether with regard to the old land a capital yields 50 pc$^t$ (rent and profit together) or 20 pc$^t$ In either case the price of corn on such land has nothing to do with the cost of production." I do not see how the admission of this fact can assist your argument, which relates only to the ratio of the surplus produce to the whole capital employed.

I cannot conceive by what argument you could shew that it might be possible that the addition of another labourer on the land would not pay his expences although not more than ¼ of the population were employed upon the land. Allowing as I most fully do that no pressure can destroy rents, yet as the last portions of capital employed on the land pay no rent, it is to me inconceivable that there would be no inducement to employ more labourers whilst their average production should be 3 times more food than they could themselves consume. If the whole of this surplus, after maintaining in the most frugal manner the owners of stock, were absorbed by the landlords as rent, they would increase their revenue, and employ more labourers on the land, if any among them saved any part of his income and lent it at the common rate of interest.

I am sorry you do not come to town for the next club.

Y$^{rs}$ truly

DAVID RICARDO

## 86. MALTHUS TO RICARDO[1]

[*Reply to 85.—Answered by 87*]

E I Coll March 24th [1815]

My dear Sir

What a dreadful reverse![2] and what a prospect we have 24 March 1815
before us! It is scarcely possible not to be always thinking of
it; but it is of no use; so that we may as well distract our
attention as much as we can by other subjects.

I think you push my principle much too far; and do not
recollect the limitations to which it must necessarily be
subject. In the first place all depends upon the relation between corn and other commodities, and as labour and corn
enter into the price of all commodities, the difference between
corn and other commodities cannot possibly increase in any
proportion to the increase in the money price of corn. I have
supposed that $\frac{2}{3}$ of the farmers advances still consist necessarily of raw produce; and even if the fixed, and other parts
of the capital besides food could be had for nothing, and the
whole remaining $\frac{1}{3}$ went in profits and rent, the principle
of population would not be destroyed by it. There is no more
food produced, on the old land. It is only that there is a
difference in the distribution of it, and a larger share of the
raw produce remains for profit and rent, chiefly of course the
latter. Before,—the farmer to pay his money wages and
purchase his fixed capital, was obliged to sell more corn:—
Now, he can do this with less, and will have a larger remainder, but the same quantity of corn, neither more nor
less, is distributed to the public, and as we dont suppose the
people to live worse, precisely the same number are supported
from the old land.

[1] Addressed: 'D. Ricardo Esqr /
Upper Brook Street / Grosvenor
Square.' Postmark, 1815.

MS in *R.P.*
[2] Napoleon had entered Paris on
20 March.

On the new land brought into cultivation in consequence
of the demand, more men are employed in proportion to the
quantity of corn produced, and as the same number of men
as before are employed to obtain the old produce, there will
be a greater number of men employed in proportion to the
whole produce. But if the new produce be inconsiderable
compared with the old, it appears to me quite certain that the
increased corn expenditure of the former will be more than
counterbalanced, by the diminished corn expenditure of the
latter; and owing to the increased value of corn, the whole
money cost of production on the land will bear a less proportion to the money value of the whole produce. On the
other hand, if the new produce is so large, as to require
2 milllons of labourers to obtain it, the increased corn expenditure owing to the additional number of persons employed, will more than counterbalance the diminished corn
expenditure arising from the increased relative value of corn.
It is of course quite impossible to suppose that the relative
value of corn to other commodities can continue regularly increasing in proportion to any additional number of men which
we may chuse to suppose employed upon the land. There
will be in fact a constant reaction to prevent such increasing
difference. The increased profits of agriculture, and diminished
profits of other employments will increase the quantity of raw
produce compared with other commodities, and this joined
to the increased money price of corn, will be continually
raising the money price of commodities, and bringing them
again nearer to a level. I think further that the increased price
of corn is in the order of things rather a cause than a consequence of more men being employed. The price rises first
from increased demand, and this rise, by increasing the value
of produce compared with the instruments of production
determines what poor lands can be cultivated. No greater

number of men can be employed at the same wages till the 24 March 1815
price rises.

I have been wrong however in supposing as I did at one
time that a greater quantity of raw produce would be set free
from the old land for the use and encouragement of the
manufacturing and mercantile classes. While the same number of men are employed on the old land without a greater
production, and living as well, this cannot be the ease. In
fact, while that capital the produce of which relatively rises
in value becomes more productive, those capitals the produce
of which relatively falls in value will become less productive,
or yield less profits. But then the greatly increased money
value of the corn in the country arising both from its increased quantity and increased price cannot fail to occasion
such an increased demand for manufactured and foreign
products as to encourage the growth of them and to render
improvements in machinery particularly advantageous.
Under such circumstances general profits may rise with
rising prices of corn, and fall with falling prices, as we find
from experience, though such periods are not likely to be of
long continuence. The subject is very curious, and the principle when properly matured will I think throw some light
on it. I have had little or no leisure lately, and am expecting
company in the house. I have written part of answer to
Torrens for a new Edition of the Grounds,[1] but I think it
would be too long, and as I hear of more attacks,[2] I fear if I
begin to answer I shall be led too much into publick contro-

[1] Cp. above pp. 182 and 186. Malthus did not publish a second
edition of The Grounds of an
Opinion.
[2] The latest attack was a pamphlet, advertised in The Times of
23 March, on The Policy of a
Restriction on the Importation of
Corn, argued on the Principles of
Political Economy, and proved to
be inconsistent with the Prosperity
of the English Nation...in Reply
to the Pamphlets of Professor
Malthus. By Philalethes, London, J. M. Richardson, 1815.

24 March 1815 versies, which I had rather avoid. Do you know whether Torrens is much read. I think he has treated me unjustly in the preface and that the instances of inconsistency which he produces, even if established, would by no means warrant his sweeping accusation.[1]

If you would lay a tax on foreign corn on account of a tax on our own; does not the same principle apply to the indirect taxes that raise the price of labour? As rents cannot be absorbed, profits and rents together must be high when population stops.

Ever Yours

T R MALTHUS

Can you come and see us Saturday sennight?

## 87. RICARDO TO MALTHUS[2]

[*Reply to* 86.—*Answered by* 88]

My dear Sir

London 27th March 1815

27 March 1815 No political event which I recollect ever occasioned so great a gloom as the late lamentable reverse.—At present we have the most dismal forebodings of war, and its consequences, on our finances,—the truth is our courage is not screwed up to the proper pitch,—like every thing else we shall be easy under our new situation in another fortnight. I am glad however to turn my attention to other subjects.

[1] 'In the writings of the professor he [Torrens] found hints for reflection, and suggestions for farther thought; but he looked in vain either for a development of principles before undiscovered, or for consistent deductions from those already established. It is a singular fact, and one which it is not improper to impress upon the public, that, in the leading questions of economical science, Mr. Malthus scarcely ever embraced a principle, which he did not subsequently abandon' (*Essay on the External Corn Trade*, pp. viii–ix).

[2] Addressed: 'To / The Revᵈ T R Malthus / East India College / Hertford'.

MS at Albury.—*Letters to Malthus*, XXIX.

I have observed in the bullion pamphlet[1] that many who   27 March 1815
say they consider money only as a commodity, and subject
to the same laws of variation in value from demand and
supply as other commodities, seldom proceed far in their
reasoning about money without shewing that they really
consider money as something peculiar,—varying from causes
totally different from those which affect other commodities.
Do you not fall into this error when you say "In the first
place all depends upon the relation between corn and other
commodities, and as labour and corn enter into the prices of
all commodities the difference between corn and other commodities cannot possibly increase in any proportion to the
increase in the money price of corn"? If money be a commodity does not corn and labour enter into its price or value?
and if they do, why should not money vary as compared
with corn and labour by the same law as all other commodities
do? As far as this question regards the importation of corn
you are much more interested than I am in maintaining the
uniform value of commodities, because if the rise of the price
of corn and labour will as you contend raise the price of our
commodities, this is an additional reason why we should not
impose restrictions on the importation of corn, as it will
subject us to a decided disadvantage in our competition with
foreigners for the sale of our commodities. Not however to
dwell on this very essential point,—I agree with you that a
rise in the price of corn occasions a different distribution of
the produce from the old land. It does this by lowering
profits. Instead of a manufacturer having it in his power to
maintain a servant or mechanic who may contribute to his
enjoyment, that power will be transferred to the landlord
and this will arise from the lower corn value of manufactured
goods. Indeed I see no limit to the fall of the corn value of

[1] Above, III, 103–4.

27 March 1815 goods but the impossibility of manufacturing them with any
the least return of profit, and this will not happen till the
landlord has appropriated to himself in the form of rent
nearly the whole surplus produce of the land. It appears to
me that the progress of wealth, whilst it encourages accumulation, has a natural tendency to produce this effect and is as
certain as the principle of gravitation.

You have I think totally changed your proposition. You
before contended that in consequence of increasing wealth
and the cultivation of poorer land, the whole *corn* cost of production on the land would bear a *less* proportion to the whole
*corn* produce,—but now you say that the *money* cost of production on the land will bear a less proportion to the *money*
value of the whole produce. Between these propositions
there is a very material difference, as the latter might be true,
at the very time that the former was false. To admit what you
now contend for would not affect my theory, as though it
would prove that the landlord and tenant (together) got
more money revenue, or if you will a greater proportion of
money revenue as compared to the money capital employed,
yet the tenant might and I think would get a less proportion,
and therefore the rate of profits would fall. Such a state
of price is quite compatible with a greater proportion of
men, as compared with the produce obtained, being employed on the land;—but it is wholly irreconcileable with
the net corn produce bearing a larger proportion to the
gross corn produce,—which was the principle before contended for.

I agree with you that the increased price of corn in the
order of things is rather a cause than a consequence of a
greater than the usual number of men being employed to
obtain the same quantity of produce from new land, because
profits from such an employment of capital may be higher

than other profits,—but this difference of profit may be owing to a general fall in the rate of profits on other concerns rather than to[1] the actual elevation of the profits on land, and I am of opinion that a rise in the price of corn always lowers general profits by increasing wages. I can in no way satisfy myself that general profits can rise with a rising price of corn and fall with falling prices, unless they are raised or lowered by diminishing or increasing wages, and then they can be but of short duration. In the ordinary course of things as a high price of corn attends a state of progression, wages of labour will be really high, and profits cannot rise because of wages being low.

I am decidedly of opinion that Torrens has treated you unjustly in his remarks in the preface of his book. If I recollect right you acknowledged an alteration in your opinion respecting the corn laws, since you wrote your essay on population, in your "Observations on the Corn Laws."[2] I think too that you have always held the opinion you now do that the difference between the value of gold and paper was partly owing to the rise of the value of gold.[3] Is not his criticism very much strained as to the use of the word depreciation?[4] But if he be right in all, the instances are much too few to justify his severe observation. At the Geological Club his book was spoken of the other day with great

[1] 'rather than to' replaces 'as by'.
[2] 1st ed., 1814, p. 3.
[3] According to Torrens (*Essay on the External Corn Trade*, p. x) at the time of the Bullion Controversy Malthus 'was known to be a strenuous supporter' of the contrary opinion.
[4] Torrens (p. xi, note) takes Malthus to task for having spoken (in *Grounds of an Opinion*, p. 9) of depreciation of the currency in a case in which the difference between currency and bullion was produced, not 'by a fall in currency', but 'by bullion having risen'. 'The very inaccurate and unphilosophical language which Mr. Malthus employs when alluding to our monetary system, shews that he has not yet attained any accurate conceptions on the question of the currency.'

27 March 1815 approbation. Mr. Blake[1] and Mr. Greenough[2] think that he has exhausted the subject and that his arguments cannot be controverted.—I should think that he is very generally read.[3]

"If I would lay a tax on foreign corn" you ask "on account of a tax on our own; does not the same principle apply to the indirect taxes that raise the price of labour?" I think not because a tax on corn will raise the price of corn twice, once on account of the tax and a second time on account of the rise of wages, but as this second rise is common to all things in which labour enters and will be corrected by a new value of money, it will not be of long duration. The indirect taxes which only raise the wages of labour produce I think the same effects as the second rise in the price of corn of which I have just been speaking. Whenever a tax bore with unequal effect on the land, when it did not affect labour bestowed in other employments a countervailing duty on importation should I think be also imposed.—I fear I cannot be with you on saturday. If you do not hear from me by wednesday's Post, conclude that I cannot leave home. Comp[ts] to Mrs. Malthus.

Ever Y[rs]

DAVID RICARDO

[1] William Blake (*ca.* 1774–1852), F.R.S., the writer on foreign exchanges, was President of the Geological Society in 1815–16. The Society dined together once a month from November to June at the Freemasons' Tavern. (H. B. Woodward, *History of the Geological Society of London,* 1907, pp. 16 and 286.)

[2] George Bellas Greenough (1778–1855), F.R.S., geographer and geologist; the first President of the Geological Society, and at this time one of its Vice-Presidents.

[3] Later, however, Ricardo tells Malthus that the sale of Torrens's book 'was very limited' (below, VII, 141).

## 88. MALTHUS TO RICARDO[1]
*[Reply to 87.—Answered by 89]*

My dear Sir,

E I Coll April 2nd 1815

You understood my proposition as going farther than I  2 April 1815
intended, at first; and now perhaps not quite far enough.
Although I suppose no more corn to be produced by the
same number of labourers on the old land, and no less corn
actually to be consumed by them, yet I still think the corn
expences are diminished compared with the corn profits.
Each family on the land instead of receiving 8 quarters a
year receives now only 7. In both cases it actually consumes
4, and spends the remainder in manufactures and foreign
commodities. In the latter case, owing to the increased
relative value of corn, the remainder 3 is as effectual as 4 was
before. And not only a greater money value, but a greater
quantity of raw produce will remain to the farmer and landlord.

I own I think it affects your theory essentially; because it
shews that there is ample room for an increase of profits upon
the land; and if this increase of profit be prevented from taking
place, it can only be owing to the diminished profits in manufactures, and consequently it would appear that manufacturing profits determined the profits upon the land, and not
the profits upon the land, manufacturing profits. I cannot
however help thinking that the increasing demand for
manufactured commodities must prevent the profits upon
them from falling for any length of time. If five coats be now
necessary to purchase the same quantity of corn as could be
purchased formerly by four, will it not to a certainty follow,
that the whole quantity of corn in the country will exchange

[1] Addressed: 'D. Ricardo Esqr / Upper Brook Street / Grosvenor
Square'.—MS in *R.P.*

2 April 1815  for a greater number of coats than before; and consequently that there will be both the power and will to purchase with the raw produce of the country, a greater quantity of manufactured and foreign commodities. This is a most important and vital question as it appears to me, and I wish you to give me your opinion upon it. If the value of the whole raw produce falls compared with manufactured and foreign produce does not such fall necessarily involve a diminution of demand for manufactured and foreign produce?

Surely you don't seem to be sufficiently aware of the necessary limits to the separation in price of manufactured commodities and [raw][1] produce.

If 400 yards of cloth require ten persons to produce them, and a hundred quarters of corn (last added) require ten persons, each at a profit of ten per cent (the last of course without rent) is it physically possible that the labour employed in producing the 100 quarters of corn should be increased so much as one third, while the people continue to eat the same quantity of corn as before.

Of course I presume that no person will employ an additional labourer upon his land, whose wages are more than the value of what he adds to the former produce. Upon this supposition which is unquestionably the true one, when the profits on land are only ten per cent and no rent, the limits to the number of persons which can be employed with advantage on the land are a good deal confined. And such suppositions as you made in a former letter are not admissible. We cannot say for instance "Suppose now the 100 quarters of corn in the progress of society to require for their production 25 men instead of ten.["] The thing is physically impossible consistently with giving the labourers the same quantity of food, which we have all along taken for granted.

[1] Word covered by seal.

On account of paper money, the distance of the mines, and 2 April 1815 the small effect on the market of a few years produce the precious metals are not in fact affected like other commodities. Of this there are abundant proofs.

I am sorry you could not come. Can you next saturday.

Ever truly Yours
T R MALTHUS

89. RICARDO TO MALTHUS[1]
[Reply to 88.—Answered by 90]

My dear Sir                                London 4 April 1815

You think that my theory of a diminishing rate of 4 April 1815 profit, in consequence of being obliged to cultivate poorer lands, is affected by my admission that there will be a greater quantity of surplus produce and a greater money value from the old land. This would be true, if any part of either the additional quantity or additional value, belonged to the owner of stock. You however expressly say that this additional value or quantity "will remain to the farmer and landlord.["] Before my theory is affected it must be shewn that the whole will not remain with the landlord, as if the farmer gets no share of it his rate of profits cannot be raised.—

I agree with you that when the exchangeable value of corn rises "the whole quantity of corn in the country will exchange for a greater number of coats than before, and consequently that there will be both the power and will to purchase with the raw produce of the country, a greater quantity of manufactured and foreign commodities." In a progressive country I can easily conceive this power and will

[1] Addressed: 'To / The Rev^d / T R Malthus / East India College / Hertford'.  MS. at Albury.—Letters to Malthus, XXX.

4 April 1815 to be doubled or trebled, as well as the commodities on which they are exercised; but this admission does not affect the question of profits. There may be a great demand for home and foreign commodities without their price being permanently raised, as no new difficulties may attend their production. When America becomes populous and wealthy, in the same proportion as the most wealthy country of Europe, will not her corn exchange at a higher value, both for money and commodities, although it will have much increased in quantity? Will not all foreign and home commodities in America be double or treble their present amount, —yet will not the profits of stock be less there than they now are? On this question I could not have thought that the slightest doubt could exist,—all theory, all experience is in favour of this opinion.

Whilst the labour of ten persons employed on land paying no rent can produce 100 quarters of wheat it appears to me possible and probable that one third more labour might be profitably employed on that land, not indeed in producing only 100 quarters of wheat, but an additional quantity more than the additional labourers would consume. Whilst the labour of ten men can produce 100 quarters of wheat it is difficult to suppose profits only 10 pc$^t$,—and more difficult to conceive that many more men might not be profitably employed in increasing the produce off such land. In theory, land which yields no rent, according to your supposition, would have more and more capital profitably expended on it whilst the additional quantity of produce obtained, exceeded the quantity paid to the additional labourers. Capital might be so expended whilst the profits of stock gave any return not 10 pc$^t$ but 1 pc$^t$ or $\frac{1}{2}$ pc$^t$—

No doubt money varies more slowly than other commodities for the reason you mention; nevertheless its value

like every other foreign commodity depends on the labour   4 April 1815
and expence of bringing it to market.—

I expect some friends to dine with me on saturday and on
monday I am engaged out to dinner,—yet if the weather is
tolerably fine I will be with you by the time you leave chapel
on sunday, but I must get home next day. If this is not quite
convenient pray let me know.

Ever Y<sup>rs</sup>

DAVID RICARDO

90. MALTHUS TO RICARDO[1]

[Reply to 89]

My dear Sir,                 E I Coll April 5<sup>th</sup> 1815

I write a line to say that your visit on sunday will be   5 April 1815
perfectly convenient, and very agreeable to us, and we are
only sorry that you cannot make it longer.

Would it be inconvenient to you to call some time before
you come down at Murray's, and say that I have been expecting a letter from him in answer to one I wrote about a
week ago. I wished to know whether from the new turn that
affairs had taken in Europe, the question of the corn laws
was so completely at an end, as that the public would not be
inclined to listen to any further discussion on the subject, in
which case I would say what I had to say in a new edition
of the Rents, without directly answering Mr. Torrens; or
whether it would be adviseable to make a reply to his work
in a long note at the end of the Grounds.[2] I have felt so much
doubt lately as to which of the two plans would be the best,

---

[1] Addressed: 'D. Ricardo Esqr /
Upper Brook Street / Grosvenor
Square'.
MS in *R.P.*

[2] Cp. above, p. 201. Neither of
Malthus's pamphlets had a second
edition.

5 April 1815 that with the assistance of idleness and engagements I have not proceeded in the execution of either. I think Mr. Torrens's publication is an able one in many respects. At the same time I think him wrong in many important points, and cannot consider him as having taken a just view of the whole subject. He is particularly wrong respecting rent, which he uniformly views as so much increase of the expence of production, instead of a measure of the excess of produce above that expence.

But we will talk of these things when I have the pleasure of seeing you. I shall rely upon your coming on sunday.

I hope there is yet a small chance of peace, though I fear our ministers are not that way inclined. We ought not to give Buonaparte the moral strength which he will derive from our beginning the attack.

Ever truly Yours<br>T R MALTHUS

## 91. RICARDO TO MALTHUS[1]
### [Answered by 92]

London 17 April 1815

My dear Sir

17 April 1815    You, I think, agree with Mr. Torrens[2] that a rise in the price of corn will be followed by a rise in the price of home commodities;—but your theory requires that there should be no rise in the price of those commodities on which the wages of labour are expended, for if they rose in the same proportion as corn, there could be no fall in the corn wages of labour. Is it not however very improbable that all manu-

---

[1] Addressed: 'To / The Rev.ᵈ T R Malthus / East India College / Hertford'.

MS at Albury.—*Letters to Malthus*, XXXI.
[2] *Essay on the External Corn Trade*, p. 81 ff.

factures should rise at home and yet that those on which labour[1] are expended should not rise? Is not the price of soap, candles &c.ª, though foreign commodities, necessarily affected by the rise in the price of those home goods which are given in exchange for them.

Mr. Torrens theory however on this part of the subject appears to me defective, as I think that the price of commodities will be very slightly affected either by a rise or fall in the price of corn. If so every rise in the price of corn must affect profits on manufactures, and it is impossible that agricultural profits can materially deviate from them.

I will however suppose that you and Mr. Torrens are correct, and that commodities do rise in price with every increased price of corn. The value of fixed capital as well as of circulating capital employed on the land will then rise also, and altho' the money value of the produce should be increased on the old land it will still bear the same proportion to the money value of the capital employed, and as this produce will be divided in different proportions between the landlord and the farmer the rate of profits of the latter will fall. For the purpose of examining the effects let us suppose that all commodities rise, with the rise of the price of corn, excepting those only on which the wages of labour are expended, and that in consequence the corn wages of labour fall. Suppose the price of corn £4 and that on the old land the labour of 8 men was necessary to raise 80 q$^{rs}$ of corn, that no rent was paid, and that each labourer had 8 quarters annually for his wages of which one half was expended on commodities. The gain of the farmer when the price was £4 would be £64 or 16 q$^{rs}$ and besides his fixed capital, horses, seed, &c.ª he would require the value of 64 q$^{rs}$ or £256 to pay the annual wages of his labourers, consequently his

[1] Should be 'the wages of labour'.

17 April 1815 profits would be in the proportion of £25 to £100 of wages, for 256 : 64 :: 100 : 25

Now suppose corn to rise to £4. 10, wages would vary only 10/- on 4 quarters, and consequently would rise to £34 annually p$^r$ man or £272 on the old land,—but the 80 q$^{rs}$ of corn would sell for £360 – leaving a produce[1] of £88 to be divided between farmer and landlord,—and 88 would be to 272 as 32 to 100.

But on the new land the labour of 8 men and a half might be required to obtain 80 q$^{rs}$ or £360,—the labour of 8½ men would cost at £34 each £289 consequently the profit would be £71—which is to the whole expence of £360 as £19·7 to £100

£100 Capital, or expences, on the old land will yield £32

$$100 — D^o — D^o — \text{new land} — — 19\cdot7$$

$$\text{rent } 2\cdot3^2$$

It appears then that the profit on new land which regulates the profit on all other land would be 19·7 pc$^t$ when the price of corn was £4. 10 –. It was 25 pc$^t$ when the price was £4. –

If indeed under the same circumstances we had supposed the price of corn to rise to £6 then profits would be increased and would be much more than 25 pc$^t$ but some adequate cause must be shewn for such rise and it cannot be arbitrarily assumed. Your theory supposes too what is impossible that the demand for manufactures will increase in the same proportion as the demand for corn at the very time that more men are employed on the land to obtain a less proportion of produce. The whole appears to me a labyrinth of difficulties; one is no sooner got over than another presents itself, and so in endless succession. Let me intreat you to give my simple doctrine fair consideration, and you must allow that it accounts for all the phenomena in an easy, natural manner.

----

[1] Replaces 'profit'.                    [2] Should be '12·3'.

I yesterday met Mr. Smyth, your friend, and Mr. Torrens, 17 April 1815 at Mr. Phillips. I passed a very pleasant day. Mr. Smyth was exceedingly agreeable, I like him very much. The corn question was occasionally introduced and I had an opportunity of stating some of my objections to Mr. Torrens theory.—I have no reason to think that I convinced him. I defended the use of the word depreciation in the sense which you had used it;[1] and I believe I had every one with me. I fancy that his arguments in his book on currency[2] are founded on the sense in which he uses the word. We spoke on the other points of difference between him and you.

Mr. Smyth, Mr. Phillips and Mr. Torrens have agreed to dine with me on wednesday, which has induced me to write to you a day or two sooner than I otherwise should have done, that I might express my wish that you would join us.

If you will, we will dine as late as you please. There will be a bed at your service, and I need not say that you will add considerably to my pleasure.

Y<sup>rs</sup> very truly<br>DAVID RICARDO

## 92. MALTHUS TO RICARDO[3]

[Reply to 91.—Answered by 93]

My dear Sir                    [East India College, 18 April 1815]

I should have great pleasure in joining your party on 18 April 1815 wednesday, but of all the days in the week, that is the one, when it is least possible for me to leave College, as it is the

---

[1] See above, p. 205, n. 4.
[2] *An Essay on Money and Paper Currency,* London, Johnson, 1812.
[3] Addressed: 'D. Ricardo Esqr. / Upper Brook Street / Grosvenor Square.' Postmarks: Hertford, undated; London, 19 April 1815. Tuesday the 18th is probably the date of the letter. MS in *R.P.*

18 April 1815 first of my two lectures days. I rather believe that I shall be in Town with Mrs. Malthus for two or three days towards the latter end of the next week, when I hope we shall have an opportunity of meeting.

Do you not perceive that the conclusion you have drawn from your calculation depends entirely upon the arbitrary assumption that the next portion of land taken into cultivation will require 8½ men to produce 80 quarters of corn. But as you have distinctly allowed that, on account of the rise of price occasioned by demand, from 4£ to £4. 10$^s$, the profits on the old land will rise from 25 to 32 per cent, surely there is land that may be brought into cultivation at all the intermediate gradations of profit from 32 per cent to 25, and 19.7 and nothing can be so improbable as that if the last land yielded 32 the next taken into cultivation should yield only 19.7. I suppose in this case the rise in the price of corn to be occasioned by demand, and to be its market price. What additional quantity of labour will be employed on new land will depend entirely upon circumstances—upon the causes which determine the general rate profits.

I assure you I have been reading over your essay again, and giving it great attention, as I particularly wish to get to the bottom of this subject.

I think your theory simple just and consistent as far as it goes; but I think you wrong in the application of it, that is, you expect similar results when the premises are essentially different. The source of this error, as it appears to me, is, that because a relative rise in the price of corn (or rather perhaps fall in the price of manufactures) always accompanies an accumulation of stock and fall of profits, you assume such rise in the price of corn as the *cause*, when in fact the whole operation of this rise as far as relates to the land, goes the other way, and tends to raise rather than to lower profits, although of course when the rise is absolutely occasioned by the fall of profits, such fall must overcome the tendency, and all the advantage derived from it will go, as you justly observe to the Landlord.

But there are other causes of a relative rise in the price of corn besides the fall of profits, such as a foreign demand for it, a greater home demand occasioned by restrictions on importation, and a prosperous foreign trade, by which we can at once import a great abundance and a great value of foreign commodities. These are causes (particularly the two former) of a rise in the relative price of corn in no respect necessarily connected with a fall of profits, and under the influence of these causes fresh land may be taken into cultivation, at various profits (to refer to your instance) from 32 to 26 per cent. With regard to manufactures in this case, if they did not rise immediately from increased demand, some of the capital vested in them would go to the land till the level was restored.

Now the error you appear to me to fall into is, that, of applying your neat simple and ingenious table[1] to a state of things not contemplated in it, and to which it does not apply. The high profits of stock which appear in the early periods of your table are owing, not to the low relative price of corn (which in fact has a contrary tendency) but to the small quantity of capital in the country compared with the means of employing it, and particularly to the small quantity of capital employed in manufactures, which unless furnished very sparingly could never bring such high profits as could be obtained from the land. But this state of things cannot surely be brought back by a low price of corn not occasioned by scantiness of capital and high profits, and if it be not preceded by these causes, its effects will be to lower not to raise the profits of agriculture. A large tract of rich land added to

[1] *Essay on Profits*, above, IV, 17.

18 April 1815 the Island, would indeed restore the state contemplated in your table. Before any fall of price had taken place, capital would be removing fast both from the old land and from manufactures. There would be a real want of stock compared with the means of profitably employing it; manufactures would rise considerably in price, from higher profits, and corn not rising, on account of the abundance of rich land, the relative price of corn would become low; but as a *consequence* (remark) not as a *cause* of high profits.

The case would be quite different if you begin by a fall in the price of corn, not occasioned by high profits, such as the opening of the ports or the stoppage of a foreign demand for corn. Capital would in this case be expelled from the land slowly by low profits, instead of removing with alacrity for high profits. Manufactures would be overloaded with capital instead of being very scantily furnished with it; and nothing I conceive but the immediate vicinity of such a country could under such circumstances so increase the prices of manufactures as to occasion generally high profits.

In your table, by the by, putting the affair of mining out of the question which it is difficult to estimate, I should say that the regular progress would be a fall in the price of manufactures from lower profits, and a stationary price of corn, rather than a rising price of corn, and a stationary one of manufactures. And this I think accords best with experience, but it is of no great consequence which, except perhaps, as it might serve to distinguish a rise occasioned by demand from a rise by a fall of profits.

You did not tell me how you liked Mr. Torrens. Did you set him right as to the consistency of my bullion opinions.[1]

Ever truly Yours

T R MALTHUS

[1] Above, p. 205, nn. 3 and 4.

## 93. RICARDO TO MALTHUS[1]

[*Reply to 92.—Answered by* 94]

My dear Sir

London 21 April 1815

I was sorry you could not join our party on wednesday. 21 April 1815
Mr. Smyth has left a pleasing impression on the minds of all
those who met him, and I had every reason to confirm me
in the favorable opinion which I had formed of him at our
first meeting. Mr. Torrens is a very gentlemanly man. He
had sent me his book on bullion[2] before he came, and I fear
that too much of the conversation was bestowed on the
differences between his opinion and mine on the subject of
paper currency and the exchanges. The latter he does not
appear to me correctly to understand. I insisted on the consistency of your former and present opinions on the bullion
question, and asked him from whence he had derived his
knowledge of your views on that subject. He said that Dr.
Crombie and you had met purposely to discuss the question
and from him he had understood that you ascribed the whole
effects on the price of bullion to the abundance of paper.

He as well as Mons[r] Say finds it difficult to support his
opinions and answer objections in conversation,—he says all
such discussions should be carried on in writing.

We have just rec[d] notice that Mr. and Mrs. Clutterbuck
will be in London on Monday, and as on saturday our boys
come home and Osman is at present with us we are pre-
cluded from asking you and Mrs. Malthus to stay at our
house. I very much regret it, and hope you will be with us
as much as you can.

---

[1] Addressed: 'To / The Rev[d]
T R Malthus / East India College /
Hertford'.
MS at Albury.—*Letters to Mal-
thus*, XXXII.

[2] *An Essay on Money and Paper
Currency*, 1812. The copy presented to Ricardo is preserved
in the library at Gatcombe.

21 April 1815    On saturday[1] I shall meet you at the King of Clubs, to
which I am invited by Mr. Whishaw, and on sunday I wish
you and Mrs. Malthus will oblige Mrs. Ricardo and me with
your company to dinner. If you can I will ask Mr. Whishaw
and Mr. Smyth to meet you. Perhaps too you will breakfast
with me on saturday or sunday morning.

It appears to me that my table is applicable to all cases in
which the relative price of corn rises from more labour being
required to produce it, and under no other circumstances can
there be a rise, however great the demand may be, unless
commodities fall in value from less labour being required for
their production. It is not probable that the relative[2] price
of corn will fall so low with an abundant capital in the
country, as when capital was very limited, but, if it could,
the same effects on profits and on rent would follow, as it
would demonstrate that land only of the best quality was in
cultivation. You agree with me that if a large tract of rich
land were added to the Island it would restore the state contemplated in my table. Though we agree in the conclusion
we differ materially in our opinion of the means by which it
would be brought about. You think that "before any fall of
price had taken place capital would be removing fast from
the old land, *and from manufactures,*"—I think that capital
would go from the old land to manufactures, because a given
quantity of food only being required, that quantity could be
raised on the rich land added to the Island, with much less
capital than was employed on the old, and consequently all
the surplus would go to [manu]factures[3] to procure other
enjoyments for the society, and profits on the land would
rise at the expence of the rent of the landlord, whilst the
cheaper price of corn would raise the profits on all manu-

[1] 29 April.                          [3] MS torn.
[2] 'relative' is ins.

facturing capital. I confess it appears to me impossible that under the circumstances you have supposed the relative value[1] of corn would fall, not from the facility of procuring it, but from a rise in the value of manufactures. You suppose that corn would remain at the same price whilst manufactures rose in price,—I on the contrary think that the price of manufactures would continue nearly stationary whilst the price of corn would fall. Is not this the natural consequence of more capital being employed on manufactures and less on agriculture? Have you not too uniformly supported the opinion that a fall in the price of corn will occasion a fall in the price of commodities? If they act on each other as you think but to which I do not agree, how can manufactures rise in price with a stationary price of corn? I should have thought that on your principles such an effect would be deemed impossible.

21 April 1815

Ever truly Y[rs]

DAVID RICARDO


### 94. MALTHUS TO RICARDO[2]
[*Reply to* 93]

My dear Sir,

E I Coll April 23. 1815.

We will dine with you on monday with great pleasure, but I fear we cannot engage for sunday, and as we shall only stay in Town till tuesday, we will not put you to the trouble of a bed, though we are much obliged to you and Mrs. Ricardo for the kind offer. I will endeavour to breakfast with you one or two of the mornings I am in Town.

We do indeed differ materially as to the mode by [which][3]

23 April 1815

---

[1] 'value' replaces 'price'.
[2] Addressed: 'D. Ricardo Esqr / Upper Brook Street / Grosvenor Square'.—MS. in *R.P.*
[3] Omitted in MS.

23 April 1815 a large additional tract of rich land would bring things back to the state contemplated in the early parts of your table. If as you suppose more capital would go to manufactures, from the impossibility of employing it with advantage on the land, no two cases could well have less resemblance; and nothing certainly but the continued absorption of fresh capital on the land, to supply the wants of a rapidly increasing population could put a manufacturing country into the state [of] [1] America. If any cause were to stop the rapid increase of population, the profits of stock would almost immediately fall.

Surely you are wrong in your view of the subject. For what is it in fact that you maintain. It is this that a *given* quantity of food, fallen in relative value compared with manufactures to one half, should not only exchange for the same mass of manufactures as before, but a much greater mass. Under the circumstances that you suppose it is contrary to every principle of supply and demand that your manufactures should keep up their price. At the old prices and in such quantities it is not in the nature of things that there should be a demand for them.

Surely I have always maintained that when corn rises, though other commodities would rise they would not rise in proportion. I do not see then why it should be contrary to my principles, as you intimate, that manufactures should rise in price from the comparative scarcity of capital, and consequent high profits; while the same scarcity of capital should not raise the price of corn, on account of the superior fertility of the land employed. You ask whether the natural consequence of employing more capital in manufactures, is not their *stationary* price. I should say that according to the usual doctrines of political Economy, it would be on the contrary a fall in their price, from a fall of profits.

[1] Omitted in MS.

The more I consider the subject, the more I am inclined 23 April 1815
to think that in the natural progress of accumulation the fall
in the profits of stock employed in manufactures is occasioned
rather by the fall in their price owing to the abundant supply
occasioned by such accumulation, than to the rise in the
price of wages.

The bell rings I must finish

Ever truly Yours

T R Malthus

## 95. MALTHUS TO RICARDO[1]

*[Answered by 96]*

E I Coll May 5th 1815

My dear Sir,

You will find in page 298 and two or three following, 5 May 1815
some of the passages which I mentioned to you. Low
profits and low rents are not a usual combination, and yet
I am inclined to agree with Mr. Torrens that in the case
supposed they would be united, though not to the advantage
of the country.[2] When it is considered that a fall in the price of
corn would not occasion an equal fall in labour, and still less
of an equal fall in the other advances of the farmer, such as

---

[1] Addressed: 'D. Ricardo Esqr. /
Upper Brook Street, / Grosvenor
Square'.
   MS in *R.P.*

[2] The case supposed by Torrens is
that of 'a free external corn
trade'. He claims to have shown,
first, that 'in the present circumstances of these countries, an unrestrained corn trade would lower
the price of corn, and bring down
the monopoly rents occasioned by
the war'; secondly, that 'a reduction in the value of corn
reduces wages'; and thirdly,

'that the low natural price of
subsistence heightens the productive powers of industry; that
these heightened powers accelerate
the accumulation of stock; and
that this accumulation lowers the
rate of profit.' Thus, he con-
cludes, 'a free external trade in
corn...would effect a reduction
in rents, wages, and profits'
(*Essay on the External Corn Trade*,
p. 298); subsequent pages describe
the beneficial effects of this reduction.

5 May 1815  timber bricks leather, &c: &c: I own it appears to me quite impossible that the profits of capital employed on the land should not diminish, notwithstanding a very great reduction of the cultivation, particularly as some of these advances of the farmer cannot fall very much, on account of the demand and difficulty of supply occasioned by a full population, and the necessary and permanent rise of price occasioned by taxation. Under these circumstances I really think that a fall in rent profits and wages at the same time would be compatible, though I should consider it as a great national misfortune. But, to leave this subject; I have been considering the case that we discussed when I had the pleasure of seeing you, and I am convinced that the effects of the facility of production supposed, would go exclusively to wages not profits; indeed I cannot help thinking that you are fundamentally wrong in measuring the rate of profits by the facility of production. For what in fact is meant by facility of production? It is that a days labour instead of producing two measures of corn cloth and cotton will produce four. And what is the natural consequence of this facility? why, that four measures of corn cloth and cotton are worth only the price of a days labour; and nothing can prevent this consequence, but a scarcity of capital compared with the means of imploying it profitably. But the means of imploying capital profitably can never coexist with an abundant capital and produce and a *stationary* population, on account of the necessary effect of such a state of things in increasing the real price of labour.

Facility of production (which includes of course, the facility of producing the materials of capital, and which tends therefore to make the other materials of capital besides labour as plentiful as the commodities produced for consumption) mainly affects the real wages of labour, and not the rate of profits; and if at any one time in the early periods of society population were to be stopped and accumulation were to go on, profits would fall extremely low although at the same time the labour of one man might be able to produce the food for ten or twenty. In this case everything would be in abundance and cheap except labour; and probably labourers would only work $\frac{1}{4}$ of their time and yet live luxuriously. This shews that profits do not depend upon facility of production, although they may be often high when the facility of production is great; because capital is often scarce, and generally so indeed, at the time that land is most productive.

The rate of profits depends upon the scanty or abundant supply of capital compared with the means of employing it profitably. And these means will upon the common principles of supply and demand be increased either by a diminution of capital, [or by] [1] an extension of the market for it, by the opening of new channels of trade and by improvements in agriculture and manufactures, when accompanied as is almost invariably the case, by an increase of population and demand.

The principle of demand depending entirely on the power of production is true as long as each sort of commodity is in the proper proportions, and above all, food so as to keep up demand by a progressive population. But the principle is not true when population cannot be made to increase proportionally. If it be supposed stationary, capital may very easily increase beyond the powers of employing it productively.

I am interrupted by the Postman and must conclude.

Ever truly Yours<br>T R MALTHUS.

I hope we shall see you some time this month.

[1] Covered by seal.

## 96. RICARDO TO MALTHUS[1]
### [*Reply to* 95]

My dear Sir                              [London, 8 May 1815][2]

8 May 1815    I have an account before me of the Capital actually employed on a farm of 200 Acres in Essex. It amounts to
£3433. – or about £17 p$^r$ Acre, of which not more than
£1100, or £1200 is of that description which is not subject
to the same variation of value as the produce of the land
itself; for £2200 – consists of the value of the seeds in the
ground, the advances for labour,—the horses and live stock
&c$^a$ &c$^a$. If then the money value of the produce from the
land should fall, *from facility of production*, it must ever continue to bear a greater ratio to the whole money value of
the capital employed on the land, for there will be a great
increase of average produce per acre, whilst the fall in money
value will be common to both capital and produce[3] and it
cannot therefore be true that rent, profits, and wages, can all
*really* fall at the same time.

The effect of high or low wages on profits has always been
distinctly recognized by me;—till the population increases
to the proportion which the increased capital can employ,
wages will rise, and may absorb a larger portion of the whole
produce. But this effect will only take place with an increase
of capital, and has nothing to do with new facilities of production. Wages do not depend upon the quantity of a commodity which a day's labour will produce, and I can not help
thinking you quite incorrect when you say that the natural

---

[1] Addressed: 'The Rev$^d$ T. R
Malthus / East India College /
Hertford'.
  MS at Albury.—*Letters to Mal-
thus*, XXXVII, where it is mis-
dated 'Oct. 1815?'

[2] Undated. London postmark, 8
May 1815.
[3] The last three lines, beginning
'for there will be', are ins.

consequence of the facility of production being so increased that a day's labour will produce four measures of corn, cloth and cotton instead of two measures, will be, that 4 measures of corn cloth and cotton will be worth only the price of a day's labour instead of 2. It appears to me that if, instead of 4, ten measures could be produced by a day's labour no rise would take place in wages, no greater portion of corn, cloth or cotton would be given to the labourer unless a portion of the increased produce were employed as capital, and then the rise in wages would be in proportion to the new demand for labour, and not at all in proportion to the increase in the quantity of commodities produced. This increase would be exclusively[1] enjoyed by the owner of stock, and if he consumed in his family the whole increased produce, without augmenting his capital, wages would remain stationary, and not be in any way affected by the increased facility of production.

I cannot agree with your proposition namely ["]That the means of employing capital profitably can never co-exist with an abundant capital and produce and a stationary population, on account of the necessary effect of such a state of things in increasing the real price of labour," because I consider the rise of wages as by no means a necessary effect of an abundant capital and produce, for it may be accompanied with new facilities in procuring corn, and then wages[2] even if they should rise would not lessen profits, they will only keep them lower than they otherwise would be. In the case which we were considering the other night, if every lady made her own shoes, a part of the capital now employed in making shoes by the shoemakers would be otherwise employed. The same labour would be bestowed in the produc-

---

[1] 'the reward' is del. here.      [2] The remainder of the sentence replaces 'will not lessen profits.'

8 May 1815 tion of other objects desirable to these lady shoemakers, who would have both the power and the will to purchase them from the savings which would accrue to them by employing their labour productively.—

There is a great difference between [the]¹ common effects of an accumulation of capital, and the employing the same capital more productively. The first is generally attended with a rise of wages and a fall of profits for a time at least,—but the second may exist for an indefinite length of time without producing any such effects. In the case of great improvements in machinery,—capital is liberated for other employments and at the same time the labour necessary for those employments is also liberated,—so that no demand for additional labour will take place unless the increased production in consequence of the improvement should lead to further accumulation of capital, and then the effect on wages is to be ascribed to the accumulation of capital and not to the better employment of the same capital.

If the population were to be stopped whilst accumulation continued the effects which you enumerate would undoubtedly follow, but this would arise from the demand for labour not being adequately supplied,—it would be the effect of accumulation which would operate so powerfully that it would be but slightly checked by the facility of production,—but it would not by any means be the consequence of such facility.

It is true that the rate of profits depends upon the scanty or abundant supply of capital compared with the means of employing it profitably,—and these means will as you say upon the common principles of supply and demand be increased either by a diminution of capital or by an extension of the market for it. Our enquiry is in fact what the causes

¹ Covered by seal.

are of an extension of the market and I hold that the most   8 May 1815
powerful and the only one which operates permanently, is a
reduction in the relative value of food. You appear to me to
concede a little respecting demand being regulated by the
power of production,—but you are yet very far from yielding all that I demand.

I hope we shall meet this month but I cannot yet say
whether I can leave London.

Y<sup>rs</sup> very truly<br>
D. RICARDO

## 97. MALTHUS TO RICARDO[1]

Weston House Guildford<br>
June 11<sup>th</sup> 1815.

My dear Sir,

The Champ de Mai[2] has passed off so well for Buonaparte,   11 June 1815
and I am so much inclined to think that he will make a
formidable resistance, that I expect the Stocks will be rather
lower than higher some months hence. I may very likely be
quite mistaken; but under this impression I should naturally
be disposed to take an early opportunity of realising a small
profit on the share you have been so good as to promise me.[3]
I will not however do this if it is either wrong, or inconvenient to you, and whatever may occur, you may depend
upon it, that I shall always, be sensible of your kindness, and
not disposed to repine.

We expect to stay here about a week longer.

Supposing two nations with the same population and
wealth, and the same rate of profits; and one of them to be

---

[1] Addressed: 'D. Ricardo Esqr /
Upper Brook Street / Gosvenor
Square'.
    MS in *R.P.*

[2] The ceremony on 1 June at
which Napoleon proclaimed the
new Constitution.
[3] See above, p. 122.

11 June 1815 merely manufacturing and commercial, and the other mainly agricultural, would you not say, that the agricultural country would produce the given quantity of wealth and population with less labour, and would therefore have a greater mass of disposeable wealth, and could maintain larger fleets and armies?

The postman is here

Ever truly Yours<br>T ROB<sup>T</sup> MALTHUS.

If this be not allowed, it is saying, that the possession of such an instrument as the land, is of little or no use.

## 98. RICARDO TO MURRAY[1]

Dear Sir

12 June 1815    Should you like a little of the loan[2] which is to be bid for on wednesday? If you should be so good as to let me know, to-day, or to-morrow, how much you wish to have.

Y<sup>rs</sup> truly<br>DAVID RICARDO

Upper Brook Street
    12 June 1815

I hope you are no worse for the attack which was made on you.[3]

---

[1] Addressed: 'Mr. Murray/Albermale Street'.
    MS in the possession of Sir John Murray.
[2] See below, p. 231, n. 2.
[3] 'Mr Murray, bookseller, in Albemarle-street, on his return to town from Stoke Newington over the fields, on Wednesday last, was assailed by two ruffians, who knocked him down, and robbed him of his money, but declined taking his watch.' (*Morning Post*, Monday 12 June 1815.)

## 99. MALTHUS TO RICARDO[1]

[*Answered by* 100]

Weston House. Guildford
June 19th 1815

My dear Sir

We leave this place tomorrow for the Bath country, 19 June 1815
and aware of your engagements at present, I will not take up
more of your time than to say how much obliged to you I am
for your kindness about the Loan, and the trouble you have
taken for me. Should the Allies be successful at the commencement of the campaign, omnium will certainly rise very
considerably; but on the other hand if Bonaparte should
begin prosperously, I think there might be a panic which
would occasion a rapid fall; and tho on the whole the
probabilities of a rise are perhaps the greatest, yet I am fully
and entirely satisfied with what you have done and beg to
thank you sincerely.[2]

I saw Lord King last night. He speaks of having heard of
very general distress among farmers and shopkeepers all over
the country. I confess I feel more and more convinced of the
unavoidable evils attending a general fall of prices, and of the
unobserved advantages attending the high prices of corn and
labour (when not arising solely from diff[y] of production[)].
I mentioned the subject to Lord K. but we had not time to
discuss it. He said he would consider it, and that the view
which I took of the effect of such prices on foreign commerce
appeared to him to be quite new.

---

[1] Addressed: 'D. Ricardo Esqr /
56. Upper Brook Street / Grosvenor Square'.—MS in *R.P.*
[2] A loan of £36,000,000 had
been contracted for by Ricardo
and others on 14 June. Ricardo
had presumably sold the share of
£5000, which he had reserved for

Malthus, on the same day, when
the Omnium was quoted at 2¼ to
3¼ per cent. premium. The news
of Waterloo (18 June 1815) did
not reach London till the evening
of 20 June, and on the following
day the Omnium rose to 6 per
cent. premium.

19 June 1815   By the by I have just obtained the prices of wheat and labour in America. Before the late war, labour was about 4$^s$ 6. or 5 shillings stirling a day and wheat about 11$^s$ 3$^d$ a bushel. I am surprised at these prices in a specie currency. —But I am doing what I did not intend.

Mrs. M desires to be kindly remembered to Mrs. Ricardo.

Believe me

very truly Yours

T R MALTHUS.

My address in a few days will be Claverton House near Bath.

## 100. RICARDO TO MALTHUS[1]

*[Reply to 99.—Answered by 101]*

Upper Brook Street
27$^{th}$ June 1815

My dear Sir

27 June 1815   I have been for two or three days at Tunbridge Wells, and have been agreeably surprised to day on my arrival in London, to hear of the great events which are taking place in France, in consequence of the great victory obtained by the Duke of Wellington and his brave army over Bonaparte. With the deposition of Bonaparte I hope there may be no other obstacles to peace, and that we may at length be rewarded for the blood and treasure which we have expended with a long period of tranquility,—which I have no doubt will also prove a long period of prosperity. I think with Mr. Whitbread[2] that great credit is due to ministers for the energy

[1] Addressed: 'To / The Rev$^d$ T R Malthus / Claverton House / near / Bath'.

MS at Albury.—*Letters to Malthus*, XXXIII.

[2] Samuel Whitbread, who in April had protested in the House of Commons against the resumption of war, had now (on 23 June) made a speech in support of the proposed grant of £200,000 to the Duke of Wellington. On 6 July Whitbread died by cutting his throat.

which they have displayed in the prosecution of this contest.
Having determined on war their preparations have been on
such a scale as to give from the commencement the best
hopes of success, and we appear at last to have adopted the
wise policy of making one grand effort in preference to a
series of puny efforts each just sufficient to keep the contest
alive without making the least advance to its ultimate object.

The effect on the price of Omnium has been no more than
what might have been expected.[1] I am sorry that you have
not profited by the rise.—As for myself I have all my stock,
by which I mean I have all my money invested in Stock, and
this is as great an advantage as ever I expect or wish to make
by a rise. I have been a considerable gainer by the loan; in
the first place by replacing the stock which I had sold before
the contract with the minister at a much lower price, and
secondly by a moderate gain on such part of the loan as I
ventured to take over and above my stock This portion I
sold at a premium of from 3 to 5 pc.$^t$ and I have every reason
to be well contented. Perhaps no loan was ever more
generally profitable to the Stock Exchange.

Now for a little of our old subject.

It appears to me that there are two causes which may
cause a rise of prices,—one the depreciation of money, the
other the difficulty of producing. The latter can in no case
be advantageous to a society.—It is always a sign of prosperity but never the cause of it. Depreciation of money
may be beneficial because it generally favours that class who
are disposed to accumulate,—but I should say that it augmented riches by diminishing happiness, that it was advantageous only by occasioning a great pressure on the labouring classes and on those who lived on fixed incomes. You
I think concur in this opinion for you say that you are con-

[1] The Omnium was now quoted at 11½ to 13 per cent. premium.

27 June 1815 vinced that there are unobserved advantages attending the high price of corn and labour "when not arising solely from difficulty of production," by which I think you imply that no such advantages would attend high prices if attended with difficulty of production.

This opinion is however a little at variance with that which you have long been supporting, for you have said that the high price of corn and labour in this country at this time was an advantage, although it is universally allowed that that high price is mainly owing to difficulty of production. The farmers and shopkeepers may suffer very general distress from a sudden and general fall of prices, but I hold that this would be no criterion by which to judge of the general or permanent prosperity of a country.

The accounts in which I am at present engaged will I fear keep me in London till the very latter end of July. I shall very much regret if you quit Bath without my seeing you.— I quite depended on having a visit from you at Gatcomb this year, and I yet hope that it may be accomplished. I shall certainly leave London the very earliest day possible.

The price of labour in America appears to me enormously high as compared with the price of wheat but we should not fail to remember how very low the exchangeable value of wheat is there and how much of it must be given for the manufactured necessaries and comforts of life. Kind regards to Mrs. Malthus.

Ever truly yours
DAVID RICARDO

## 101. MALTHUS TO RICARDO[1]

*[Reply to 100.—Answered by 103]*

Claverton House. Bath
July 16th 1815.

My dear Sir

I hope the victory of the Duke of Wellington will be   16 July 1815
the means of giving Europe some permanent repose. It has
been purchased by a tremendous sacrifice, and I do not quite
like the idea of imposing the Bourbons upon France by force,
but if it leads to a lasting peace, it will be worth all that it has
cost. I think Louis in order to be safe himself must disband
nearly the whole army, and this must powerfully contribute
to the safety and repose of Europe, though this second successful combination of Sovereigns will I fear be unfavourable
to its liberty and improvement.

I was disappointed to find that you had not sold any of
your omnium at a higher price than five per cent premium.
I was in hopes that you had got some of the high prices, tho
I had missed them. I confess I thought that the chances of
the first battle were in favour of Buonaparte, who had the
choice of attack; and it appears indeed from the Duke of
Wellington's despatches that he was at one time very near
succeeding. From what has happened since however it seems
certain that the French were not so well prepared as they
ought to have been. If there had been the energy and en-
thusiasm which might have been expected in the defence of
their independence, one battle however sanguinary and complete could not have decided the fate of France.

We shall leave our friends here on the 25th and must be at
Haileybury on the 26th, so that even if you were at Gatcomb

---

[1] Addressed: 'D. Ricardo Esqr / 56. Upper Brook Street / Grosvenor Square / London'.—MS in *R.P.*

16 July 1815 we could hardly pay you a visit this time, and must therefore defer that pleasure till a better opportunity.

I certainly do not mean to consider a difficulty of producing as desirable in itself; but I think that a high price of corn when not occasioned by such difficulty is a decided advantage, and that it is at all times the best remedy for that difficulty of producing food, which in the progress of society is absolutely unavoidable. In our own case I believe that a great part of our high bullion prices is attributable to other causes besides the barrenness of the land to be taken into cultivation; and I feel a strong conviction that we should not have been able, during the last 20 years to subsidize Europe, and make such extraordinary exertions as we have done, if by open ports we could have kept our corn and labour on a level with the rest of Europe. If the wages of labour are mainly determined by the price of food, I do not see why an increase of money prices should diminish happiness. It will injure some undoubtedly, but will benefit a much greater number; and it is consolatory to reflect that even when it arises from difficulty of production, the high relative value of corn constantly counterbalances in a considerable degree the evil of reduced corn wages.

Are you not surprised at the high money price of corn in America as well as the high money price of labour, with a currency convertible into specie.

Mrs. M desires to be kindly remembered. Ever truly Yours

T R MALTHUS.

There are many causes of a high relative price of corn—Division of labour in manufactures; machinery; Demand for corn abroad; Restrictions on importations; Prosperous foreign commerce &c: None of these involve diminished profits.

## 102. TROWER TO RICARDO[1]

Unsted Wood—Godalming—
[*ca.* 23 July 1815]

Dear Ricardo

I trust that this will catch you before you have spread  23 July 1815
your wings, and taken flight to the Westward—Even *you*
must, by this time, be parched and panting for the Country;
and impatient to turn your back upon the modern Babylon.
—I am rejoiced to find, that you have wisely determined no
longer to subject yourself to the anxieties and vexations of
business. Rest assured, that you will daily find occasion to
applaud the wisdom of your resolve; and that you will become
more enamoured of the vegetable part of the creation the better
you are acquainted with it.—I depend upon your devoting a
portion of your time and attention to farming, and especially
to that most interesting and important branch of it, the growth
and culture of Trees.—Remember to carry with you into the
Country Dr Hunters edition of Evlyns Silva,[2] and Nichols
Planters Kalendar.[3]—You will find, that an attention to this
subject will give a great additional interest to your landed
possessions, and afford you an unlimited pleasureable pursuit.

You ask me the fate of my Omnium. I sold it at 10. and
might have obtained a higher price had I not been too sanguine.[4] I entertained a confident opinion that the result would
be such as it has proved, and expected that one so glorious

[1] Addressed: 'To/David Ricardo
Esqr. / Upper Brook Street / Grosvenor Square'. London postmark, 24 July; the contents show
that the year must be 1815.
MS (in Trower's handwriting)
in *R.P.*
[2] *Silva: or, A Discourse of Forest-
Trees,...* by John Evelyn, with
Notes by A. Hunter, 2 vols., 4th
ed., York, 1812.

[3] *The Planter's Kalendar; or the
Nurseryman's & Forester's Guide
in the operations of the Nursery, the
Forest, and the Grove,* by Walter
Nicoll, ed. by E. Sang, Edinburgh, 1812.
[4] The Omnium, after rising to
13 per cent. premium on 28 June,
had fallen gradually and was now
at 8⅜ premium.

23 July 1815 and important would have produced a greater effect upon the Funds. But there is no reasoning upon them, therefore the less one has to do with them the better. *Excepting* upon those golden opportunities which Loans *judiciously taken* generally afford.—

Bonaparte captive! That one word will in [the eyes][1] of posterity efface the whole glory of his lif[e. He] should have died with "the harness on h[is back" or] must have afforded a mark for scorn to p[oint a] finger at. Really the close of his career [makes] him appear contemptibly ridiculous, and ridicu[lously] contemptible.—What will become of him I k[now not.] But sure I am, that justice requires h[im to] expiate his offences on the block. Europe [...] Europe cries for vengeance on his head—[His] life is forfeited to France— Should *we* have spared the life of the Pretender? Was he not proscribed when the event was *doubtful,* and now that *certainty* has made him theirs shall they hesitate to act? In surrendering to *us*, he has in fact surrendered to the *Allies*; the Allies should deliver him up to the french Government, and they should consign him to the Devil.—It is a sacrifice necessary for the happiness of France and for the peace of Europe. As long as he is above ground, dispose of him as you will, he will form a nucleus round which the [? discontented] will collect and gather.—Adieu my Dear [Ricardo. Our] united Compliments to Mrs. Ricardo [and family.] Most probably when next I write to you [I shall have] to announce an addition to my own.[2]

Remember your letters will at all times be most acceptable to me, and be assured that I shall estimate their value in a manner very different from that in which it appears you have done—

---

[1] MS torn here and below.　　[2] The signature is omitted in MS.

## 103. RICARDO TO MALTHUS[1]
*[Reply to* 101.—*Answered by* 110]*

Gatcomb Park. 30 July 1815

My dear Sir

I bore with great patience the fatigues of the last fort- 30 July 1815
night in London in the hope that on my arrival at Gatcomb I should have the pleasure of your company for a few
days previously to your return to London. It was a great
disappointment to me to learn that you would be travelling
to London the very day after I quitted it, and I see little
prospect of having a visit from you here for some time to
come, as your convenience or inclination will probably lead
you to a different part of the country next year.

I most cordially join with you in the wish that the victory
of the Duke of Wellington will be the means of giving
Europe some permanent repose. There appears every probability that it will be attended with that happy effect, and
I should hope that the late stormy times will afford instruction both to sovereigns and people, and will secure the world
from the evils of anarchy as well as from those of tyranny
and despotism.

David's ill health has induced us to take him from the
Charterhouse and we have been particularly recommended
to keep him under our own eye. This plan has materially in-
terfered with those arrangements which are most conducive
to my comforts, but his health and safety were objects too
great to be hazarded. I thought they would run little risk if we
placed him with a gentleman who took only a very limited
number of pupils, but his mother was full of terror and alarm,
I have therefore been obliged to get a gentleman to live with

[1] Addressed: 'The Rev^d T R     MS at Albury.—*Letters to Mal-*
Malthus / East India College /     *thus,* XXXIV.
Hertford'.

30 July 1815 us as tutor. In your absence I took the liberty of calling on Mr. Whishaw where I met Mr. Smyth. They both gave me much useful information, and pointed out the difficulties which I should encounter in getting a respectable gentleman to undertake the office. Those difficulties I found it no easy task to surmount, but I believe I have at last succeeded; and in a few days I expect a gentleman in orders, who has very much distinguished himself at Oxford and who is very strongly recommended by the vice principal of Mary's Hall College Oxford,[1] to take care of David and Mortimer's education. He is about 24 and his appearance is gentlemanly and agreeable.[2]

Mr. Clerk a neighbour of mine here in Glostershire, and who is brother to the East India Director of that name, has just sent his son George[3] to the East India College and knowing my intimacy with you has called upon me to request me to write to you on behalf of his son,—that in case he may st[and in][4] need of any friendly advice or assistance you [would have] the goodness to give it to him. I hope [I] am not taking too great a liberty in asking you to comply with his father's wishes.

The immense concerns in business which I have lately had on my mind had nearly banished all consideration of subjects connected with political economy from it. Those concerns are now settled, but they have given me incessant work in arranging and balancing my accounts ever since I have been

---

[1] John Radcliffe (*Oxford University Calendar for 1815*).
[2] The tutor was James Hitchings (*ca.* 1790–1850), of Christ Church, Oxford. He remained with the Ricardos three years, and afterwards obtained a curacy at Sunninghill, near Windsor, when he took Ricardo's younger boys as pupils in his house.
[3] George Russell Clerk (1800–1889), afterwards Governor of Bombay, Secretary to the India Board (1857) and Permanent Under-Secretary of State for India (1858).
[4] MS torn here and below.

here. I recur now however with pleasure to corn, labour, 30 July 1815
and bullion. A really high price of corn is always an evil; in
this opinion I think you would concur because it is always
occasioned by difficulty of production. I know of no other
cause and you allow difficulty of production not to be desirable in itself. In our own case the high bullion price of corn
is not wholly owing to the barrenness of the land to be taken
into cultivation, but from whatever cause it has arisen it
cannot I think have enabled us to grant greater subsidies than
we should otherwise have done for subsidies as well as all
services performed for us are paid for by the produce of the
land and labour of the people of England. It surely is a
palpable contradiction to say that our power of commanding
services is increased whilst our productions with which
those services are paid are diminished. The principle may be
true when confined to a few commodities of which we either
have a monopoly or peculiar facilities in the production of
them but as a general proposition it appears to me to be at
variance with the best established doctrines.

If a free trade in corn were allowed with America I should
not expect that the prices would differ more, here and there,
than the expences and profits of sending it,—as it is I am
surprised the price should be so high. A high money price
of wages is I think quite natural.

Ever Y<sup>rs</sup>

DAVID RICARDO


104. GRENFELL TO RICARDO[1]

My dear Sir               Taplow House 1 August 1815

The modesty with which you speak of your own 1 Aug. 1815
Qualifications, makes me the more anxious and desirous that

[1] MS in R.P.

1 Aug. 1815 you should feel an inclination to undertake, in the course of the approaching Autumn—or rather I would say—before the next Bank Court in September or October—to write a Short Pamphlet on the Subject to which I have lately called the attention of Parliament[1]—and which I am sure no person is better qualified to do than yourself, and which I am equally certain would acquire a Sanction, and favourable Introduction to the Public, from the merited Reputation of your Name as a writer upon subjects of the like Nature—

If however you should be averse to the undertaking in a distinct Pamphlet (which would be a Short and as you say an easy Task) I shall be gratified by seeing the Subject referred to, in the work which you have in Contemplation on the Corn Trade[2]—There is a Book of *Allardyce* on Bank Affairs[3] containing many details and Facts, which you will find it convenient and desirable to be possessed of, if you determine (as I anxiously hope you will do) to write a short Pamphlet on this subject—And if you have not this Book, I shall be happy to Send it to you, with a few observations of my own—Coaches pass my Door here, to Worcester and Glôster daily—and I would direct a Parcel to you containing this Book, in any way you may point out.

I think the discussion—and a more general diffusion of the Facts which refer to this Subject, may have the Effect of benefitting the Public (my only motive for originating it) and at the same time accelerate to the Proprietors of Bank Stock, the participation in the immense Profits already

[1] See Grenfell's Resolutions on the Bank of England, proposed on 13 June, above, IV, 136. As a result of Grenfell's suggestion Ricardo wrote *Economical and Secure Currency*.

[2] This probably refers to the project of Ricardo's rewriting 'more at large' the *Essay on Profits*, on which see below, p. 249.

[3] On Allardyce's two books on Bank affairs see above, IV, 103 and 106.

made by the Bank, to which there can be no doubt, their ₁ Aug. 1815
Charters and every principle of Justice and equity entitle
them.

I write this in haste, being called to Town suddenly by the
Death of a Relation—But I will not leave the Country without thanking you for your Letter, intreating you to undertake the Pamphlet, and assuring you that I am My dear Sir

Most truly and faithfully Yours

PASCOE GRENFELL[1]

David Ricardo Esq.

## 105. WHISHAW TO RICARDO[2]

Lincolns Inn
August 8, 1815

My dear Sir

I have to acknowledge your attention in acquainting ₈ Aug. 1815
me that you had succeeded in making a satisfactory
arrangement for your Son's domestic education;[3] a circumstance, which it gave me great pleasure to hear, and which
makes it unnecessary for me to prosecute some enquiries
on the same subject, which I had set on foot, but which
did not promise any very satisfactory result.

Mr Smyth is gone, some time since, into Cheshire; but
when I write, I will acquaint him with your obliging
communication and wish to see him at Gatcombe. If anything should lead him your way, I am sure he will make
a point of calling on you.—With respect to myself I am
vibrating, at present, between town and country, making
occasional excursions to the latter, whilst I am detained
here for the greater part of this month by business.—
Last week I was to have gone to Malthus for a few days,

[1] A postscript, reading 'Direct always to Spring Garden, London', is del. here.
[2] Addressed: 'David Ricardo
Esqr / Minchin hampton / (Gatcomb Park)/Gloucestershire.'
MS in *R.P.*
[3] See above, p. 240.

8 Aug. 1815 but some circumstances prevented me; and I must endeavour to accomplish a visit to him before I quit London for my vacation. It was very ill-managed, as I told him, when he passed through London in his way from Bath, that he and Mrs Malthus did not contrive to see Gatcombe and your beautiful neighbourhood.

In the course of next month Mr Warburton and I hope to pay a visit at Easton Grey; and I trust we shall then pay our respects to you. I heard lately from the Smiths, who were then very well and much pleased with their Irish expedition. They were about to leave Dublin, and must at this time be in the South of Ireland, probably at Cork or Killarney.—Almost all our friends are dispersed. Mr Sharp is gone to Holland and the Netherlands, and ends his tour by a short stay at Paris. Mr A. Baring went last week with his family to Switzerland through Germany; it being considered unsafe to travel through the South of France.

With the assistance of Mr Warburton, I have written a short Memoir of the Life of poor Mr Tennant for insertion in Dr Thomson's Scientific Journal. A few copies will be printed off for distribution among his friends;[1] and I propose sending one to your house, together with some *addenda* to Park's Journal, which I am putting together for a new Edition.[2]

I remain, with best Compl[ts] to Mrs Ricardo,

My dear Sir,

Y[rs] most faithfully

J. WHISHAW.

[1] *Some Account of the late Smithson Tennant, Esq. F.R.S. Professor of Chemistry in the University of Cambridge*, London, 1815, pp. 46 [reprinted from Thomson's *Annals of Philosophy*]. Tennant had been killed in February 1815 near Boulogne by the collapse of a bridge over which he was riding. [2] *The Journal of a Mission to the Interior of Africa, in the year 1805*, by Mungo Park, 'to which is

## 106. SAY TO RICARDO[1]

*[Answered by 107]*

Je profite, Monsieur, de la complaisance de M. Basevi[2] 2 Aug. 1815
pour vous adresser un Catéchisme d'Economie politique qui
contient en style familier l'exposé de nos grands principes.[3]
Je les reproduirai sous toutes les formes aussi longtems que
j'aurai un souffle de vie; et je mourrai probablement avant
qu'ils soient devenus populaires, surtout en France où l'on
est généralement moins avancé que chez vous. Je me persuade cependant qu'on finira par savoir tout cela jusque dans
les chaumières, et les resultats en seront immenses. Travaillez
de votre côté, Monsieur, à une si bonne Œuvre en protègeant
les bons écrits, en écrivant vous-même dans votre char-
mante retraite de Gat-combe Park; cela vous procurera de
doux momens et la conscience d'avoir été utile aux hommes.

J'ai appris avec bien du plaisir, Monsieur, les bonnes
nouvelles qu'on m'a données de votre respectable famille et
de vous. Vos spéculations financieres ont dû être favorables

prefixed *An Account of the Life
of Mr. Park* [Anon., by John
Whishaw]', London, Murray,
1815, 4° (Introduction dated 1
March 1815).—*The Journal*...
'Second Edition,Revised andCor-
rected, with Additions', *ib.* 1815,
4° (Introduction dated 1 Aug.
1815). The *Addenda* to the *Account of the Life* in the 2nd ed.
were also printed separately, *n.d.*,
*n.p.* xxvii pp., 4°.
[1] MS in *R.P.*—This letter cannot
have reached Ricardo before 14
August (see next footnote).
[2] Naphtali Basevi (1792–1869),
son of Ricardo's friend George
Basevi, sen. (see below, VII, 10,
n. 1). A letter from N. Basevi to

Ricardo, giving an account of his
visit to Paris, accompanied Say's
book and letter. It is dated
Montague St., 13 Aug. 1815 and
addressed to Gatcomb Park; the
MS is in *R.P.*
[3] *Catéchisme d'Économie politique,
ou instruction familière qui montre
de quelle façon les richesses sont
produites, distribuées et consommées dans la société; Ouvrage fondé
sur les faits, et utile aux différentes
classes d'hommes, en ce qu'il in-
dique les avantages que chacun peut
retirer de sa position et de ses talens,*
Paris, chez l'Auteur, rue des
Fossés-St-Jacques, n° 13, près
l'Estrapade, 1815.

2 Aug. 1815  autant que vastes, et je m'en réjouis; la fortune ne pouvait
s'adresser mieux, et elle ne passerait pas pour aveugle si elle
se conduisait toujours de même. Il est vrai qu'elle est rare-
ment secondée par un jugement aussi sûr.

Vous avez renoncé à visiter la france cette année, et vous
avez bien fait. Il y a peu de divertissement à voir des villages
incendiés et ravagés par la guerre et des villes écrasées de
contributions militaires. Si de tout cela il pouvait sortir un
bon gouvernement et la tranquilité, il y aurait de quoi se
consoler; mais je crains bien qu'il n'en sorte rien de bon, du
moins prochainement. Je voulais rentrer dans les fonctions
publiques, mais j'y ai renoncé par l'impossibilité d'y faire le
bien; je formerai quelqu'entreprise particuliere quand nous
serons debarrassés des gens de guerre.

Agréez, Monsieur, l'assurance de ma sincère estime et de
mon dévouement sans bornes

J. B. Say

Paris 2 août 1815

David Ricardo Esq$^{re}$

## 107. RICARDO TO SAY[1]

[*Reply to* 106.—*Answered by* 117]

Gatcomb Park, Minchinhampton
Gloucestershire
18$^{th}$ Aug$^t$ 1815

Dear Sir

18 Aug. 1815      I received with very great pleasure the book and letter
which Mr. Basevi delivered me from you. I was exceedingly
happy to hear that you were well, as I had very often thought

---

[1] Addressed: 'J. B. Say Esq$^{re}$ /
Paris.' Not passed through the
post (cp. the opening of letter
117 below). Marked by Say:
'Repondu le 10 Septembre'.

MS in the possession of
M. Raoul-Duval.—*Mélanges*, pp.
92–6; *Œuvres diverses*, pp. 409–11
(in French translation).

of you, during the almost incredible occurrences which have
in the last few months taken place in France, with apprehensions that they might interfere with your ease and comfort. I regret, as all the friends of peace must, the renewal of
those military outrages which had so long desolated Europe,
and to which I hoped there had been a termination for many
years. May your country be soon relieved from the terrible
scourge under which it is now suffering, and may the smiling
days of peace, tranquility and good government compensate
you for the evils which you have endured.

Surrounded as I am by a large family I shall find some
difficulty in arranging a visit to Paris,—I hope however to
accomplish it next spring. I shall be glad to find you actively
employed in some public situation, devoting your energy
and talents in the service of a free government and in the
establishment of those sound principles of Political Economy
which your writings have already so ably developed.

I have read with much satisfaction your Catechisme
D'Economie Politique. I think it excellent. All the grand
principles are perspicuously and forcibly laid down, and I
am convinced that not only the student but the initiated will
find considerable advantage from consulting it.

You have I perceive a little modified the definition of the
word *value* as far as it is dependent on utility, but with great
diffidence, I observe, that I do not think you have mastered
the difficulties which attach to the explanation of that difficult
word. Utility is certainly the foundation of value, but the
degree of utility can never be the measure by which to
estimate value. A commodity difficult of production will
always be more valuable than one which is easily produced
although all men should agree that the latter is more useful
than the former. A commodity must be useful to have value
but the difficulty of its production is the true measure of its

value. For this reason Iron though more useful is of less value than gold.

Riches are valuable only as they can procure us enjoyments. That man is most rich, and has most valuables, who can procure in exchange for his commodities, not those things which he himself or the world generally consider as most desireable, because they may possibly be procured at little cost, but those things which are of difficult production, which is always the foundation of great value. It appears to me therefore incorrect to say as you do page 95 that that man is superlatively rich, *although he has few valuables*, who can procure easily or for nothing those things which he wishes to consume. He may only wish to consume bread and water and may be able to procure no more. He cannot be so rich as his neighbour who has abundance of valuables which he can exchange for all the luxuries of life, which it [is]¹ his desire to consume. Riches are measured by the quantity of valuables which a man possesses, not by the moderation of his wants.

You will excuse me for offering one more observation. In page 21 you say that a manufacturer to ascertain whether the value of his capital is increased must make an inventory of all that he possesses valuing each commodity at its current price. Such a process would inform him only whether the money value of his capital had increased:—it might be satisfactory to him, but it is not the mode by which a political economist should judge of the increased value of capital. During the depreciation of our currency (Bank notes) many men thought the value of their capital had increased, when possibly it had diminished, merely because it was worth a greater number of pounds sterling. Money, whether metallic, or paper money, may always fall in value, and cannot

¹ Omitted in MS.

therefore correctly measure the value of other commodities for six months together. An increase of capital is to be ascertained only by its power of employing more industry and of adding to the produce of the land and labour of the country. The principle I know you fully recognize but I question whether you have not lost sight of it in the above passage.

My pleasure in reading and studying works on political economy has suffered no abatement and I would readily devote my time to the discussion of such points as appear to me to want elucidation if my want of talent for composition did not prevent me. I ventured however notwithstanding this defect to publish the small pamphlet which I sent you in the spring.[1] I should have been glad to have had your opinion of the particular doctrines which I hold respecting rent and profit in opposition to Mr. Malthus. Possibly you may think as I understand from Mr. Mill many able persons think here that I have not been sufficiently diffuse, and therefore do not understand me. Mr. Mill wishes me to write it over again more at large. I fear the undertaking exceeds my powers.

I thank you much for your kind expressions with regard to my successful operations in business, and with best wishes for your happiness and prosperity

I am My dear Sir

very respectfully Yours

DAVID RICARDO

[1] *Essay on Profits.*

## 108. RICARDO TO [SAY][1]

[*Answered by* 117]

My dear Sir                                    London 26ᵗʰ Aug. 1815

26 Aug. 1815       I am just going to leave London for Gatcomb Park, and I have this instant been informed by my brother Ralph Ricardo that he intends visiting Paris next week in company with Mr. George Basevi,[2] brother to the Mr. Basevi you have lately seen.[3] I am afraid that you may think me troublesome, but I could not refuse to give them this letter of introduction to you, as it is of considerable advantage to a stranger to be known to some respectable person when he visits a foreign country. If I am presuming too much it is your fault, your kind letter,[4] and flattering manner to me whilst in this country have added to my natural vanity.

I am Dear Sir with great esteem

Your's very truly

DAVID RICARDO

## 109. MILL TO RICARDO[5]

[*Answered by* 114]

My dear Sir                          Ford Abbey  Chard  Augᵗ 23ᵈ 1815

23 Aug. 1815       It appears to me to be high time that I were hearing something of the history of all of you. I know not how long,

[1] MS in Moscow Historical Museum. (In the collection of autographs formerly of Count Orlov Davidov, Russian Ambassador to England, who purchased it at a London auction in 1868. See *Daily Worker*, 27 April 1934.) I am indebted to R. Page Arnot for a photostat.

The contents of the letter suggest that it was addressed to Say;

cp. also letter 117 (postscript) and letter 135.
[2] George Basevi, junr. (1794–1845), the architect, son of Ricardo's friend of the same name.
[3] N. Basevi; see above, p. 245.
[4] Letter 106.
[5] Addressed: 'David Ricardo Esq / Gatcomb Park / Mincing Hampton / Gloucester Shire'.—MS in *R.P.* (Recᵈ 26 Aug.; see reply.)

however, I might wait for such a thing, before you would give it to a body of your own accord. For this, as for I doubt not many other sins, you have much need of repentance and amendment of life.

Of intelligence respecting you I have not had a syllable, since the day of dining last at Chingford,[1] where we wanted only your presence and that of your ladies, could that have been obtained, to have rendered the enjoyment complete. Mr. Bentham was highly delighted with both ladies and gentlemen, at that same place of abode; and I should have had a poor opinion of his taste, if he had not. It is not every day in this world of ours that you meet with as many people by whom you are impressed with an immediate conviction that they have some of the highest claims to your love; and who have so much of the art of compelling you to bestow it upon them. Well then, since that day, I know any thing of you by guess merely. I conclude that you remained at least a month longer in town; and that you employed it in making great quantities of money; and that you are now—Bless us all! no body can tell *how* rich!

Well, this much I hope from it, as you have now made quite as much money for all your family, as will be conducive to their happiness, which after all is a better thing than superiority, that, resting contented with your acquisitions of that description, you will now have leisure for other pursuits. That you will devote yourself to them, in that case, with a calm but vigorous perseverance, I have no doubt; for that is part of your nature. I should advise you to do so, if I had nothing in view but to promote the happiness of a friend; even if I had no hopes of your gaining any illustration to your name, and sharing in the dignity which does attend

[1] Probably at Chingford Hatch, the residence of Ricardo's brother Ralph.

23 Aug. 1815 upon the reputation for talents, and profound knowledge of an important subject. When I am satisfied, however, that you can not only acquire that reputation, but that you can very greatly improve a science on which the progress of human happiness to a singular degree depends; in fact that you can improve so important a science far more than any other man who is devoting his attention to it, or likely to do so, for Lord knows how many years—my friendship for you, for mankind, and for science, all prompt me to give you no rest, till you are plunged over head and ears in political economy.

I have other projects upon you, however, besides. You now can have no excuse for not going into parliament, and doing what you can to improve that most imperfect instrument of government. On all subjects of political economy, you will have no match; and you express yourself on those subjects so correctly, and so clearly, that in a short time you would be a very instructive, and a very impressive speaker. Of the innumerable ways in which the parliament, as at present constituted, is an instrument of misgovernment, you have already no little knowledge; and as soon as you have more leisure for reading, or rather for meditation, the discovery will pour in upon you every day. There is not much difficulty in finding out the principles on which alone good government must of necessity depend; and when all this is as clearly in that head of yours, as that head knows how to put it, the utility in parliament, of even you, in spite of all your modesty, would be very great. You would be thoroughly honest; nothing would you do but what you purely and genuinely thought right. Upon my life, I question, (such is the manner in which improper motives are ensured in the bosoms of members of parliament, by the manner in which that assembly is constituted), I do question whether another

man would be found in it, not ready to sell his country—
some of them to a greater, some of them to a less extent—
and almost all of them would stop, at a certain stage of
treachery—but not a man is there I fear in that house, who
would not compromise the good of his country in many, and
these far from trifling particulars, to gain the favour of a
ministry, of a party, or if despising the favour of ministers
and parties, to push some other personal end. That many of
them have sets of opinions conformable with their practice,
I admit; which gives them an air of sincerity: but it is an
easy thing to contract opinions which favour ones corrupt
inclinations. When the man who is hunting after a share in
the plunder of the people, adopts a set of opinions calculated
to recommend him to those in whose hands is the division of
the spoil, opinions the fruit of which would be to exclude
good government, that is human happiness, from the face of
the earth, I may not doubt the reality of his belief, but I well
know from what fountain it is derived. The wish in most
minds goes three parts in four to the procreation of the belief.
It is curious to trace, even in those who seem to be the
farthest removed from the hope of directly sharing in the
plunder, by what secret links the opinions which favour misgovernment are really and in fact connected with the feelings
of the plunderers; even by vain imitation; an idea that it
gives them an aristocratical air, where there is not a stronger
bond of connection—but in truth I have very seldom,
indeed, found in real life, any man a friend to bad principles
of government, who did not some way or another foster the
idea of deriving advantage from them. Even when education
has produced all its effects, it requires some association or
another with ideas of interest to make any man a convert to
doctrines which would render the whole of the human race
for ever slaves, for the benefit of a few. Yet these are the

23 Aug. 1815 doctrines which more than 99 in 100 of all the rich and great men in England perpetually preach: to such a degree by the operation of the bad principles of our government, are the intellectual and moral parts of the mind among the leading orders corrupted and depraved.

But, so, ho! who thought of this ebullition, about good government and bad government; about good national principles and bad national principles? I have left myself hardly any room to give you any of my own history. Happily it may be all given in a line—that we arrived here I fancy two months ago, or rather more—and that one day has passed almost exactly like another, all the time. We have had but few people with us. And the time has passed in a succession of study and exercise, the young as actively employed as the old. With best regards to all, and great desire to hear of all your doings believe yours,

J. MILL

## 110. MALTHUS TO RICARDO[1]

*[Reply to 103.—Answered by 116]*

E I Coll August 26th 1815

My dear Sir

26 Aug. 1815    I called at your house in Brook Street as I passed thro Town,[2] and was sorry to find that you had left it the day before. Our vacation is so early that I fear we shall not easily catch you at Gatcomb; but we will still hope for better success at some future time, when the war is over, and you are not detained in Town by so tremendous a loan. I don't wonder that the business relating to it pursued you even into

---

[1] Addressed: 'D. Ricardo Esqr. / Gatcomb Park. / Minching Hampton. / Gloucestershire'.
MS in *R.P.*

[2] On 25 July; cp. above, pp. 235 and 239.

the country. As it is now over, however, what say you to reviewing Mr. Say. I know he will be disappointed if he does not get a place in the Edinburgh and unless you do it I fear it will not be done.[1]

I am quite concerned to hear that David's health has been in so uncomfortable a state. Whishaw was here last saturday and told me that you had consulted him about a Tutor. I am very glad to find that you have got one that is likely to suit you.

I hear there is great scarcity of money in Town and the stocks seem to shew it. With Bonaparte at S$^t$ Helena I think they ought to be higher, but I suppose people are of opinion that there is no prospect of a speedy and satisfactory settlment of affairs in France—indeed it is very difficult to see how the matter can be arranged so as to produce the desireable object of peace and quiet. I fear it must be allowed that we have not kept our pledge, and that we are in the most direct manner interfering in the domestic concerns of France.

I do not, I confess, see how it is possible to resist the conclusion, that, if the nominal price of your corn and labour be double that of surrounding nations, in every million's worth of goods you exchange, or every million of subsidy you grant, you are able to command twice as much foreign labour, as if your corn and labour were of the same price with your neighbour's. But of course this state of things is not affected by the mere difficulty of producing corn. I do not indeed see how it is possible that the necessity of much more labour in the production of corn can ever have the effect of filling a country with the precious metals, and of enabling it to circulate all its commodities at a high price. A high permanent price of corn and labour *compared with other countries*, can only be caused in my opinion by great facility

[1] Say's books were not reviewed.

26 Aug. 1815 of production in manufactures, or in some peculiar natural products, and is therefore really the consequence of facility, rather than of difficulty of production. Without some such peculiar advantages, difficulty of production, or taxes on labour, would not permanently raise prices, relatively to other countries. In our own case, I conceive that the restrictions upon importation have increased in a slight, but only in a slight degree the difficulty of producing corn, while by preventing the home competition from lowering to a very much greater extent the prices of our exportable commodities, it has rendered our manufacturing labour vastly more productive than it would have been otherwise, and greatly overbalanced the trifling disadvantage that has been felt in a very slight increase of the difficulty of raising corn. You see therefore that I attribute the power of granting subsidies in this [case]¹ to a general *facility* rather than difficulty of production; and I am very far from agreeing with you in thinking, that high relative prices, with regard to other countries arise solely from the real difficulty of production. They may indeed, and do arise from the high price of the materials of capital, but by no means always from the greater quantity of labour required. In a country without land what determines the profits of stock. The bell rings

truly Yours

in great haste

T R MALTHUS.

¹ Omitted in MS.

## III. GRENFELL TO RICARDO[1]

Taplow House
My dear Sir                                   August 27: 1815

I dictated a Letter to you on Friday[2] in great haste   27 Aug. 1815
whilst I was preparing to leave Town and arranging my
Papers for that purpose. I had not time to read over what
was written; you will therefore have the goodness to excuse
any inaccuracy resulting from a hasty dictation—

I now send you herewith four Parliamentary Papers,
containing much useful information and detail on the subject
of the Bank of England—the Principles which apply to the
Deposits of Public Money there, the Charter &c &c[3]—As
these are Parliamentary Papers my Privilege enables me to
Frank them to you, whatever their Weight may be; and
when you have perused them, you will have the goodness
to return them to me in the same manner, leaving both Ends
of the Cover open and writing "Parliamentary proceedings" on the address.—I could wish to have these Papers
returned to me by the middle of September, if possible: they
are valuable to me, as I have no Duplicates of them.

I am My dear Sir   Very sincerely yours
PASCOE GRENFELL.

Be so good as to acknowledge the Receipt of these Papers.

David Ricardo Esq[r]

P:S: I also send herewith under 3 Covers some observations of my own which I drew up for the purpose of explaining

---

[1] MS in *R.P.*—Dictated; only
the signature, the line that follows
it, and the last two lines of the
postscript are in Grenfell's hand.
[2] Letter 113 of Friday 25 August,
*below*, p. 260.
[3] A great number of accounts relating to the Bank of England,
including accounts of public balances in the hands of the Bank,
were moved for by Grenfell and
ordered to be printed by the
House of Commons in May and
June 1815. (See *Parliamentary
Papers*, 1814–15, vol. x.)

27 Aug. 1815  to some Friends of mine in Parliament, the Case of the Bank
with reference to the Stamp Duties. These Papers will explain
themselves. When I stated in the House the Facts which you
will find in No 1:, Mr. Sam Thornton the Bank Director,
(whose Memory does not appear to be a very correct one)
boldly asserted that when the composition for Stamps was
made with Mr. Pitt in 1799, it was understood, distinctly,
that the Bank were *not* to pay an equivalent for the Stamp
Duties on their circulation, and that in fact they enjoyed a
Bonus on that occasion.[1] I had no means at the moment of
contradicting Mr. Thornton and indeed was impressed with
a Notion, that he would not have advanced such a fact but
upon some foundation. Upon reference however to Parliamentary Documents, and other Materials, a few days afterwards, I discovered that so far from any Bonus having been
given to the Bank by Mr. Pitt in 1799, the £20,000 then fixed
as the Composition for the Stamp Duty on Notes above 40
Shillings greatly exceeded what the Duties would actually
have amounted to, on *the circulation* of Notes of that description at that Period; and to prove this I drew up the
observations in Paper No 2: I also took the first opportunity
of correcting Mr. Thorntons mis-statement from my Place
in the House, and in Mr. Thorntons presence: and he gave
a very lame explanation of the mistake he had made in his
former statement[2]—

    Be so good also to return these Papers to me—Excuse my
using an Amanuensis—Writing is a painful Operation to
me—

:P G:

[1] Debate on the Stamp Duties
Bill, 27 June 1815. (*Hansard*,
XXXI, 1012–13.)

[2] In the same debate, 29 June
1815. (*Hansard*, XXXI, 1057–8,
1060.)

## 112. GRENFELL TO RICARDO[1]

[*Fragment*]

[*ca.* 29 Aug. 1815]

[...] their *Circulation*—A private Banker may issue £50000  29 Aug. 1815
(and of course must pay for Stamps to this amount) whereas
perhaps his permanent Average Circulation may not be
more than 40,000.

' I sent my letter of Friday last[2] with a printed Return of
Notes in Circulation, to your House in Brook Street—where
I suppose it now may be.

I am my dear Sir<br>
Very truly Yours<br>
PASCOE GRENFELL.

David Ricardo Esq

The Bank as you may imagine were not very forward in
yielding to my Demands for Papers on the subject of their
Issues of Notes—*nor very active* in producing them when
ordered—The enclosed Paper on their Circulation of Bank
Post Bills was presented *after* the discussion on the Stamp
Bill had terminated—and has been printed since the Close
of the Session[3]—

[1] MS in *R.P.*—The last sheet only is preserved; paper water-marked 1814. For dating cp. the next footnote and the opening of letter 115 from which it appears that Ricardo replied on 2 September.

[2] Letter 113 of Friday 25 August, *below*, p. 260.

[3] 'An Account of the Amount of Bank Post Bills in Circulation, on the 1st of July 1814...', ordered by the House of Commons to be printed, 11 July 1815. (*Parliamentary Papers*, 1814–15 vol. x.)

## 113 GRENFELL TO RICARDO[1]

My dear Sir, Spring Garden 25<sup>th</sup> August 1815

25 Aug. 1815     I have desired my Bookseller Mr. Bagster to send you Allardyce,[2] which he thinks he shall be able to do in the course of this day in which Case you will have the goodness to return me my Book, but if he should fail herein, you will take mine out of Town with you—Yours will be sent to me by Bagster, and we may exchange them the first time you come to Town again, there being some references in pencil in the beginning of my Book, which would make me prefer it to another Copy—

I inclose one of my Bank Papers, which I moved for, for the purpose of calculating what the Bank would have had to pay for Stamps on their Circulation of Notes last Year, supposing them to have used Stamps[3]—The Calculation upon which I founded this paper, is amongst my Papers at Taplow, from whence I will send you a Copy of it.—The Result upon Arithmetical Proof shewed that supposing Bank Notes to last three Years, the Bank ought to have paid for Stamps at the rate of their Circulation (not their issue for you will be aware of the difference between their issue and what may be called their permanent circulation) £80,879. –. –[4] exclusive altogether of the Stamp Duties on their Bank post

[1] MS in *R.P.*—Dictated; only the signature is in Grenfell's hand.
    This letter, written while Ricardo was on a visit to London (see the opening of Letter 108), must have reached his house in Brook Street after he had left for Gatcomb, and it appears to have been still there on 29 August (see Grenfell's letters of 27 and 29 August, above, pp. 257 and 259).
[2] See above, p. 242.

[3] Probably 'An Account of the Amount of Bank Notes in Circulation on the 1st and 15th days of each Month, from the 1st of June 1814 to the 15th of May 1815 inclusive; distinguishing the Amount of Notes under the following Classes...', ordered by the House of Commons to be printed, 7 June 1815. (*Parliamentary Papers*, 1814–15, vol. x.)
[4] Replaces '£99,572. 0. 0'.

Bills, of which I had no distinct account,[1] when I formed   25 Aug. 1815
this Calculation, instead of which they paid no more than
£42,000.

I also calculated upon the best parliamentary Documents,
produced upon the Subject, that from the Year 1799 to 1815
the amount of Stamp Duty upon the Bank circulation would
have been ... ... ... ... ... ... ...   £1,076,183
whereas upon the several stipulated composi-
tions, they actually paid during that period no
more than ... ... ... ... ... ... ...       542,000
                        the difference being   £534,183
was lost to the Public and gained to the Bank in consequence
of the injudicious Bargains made with them by Lord Sid-
mouth in 1804, and by Mr. Percival in 1808, upon this
subject, and which System would no doubt have been continued, but for the discussions which took place in the House
of Commons in the last sessions hereon; notwithstanding
what the Bank directors and the Chancellor of the Exchequer
have said to the contrary since the discussion took place.[2]

(Just leaving Town)   I am My dear Sir,
                    very truly Yours
                    PASCOE GRENFELL.


### 114. RICARDO TO MILL[3]
[*Reply to* 109.—*Answered by* 134]

                                      Gatcomb Park
My dear Sir                          30th Aug 1815

You would soon have had a history from me of our   30 Aug. 1815
proceedings if I had not received your letter, which I found

---

[1] Cp. letter 112, postscript.
[2] On the question of Stamp
Duties, see above, IV, 94–5.

[3] Addressed: 'James Mill Esqr /
Ford Abbey / Chard / Somersetshire'. MS in Mill-Ricardo papers.

30 Aug. 1815 here on my return from London,[1] where I was obliged to go for 3 or 4 days. I began indeed to think that there was no other way of obtaining some account of you but by writing first. I thought it probable that you had quite determined that I should, this time, make the first move; and I did not in my heart blame you for your determination, because you had a clear right to expect it of me. Disposed, as all men are, to view my own omissions in a favourable light, I consider my disinclination to write rather as a misfortune which deserves your pity, than one amongst the number of my sins which calls for repentance. If you do not so regard it I am sorry for your want of charity.

You are right in some part of your conclusions respecting our movements after you quitted London. We remained there at least a month after you. I was employed, very busily employed during that month in making money, but not in such quantities as you seem to intimate, and though sufficiently rich to satisfy all my desires, and the reasonable desires of all those about me, I am not "Bless me how rich!!" On that plea then I have no excuse for not devoting my time to those pursuits in which you think by perseverance I should succeed in making myself a name in the world. Whether it be art in you, knowing how effectual the desire of distinction is in calling forth exertion and talent, to persuade me that I have certain capabilities, in order by the reward which you display in such glowing colours, and to which I am feelingly alive, to stimulate me to exertion and put my power to the test,—or whether you are really satisfied that I have those capabilities I am not quite sure,—but of this I am certain that if the latter is your opinion you are completely deceived. If you could witness the small progress which I make in writing on the subject which I have most considered you

[1] On 26 August; see letter 108.

would be convinced of your error, and as my friend would
recommend to me to be satisfied with a private station, and
not by attempts which are beyond my strength court unhap-
piness and disappointment. The experiment shall however
be tried,—I will devote as much time as I can to think and
write on my favorite subject,—I will give myself a chance
for success and at any rate the employment itself will, if
nothing else comes of it, have afforded me instruction and
amusement. I find, that at this season of the year, the visits
of friends make great encroachments on my time; and the
temptation of being out in the air in fine weather frequently
draws me from my books, but with proper management I
shall no doubt find leisure for all these objects. Your other
project—your parliamentary scheme is above all others unfit
for me,—my inclination does not in the least point that way.
Speak indeed! I could not, I am sure, utter three sentences
coherently, and if I attempted it should probably from vexa-
tion and disappointment turn my back on the house for ever.
Your favourable opinion of my honesty is in striking contrast with your opinion of the honesty of those who at
present constitute the house of Commons. On this subject
you are, as I have often thought you unjustly severe. That
there are many venal men in Parliament who get there with
no other view but to forward their own personal ends, no
one can doubt,—but as a body they have more virtue than
you are willing to give them credit for. No other assembly
is perhaps so much under the influence of public opinion
which you will allow is a great security for virtue. The bias
of private interest will always have its effect. No human
assembly can I think be constituted where its voice will not
be heard. Our efforts should therefore be directed so to
constitute Parliament that no particular interest should be
predominant, or rather that no man could better serve him-

self, or better promote his own happiness than by serving the public. Whether this be attainable I have great doubts, yet I am convinced if any thing will tend to produce so desirable an end, it is general information. Where all men are enlightened as to what their own happiness and welfare consists in they will be more likely to enter into a judicious compromise by which each in giving up a little will best secure to himself the greatest attainable sum of good.

I am very much pleased that my brothers and sisters made so favourable an impression on Mr. Bentham's mind. You, I knew before, were very partial to them. Their union, and affection for each other, I delight to contemplate, and often congratulate myself that I am one amongst them loving and I hope beloved by them. I know no people less selfish— none more disposed to make sacrifices for their mutual comfort. If you witnessed the sufferings of my poor sister Sally your heart would be filled with commisseration. If you saw the daily attention of my brothers and sisters to her your sympathy would be still further excited, but if you beheld the absolute devotion of all my sister Esther's time, amusements and recreations to the one object of lightening Sally's afflictions admiration would be added to your other feelings. Perhaps it is hardly pardonable to pronounce so warm a panegyric on those so nearly related to me but I remember Mr. Bentham's and your argument that nothing should be suppressed which tends to elucidate the history of the human mind and in this instance it appears under a pleasing form.

Do you and Mr. Bentham mean to return my visit here this year? I have few temptations to offer you, I can only engage for a hearty welcome and for my best endeavors to make your stay agreeable.

Have you seen Mr. Say's Catéchisme D'Economie Politique? He sent it to me by young Basevi who saw him in

Paris. I like it very much though he has not altered the 30 Aug. 1815
definitions to which you and I objected last year. I hope
Mrs. Mill is well,—pray remember me most kindly to her.

Y$^{rs}$ ever

DAVID RICARDO


## 115. GRENFELL TO RICARDO[1]

Spring Garden Friday 8 Sept: 1815

My dear Sir

    I have received your Letter of the 2$^d$ and all my Papers 8 Sept. 1815
safely returned. I find too my Allardyce *here*—And my
Bookseller has, after much difficulty, he says, found another
Copy for you—which he has sent to me—and which I have
dispatched to your House in Town—from whence you may
order it into the Country, if you desire to have it before you
come to Town.

    The old Duty on £1– Notes was 4$^d$ and on £2 Notes—8$^d$
The new Duty  –          –   5   –     –        10
in other words the old Duty was at the rate of 4$^d$ in the £1–
           the new  –   –   at the rate of 5$^d$   –   –

    The next Class comprizes Notes *above* £2—and not
exceeding *£5.* and the old Duty hereon was 1/– the
new 1/3.

    Notes therefore of £3– or £4– would be subject to the
same Stamp Duty as Notes of £5– that is 1/ for *old*—1/3 for
new Duty—But in point of Fact neither the Bank of Eng.
nor private Bankers (so far [as][2] I have been informed) have
ever issued Notes of £3– or of £4–

    If £20000 (the Composition of 1799 for Notes *above* £2)
was admitted as a fair and just equivalent for *Notes of this
Class* upon the *then* Circulation, the Duty of 1804 being

---

[1] MS in *R.P.*                    [2] Omitted in MS.

8 Sept. 1815 50 p Ct would necessarily have carried that Composition to £30,000—And again the Duty of 1808 being 33 p Cᵗ would have carried £30000– to £40,000.—even supposing the Circulation of Notes *of this Class* not to have increased— (*an Increase however of some millions took place in point of Fact*)—Observe this applies *only* to Notes of £5– and upwards—and excludes all Duty on Notes under £5–

Instead however of the Bank paying £40000—for their Notes of £5 and upwards—and a fair Composition for Notes of the Class under £5 (*which Class is more productive of Duty than all the other Classes together*) they have paid since 1808 Only *£42000* for *all* their Notes—!

By this shameful neglect on the part of Government—in 1804—and 1808—the public Revenue has suffered and the Bank pocketted £535.000!

The Composition fixed by the Act of last Session[1] is upon this principle—that upon the Average Circulation of *three* preceding years, they are to pay at the rate of *£3500 ℔ million* —without reference to the Classes or Value of the Notes of which that aggregate Circulation may consist. The Bank produced therefore during the Discussion, the enclosed Account[2]—making an average of 25.102.600. and upon this average they will pay this year *about* £87,500.

I contended that they ought to pay upon their average *Circulation* of the last Year—which would have made the Composition £99572—*exclusive* of their Bank Post Bills, but I was beat (for I divided the House upon it) in a very thin House, by a small Majority.[3]

[1] The Stamp Duties Act of 1815 (55 Geo. III, c. 184).
[2] 'An Account of the Average Amount of Bank Notes in Circulation, including Bank Post Bills; for the Three Years ending the 5th April 1808, and for the Three Years ending the 5th April 1815'; ordered by the House of Commons to be printed, 13 June 1815. (*Parliamentary Papers*, 1814–15, vol. x.)
[3] See debate on 29 June 1815, in *Hansard*, XXXI, 1057ff.

Next year the average will be taken upon 3 Years including *this* Year, and the Duty will of course vary annually [1]—
Have I made the subject intelligible to you?

I am ever My dear Sir

Most truly Yours

PASCOE GRENFELL.

David Ricardo Esq


## 116. RICARDO TO MALTHUS[2]

[*Reply to* 110.—*Answered by* 126]

My dear Sir        Gatcomb Park 10 Sep.[r] 1815

Nothing could be more unlucky than our missing each
other as we did this year. I should think there would be no
obstacle to our leaving town a little earlier next year, when I
hope we shall at length have the pleasure of seeing Mrs.
Malthus and you at Gatcomb.—

It is the general remark in our part of the country that a
finer season was never remembered. The rain, of which we
have certainly had a deficiency, has generally come at night,
and the days which have followed have been beautiful. The
temptation to enjoy it has been so great that I have been incessantly out with someone or other of my friends, who have
been staying with me,—either riding or walking—which
makes such inroads on my time that I find I have much less
leisure here for reading and study than I have in London.

Before I came here I often saw Mr. Grenfell who is very
warm on the subject of the Bank, and the advantageous bargains which it has always made with Government, as well

---

[1] Ricardo uses the last three paragraphs in *Economical Currency*, above, IV, 95.
[2] Addressed: 'The Rev.[d] T. R

Malthus / East India College / Hertford'.
MS at Albury.—*Letters to Malthus*, XXXV.

10 Sept. 1815 for the management of the National Debt,—the composition which it has hitherto paid for stamps, as for the compensation which Government has received in the way of Loan for the enormous average deposits left with the Bank. I am quite of his opinion, and indeed I go much further. I think the Bank an unnecessary establishment getting rich by those profits which fairly belong to the public. I cannot help considering the issuing of paper money as a privilege which belongs exclusively to the state.—I regard it as a sort of seignorage, and I am convinced, if the principles of currency were rightly understood, that Commissioners might be appointed independent of all ministerial controul who should be the sole issuers of paper money,—by which I think a profit of from two to three millions might be secured to the public, at the same time that we should be protected from the abuses of the country Banks, who are the cause of much mischief all over the Kingdom. These Commissioners should also have the management of the public debt, and should act as Bankers to all the different public departments. They might invest the 11 millions which is the average of public deposits in Exchequer Bills, a part of which might be sold whenever occasion required. This, of course (at least all of it) could not be effected till the expiration of the Bank Charter in 1833, but it is never too soon to give due consideration to important principles, which might be recognized tho' not yet acted on. In looking over the papers which have from time to time been laid before Parliament I think it might clearly be proved that the profits of the Bank have been enormous,—I should think they must have a hoard nearly equal to their Capital. By their Charter they are bound to make an annual division of their profits, and to lay a statement of their accounts before the Proprietors,—but they appear to set all law at defiance. I always enjoy any attack

upon the Bank and if I had sufficient courage I would be a party to it.[1]

Though I have been thinking on this subject lately I am not less interested about our old subject,—of the advantages or disadvantages of high prices for raw produce. If I agreed with Mr. Torrens[2] that such high prices were accompanied with a rise in the prices of commodities,—and if I thought that such rise would not preclude the usual exchanges with foreign countries, I should of course agree with you that with such general high prices we should command a greater quantity of foreign commodities in exchange for a given quantity of ours,—but I cannot admit in the first place that commodities would rise because corn rose, and secondly if they did so rise there are but very few which we could sell in equal quantity at the advanced price to foreigners, and if we sold less to them we could buy less of them and thus would our general commerce suffer. I can see great advantages attending low general prices but none in high prices. On this subject we are not likely to agree.

I hope you are diligently employed, and that early in the year we shall see something new from your pen. I have some curiosity to see a pamphlet just advertised, in the title page of which your name is mentioned.[3]

Ever Y<sup>rs</sup>

DAVID RICARDO

Kind regards to Mrs. Malthus.

Have you seen Mons<sup>r</sup> Say's Catéchisme D'Economie Politique? He has softened but not removed the objectionable definitions.

---

[1] See his speech at the Bank Court, 21 Dec. 1815, below, p. 335, and above, V, 463.
[2] *Essay on the External Corn Trade*, 1815, p. 81.

[3] *An Address to the Nation on the Relative Importance of Agriculture and Manufactures, and the Means of Advancing them both to the Highest Degree of Improvement of which*

## 117. SAY TO RICARDO[1]

[*Reply to* 107 & 108]

10 Sept. 1815    J'ai reçu, Monsieur, la lettre que vous avez chargé Messieurs Stoke et Baily[2] de me remettre et j'y ai trouvé avec grand plaisir des détails et des discussions d'Economie politique qui me sont toujours agréables et profitables lorsqu'elles me viennent de votre part. Je ne sais réellement pas où j'avais la tête quand je vous ai ecrit par Mr. Basevi, puisque je ne vous ai point parlé de votre *Essay on the influence of a low price of corn* etc.—J'ai bien reçu dans le tems cet interessant opuscule, et je l'ai lu avec tant de fruit que je l'ai mis à contribution et l'ai cité dans la troisième édition que je prépare de mon Traité d'Economie politique.[3] Je dois vous dire en attendant que je partage votre opinion dans tous les principes que vous établissez, et que j'ai été fort aise de trouver de nouveaux et solides argumens en faveur de la liberté du commerce. Je pense bien, comme M. Mill, que si vous aviez developé chaque proposition abstraite, par quelques applications et par des exemples, vous auriez été plus facilement entendu. Mais je ne conçois pas que vous puissiez croire cette tâche au dessus de vos forces, puisque ce que vous avez fait, j'entends l'établissement des principes, etait précisément ce qu'il y avait de plus difficile et ce qui exigeait la plus grande exertion de ce que vous me permettrez d'appeler un génie très profond.

*they are capable; together with Remarks on the Doctrines lately advanced by Mr. Malthus, on the Nature of Rent, and the Relation it has to the Amount of National Income...*, By the Author of *Observations on the National Debt, Thoughts on Peace...*, &c. &c., London, Longman, 1815. Advertised in the *Morning Chronicle* of 6 September.

[1] MS in *R.P.*—See note at the end of this letter.
[2] Charles Stokes and Francis Baily, stockbrokers: cp. below, VII, 14.
[3] Vol. I, p. 264 of the 3rd ed. (not published till 1817).

Apres vous avoir dit que je partage votre opinion, je vous dirai que vous partagez la mienne, nonobstant les observations que vous me faites sur le mot *Valeur* dans mon *Catéchisme*. Vous avez été fondé à croire que je regardais l'*Utilité* (c'est à dire la faculté de pouvoir servir) comme l'unique fondement de la *valeur des choses* parce qu'afin de ne pas brouiller l'esprit des commençans, je n'ai pas dit tout de suite les restrictions qu'il faut mettre à cette proposition; mais je pose les restrictions un peu plus loin, page 31 et 33. Il resulte du tout que l'*utilité* n'est pas l'*unique* mais la *premiere* cause de la valeur; car enfin une chose qui ne serait d'aucun usage ne serait nullement demandée, on n'y mettrait point de prix, elle n'aurait point de valeur. Mais il faut que le prix, que son utilité détermine les gens à y mettre, suffise pour payer ses frais de production (what you call *the difficulty of its production*) et c'est ce qui fait que son prix ne peut pas tomber au dessous de ce taux. Je dis donc, comme vous, que les frais de production d'une chose, déterminent la plus basse limite de son prix; mais ils ne sont pas la cause premiere du prix qu'on en offre.

Il me semble qu'il n'y a rien là de contraire à ce que vous etablissez.

Quant à l'observation que vous me faites sur la page 95, je crains de n'avoir pas été suffisamment compris. Vous dites: *He may only wish to consume bread and water...he cannot be so rich as his neighbour who has abundance of valuables which he can exchange for all the luxuries of life.* Mais je prétends dire que l'on serait au comble de la richesse, quelque peu de valeur qu'on possedât, si l'on pouvait se procurer pour rien, non seulement du pain et de l'eau, mais *tout ce que l'on voudrait consommer*, EVEN THE LUXURIES OF LIFE. Et la proposition ne me semble pas susceptible d'etre niée.

Je ne dis pas comme Epictète que la richesse est d'autant

10 Sept. 1815 plus grande que les desirs sont plus moderés, mais d'autant plus grande que les choses qu'*on veut avoir sont moins chères.*

En un mot toute valeur est relative, et la richesse n'etant que de la valeur, est relative aussi.

A l'égard de l'appréciation par le moyen d'un inventaire des biens qu'on possède, je vous dirai que je n'oblige pas qu'on se serve pour cette appréciation d'une marchandise plutôt que d'une autre, de la monnaie, ou du papier-monnaie, plutôt que du blé. Pour comparer sa fortune de l'année derniere, avec sa fortune de l'année presente, il vaut mieux les évaluer en une marchandise qui varie peu en valeur d'une année à l'autre, comme l'argent, plutot qu'en une marchandise qui peut varier beaucoup, comme le papier-monnaye. Un inventaire n'est proprement que la réduction en une valeur homogène d'un grand nombre de valeurs de nature diverse. En disant: *The increase of capital is to be ascertained only by the power of employing more industry,* c'est préferer la mesure des valeurs proposée par Smith, c'est à dire la valeur du travail. Le travail est une marchandise du prix de laquelle on peut se servir, si l'on veut, pour faire une évaluation; mais je crois ce prix plus variable que celui de l'argent, plus difficile a etablir clairement et d'un emploi plus pénible.

Voila, Monsieur et respectable ami, mes observations sur vos observations. Elles m'ont obligé à remanier le sujet, et quand je réimprimerai mon catéchisme, j'aurai soin de mettre plus de clarté aux endroits que vous m'indiquez. Que si vous y trouvez encore bien des passages criticables, accordez-moi votre indulgence en songeant à la quantité d'idées justes encore entierement ignorées ou combattues, qu'il peut répandre, et tout le bien qui resulterait pour l'humanité de la diffusion de ces lumieres, de ce seul corollaire qui resulte de nos principes, que chaque nation est interessée à la prosperité de toutes les autres.

Agréez, Monsieur, mes salutations bien sincères et 10 Sept. 1815 l'assurance de mon inviolable attachement

J. B. SAY

Comme je finissais cette lettre, j'ai vu entrer chez moi Mr. votre frere.[1] Je ferai ce qui dépendra de moi pour lui etre utile en ce pays-ci.

Paris 10 septembre 1815.

David Ricardo Esq$^{re}$

[The above letter has not been published before. Another reply to Ricardo's letter 107, however, was published in Say's *Mélanges*, pp. 97–100 and *Œuvres diverses*, pp. 411–13, and is reprinted below; Say's editors must have found it among his papers, but the MS is no longer extant. It may be conjectured that Say, forgetting that he had already replied on 10 September, wrote the second letter and, when he discovered his error (cp. above, p. 246, n. 1), refrained from sending it.

SAY TO RICARDO

Paris, 2 décembre 1815.

Mon cher Monsieur,

Je me reproche de ne vous avoir pas répondu plus promptement. 2 Dec. 1815 Nous nous occupons heureusement, vous et moi, de choses de tous les temps, plutôt que de celles du moment actuel, qui ne sont pas gaies, malgré les fêtes que l'on donne pour faire croire aux peuples qu'ils sont heureux. En attendant, ils sont dépouillés par leurs amis et par leurs ennemis; les uns les tourmentent par leur ambition; les autres, par leurs vengeances; et les lumières, aussi bien que le courage civil, leur manquent pour résister à propos.

Le sujet des valeurs est, comme vous le dites, difficile et compliqué, et je suis un peu confus qu'avec la prétention que j'ai eue de me mettre à la portée des esprits les plus ordinaires, je ne sois pas entièrement compris des hommes les plus distingués. Il faut que je me sois bien mal expliqué, puisque vous m'accusez d'avoir dit que l'utilité était la mesure de la valeur; tandis que je croyais avoir toujours dit que la valeur que les hommes attachent à une chose est la mesure de l'utilité qu'ils trouvent en elle; et quand vous ajoutez: "Riches are valuable only as they can procure us enjoyments; and the man is most rich who has most valuables," vous tenez exactement le même langage que moi.

[1] Ralph Ricardo.

2 Dec. 1815  Je conviens de même, avec vous, que la valeur d'un produit ne peut pas baisser au-dessous de ce que coûtent les difficultés de sa production. Si les hommes estiment que son utilité vaut ce prix-là, ils le produisent; s'ils estiment que son utilité ne vaut pas ce prix-là, ils ne le produisent pas.

Je m'aperçois que je me suis encore mal exprimé dans un autre endroit (page 95), en disant que: "le comble de la richesse, quelque peu de valeurs qu'on possédât, serait de pouvoir se procurer pour rien tous les objets qu'on voudrait consommer." Je n'ai point voulu dire comme les stoïciens, et comme vous m'en accusez, qu'on est d'autant plus riche qu'on a moins de désirs, mais d'autant plus, qu'on peut acquérir à meilleur marché les choses qu'on désire, *quelles qu'elles soient*, c'est-à-dire des maisons, des domestiques, des chevaux, si on les désire; ce qui arriverait, en effet, dans la supposition où les difficultés des frais de production se réduiraient à peu de chose ou à rien. Cette supposition est inadmissible dans son excès, je le sais; mais, ce qui ne l'est pas, ce sont les différents degrés de bon marché (*cheapness*) qui s'éloignent ou se rapprochent plus ou moins du bon marché absolu.

Vous avez bien raison en disant qu'un manufacturier qui, pendant la dépréciation de votre papier-monnaie, aurait fait son inventaire en livres sterling, aurait pu croire son capital augmenté, tandis qu'en effet il aurait diminué. Il est bien évident que, lorsque j'ai dit que ce n'est que par un inventaire qu'on peut savoir si le capital qu'on a est accru ou diminué, c'était avec cette restriction nécessaire: *en supposant que la monnaie* (the currency) *qui sert à inventorier n'a pas changé de valeur*. Je sens maintenant la nécessité d'exprimer ce qui me paraissait évident, et j'aurai soin de l'exprimer dans les prochaines éditions de mon Catéchisme, si le public accueille ce petit ouvrage.

Que vous dirai-je à l'égard de votre polémique avec M. Malthus? Vous avez l'un et l'autre étudié la question *of rent and profits* sans doute beaucoup mieux que moi; et puis je vous confesse que ma façon d'envisager les profits, soit d'un capital, soit d'un fonds de terre, rend très difficile pour moi la tâche de débrouiller cette question. Je ne peux m'empêcher de faire entrer pour beaucoup, dans l'appréciation des profits, le talent, la capacité industrielle de celui qui fait valoir un terrain ou un capital; et je regarde comme comparativement peu important le profit propre, le profit inhérent à ces deux instruments. Au surplus, je dois me défier beaucoup de mon opinion, et je crains de l'énoncer à côté de la vôtre. Je me bornerai donc à souhaiter, avec M. Mill, que vous développiez vos idées dans un ouvrage *ad hoc*. J'y gagnerai, et le public aussi. Que j'envie votre sort de faire de l'économie politique

dans votre belle retraite de Gatcomb-Park! Je n'oublierai jamais les trop    2 Dec. 1815
courts moments que j'y ai passés, ni les charmes de votre conversation.

Agréez, mon cher Monsieur, les assurances de ma haute estime et de
mon sincère attachement,

J.-B. Say.]

## 118. GRENFELL TO RICARDO[1]

Spring Garden
20 Sept 1815

My dear Sir

    I have your Letter of the 17$^{th}$—I cannot now reply to   20 Sept. 1815
your Calculations—Where is the calculation of Mr. Morgan,[2]
as to the Cash and Bullion of the Bank in 1793 &c.?—No
doubt the Bank must have lost a large Sum, prior to their
Suspension of Cash payments in 1797, in the purchase of
Bullion, above the Mint price; but that loss had been in-
curred, when Parliament examined into their affairs in 97,
and when they reported a Surplus Capital of £3,826,890:
we are to consider therefore, what additions may have been
made to this Surplus, since the 25 February 1797, to which
period the Accounts laid before Parliament were made up.—
I do not believe there is any parliamentary account, that
shews in one view, what the Bank has received for managing
the public Debt in each Year, but you are no doubt aware
of the rate per Million charged on the existing Debt of each
Year, and the rate of allowance for each Loan and Lottery.—
The amount of Bank Notes in circulation since 1810, may
be found in any Collection of parliamentary documents.

    I do not recollect to have seen any return of public de-
posits for each Year between 1800 and 1807.

    The Income Tax was raised to 10 ℔ Cent in Mr. Fox's
Administration in 1806, before which I think it was 6$\frac{1}{4}$.—

---

[1] MS in *R.P.*—Dictated; only
the signature and the postscript
are in Grenfell's hand.

[2] On William Morgan and his
calculations see above, IV, 416.

20 Sept. 1815  I believe with you, that the "Old Proprietor"[1] has estimated the Expences of the Bank upon the whole, much too high, but Mr Thornton stated in the House of Commons that the number of their Clerks has increased to one thousand.[2] The £4000 for House Allowance has not been discontinued, and £1898 continues to be paid for the management of the South Sea Capital; at least Mr Mellish did not deny this, when I stated it in the House of Commons.[3]—The General Court "for considering a Dividend" is to be held to morrow.— Not having seen it advertised, I knew nothing of it till yesterday, when I heard it accidentally mentioned.—It is not my intention to be present, unless I should be called into the City upon other Business—I hear much discussion, however, is expected on the Subject of the Dividend.—Your Letter of Sunday[4] reached me this Morning from Taplow, as I have been in Town since Monday. I can only add by this post, that I am,

My dear Sir, very truly Yours.

PASCOE GRENFELL.

As I think it would be unadviseable for me to take any part in any discussion tomorrow on the subject of Dividend, it appears to me that I may as well not be there.

David Ricardo Esq[r]

[1] A series of letters over this signature was appearing in the press; they were afterwards collected in a pamphlet with the title *Letters addressed to the Proprietors of Bank Stock. By an Old Proprietor*, London, 1816. In one of his letters, which is dated 7 Sept. 1815, the Old Proprietor estimates the expenses of the Bank of England as follows: 'Salaries to 1000 Clerks £200,000, Property Duty, suppose £150,000, In Buildings, Salaries of Directors, Stationary, Porters, Coals, and all other expences of the establishment £150,000'.

[2] See Samuel Thornton's speech on Grenfell's Motion respecting the profits of the Bank of England, 13 June 1815, in *Hansard*, XXXI, 770.

[3] See Grenfell's speech on his own Motion respecting Balances in the hands of the Bank of England, 26 April 1815, in *Hansard*, XXX, 873 and cp. 875.

[4] 17 September.

## 119. GRENFELL TO RICARDO[1]

Spring Garden,
21 Sept.[r] 1815

My dear Sir

Being in the City this Morning, I attended the Bank 21 Sept. 1815
Court, which was very thin in numbers—Upon the motion
of a Dividend of 5 ℔ Cent for the half Year being proposed,
a young Man, Mr Bouverie,[2] the Son of the Earl of Radnor,
after referring to the Parliamentary Papers upon the subject,
(which he did in a way, that proved he understood little
about them, or indeed about the subject generally) moved
that instead of 5,—10 ℔ Cent should be the Dividend for the
half Year—Nobody seconded this Amendment, but a Mr
Terry, or Cherry,[3] who I understand is a great dealer in
Bank Stock, after complaining that no accounts were laid
before the Proprietors by the Directors, and expressing an
opinion, that a much larger dividend ought to be made,
concluded, by moving as an Amendment, that *Six* ℔ Cent,
should be substituted for *five*!—This Amendment was
seconded by Mr Bouverie, and upon a shew of hands *was
carried*, which put the Gentlemen behind the Bar in no little
dismay. They then discovered, however, that no increase of
Dividend could be made, but by a Ballot—If Mr Terry and
Mr Bouverie had had their wits about them, they would have
called for such Ballot, instead of which, a very desultory
conversation took place, during which, the Ballot seemed to
have been lost sight of altogether—The Governor then
again went back to the Vote of the 5 or 6 ℔ Cent, (a most
irregular proceeding I should conceive, as that point had
already been decided) and upon the number of hands being

[1] MS in *R.P.*—Dictated; only
the signature is Grenfell's.
[2] Philip Pleydell Bouverie (1788–
1872), brother of Lord Folkestone

and partner of Bouverie and An-
trobus, bankers in the Strand.
[3] Christopher Terry, a stockbroker.

21 Sept. 1815 even, twelve I think on each side, the Governor gave his casting vote, of course, in favor of his own Motion of 5 ℔ Cent! and declared the Business concluded! I never saw a Business more clumsily managed on the one side, or with so much informality on the other, as what passed this Morning. —I should think two thirds of those who were in the Court declined holding up their hands on either side, but I am sure any person at all conversant with the subject, and at all in the habit of public speaking would have carried the Court along with him, and left the Directors in a minority.—I determined before I entered the Room, to take no part whatever in any discussion that might arise, nor did I hold up my hand on either of the two occasions when the sense of the Court was taken; my feeling being, that until I have finished what I have undertaken in the House of Commons, it is best that I should abstain from taking any part at the Bank in a question respecting the rate of Dividend. I inclose a third Letter from "An Old Proprietor" which appeared in the Press this Morning.

I am, My dear Sir
very truly Yours
PASCOE GRENFELL

David Ricardo Esq

## 120. TROWER TO RICARDO[1]
[*Answered by* 136]

Unsted Wood—Godalming—
21. September 1815—
Dear Ricardo

21 Sept. 1815 When I cast my eye on the date of your letter[2] I feel ashamed it has remained so long unanswered. The fact is I

[1] Addressed: 'To/David Ricardo Esqr. / Gatcomb Park / Minchinhampton / Gloucestershire'.

MS in *R.P.*
[2] Ricardo's letter is wanting.

have had friends staying with me for some time past, and that circumstance always unsettles our regular habits. My wife's confinement too has contributed to the dissipation of my time. She has added a little girl to our family, and I am happy to say they are both quite well.

I am rejoiced to find, that the subject of Political Economy still occupies your thoughts, and should regret exceedingly if it were to give way to the humbler pursuits of farming, and planting. These do well enough to fill a vacant space, but have no pretensions to obtrude where weightier thoughts inhabit.—

Devoting, as you have done, so large a portion of your leisure hours, to this your favorite subject, it would be *unpardonable* with the encreased opportunity you now enjoy not to collect, condense, combine, and *embody* the substance of your former meditations. The difficulty of composing you speak of is common to all young authors, and is to be surmounted only by practice habit, and labor.—It has been felt, encountered and surmounted by an Addison and a Gibbon, and so it may be by a Ricardo—

I am desirous of knowing the remedy you have in view to obviate the evils arising from the too sudden fluctuations in the amount of the circulating medium. The Bank already possess the means if they knew how to use them rightly. That they have fattened too much at the expence of the public I admit, and that they should disgorge I heartily approve. But, I confess, I should view with great distrust and alarm so powerful an engine as the Bank direct placed in the hands of Government. The temptation to abuse it would be strong and constant, and the means easy—In the hands of the Bank this machine may be worked improperly nay mischievously, from ignorance, but there is little fear that it should be so from dishonesty.

21 Sept. 1815   What think you of the last number of the Edinburgh
Review. I was highly amused in hearing the circumstance
which occasioned its late appearance. It contained a long and
labored article written by S^r James Mackintosh, abusing the
confederacy against France most unmercifully, prognosti-
cating the utter ruin and disgrace of the Allies, and the
triumph of Bonaparte. This was ready printed, when lo! the
accounts of the victory of Waterloo arrived; and it became
necessary to suppress this article, and reprint the edition!

So much for these pseudo northern prophets from
Brougham to Mackintosh—This rejected Edition will form
a rare article in the libraries of Vertuosi!

I admire your ingenious defence of Bonaparte. "A man's
glory cannot be *effaced* by his subsequent faults." With
submission, I apprehend there is some sophistry in this.
Every *individual action* considered by itself, must stand or fall
upon its own merit, without any reference to circumstances
not necessarily connected with it. But a man's *character*, his
reputation, his renown, must be estimated upon a reference
to the *whole of his conduct*. It is not a single action, which
constitutes a man either virtuous or vicious. It is the *habit*
the practice of a man's life, which must stamp his character.
We must cast up the account of his good and bad qualities
and strike the balance. None are so base as not to evince
some momentary moments of virtue; and none, I fear, so
good as not to discover, on some occasions, slight stains of
vice—How then will Bonaparte stand the test of this strict
account—So far from not doing him justice, it appears to
me that the world are disposed to favor him too highly.
There is a sort of splendor that accompanies his exploits
which dazzles our eyes and renders us blind to his deformities
—Talent, great talent, he undoubtedly possesses, and that is
the divinity principally worshipped in this age of intellect.

I greatly doubt therefore whether the advocates of Bonaparte   21 Sept. 1815
will successfully appeal from the present times to posterity.

Pray make our united regards to Mrs. Ricardo and family,
and believe me

Yours very sincerely,<br>HUTCHES TROWER.

Vegitation with us is rapidly disappearing, and if the dry
weather continues much longer we shall be burnt to a cinder.


## 121. GRENFELL TO RICARDO[1]

Taplow House<br>September 24<sup>th</sup>. 1815

My dear Sir

    I have now to acknowledge your Letter of the 27<sup>th</sup> [2] and   24 Sept. 1815
am much gratified that you are occupied upon Bank Affairs
and I look forward with much interest to what you announce
to me by the Coach to Spring Garden. I send you herewith
Parliamentary Papers which may be of use to you in ascertaining the amount of Circulation for some Years past,
particularly that marked C: Page 6: in which you will find
the amount stated for every Year from 1761 to 1810.[3] Have
you got the Accounts since 1810? If not, I can furnish you
with them when I go to Town without giving you the
trouble of searching the Papers at the Institution.[4] In the
mean time you have from my Papers here D: A and B: the
circulation from April 1812 to February 1815: so that you
only now want the Account from 1810, to 1812.

---

[1] MS in *R.P.*—Dictated; only
the close and the postscript are in
Grenfell's hand.
[2] A slip, probably for '22<sup>nd</sup>'.
[3] 'Bank of England. Accounts relating to Bank Notes in Circulation, and to Prices and Sales of

Bullion and Silver', ordered by
the House of Commons to be
printed, 22 Feb. 1811. (*Parliamentary Papers*, 1810–11, vol. x.)
[4] The London Institution, which
had an extensive library.

24 Sept. 1815    I must trouble you to take care of and return to me 4 of these Papers viz A: B: C: and D: as I have no Duplicates of them. You may keep the other, being the 3 Years Average— a Paper produced by the Bank and which, if I mistake not, I sent you before.[1]

Since I last wrote to you I have fully considered the Basis upon which you have calculated in your former Letter of the 17$^{th}$ the Bank Profits: and it is very intelligible and as a Principle correct and ingenious.[2] To work upon it however, with a View to coming to a correct Arithmetical result, would require a knowledge of many particulars that could only be furnished by those who are in the Secret at the Bank. But these particulars are of a Nature to allow of their being guest at with sufficient accuracy to Answer the purpose of a calculation of this kind.

The Account of Deposits in 1797 included Public and *private* deposits. That lately laid before Parl! which stated, as you say, the Average in 1800 at 5,625,000 referred to Public deposits only.

You assume, I think, that the 10$\frac{3}{4}$ p$^r$ Cent divided in the 4 Years to 1801 included the *whole* of their Profits made during that period—but I should rather doubt this fact.

The Income Tax commenced in 1798 but I think in 1803 it was not at 10 p$^r$ Cent. I have no doubt but that the number of Clerks in 1807 was correctly stated by the Committee at 450.[3] I think however the Committee under rated the Law expenses and losses by Forgeries at £10,000; but the Bank must annually gain a great deal from the distruction and loss of their Notes; I have heard intelligent Men give it as their

[1] Cp. above, p. 266, n. 2.
[2] See Appendix to *Economical and Secure Currency*, above, IV, 119 ff.
[3] See 'Second Report from the Committee on the Public Ex-

penditure, &c. of the United Kingdom. The Bank', ordered to be printed 10 Aug. 1807, p. 71. (*Parliamentary Papers*, 1807, vol. II.)

opinion that what they gain from this must be equal to the whole expenses of their establishment! I understand the sum stated by the Committee to be meant as their whole expense in 1807: I really cannot venture an Opinion upon its increase since Mr Thornton told us that the present number of Clerks was 1000,[1] but I am confident the "old Proprietor" has considerably over rated the expenses of the Bank.[2]

I have no doubt but that the Bank might at their present rate of Profit divide 20 to 25 p$^r$ Cent.

I know not any other mode of calculating the Annual Income for managing the Debt from Year to Year, but by referring to the Amount of the National Debt of each Year and calculating the Commission per Million which from 91 to 1808 was £450 and since 1808, £340—to which must be added the allowance on Loans and Lotteries. I understand that the allowance in 1807 exceeded [that][3] of 1797 by £155000. Mr Perceval proposed that the £4000 for House allowance should cease, but upon the Bank objecting to it, he gave way.

I am my dear Sir

very truly yours

Pascoe Grenfell

Excuse a female Amanuensis—and very rapid dictation—which I have hardly time to read over.

David Ricardo Esq

---

[1] See above, p. 276, n. 2.　　[3] Omitted in MS.
[2] See above, p. 276, n. 1.

## 122. GRENFELL TO RICARDO[1]

My dear Sir                          Taplow 27 Sep: 1815

27 Sept. 1815     I have your letter from Cheltenham—and you will before now have received mine written on the same day.[2] I hope to find your Manuscript[3] on my arrival in Spring Garden tomorrow—and I will very readily give you, and in the way you suggest, what may occur to me on reading it— It shall be returned to you at your office—and by the time you arrive in Town—when I will make a point of meeting you. I expect to be there myself on Wednesday the 11 October—Suppose we agree to meet at the Assurance Office[4] on that day at *One* oClock?

The Papers which I sent to you on Sunday will have added something to your Knowledge on the Circulation of Bank Paper—and I will supply you with what may yet be necessary on this part of the subject—The Charge for managing the Debt since 1808 has been £340 ⅌ million as far as 600 millions—and £300—for all beyond 600 millions —the Capital of the Annuities ascertained for the purpose of making this charge by considering them at 25 Years purchase—£800 ⅌ million upon the amount of each Loan raised —and £1000 upon each Lottery Contract—one of *my* Papers *N?* *3* which I sent to you in the early part of the Summer[5] states this—and the *least* Amount received in each of the *two last* Years—Are you not in possession of the Amount of the Debt in each year for many years past? The

---

[1] Addressed: 'David Ricardo Esq[r] / Gatcomb Park / Minchinhampton'. Franked by Grenfell, from Maidenhead.
MS in *R.P.*
[2] Letter 121, of Sunday, 24 September.

[3] *Economical and Secure Currency.*
[4] The Royal Exchange Assurance Office, of which Grenfell was Deputy-Governor. (A. Johnstone's *London Commercial Guide*, 1817.)
[5] Cp. postscript to letter 111.

annual Finance Papers presented by the House of Commons shew this—and by applying the Rate of Charge
(which before 1808 was £450 ⅌ million on the whole Debt)
you get at the exact Income derived from this Source.

I should think (but without Calculation) that the Bank
must have added more than 7 millions to their Surplus
Profit since 1797—which however is not the case, if your
Estimate of 10 millions be correct—

You will have seen from my last Letter that the Principle
—the Basis—of your Calculation is perfectly well understood by me—

If you write tomorrow or on Friday direct to Spring
Garden—I shall not leave Town to return to this place
before Saturday—

I am my dear Sir

Very truly yours

Pascoe Grenfell

If you are a Farmer, as I conclude you are, this Rain I hope
has reached and rejoiced you.

I still hope you'll publish something on Bank Affairs
before Parliament meets—


123. GRENFELL TO RICARDO[1]

Taplow 28 Sep. 1815

My dear Sir

After I had sent off my Letter to you yesterday, I received by Coach from Spring Garden, your Manuscript[2]—
of which I read in the Evening about 60 pages with much
Avidity and Satisfaction—I shall finish it—and read it a
second time before I return from Town—which will be on
Sunday—in the mean time I cannot refrain from telling you,

---

[1] MS in *R.P.*      [2] *Economical and Secure Currency.*

28 Sept. 1815 that so far as I am a Judge, what I have read is excellent—
Your Idea of making Paper convertible into Bullion and not
into Coin is quite new to me, and as it now presents itself
to me, is admirable—You had before if you recollect, stated
to me your Expedient for economizing Currency at the Eve
of each Quarter by an Issue of the Dividend Warrants some
days previous to the Dividends being due—but payable *as
now* when due—I am aware of no practical objection to this
—and it seems calculated to secure the object for which you
intend it[1]—

You say more of my Exertions in Parliament than they
deserve[2]—You *under* rate the Sum gained by the Bank and
lost by the Public in Stamp Duties on the Bank Circulation
from 1799—to 1815[3]—which upon a Calculation accurately
made by me—*exceeded* £534,183—I say *exceeded*—because
in my Calculation I suppressed the fractional parts of *100,000*
—in order to simplify the Calculation—feeling too that after
giving *this* advantage to the Bank, the Result would exhibit
a Sum of *Loss* to the Public under this head sufficiently large
for my Purpose—That you may be satisfied that I advanced
nothing without Calculation, I enclose my original Papers
3 in Number containing the Bases of my Calculations which
were made (I mean the mere mechanical parts by Rule of 3)
by a very accurate person in my Employ and checked by
another—So that I am confident of their arithmetical accuracy—I doubt whether you will understand my Basis of
Calculation—but I am particularly desirous you should see
the Paper which I have marked X because it shews a regular
Series of Bank Circulation in each year from 1799 to 1815—
the first Column being the amount of Notes of £1—and £2
—and the second—of Notes and Bank Post Bills of *all*

[1] See above, IV, 74.          [3] 'A sum little less than 500,000*l.*';
[2] See above, IV, 54.          see above, IV, 95.

Denominations including £1 and £2—*Suppressing the* 28 Sept. 1815
*fractional parts in most instances of £100000*—Another Paper
accompanies these three—When you have done with, return
them to me. I am just starting and can only add

My dear Sir

Yours very truly

P: G:

D. Ricardo Esq

## 124. GRENFELL TO RICARDO[1]

Spring Garden,
28 Sept 1815.

My dear Sir

I am in the act of dressing, and can only ask you, 28 Sept. 1815
whether there is not an error in the inclosed at the top of the
Page marked G. and which instead of £250,000, you ought
not to have put down £750,000, being the fourth part of
three Millions.[2]—It has puzzled me a good deal, on my way
up, and I did not at first understand its making any part of
the calculation; but by substituting £750,000 for £250,000,
I now think it correct—If it be an oversight on your part,
it affects the whole Series of Calculation from 1801 down-
wards, but the effect of the Alteration will be to show a
greater annual profit than you have stated.

Have the goodness to return me the inclosed to Taplow
from where I sent you two Covers this Morning, and where
I shall be till Monday, after the Post comes in, when I shall
return to Town.

I am

My dear Sir

very truly yours,

PASCOE GRENFELL.

David Ricardo Esq

[1] MS in *R.P.*—Dictated; signed
by Grenfell.

[2] This part of the calculation
(which from what follows appears

## 125. GRENFELL TO RICARDO[1]

My dear Sir                    Spring G. Saturday [30 Sept. 1815]

30 Sept. 1815    Another Letter from the "Old Proprietor" in yesterday's Press[2] has just attracted my Notice—and having obtained *two* of the Papers I inclose you *one* to add to your
Collection. He gives I think a very correct Report of what
passed—except in converting *Mr. Thornton* into the Secretary.

I am just starting for Taplow—to return here on Monday.

Ever truly yours

P S.                                          P: G:

Since I wrote what is within I have yours of yesterday
from Cheltenham. You will have found on your Return, *3*
Covers from me of Thursday.[3] I have referred to the House
of Commons Papers you allude to—What was the voluntary
Subscription of 200000?[4]

## 126. MALTHUS TO RICARDO[5]

*[Reply to 116.—Answered by 127]*

My dear Sir                              Oct^r 1^st [1815]

1 Oct. 1815    I dare say you have been enjoying greatly the late fine
season, and have found but little time for study. I felt
myself in the same predicament at Claverton in the summer,

to refer to the three millions lent
by the Bank to Government in
1800; see above, IV, 121) is not
to be found in the published
*Economical and Secure Currency.*
[1] MS in *R.P.*—For dating see
below, note 3.
[2] Cp. above, p. 276, n. 1.
[3] 28 September (letter 124; cp. its
second paragraph).
[4] See above, IV, 119. The

£200,000 were a voluntary contribution of the Bank of England
for the defence of the country in
1798. (See A. Allardyce, *A Second
Address to the Proprietors of Bank
of England Stock,* 1801, p. 8.)
[5] Addressed: 'D. Ricardo Esqr /
Gatcomb Park / Minchinghamp-
ton / Gloucestershire'. Postmark,
1815.
MS in *R.P.*

and in consequence did nothing. I am now thinking about a new edition of the Essay[1] which Murray wishes to have finished before anything else is done. I am now casting the chapters about the agricultural and commercial systems, and making them apply more directly to the main subject; but am greatly puzzled about what to do with the chapter on the bounty, the greatest part of which I still think quite correct, and am unwilling therefore to throw out, lest it should give rise to charges of a change of opinion which I do not feel. My real change of opinion is very *partial* indeed.

I hope you have begun to do something now the weather has altered. I quite agree with you in thinking that the Government ought to participate more largely in the profits of a paper circulation, but from the experience of the last 5 or 6 years I own I feel great doubts of the practicability of keeping a very large paper circulation on a level with the precious metals, without great and distressing variations in the whole quantity of currency. What has happened clearly proves that there may be a great demand for the precious metals in times of war and convulsion, on account of their superior convenience; and such a demand operating upon a country possessing a small quantity of them, must occasion either a great rise of price, or an extraordinary and most inconvenient diminution of currency. To keep a paper currency on a level with the precious metals without great fluctuations in the value of the currency, I fear we must have *hoards*, and a partial metallic circulation.

The more I consider our old subject, the less I find I can agree with you in the new view which you have taken of capital as depending with respect to profits, on facility of production rather than as was formerly supposed on quantity and competition. Because of small quantity of capital com-

[1] The 5th ed. of the *Essay on Population* was not published till 1817.

pared with the means of employing it is always accompanied with facility of production, you attribute the high profits which are yielded in this case, to the latter cause instead of the former; although it is quite certain that great facility of production, accompanied by *abundant* capital compared with the demand, could only shew itself in increased rents and wages, and could not possibly appear in the shape of profits. In Otaheite where perhaps the facility of production is the greatest of any country we know, there is scarcely any capital wanted, and almost the whole of the produce goes to rent and wages. Universally where land is limited in quantity, the facility of production upon it, will go mainly to rent; and the soil of a country might be of such fertility as to yield 60 fold instead of 8 or 10, and yet the profits of stock be only 6 per cent, and the wages of labour both nominally and really low;—only just sufficient, in short, to support a stationary population.

You appear to me to overlook a most important distinction between productiveness of industry and productiveness of capital. They are in fact very different, and do not necessarily go together except perhaps in the last capital that can be employed on the land, where the productiveness of industry finally limits the productiveness of capital. In manufactures they have very little indeed to do with each other; and in land except in the case above mentioned, they seldom increase and decrease in the same proportion. I have no doubt, it frequently happens that with regard to the last capital employed upon the land in two countries, the soil of one may be such as to yield ten fold, and the soil of the other only eight fold, and yet the capital on the latter, from the greater demand for corn, and the greater relative price, may yield a higher per centage profit.

When you speak of difficulty or facility of production, do

you mean to refer to industry or capital. If you refer to capital, of course difficulty or facility of production must be synonimous with low, or high profits, and our difference is merely verbal. If you refer to industry or labour, the difference is real, and I am not I fear likely to see the subject in the same light with you. Pray give me a definition of productiveness in your next.

Your doctrine that high profits depend upon the low money price of corn appears to me still more objectionable and still more uniformly contradicted by experience, than the dependance of profits upon facility of production. Facility of production on land does not always *necessarily* occasion a cheap money price, the high profits often counterbalancing such facility; and in a similar manner low profits will often counterbalance in price, difficulty of production. For a hundred and fifty years after the reign of Edward the third, corn continued to fall, and so it did from 1640 to 1750—profits falling at the same time.

By the by surely we have been both wrong in thinking that in the progressive cultivation of poor land, the price of corn compared with manufactures would very greatly rise. I much question whether the natural and necessary rise of the raw material will not in general be nearly in proportion to the additional labour employed on the land. In wool, leather, and flax, I have little doubt that this is the case. Is it possible that a difficulty in the production of corn, should, without the operation of any other peculiar cause, make the precious metals abundant and cheap in a country, and greatly raise the price of labour compared with other states. Surely with regard to money prices, we have attributed too much to difficulty of production.

We have had young Clarke[1] to tea who seems a nice lad,

---

[1] George Clerk; see above, p. 240, n. 3.

1 Oct. 1815 and I believe is doing very well. Mrs. M desires to be kindly remembered to Mrs. Ricardo.

Believe me most truly Yours

T R Malthus.

### 127. RICARDO TO MALTHUS[1]

*[Reply to* 126.—*Answered by* 128]*

My dear Sir                                                    7ᵗʰ Octʳ 1815

7 Oct. 1815     By facility of production I do not mean to consider the productiveness of the soil only, but the skill, machinery, and labour joined to the natural fertility of the earth. It does not therefore follow that because Othaeite[2] has an abundance of fertile land that profits should be there at the highest rate, because the skill, and the means of abridging labour may in Europe more than compensate this natural advantage of Othaeite. The question is this, If part of[3] the skill and capital of England were employed in Othaeite to produce 100,000 quarters of corn, would not the persons employing that capital obtain greater profits in Othaeite than they would if they employed the same capital for the same purpose here, and would not rent be lower there than here? You must at any rate allow that the quantity of corn produced with a given quantity of capital, supposing the same skill to be employed, must be greater there than here, or there is no meaning in fertility of soil. You must allow too that in proportion to the fertility of Othaeite and to its extent compared with the population will be the lowness of rent, notwithstanding its abundant rate of produce. I can easily *conceive* that with

[1] Addressed: 'To / The Revᵈ T R Malthus/East India College/ Hertford'. Written at Gatcomb but posted in London (postmark, 9 Oct.).

MS at Albury.—*Letters to Malthus*, XXXVI.
[2] Ricardo's spelling, here and below.
[3] 'part of' is ins.

the imperfect tillage the people of Othaeite now give their 7 Oct. 1815
land, the population may be just sufficiently numerous to
require that the whole of their lands should be in cultivation,
and consequently that they should bear a rent,—but let 100
Europeans only join them with our improved machinery,
and perfectly skilled in husbandry, and the immediate consequence would be that $\frac{3}{4}$ of their lands would for a time[1]
become perfectly useless to them as the $\frac{1}{4}$ might produce
them more food than all the inhabitants could possibly consume. Now I ask whether it be possible that $\frac{3}{4}$ of the land of
a country can be suffered to pass from a state of tillage to a
state of nature without occasioning a fall in rents? If land is
less in demand must not the rent of it fall? If you say no,
there is no truth in the proposition that value depends upon
the proportion between supply and demand.

Now Suppose England in the state in which I have been
fancying Othaeite, and she is actually in that state, all or most
of[2] her land being in cultivation; and suppose further that
there is another country totally unknown to us whose skill
and machinery in husbandry as far surpasses ours, as ours
do that of the Othaeitians. If 100 of these persons were to
come amongst us with their capital, skill &c[a],— would not
the same consequences follow as I have just stated? Now
every improvement in machinery is precisely, on a small
scale, what I have been here supposing on a large scale, and
I am quite astonished that you should yet maintain that
"Universally where land is limited in quantity, the facility of
production upon it, will go mainly to rent, and the soil of a
country might be of such fertility as to yield 60 fold instead
of 8 or 10 and yet the profits of stock be only 6 pc[t] and the
wages of labour both nominally and really low." Land like
every thing else rises or falls in proportion to the demand for

[1] 'for a time' is ins.     [2] 'or most of' is ins.

7 Oct. 1815 it; every improvement which shall enable you to raise the same quantity of produce on a less quantity of land, or which is the same thing, a larger quantity of produce on the same quantity of land can not increase the demand for land, and therefore can not raise rents.

I do not clearly see the distinction which you think important between productiveness of industry and productiveness of capital. Every machine which abridges labour adds to the productiveness of industry, but it adds also to the productiveness of capital. England with machinery and with a given capital will obtain a greater real net[1] produce, than Othaeite with the same capital, without machinery, whether it be in manufactures or in the produce of the soil. It will do so because it employs much fewer hands to obtain the same produce. Industry is more productive, so is Capital. It appears to me that one is a necessary consequence of the other and that the opinion which I have advanced and which you are combating is that in the progress of society, independently of all improvements in skill and machinery, the produce of industry constantly diminishes as far as the land is concerned, and consequently capital becomes less productive. That this diminution of produce is beneficial to all owners of land, but that it is so at the expence of manufacturers, amongst which I include farmers, first by rendering the commodities which they manufacture of less exchangeable value than they before were for corn, and secondly by raising the cost of production by raising the price of labour.

I shall put this letter in the Post office in London where I am going to morrow for a few days. I have been writing in my unconnected and confined stile my opinions on the profits of the Bank, and on the advantages of a paper and nothing but a paper currency.[2] I am too little pleased with it

---

[1] 'net' is ins.     [2] *Economical and Secure Currency.*

to think of publishing. The whole is too little for a pam- 7 Oct. 1815
phlet. Mr. Grenfell is I think anxious that something should
be said about the Bank before the meeting of Parliament,
and I too wish some able hand would undertake it.

I am always glad to hear that you are preparing for the
press, for though I do not always agree in opinion with you
I am sure that your writings will contribute towards the
progress of a science in which I take great interest. I should
be more pleased that we did not so materially differ. If I am
too theoretical which I really believe is the case,—you I
think are too practical. There are so many combinations,—
so many operating causes in Political Economy, that there is
great danger in appealing to experience in favor of a particular doctrine, unless we are sure that all the causes of
variation are seen and their effects duly estimated.

Mr. Whishaw and Mr. Warburton have been at Mr.
Smith's for some time.—I have been absent from home unfortunately, and have seen but little of them. I yesterday
dined with Mr. Whishaw, he talked of leaving Mr. Smith
immediately.

Mrs. Ricardo joins in kind compliments to Mrs. Malthus.

Y<sup>rs</sup>

DAVID RICARDO

I thank you for noticing Clerk.


128. MALTHUS TO RICARDO[1]

[*Reply to* 127.—*Answered by* 130]

My dear Sir,                    E I Coll Oct<sup>r</sup> 11<sup>th</sup> 1815

   I returned from Town yesterday where I had been 11 Oct. 1815
spending some days with my brother[2] previous to his leaving

[1] Addressed: 'D. Ricardo Esqr. / 56. Upper Brook St. / Grosvenor
Square'.—MS in *R.P.*          [2] Sydenham Malthus.

11 Oct. 1815 England for Italy. I was quite sorry to find upon receiving your letter, that I had missed seeing you in Town. I wish you could make it up to me by coming down for a couple of nights before you return to Gatcomb. We could then look over together your remarks upon the Bank, and determine whether it would be adviseable to publish them. If you can give us a couple of days now, I will try and return them to you during the Xmas vacation at Gatcomb, if I possibly can. I think it possible that we may be going another way next summer.

You have rather misapprehended my illustration from Otaheite. I did not mean, that from want of skill their capital yielded but little, though their soil was extremely fertile; but that from the nature of their products, consisting chiefly of the spontaneous fruits of the earth, scarcely any advances in the shape of capital were necessary, and consequently that all the richness of their soil must go to rents and labour, but chiefly to rents.

I have always distinctly allowed, and ever shall allow in future that any causes which tend to make land less in demand will lower rents. I only want to make you allow, according to the same great principle of supply and demand, that any causes which tend to make *capital* less in demand, will lower *profits*; but you appear to me to except profits from the laws which operate upon all other commodities, and will not allow that they will be low for the same reasons that the rents of land and the wages of labour are low.

You are astonished that I maintain that when land is limited in quantity, the facility of production upon it will go mainly to rent and that though it might yield 60 fold instead of ten, profits might be only 8 per cent. Now I would ask distinctly what would happen with respect to profits in a country limited to 100,000 acres all of the richest conceivable

quality, yet peopled and capital'd up to the utmost limits of
its produce. Would not both the profits of stock and the
wages of labour be very low, although the quantity of produce yielded by a given capital *including rent* might be 100 per
cent. I believe I mentioned to you some farms in Scotland
the value of the produce of which compared with the capital
employed is 56 per cent: and I have very little doubt that
the whole landed produce of great Britain is much above
twenty per cent on the whole of the labour and capital employed upon the soil, and yet the common profits of farming
stock and of other stock in general are not more than ten per
cent. Are not these instances of the benefit derived by rents
from the fertility of our soil, and our skill in agriculture; and
if both were greatly to improve, would not rents very greatly
rise, as soon at least as the population had reached the limits
of the more abundant produce which would be in a short
time comparetively. Fertility is in fact the essence of high
rents, and low rents are the necessary result of barrenness
however scarce corn may be. If land will support no more
than those who work upon it, there can be no rent.

I am rather surprised that you do not see the distinction
between productiveness of industry and productiveness of
capital which I still think most important. They often go
together but by no means always. The machine which does
the work of five people, yields often no more profit than the
commonest instrument.—

I have not time to read over my letter you must take it
as it is

Ever truly Yours<br>
T R Malthus

## 129. MALTHUS TO RICARDO[1]

*[Answered by 130]*

My dear Sir,

E I Coll Oct 15<sup>th</sup> 1815

15 Oct. 1815    I am very sorry that you cannot come to us now; but I do not mean to retaliate, in consequence, if I can help it. If however I should be able to come, which is problematical, it will not be for above 2 or 3 days, and without Mrs. Malthus. We keep no governess, and cannot in consequence leave our children.[2] My boy will also be at home from school, so that I cannot be absent but for a very short time. You must not therefore depend upon me, nor forego any other engagements whatever on my account, but if I can manage it, and it should happen not to be inconvenient to you at the time, I will endeavour to pay you a visit at Gatcomb for a few days.

I have read your manuscript with attention, and think it important and well worthy the attention of the public; but I doubt whether it is so well written in point of style and arrangement, as your two first pamphlets. With regard to the matter I agree almost entirely with you, except that I do not think you have considered all the variations to which such a currency as you propose must be subject, particularly the great variation that is likely to arise from a sudden demand for bullion operating upon the scanty supply which is likely to take place upon your plan. If Mr. Vansittart wanted suddenly to send four millions in specie to Spain, as he did one year, I cannot help thinking that it would occasion upon your system a most distressing diminution of currency. If you recollect, we found upon calculation that the value of gold in

[1] Addressed: 'D. Ricardo Esqr / Stock Exchange / London'.
MS in *R.P.*
This letter is a reply to a missing one of Ricardo, which accompanied the MS of *Economical and Secure Currency*.
[2] Malthus had three children: Henry, then ten years old, and two girls.

this country at some periods during the Peninsular war was ten and fifteen per cent higher than at Amsterdam and Hamburgh;[1] and I feel no doubt that, without very extra-ordinary stores in the Banks, the variations in the value of the precious metals would always be found the greatest, (from sudden demand) in those countries in which a paper currency was most universal. I have no doubt that the precious metals during the last ten years experienced less variation, (with regard to commodities) in France than in this country.

I am not sure whether I should not myself propose silver instead [of][2] gold as a standard, to prevent the run upon the bank which might be occasioned by an alteration in the relative value of the two precious metals.

I am much pleased with your proposal for remedying the temporary distress for money in the market at certain seasons; and should think that it would fully answer. You have made out your case about the bank very clearly; but I expect that the directors will stand upon their charter.

I will send the manuscript by tomorrows three o'clock coach which goes to the George and Blue Boar Holborn directed to you there—to be left till called for. I have made a few pencil corrections chiefly in the style which of course you will adopt or not, as you like. I wrote my last in such a hurry that I hardly know what I said, and I am not much less hurried now.

Ever truly Yours

T R Malthus.

----

[1] See above, pp. 97 and 100.          [2] Omitted in MS.

## 130. RICARDO TO MALTHUS[1]

*[Reply to 128 & 129.—Answered by 137]*

My dear Sir                                    London 17 Oct.[r] 1815

17 Oct. 1815    Mrs. Ricardo and I are sorry that Mrs. Malthus will be
prevented from accompanying you when you pay us a visit
at Gatcomb. We should have been very happy to have shewn
her some of the beauties of our county. When you come
perhaps you will bring your gun with you.—Though I am
no sportsman myself I will endeavour to procure you the
best sport that my influence can command.

I am very much obliged to you for the attention which
you have given to my MS. I am fully aware of the deficiency
in the style and arrangement;—those are faults which I shall
never conquer; I will however use my best endeavors to
elevate it to the very low standard to which you compare it.
It would be unpardonable to write worse with more practice.

I expected that you would not quite agree with my plan
of abolishing the metals from circulation, but the grounds on
which you object to it may I think be answered, and then
your objections would I hope be removed. You fear that
without a metallic circulation we could not on an emergency
supply a large sum of bullion for the exigencies of the state.
The fact is however against you for we have supplied large
sums when the metals have been absolutely banished from
circulation. This has been the case during the whole Peninsular war. If indeed on my system the Bank could keep a
less quantity of bullion in their coffers to answer the demands
of the public, the objection would be well founded, but the
only difference would be that in one case their hoards would
consist wholly of coined gold and silver,—in the other they

---

[1] Addressed: 'Rev.[d] T R Malthus / East India College / Hertford'.
MS at Albury.—*Letters to Malthus*, XXXVIII.

would consist of the uncoined metals,—but on both systems, if the Bank paid their notes on demand, the currency must be equally reduced in quantity if gold and silver should become more valuable. That argument then may be used against a currency convertible at all, into specie or bullion, but does not apply to one more than the other. I think with you that on the whole silver would be a better standard than gold, particularly if paper only were used. All objections against its greater bulk would be removed.

I find I did misapprehend your illustration, respecting profits, from Othaeite; but our difference is still very serious. I most distinctly allow that any causes which tend to make capital less in demand will lower profits, but I contend that there are no causes which will for any length of time make capital less in demand, however abundant it may become, but a comparatively high price of food and labour;—that profits do not *necessarily* fall with the increase of the quantity of capital because the demand for capital is infinite and is governed by the same law as population itself. They are both checked by the rise in the price of food, and the consequent increase in the value of labour. If there were no such rise what could prevent population and capital from increasing without limit? I acknowledge the effects of the great principle of supply and demand in every instance, but in this it appears to me that the demand will enlarge at the same rate as the supply, if there be no difficulty on the score of food and raw produce.

Fertility is as you justly observe the essence of high rents, and low rents are the necessary result of barrenness however scarce corn may be. I agree with you too that in a country limited to 100 000 acres all of the richest conceivable quantity[1], yet peopled and capital'd up to the utmost limits of its

[1] Should be 'quality'.

17 Oct. 1815 produce, the profits of stock and the wages of labour would both be very low, although the quantity of produce yielded by a given capital *including rent* might be 100 pc$^t$,—but I ask if by any miracle the produce of that land could at once be doubled would rents then continue as high as before, or could they possibly rise? We are speaking of the immediate not the ultimate effects. The improvements in skill and machinery may in 1000 years go to the Landlord but for 900 they will remain with the tenant.

Y$^{rs}$ very truly

DAVID RICARDO

I have been so busy and am yet so busy that I cannot return to Gatcomb till friday.[1]

## 131. MALTHUS TO RICARDO[2]
*[Answered by 132]*

E I Coll Oct$^r$ 16$^{th}$ 1815.

My dear Sir

16 Oct. 1815        When I wrote last night[3] I had the strongest impression that the afternoon coach went to the George and Blue Boar Holbourn. I found however this morning that I was mistaken, and that it went to the Saracens head Snow Hill, where I hope the person that you send will find it. I did not direct it to be sent to the George and Blue Boar from the Saracen's Head for fear of some mistake, and thinking that your man not finding it in Holbourn, would probably call at the other Inn.

I conclude that you have no reason to care much for the resentment of the Bank. The publication[4] will no doubt make the Directors very angry. By the by, may not the Proprietors

[1] 20 October.

[2] Addressed: 'D. Ricardo Esqr. / Stock Exchange / London'.

MS in *R.P.*

[3] Letter 129.

[4] *Economical and Secure Currency.*

claim the profits which have been made, and object to the participation of the government; but I suppose your views are prospective rather than retrospective. At all events the public ought to have some share in the enormous profits which the present paper system has allowed the Bank to make.

Pray has there been any account lately of the number of Bank of England notes in circulation. It has been said I understand that they have been much diminished lately, which is one great cause of the fall of prices. Is this so? I heard in Town that all home trade was most exceedingly slack.

Is it possible for above half the national income to fall very greatly in price, without affecting the demand and the other half. I confess I feel no doubt that the main cause of the present slackness of trade is the diminished incomes of the Landlords and Farmers. The actual produce of a country will always be sold, and the loss of the sellers will be the gain of the buyers; but it makes an infinite difference to a country whether its produce is sold at a price which will encourage production, or discourage it. During the period of a fall of prices it appears to me that all sorts of productions are pro-digiously discouraged; and that at the end of 7 or 8 years of falling prices, or 7 or 8 years of rising prices, the state of a country will be most essentially different in point of wealth.

I agree with you in your definition of facility of produc-tion,[1] but think that you have drawn wrong inferences from it. I agree with you also in thinking that in the progress of cultivation there is a regular tendency to a diminution in the productiveness of industry on the land, in the same manner as there is a regular tendency to a diminution in the real wages of labour; but it is quite erroneous I think to infer that the

[1] Above, p. 292.

16 Oct. 1815 profits of stock may not, as will the wages of labour rise for periods of some duration during the course of this progress. In fact, profits on the land will always rise, when population increases faster than capital, independently of improvement &c.

Ever truly Yours

T R MALTHUS

## 132. RICARDO TO MALTHUS[1]

[*Reply to* 131.—*Answered by* 137]

My dear Sir

London 17 Oct.ʳ 1815

17 Oct. 1815 My letter[2] was sent to the Post before I received yours of yesterday's date. The parcel you sent me has reached me safe. I am sorry you had so much trouble about it.—

My views respecting the Bank are entirely prospective. The last return of Bank notes in circulation was I think larger than any that preceded it. I have not the paper in London but I think the circulation of Bank notes then amounted (1815) to 28 000 000 or more.

It is dangerous to listen to reports respecting briskness or slackness of trade. It is I believe certain that the revenue has been uncommonly productive the last quarter which is no indication of diminished trade. As you allow that the loss of the sellers is the gain of the buyers, you appear to me to attribute effects much too great to the fall of raw produce which has lately taken place.—It does not follow that because prices are low production will be discouraged. If money were to fall very much in value whilst a country was making

---

[1] Addressed: 'Revᵈ T R Malthus / East India College / Hertford'.    MS at Albury.—*Letters to Malthus,* XXXIX.

[2] Letter 130.

great advances in prosperity would not production be 17 Oct. 1815
encouraged notwithstanding a fall of prices?—

That profits may rise on the land if population increases
faster than capital, I am not disposed to deny, but this will be
a partial rise of profits on a particular trade, for a limited
time, and is very different from a general rise of profits on
trade in general.—

This admission does not affect my principle.

Ever truly Y$^{rs}$

DAVID RICARDO

I ought to apologize for writing to you twice in one day.

### 133. GRENFELL TO RICARDO[1]

Taplow 17 Oct. 1815
Tuesday.

My dear Sir

I return Mr. Malthus's Letter,[2]—what he says will I 17 Oct. 1815
trust decide you to print and give the public the Benefit of
your Reflexions on Currency and Bank Affairs—I cannot
agree with Mr. M— in preferring Silver to Gold as the Standard—I am almost *impatient* that your Remedy for the
quarterly Distress in the Money Market should be known,
in the Hope, that when known it will be adopted—

I have determined upon going to Cheltenham on Saturday—I will give you a line from thence to Gatcomb, and
propose a day to come over to you—

Did you notice particularly that part of the *Second* Resolution of Mr Mellish,[3] where it is stated that the number of
Dividend Warrants for the year ending April 1815, was
565,600? This is a number infinitely below what I had
imagined—and proves the number of persons holding

---

[1] MS in *R.P.*                    [3] See above, IV, 138.
[2] No doubt letter 129.

17 Oct. 1815 funded property to be much fewer than they are generally supposed to be. This number includes of course *all* the Dividend Warrants issued in the four Quarters—and supposing (which we know is not the Case) that no Individual Fund holder has in his name more than one sort of Stock, for which 2 Dividend Warrants are issued to him in the Year, the Result would be (dividing the Number by 2) that there are no more than 282,800 Stock holders.—But we know in fact that there are many Individuals, who are Holders in *all* the different sorts of Stock—which would further reduce this number—on the other hand one Dividend Warrant, in *Trust* Cases, often belongs to many Individuals—The number of Accounts however cannot exceed 282,800. Is this a greater or a less Number than you may have Imagined—It appeared to Mr Tierney as well as to myself much less than we had fancied it to be—

I shall be here till Friday Evening or Saturday Morning—

Believe me My dear Sir

Most truly Yours

PASCOE GRENFELL.

D. Ricardo Esq


## 134. MILL TO RICARDO[1]

*[Reply to 114.—Answered by 135]*

My dear Sir                         Ford Abbey—Chard 10ᵗʰ Octʳ 1815

10 Oct. 1815      You quarrel with the opinions which I have formed respecting the virtue of the members of the two houses, one noble, t'other honorable. I did by no means expect you

[1] Addressed: 'David Ricardo Esq. / Gatcomb Park / Mincing Hampton / Gloucester Shire'. Ricardo, having gone to London on 8 October (above, p. 294), did not receive this letter till his return to Gatcomb, presumably on the 20th (above, p. 302); see his reply.
MS in *R.P.*

to agree with me all at once. I arrived at them slowly, and unwillingly myself; and so will you. They resulted spontaneously, and without my seeking them, from the studies in which I engaged; and I was long familiar with the premises, before I allowed myself to draw the conclusions; or could believe it possible that they were true, how infallible soever the ground of inference appeared to be. This weakness, for such it was, arose from one of the most common of our prejudices; that virtue is attached to high station, and vice to low. Suppose a quantity of *low men*, collected together, with a power of selling their country, with impunity, and praise for it to the bargain; and who, (at least among the noble and honourable members) will hesitate a moment in supposing *they* would do so? But, because they are great and high men, —oh, in that case, it is a crime to harbour any such suspicion. Yet who that has the least experience of them, their education, the circumstances in which they are placed, and the conduct they pursue, attaches virtue to that station, or accounts it less than a miracle to find it there? Did you ever find a servant who behaved to you with the same abject obsequiousness, the same base subserviency to your meanest caprices and vices, that princes universally find among the great? For their *venality*, read Windhams speech against reform[1]—not an occasion where you would expect to find the baseness of the great unnecessarily brought forward; and you will find him describing the rapacity of the members of the two houses —their insatiable, unprincipled desire to live at the expence of the public, to plunder the people for money which they may spend, in language which if I were to strive to surpass it in strength, it would be altogether out of my power.—Nor is this any thing more than the steady operation of the laws

[1] On 26 May 1809; see *Speeches in Parliament of the Rt. Hon. William Windham*, London, 1812, vol. III, p. 236 ff.

10 Oct. 1815 of human nature.—Give any other men, with the same bad
education, the same powers to prey upon their country; the
same motives to betray the principles of good government;
—money, and praise, for upholding bad government; no
money, no power, no praise, but discountenance and blame,
if they advocate the principles of good government, and they
will act in the same way as the members of the noble and
honorable houses. It is the constitution, therefore, of the
honorable houses, that does the mischief; by placing men's
interest and their duties not in concord, whence alone the
performance of the duties can be expected; but in direct
opposition, whence the violation of the duties is ensured.—
Oh, but if it is in the constitution of the houses, you say, how
are you to constitute them as to remedy this evil? First
acknowledge that the remedy is wanted—and wanted with
all the urgency which is created by the unspeakable difference
between good government, and bad. I have a genuine,
practical conviction of this necessity, to which your studies
will soon conduct you, and I shall undertake to show you a
plan, by which you yourself shall confess that the evil would
be effectually and easily remedied, without a change in any
mans circumstances, except by shutting up for the future the
channels of unjust gain—or rather by that time, you will
need none of my shewing—you will see the thing for yourself.—In the mean time, make a good sermon upon this text,
of Montesquieu—C'est une experience eternelle, que tout
homme, qui a du pouvoir, est porté à en abuser: il va
jusqu'à ce qu'il trouve des limites.[1]—I only apply under the
immediate and irresistible guidance of observation, the fruit
of this eternal experience. It is for you, either to yield to this
eternal experience, or to shew that the above-said members
have not the *power* to sell every principle of good govern-

[1] *Esprit des Loix*, Livre XI, ch. IV.

ment, and *rewards* for doing it; or if you decline this test, 10 Oct. 1815 shew that their conduct does not correspond to the theory.

We are very apt, too, in cases of this sort to deceive ourselves, by an idea of indulgence to the faults of one another. In all the private affairs of private life, no virtue should be more assiduously cultivated. But in all abuses of power, we should accustom ourselves to reflect, that sensibility to the undue pleasures of one or a few, is total insensibility to the miseries of thousands or millions. Indulgence to the abuses of power, is inhumanity upon the largest possible scale.

What is above was written shortly after your letter arrived. I have almost forgotten what it contains.—Your letter gave me no little pain by what it stated respecting Mrs. Porter,[1] who from what I heard, before leaving town, I concluded was on the way to recovery. It is an affecting case; both on account of the amiable sufferer, and of those who so acutely suffer along with her.

I expect you are by this time in a condition to give me some account of the progress you have been making in your book. I now consider you as fairly pledged to that task. The parliamentary undertakings will follow. All that sensibility you speak of as sufficing to prevent you, I should have it as strongly as you would, but strong determination, and familiarity with the scene, would in time get the better of it, and so it will in you.

You will gratify me, if you will always send in your letters as much as may be of the family history. Of mine the history is two words—*semper idem*. We study, walk, eat, drink and sleep, and that is all. The old story, my Indian history, is (thank God) now near a close[2]—but lately I have been

[1] Ricardo's sister Sarah.
[2] Mill's *History of British India*, at which he had been working since 1806, was published at the end of 1817.

10 Oct. 1815 harassed writing reviews. By the bye, our domestic history has lately been a little varied, by a visit of a dignitary of your county, whom you would not guess—the bishop of Gloucester. He comes annually into this neighbourhood, where he has an estate as Dean of Wells, and he accepted of an invitation to dine at the Abbey, and left us all very much in love with him.

Mr. Hume, with his new married lady, is to be at Cheltenham, from a tour to the lakes, about the middle of this month. Will you permit me to lay my injunctions on him, to take Gatcomb on his way to London?

Pray, what of Mr. Malthus? Is your correspondence with him as rapid as usual? Whereabouts do his opinions now stand? And what is he doing as to publication?

I beg my best respects to the circle round your fire (we have not got any here yet, though pretty cold) and am

most truly Yours,

J. MILL

### 135. RICARDO TO MILL[1]

*[Reply to 134.—Answered by 138]*

Gatcomb Park
My dear Sir                                    24th Octr 1815

24 Oct. 1815     I have been absent in London for nearly a fortnight the greatest part of which time your letter lay here waiting my return home. I lose no time in thanking you for it, and returning my answer. Against much of what you say concerning the noble and honourable houses I have nothing to offer. I have no doubt that your principle is correct, but I think you apply it too rigidly. It appears to me that you allow too much force to the stimulus of money, and the

---

[1] Addressed: 'J. Mill Esqr / Ford Abbey / near / Chard / Somersetshire'. MS in Mill-Ricardo papers.

praise of Princes, and too little to the effect of public opinion, and the consciousness of deserving approbation.—With some men these latter rewards are held so valuable that there are no difficulties which they will not incur to obtain them, which shews that badly constituted as the two houses may be in not securing every motive on the side of duty, yet that there is a natural corrective in every nation which possesses the forms of a free government which will considerably ameliorate the evil of its institutions. I do not urge this as an argument for the continuance of the evil, but as a proof that you are severe in your judgement when you say that there is no virtue to be found mixed up along with the vice. After all it is no prejudice to suppose that the high born would under similar circumstances act differently and better than the low born. Where would be the advantages of education if the balance of virtue were not on the side of those who received it, and if it did not in some measure teach us to raise our thoughts above the mere covetousness of money? Is not Montesquieu too severe when he says not only that all men are disposed to abuse the power they possess, but also to carry that abuse to its *utmost limits*?

Now for a little family history. My sister Sally was during my stay in London safely delivered of a girl. We were all apprehensive that this severe trial in her weak state would be too much for her, but she has had better nights and her skin has been less irritable since than before her accouchement. Her spirits too are improved. The child happily is healthy, strong and without a spot, and the interest which it excites in her has given a new hue to the prospect before her. Hope has not yet forsaken us that she may still recover, and enjoy health with more delight than any of us, from the contrast which it will form to the gloomy state from which it will commence its date.—

24 Oct. 1815    Ralph returned from Paris the day after I left London.—
I have not yet seen him, but I understand that he is delighted
with his journey.—He received very kind attention from
Mons.ʳ Say, to whom I gave him a letter.[1]—

Here at Gatcomb we go on much as usual,—we are
always full of visitors, some of which make great demands
on my time. I often say that I must go to London for retirement, for here not only have I to entertain the visitors who
are staying with us, but all our Gloucestershire neighbours,
living within 10 miles, in all directions, are very much
inclined to be sociable, so that with them we have to find
time, not only for the visit, but for the journey also. At the
present moment we are full to overflowing. Last night we
had a dance and sat down to supper a party of no less than
49 which did not disperse before 4 oClock this morning.
I have been satisfied with four hours bed, not so my guests,
which has given an opportunity of writing to you. Mr. and
Mrs. Basevi are here, they have a house at Cheltenham and
have come home for a few days. Mr. and Mrs. Clutterbuck are also among our guests and I am glad to say
that the latter is looking better than she has done for many
months.

After giving you this detail of our proceedings you will
not be surprised to hear that I have done very little in the
way of studying or writing. As the affairs of the Bank are
to be considered next session, I have been putting my
thoughts on paper respecting their concerns. I have endeavored to shew that a well regulated paper currency is less
variable in its value than a metallic currency, and therefore
more desirable. I have recommended a simple plan to obviate
the scarcity of money, which, to the distress of the mercantile world, always takes place before the payment of the

[1] Letter 108.

national dividends. I have again pointed out the advantages   24 Oct. 1815
which would result from making paper convertible into
bullion and not into specie. After which I have followed the
ground of Mr. Grenfell, and have endeavored to shew that
the Government in its last agreement with the Bank for a
participation of the advantages resulting from the public
deposits, and the management of the public debt, made a
very improvident bargain for the public, and recommend
more caution in the agreement now about to be made.
Finally I have attempted to calculate the present treasure of
the Bank, and have insisted (very disinterestedly for I have
only £500 Bank stock) on the right of the proprietors of
Bank Stock to a division of their enormous gains.—I have
shewn it to Mr. Grenfell and to Mr. Malthus. The former
urges me to publish it.[1] The latter agrees with almost all my
matter, but thinks, as I think myself, that the performance
is inferior *even* to my first two pamphlets.[2] I am not much
inclined for this reason to publish it, but before I finally
determine I should like to have your candid opinion about
it, and I am sure you will give me no other, and I will if
possible send it to you from Bath, the latter end of this or
beginning of next week with all its imperfections and
before I attempt to make it better, which I think I can do.—

In the Philanthropist and the Edinburgh I think I have
recognized your articles. I am glad your history is nearly
finished, I hope it will bring you abundance of fame and
money.—

I shall be very happy indeed to see Mr. Hume and his
new married lady here. If you write to them say so in the
strongest terms for me. In the mean time I will write to
Cheltenham myself for the purpose of urging the same
request.—

   [1] See letter 133.            [2] See letter 129.

24 Oct. 1815    Mr. Malthus and I continue to write to each other but not so actively as we sometimes do. We differ nearly as much as ever. There appears to me an astonishing mixture of truth and error in the opinions which he holds on the subject of rent profit and wages. Oh that I were capable of writing a book! He is preparing a new edition of his Essay on Population for the press. He ought candidly to confess that he has committed great errors in his chapters on the Agricultural and Mercantile systems, as well as in that on bounties.

I hope Mr. Bentham is well.—I have to thank him for his small pamphlet which was sent to me in Brook Street.[1] I hope soon to be able to study it.—Make my kind compliments to him and to Mrs. Mill and believe me

very truly Yours<br>DAVID RICARDO

I shall direct my MS to you at Ford Abbey near Chard.

### 136. RICARDO TO TROWER[2]

*[Reply to 120.—Answered by 141]*

Gatcomb Park Minchinhampton<br>29<sup>th</sup> Oct<sup>r</sup> 1815

Dear Trower

29 Oct. 1815    I sincerely congratulate Mrs. Trower and you on the increase of your family, which I hope will be attended with an increase of happiness.

You observe justly that having friends staying with us unsettles our regular habits. I find it very materially to interfere with my pursuits. Reading or writing, when one has an object in view, should be followed systematically, and at no

---

[1] Probably *A Table of the Springs of Action*, 32 pp., London, Taylor, 1815.
[2] Addressed: 'Hutches Trower Esq<sup>r</sup>/ Unsted Wood/Godalming/ Surry'.
MS at University College, London.—*Letters to Trower*, V.

distant intervals, for after a time our thoughts are turned into new channels and we cannot easily recal the ideas which were only beginning to be indistinctly formed in our minds. I have scarcely been a week without visitors since I have been in the country, and to that I ascribe the imperfection of the little that I have done in the writing way. So far from imitating the illustrious example, that you set before me, and improving as I go on, each successive attempt is attended with less success than the former, and it invariably happens that my last performance is the worst. I have hitherto done nothing more than write what would make a very small pamphlet on Bank affairs,[1] which I took with me to town, where I was obliged to go for a few days, a fortnight ago. I had very little intention of publishing it but I thought I might as well ask my friend Malthus' opinion of it. That opinion was not unfavourable to the matter, but was decidedly expressed respecting its inferiority in style and arrangement to my two first pamphlets.[2] Thus you see that I have no other encouragement to pursue the study of Political Economy than the pleasure which the study itself affords me, for never shall I be so fortunate however correct my opinions may become as to produce a work which shall procure me fame and distinction. I am determined however not to be daunted by common difficulties. I shall again set to work to endeavor to improve the style and arrangement of what I have just written, not that I am quite sure that I shall publish it if I succeed, but at least it will afford me an opportunity of exercising the limited powers which I possess. Mr. Malthus and I continue to differ in our views of the principles of Rent, Profit and Wages. These principles are so linked and connected with every thing belonging to the science of Political Economy that I consider the just view of them as of the first

[1] *Economical and Secure Currency.*  [2] See above, p. 298.

29 Oct. 1815 importance. It is on this subject, where my opinions differ from the great authority of Adam Smith Malthus, &c.ᵃ that I should wish to concentrate all the talent I possess, not only for the purpose of establishing what I think correct principles but of drawing important deductions from them. For my own satisfaction I shall certainly make the attempt, and perhaps with repeated revisions during a year or two I shall at last produce something that may be understood.

The anecdote you gave me respecting an article intended to have been inserted in the last number of the Edinburgh Review is very amusing. It shews that nothing is more dangerous than to set up for a prophet, unless we use such ambiguous language that with a little stretch of the imagination may suit all occurrences. Our politicians are not so wary in this particular as I should have expected, witness their prognostics concerning the war in Spain,—the utter impossibility of beating Bonaparte, not to mention the Bank restriction bill &c. &c.—

Respecting this last named personage I quite agree with [you that]¹ a man's character and renown must be estimated upon a reference to the whole of his conduct. "We must cast up the account of the good and bad qualities and strike a balance." It is by this rule that I would try Bonaparte, and by this rule he will be tried by the future historian. I thought you departed from it, when after his brilliant career for 20 years, you pronounced his glory wholly effaced by being obliged in consequence of an unsuccessful battle, bravely contested, to surrender himself a prisoner. It was the balance only that I was contending for which I still think is on the credit side of the account.

Having given you so particular an account of my employments allow me to ask what are yours? Are you amusing

¹ MS torn.

yourself with desultory reading or is your attention engaged   29 Oct. 1815
by some particular subject. If the latter I should hope that
your thoughts are turned towards the press, for one who can
stimulate others to exertion and perseverance so well, ought
himself to be animated with a desire to shine, and where
every advantage of leisure and qualifications are given it
would be unpardonable to preach a doctrine which you did
not yourself practise.

Mr. Mill writes to me that he has nearly finished his Indian
History.[1] He is this Autumn where he was last, with Mr.
Bentham at Ford Abbey, Somersetshire, where they have
both ample leisure for their literary pursuits. Mr. Malthus is
I believe engaged in preparing a new Edition of his Essay on
Population for publication.[2] Some of the doctrines on
Political Economy in that work required revision. I hope
they will receive a radical amendment. Mrs. Ricardo and my
daughter join with me in kind regards to Mrs. Trower whose
health we hope is quite restored.

Y<sup>rs</sup> very truly<br>DAVID RICARDO

## 137. MALTHUS TO RICARDO[3]
[Reply to 130 & 132]

My dear Sir Oct 30 [1815]

    I conclude you are by this time returned to Gatcomb.   30 Oct. 1815
I was sorry you could not come down to us for a day, as one
can get over more ground in conversation than in a letter. You
know I am always inclined to acknowledge the authority of
experience, and I cannot help thinking that in the point to
which you refer experience is against you. I allow most

---

[1] Above, p. 309.
[2] See above, p. 289.
[3] Addressed: 'D. Ricardo Esqr /

Gatcomb Park / Minching Hampton / Gloucestershire'. Postmark,
1815.—MS in *R.P.*

30 Oct. 1815 readily that the country *did* send the bullion, although it had none in circulation, but the demand for it and the sending it under these circumstances, certainly produced very great fluctuations in its value: and what I mean to say is, that if the whole currency by being proportionably diminished had been made to experience the same fluctuations, the mercantile world [would][1] have been extremely distressed. I do not believe that any thing like the same fluctuations in the value of the precious metals took place during the course of the war at Hamburgh Amsterdam or in France. If you recollect in some of our inquiries it appeared that the price of gold was at times considerably above ten per cent higher here than at Hamburgh,—at one time I think above fifteen. I do not mean my observation to apply to your system as paying in *bullion* instead of *coin*; but to every system in which a sudden demand may come upon a country, possessing altogether but a small quantity of the precious metals.

I have always allowed that the progress of capital and population, while they can go on together, uninterrupted by the difficulty of procuring subsistence, is absolutely unlimited; but I most distinctly deny that the demand for capital is unlimited, with a limited population; and this appears to me to be the proposition that you maintain. You seem to argue quite upon different principles in reference to land and profits. You say that the demand for capital will enlarge at the same rate as the supply; and yet think that a moderate supply of land or what is equivalent to it, of produce, will have an effect for a very considerable time in lowering rents. What can you possibly mean by the improvements in farming going to the Landlord in a thousand years? Few of these improvements have doubled the produce, and five and twenty or fifty years would proportion the population to them, and

[1] Omitted in MS.

*double the rents*, while profits would be left as they were
before notwithstanding this increased facility of production.
When before the revolutionary war, the rate of interest was
below 4 per cent and profits in proportion, might it not be
said that almost all previous improvements in machinery had
gone to the land. You say that if half the land will yield the
same produce rents will fall? Upon the same principle, if half
the capital will yield the same produce, why should not profits
fall? Where could the remaining half find employment? You
will say perhaps that though some difficulty might be found
at first, yet after a time the demand would be proportioned
to the supply; that is you ask for an interval with regard to
profits, and yet with regard to rents you say "we are speaking
of *immediate*, not ultimate effects." You allow that profits
may rise on the land if population increases faster than produce, and fall, if produce increases faster than population,
but surely in every case where a great facility of production
suddenly takes place, produce may be said to increase faster
than population. Without an increase of population in this
case profits must fall; and after a proportionate increase of
population, the facility of production will go to the land. I
am still firmly of opinion therefore that "Universally where
land is limited in quantity the facility of production upon it
will go mainly to rent,"[1] and I cannot help thinking that
your doctrine of the indefinite demand for capital without
reference to a proportionate increase of population, is an
assumption, directly in the teeth of the great principle of
Supply and demand, and *uniformly* contradicted by experience.
The rent of land depends upon its productiveness, combined
with the demand for it. Given the productiveness the rent
varies as the demand; and given the demand the rent varies
as the productiveness. In the same manner profits, depend

[1] Above, p. 293.

30 Oct. 1815 upon the productiveness of industry, and the demand for capital. To neglect the consideration of *demand* in either case, is equally erroneous. I am quite surprised that you [do][1] not see the great difference between the productiveness of industry, and of capital. You may as well say that a capital machine which every body might have for little or nothing would necessarily yield high profits.

Pray do you not think that the currency on the whole is at present diminished

truly Yours
T R M.

## 138. MILL TO RICARDO[2]

*[Reply to 135]*

My dear Sir                                   Ford Abbey  Nov. 9ᵗʰ 1815

9 Nov. 1815      For more than a week I have been expecting every day to receive the M.S.[3] of which you gave me hopes in your letter. I have also had inquiry made at Ilminster, where I thought it likely the Bath coach might have left the parcel; and I now begin to be alarmed that some accident may have happened. It is for the purpose then of making the due inquiry that I now write. The best thing to hear of, unless the parcel arrive in the mean time, is to hear that something has happened to delay the sending of it from Gatcomb. If so, I hope it will be no longer delayed, for I am very impatient to see it. Notwithstanding my passion for the science of political economy, it has so happened that for a good many

[1] Omitted in MS.
[2] Addressed: 'David Ricardo Esq / Gatcomb Park / Mincing Hampton / Gloucestershire'. Endorsed, in Mrs Ricardo's handwriting, 'I enclose this letter to Fanny'

(*i.e.* Mrs Moses Ricardo). Ricardo was now in London; see p. 322, n. 1 and the beginning of letter 140.
MS in *R.P.*
[3] *Economical and Secure Currency.*

years I have not been able to think of it, except when I was  9 Nov. 1815
excited by your instructive conversation or by your writings.
Why do you cry, "Oh that I were able to write a book!"
when there is no obstacle to your writing, but this want of
confidence in your own powers. You want some practice in
the art of laying down your thoughts, in the way most easy
of apprehension to those who have little knowledge, and
little attention; and this is to be got infallibly by a little
practice. As I am accustomed to wield the authority of a
schoolmaster, I therefore, in the genuine exercise of this
honourable capacity, lay upon you my commands, to begin
to the first of the three heads of your proposed work, rent,[1]
profit, wages—viz. *rent*, without an hours delay. If you entrust
the inspection of it to me, depend upon it I shall compell
you to make it all right, before you have done with it.

I have a long letter from our Parisian friend,[2] who says he
is delighted with what I told him, that you were now likely
to devote a considerable portion of your time to political
economy. He says he is rectifying his chapters on money to
a conformity with your ideas, for the third edition of his
book, which will probably appear next year.[3] He also says he
has written to you. He is breathing heavy sighs over the
state of his country; and something more bitter than sighs
over the British government, whose love of mankind, and
of good government has been well displayed in the measures
which they have so ardently pursued in making a government
to their liking in France. When his opinions are mentioned,
it is necessary, however, he says, that his name should
always be suppressed—for which reason you will perceive
that I have blotted it out, after it was written.

[1] 'wages' is del. here.
[2] Replaces 'Mons. Say', blotted out.
[3] *Traité d'Économie politique*, 3rd ed., 1817.

9 Nov. 1815     I do not intend this as an answer to your letter—but only a word of inquiry—and as I have been called down stairs to the parson of the parish, and kept gossiping till I have almost lost my morning, I shall cut you short. You shall have enough of it, when I return your M.S.

You delighted me much by your accounts of Mrs. Porter. My best regards to your fire side. We talk of leaving this place about the end of this month—and we shall not linger, after our determination, as we did last year. You will not be in London, I suppose, much before February

Believe most truly Yours &.c.

J. MILL

### 139. MALTHUS TO RICARDO[1]

My dear Sir,                        E I Coll. Nov$^r$ 13$^{th}$ 1815

13 Nov. 1815     We shall be extremely happy to see you on saturday; and if it is not inconvenient perhaps you would do Mrs. Malthus the favour of escorting her sister (Miss Eckersall) down to Haileybury, who I believe purposes to be with us on that day. Pray let me have a line to say whether this will be convenient, as it will save us the trouble of meeting her. She will be at Mrs. Brays[2] 57 Great Russel Street Bloomsbury, and any time of the day that you appoint will suit her. It is possible that Mr. R Bray my nephew may be able to accompany her, but this is uncertain. If he can come, you will have no objection I am sure to his making a third in the chaise; but if the plan is in any way inconvenient to you, do not think of it, as we can arrange it otherwise without difficulty.

---

[1] Addressed: 'D. Ricardo Esqr. / Stock Exchange / London'. MS in *R.P.*

[2] Malthus's sister, widow of Edward Bray.

Our great difference arises from your not sufficiently   13 Nov. 1815
considering demand; and not allowing the very marked
distinction there is, between the productiveness of industry
and the productiveness of capital. What do [you]¹ think of
land which yields sixty fold, instead of ten, without any
purchasers for the produce? Would the profits be in the one
case six times greater than in the other?

    The post waits

truly Yours

T R MALTHUS.

140. RICARDO TO MILL²

[*Answered by* 142]

My dear Sir

                              Gatcomb Park 27ᵗʰ Novʳ 1815

    Soon after I wrote my last letter to you from London,³   27 Nov. 1815
Mrs. Ricardo, to my great surprise, joined me there, impelled
partly by her wish to see her sister, who has been very ill for
a long time, and partly by her dislike to be at so formidable
a distance as 100 miles from me. We returned to Gatcomb
this morning, accompanied by Mrs. M. Ricardo who though
very little able to bear the journey was induced to accompany
us for the benefit of our pure air. We travelled very slowly
having been three days on our journey. We found your
letter to Mrs. Ricardo here, and in the course of the day
yours of the 24ᵗʰ was delivered to me. Mrs. Ricardo begs
me to thank you for the one addressed to her, and for the
kind things which it contains. Though received so late it was
in time to prevent Mr. Clutterbuck having any trouble about

¹ Omitted in MS.
² Addressed: 'J. Mill Esqʳ / Ford
Abbey / near / Chard / Somersetshire'.

MS in Mill-Ricardo papers.
³ This letter of Ricardo and that
from Mill of the 24th, mentioned
below, are missing.

27 Nov. 1815   the MS, as he and my daughter remained at Gatcomb to take care of the family during our absence, so that he had no opportunity to make enquiries after the lost MS.[1]

I have to thank you, which I do very sincerely, for sparing so much time from your avocations, as you evidently have done, in considering the matter of my MS, and although I am fully persuaded that your desire to stimulate me to persevere in writing has called forth a too flattering opinion from you of my performance, yet I am sure you would not encourage me to publish if you thought that my vanity would receive a serious mortification by so doing.

I can easily conceive that the mode you recommend of putting marginal notes to each paragraph, after having written all that occurs to one on the subject engaging one's thoughts, and then arranging the whole by an examination of these notes, must be of great assistance, particularly to an inexperienced author, and I shall certainly practise it in any future performance. You have given a complete analysis of the contents of my essay, and if the performance[2] were more elaborate and better digested, nothing could be better than the heads which you propose for each section, but I submit to you whether the contents of each section would not be in a very diminutive proportion, in this instance, to the title of it,—whether it might not be justly remarked that the title promised much more than was afterwards performed. I am fully aware of the advantages of the division into sections,— they are useful resting places and take off from the abruptness of passing from one part of the subject to another, but would it not be better to head these different sections by the shortest possible title? You know much better than I do which is best; at the same time I am sure you will not refuse to consider my objections. If not in the month of Dec.ʳ I must

---

[1] See above, p. 320, n. 3.    [2] In MS 'performarance'.

be in London in Jan.ʸ, when I shall have an opportunity of 27 Nov. 1815
shewing you my performance in the most perfect state to
which I can bring it. We will then finally determine about
the heads to the different sections. In the mean time you will
oblige me by returning the MS directed to Thomas Clutterbuck, Widcombe House, near Bath—he will immediately
forward it to me.

During my absence from home I passed two very pleasant
days with Mr. Malthus. We had as usual abundance of discussion and on the whole I think differed less in opinion.
I forgot to mention in my last that I unfortunately have been
again disappointed of Mr. Hume's visit. He did not get to
Cheltenham till long after my letter directed to him there.
He then wrote to say that he and Mrs. Hume would pass a day
or two with us on their return to London. On that very day
I was obliged to go to London, and I had barely time by the
Post to prevent his circuitous journey. I was very much
mortified at being again deprived of his company. Mr. Basevi
is coming to stay here sometime. These visits very much
interfere with my pursuits. With kind compliments to
Mrs. Mill and Mr. Bentham

> I am Very truly Yours
> DAVID RICARDO

## 141. TROWER TO RICARDO[1]
### [*Reply to* 136—*Answered by* 147]

Unsted Wood—Godalming—
November 26. 1815.

Dear Ricardo

I often lament we are so far removed from each other 26 Nov. 1815
as to prevent those discussions in which we formerly engaged

[1] Addressed: 'To / David Ricardo Esq.ʳ / Gatcomb Park / Minchinhampton / Glocestershire'.—MS in *R.P.*

26 Nov. 1815 upon the important subject of political economy, and in which I felt so much interest—I am rejoiced to find however, that you are resolved to pursue them with an energy and perseverance, that not merely deserve, but will command success. It will give me great pleasure to be made acquainted with your progress, and to learn what new views may have arisen out of a further examination of the subject. The difficulties you complain of are those of *composition*, which no doubt practice will enable you to surmount—At the same time if you have never given the subject of composition any particular attention, you might derive considerable assistance by looking a little into it. And with that view I should recommend your consulting those parts of Dr Blair's Lectures on the Belles Lettres which relate to Composition and Style[1] —I think you would find some useful hints with respect to the construction and connection of sentences and the arrangement and division of a subject.—

You ask me to give you an account of my *studies*—Alas! I fear this would be a difficult task—Of my *pursuits* I can speak more easily—These indeed are various and desultory —Some of my time is engaged in enquiring into the practice and theory of farming; some in planting and the subjects connected with it; some in the improvement of my place; some in shooting, and in discharging some of those duties, which usually devolve upon Country Gentlemen.—The

[1] *Lectures on Rhetoric and Belles Lettres*, by Hugh Blair, Professor in the University of Edinburgh, 2 vols., 4to, London, Strahan, 1783. Adam Smith had lectured on the same subject and 'it was alleged by him and his friends, that Dr. Blair had availed himself largely of his remarks, both on the construction of sentences, and on the general characters of style' (J. Hill, *Account of the Life and Writings of H. Blair*, Edinburgh, 1807, p. 55). Blair acknowledged that he had taken 'several ideas' from a manuscript shown to him by Smith (*Lectures*, vol. 1, p. 381; cp. Rae, *Life of Adam Smith*, p. 33).

complete change that has thus taken place in my pursuits and my habits, clearly shews how much we are the creatures of circumstances. Had I continued in London, moving in the midst of bustle and business, and in the centre of active spirits, I might have been stimulated to exertions, by the excitements of emulation and the ardor of ambition; but here, isolated in a manner from the World, and no longer impelled by such strong incentives, I am content to draw around me the resources a country life affords, considering that I am now,

> Fix'd like a plant to my peculiar spot,
> To draw nutrition, propagate and rot.—[1]

But I do not say this with regret—far from it. I highly applaud my choice, being fully persuaded both from reflection and experience, that

> With silent course that no loud storms annoy
> Glides the *smooth current of domestic joy*—[2]

And I am disposed fully to acquiesce in the forcible though not very elegant description of ambition, given by Lord Bacon, who compares it to a state of constant itching and scratching—[3]

Do not imagine from this however, that I look with indifference upon all those important subjects which used so much to interest me.—No. I do not lose sight of what is passing; and I am desirous of hearing your opinion of the changes that have taken place in the price of Bullion and the Exchanges: I see the Bankists exult mightily, but I think

---

[1] Pope, *Essay on Man*, II, 63.
[2] For this favourite quotation of Trower see above, p. 184.
[3] 'Ambition is like *Choler*, which is an Humour that maketh Men Active, earnest, full of Alacrity, and Stirring, if it be not stopped' (Bacon's *Essays*, 'Of Ambition').

26 Nov. 1815 without reason. To me it seems, that there is nothing in the present symptoms irreconcileable with the opinions of the Bullionists; on the contrary they are in perfect conformity with them. I have not a doubt, that the fall in Bullion is mainly attributable to a material diminution in the amount of our circulation. For, altho' the Bank circulation may remain the same, the numerous failures among the Country Bankers, and the difficulties and stagnation experienced both in internal and external commerce, must have lessened considerably the amount of the general circulation, and diminished the rapidity of its movements, which would produce a similar effect. The fall which is taking place in labor and in the prices of provisions, is another proof (accompanying as it does the fall in Bullion) of the correctness of the theory of the Bullionists. However be this as it may, I am rejoiced to see we are likely to return to a legitimate circulation, with so little difficulty, and may thank our stars for the dangers we have escaped. I am very sanguine in the view I take of things. To me it appears we are opening upon prospects of prosperity. The evidences are satisfactory. The fall in the prices of Bullion, Provisions and Labor, are the preparatory steps, I trust, which are to lead us to that natural state, in which if left to their own free course, the wealth, activity and ingenuity of this Country, must ensure its success. Give our united regards to Mrs. Ricardo and family and believe me

Yours ever sincerely<br>HUTCHES TROWER.

## 142. MILL TO RICARDO[1]

*[Reply to 140.—Answered by 143]*

Ford Abbey Dec<sup>r</sup> 1<sup>st</sup> 1815

Marginal contents, to make them the most useful, should be written, on only one side of the leaf. You can then have more of them under your eye at once—which is of great use, for seeing more easily how the paragraphs stand affected to one another—whether any of them is in substance only the same with any other—whether any of them is inconsistent with any other—whether any of them stand conjoined, which would be more useful in another situation, and so on—whether any thing is wanting to make out the point, which it is the business of the section to state or to prove.[2]

You will see, that in writing the marginal contents I now send you, I left the column, next to that on which I had written, always blank; in order to insert in it any of the remarks I might have to make, on the contents of the preceding column.

The paragraphs are numbered both in the text and in the marginals—so that you may easily refer from the one to the other.

Perhaps you will think proper to recast the first section, keeping in your view, while writing, the individual point which you desire to establish in it. The writing will thus acquire a fixity of direction, and hence an order, and a pointedness, which it never possesses, when one is writing without

1 Dec. 1815

---

[1] MS in *R.P.*

[2] 'My father made me perform an exercise..., which Mr. Bentham practised on all his own writings, making what he called "marginal contents"; a short abstract of every paragraph, to enable the writer more easily to judge of, and improve, the order of ideas, and the general character of the exposition' (J. S. Mill, *Autobiography*, p. 62).

a very precise and definite purpose. In this consists, generally, the advantage of writing any thing twice over. In the first writing, one is generally studying the subject—looking out for ideas—and then the unity of object, and fixity of direction, are impossible. The advantage is, when all the ideas are on paper, then to put them together in their proper parcels, and when they are so put up as that every parcel forms a distinct article, to write upon each article, so defined and distinguished, individually, one after another—and then arises the consummation of excellence. This is what you must do with the *opus magnum*. In the *first* writing, be not very solicitous about any thing, but about getting out all the ideas which appear to you to bear upon the subject, and to be conducive to its elucidation. When this is done, we shall have no great difficulty in marshaling them, and putting each in the place in which it will receive most light from others and shed most light upon them.

In beginning to write you will find it no slight help to invention to suppose yourself writing to a friend, of ordinary understanding, to whom you have it very much at heart to impart a complete knowledge of the subject upon which you are writing. You should suppose his mind to be in the state of an average man among those whom you expect to be your readers; and set down every thing which you think will be necessary to introduce all your own ideas into his mind: beginning with such things as he is likely to know, or acknowledge, and so passing on to others. You will, at the same time find a use in making to yourself a sort of skeleton of your ideas, before you begin to write. Beginning, for example, on the subject of rent, you should try into what propositions you can throw the ideas which seem to constitute the doctrine of rent—as for example—what is the cause of rent—on what circumstances does the operation of that cause depend—what makes it operate more productively, what less: its effects also become causes which are to be explained and so on. When these matters are written down in short notes, they remain in your eye—and operate very usefully in suggesting ideas.

To return to the M.S. I have not stopped to make any observations on the expressions. In general they are very good. I should however like to run it over before you send it to the press—merely to take security that no imperfect expression, which it is so difficult for an unpracticed writer to be sure that he has avoided, has escaped you. And even this very trifling danger you will soon be above.

I am perfectly aware of your objection to long titles for short sections—and those who dislike your conclusions will make it—but I think it ought to be disregarded—not but that it is always an advantage to make a title short, if it can be done without detriment to the instructiveness—but we must not sacrifice to *mauvaise honte*, any portion of that on which the fulfilment of our main purpose depends. The titles I have set down, I never meant to stand—they are only rough expressions to explain by examples what I meant. You must on each occasion devise a title for yourself. Perhaps you may even approve a different division and arrangement. In that case you are to follow your own ideas.—Your modesty might even be made an apology for your titles. You might say in your introduction: that a more practiced writer, who could be more sure of giving the due degree of light and prominence to his ideas, might write straight forward; and disregard the didactic helps of divisions and titles; but that you cannot afford to deprive yourself of any expedient which has been found by experience to be conducive to instruction: And, as you do not aim at eloquence, that didactic expedients ought not in your writings to appear a

1 Dec. 1815 deformity.[1] The French writers have understood the use of
frequent divisions, and distinct titles, better than the English
—Observe how very frequent they are in Voltaire, and
Montesquieu, and how often the title is nearly as long as the
section.

Mr. Hume writes to me how much he was gratified with
your attention. He goes to the continent with his lady on
the 10th—and proposes to see the principal parts of France
and Italy before he returns, when he shall endeavour he says
to renew his acquaintance with you. He is to be back early
in the summer.—We shall be here for a fortnight, or perhaps
three weeks. I am glad I shall see you so soon in London.
I was going to be jocular upon the rapid flights of your lady.
But if the health of Mrs. M.[2] is in such a state the matter is
too serious.

Gods blessing to all of you.

J. M.

### 143. RICARDO TO MILL[3]
[*Reply to* 142.—*Answered by* 145]

Gatcomb Park
9th Dec.r 1815

My dear Sir

9 Dec. 1815     The trouble which you have taken with my manuscript,
in giving a short analysis of each paragraph, and bringing so
much at once under view, shews me clearly the great use
which may be made of such a method in arranging a difficult
subject.

The encouragement you gave me to proceed made me set
to work with new energy, and I had become quite reconciled

---

[1] Ricardo did not adopt this
suggestion.
[2] Mrs Moses Ricardo.

[3] Addressed: 'J. Mill Esq.r / Ford
Abbey / near Chard / Somerset-
shire'.
MS in Mill-Ricardo papers.

to the sections and their titles, when I observed how materially
they contributed to make the subject clear and intelligible.
I found great difficulty in recasting a section, or in writing
any of the new matter which you recommended, but I proceeded with a determined spirit to overcome by perseverance
all these obstacles,—but a new one has arisen in my mind
which I think will stop me altogether. In looking over
Mr. Perceval's correspondence with the Bank Directors,
I find that in 1808, when the new agreement was made
respecting the charges to be allowed to the Bank for management, he appears fairly to acknowledge, that in virtue of their
former agreement, the Bank might insist on the rate of charge
secured to them, by that agreement, on so much of the debt
as remained unredeemed since it was entered into; but as a
new bargain might be made with respect to that part of the
debt which had been created since, and which was a very
large proportion of the whole debt, he had it in his own
power to accomplish the object which he had in view, which
was to reduce to a certain standard the allowance on the
whole debt.

If the Bank were now to insist on their agreement of 1808,
the only answer that could be given them, would be that of
Mr. Perceval,—viz that a new bargain might be made for
that portion of debt which had been created subsequently to
1808, which now however is but a small portion of the whole
debt. I doubt indeed whether that answer could now be
fairly given, for the agreement in 1808 differs from all former
ones,—it provides both for the increase, and the diminution
of the debt, and the charge is rated accordingly. It is not
my object to cancel any existing engagement, but to regulate
equitably for the public those which are about to be renewed.
I might therefore as well propose to alter the terms of their
Charter, as the terms of this agreement.

The same objection does not lie against the compensation for public deposits, that must come before Parliament before April next; but on this subject Mr. Vansittart appears to hold opinions which I think correct, and will it be desirable for me to create a host of enemies without atchieving the least good. No one holds such enmity more cheap than I do, it is so little justifiable in such a cause that I quite disregard it. I would therefore persevere if I thought I was doing myself credit, but really there appears no object for which to contend.

You will not yet have quitted Ford Abbey, and if the weather is as fine with you as it is with us, you may possibly prolong your stay,—I am not sure that I shall not be in London before you, but it will be for one night only. I am in hopes however that my journey may not be necessary. And now before I conclude let me assure you that I am very sensible of and very grateful for the very great trouble which you have had with my manuscript; it was very kind of you indeed to give me such very kind assistance. I have experienced it before, and you will encourage me to look for it again, so far it is bad policy in you, but yours is not a self regarding self-love. My best wishes to Mrs. Mill

Y$^{rs}$ very truly

DAVID RICARDO


## 144. RICARDO TO MALTHUS[1]

[*Answered by* 148]

Gatcomb Park
24$^{th}$ Dec$^r$ 1815

My dear Sir

I write to remind you that the time is come at which you once gave me hopes, almost to certainty, that I should have

[1] Addressed: 'To / The Rev$^d$ T. R Malthus / East India College / Hertford'.—MS at Albury.—*Letters to Malthus*, XL.

the pleasure of seeing you here; and even when I last saw you, you promised, if you could make it convenient, to come and pass a part of your vacation with me. The weather is beautiful, and my desire to see you as ardent as ever. Come then, and inhale the pure atmosphere of our hills, and be under no fear that your visit will retard any object to which your attention may now be devoted, for you shall be free to write, study or read, as many hours in the day as you please unmolested by any one's intrusion.

My lost manuscript is recovered.[1] Mr. Mill recommends its publication but advises me to write an introduction, and to divide it into sections. I had almost resolved to throw it aside,—but I have been again at work upon it, and though I cannot put it in any shape to please me, it is I think rather better than when you saw it, and the probability at present is that I shall venture to publish it.

I attended the Bank Court the other day.[2]—I had no intention whatever of speaking, but some very bad reasoning on the other side, and a total deviation from the question called me up, and I spoke for 5 or ten minutes with considerable inward agitation but without committing any glaring blunder. My speaking is like my writing too much compressed. —I am too apt to crowd a great deal of difficult matter into so short a space as to be incomprehensible to the generality of readers. The Chronicle, I see, has reported what he thought or heard I said, but he has imputed to me what I neither felt nor uttered. Allusions were made to the Bullion question and it was said that it had been prophecied that if the Bank Directors were corrupt, they might with the power

---

[1] The MS of *Economical and Secure Currency*; cp. letter 138.
[2] 21 December. The debate was on the motion of P. P. Bouverie ('the speaker' referred to below)

'that an account be laid before a General Court...of the amount of the surplus profits of this Company'.

they had of issuing paper occasion the greatest public distress,—no such distress however had been experienced. I observed in reply that the goodness of the system was not proved by the distress not having occurred,—that the speaker had been only paying a compliment to the integrity of the Directors, in which no one in the court was more ready to join than myself,—but if the Directors had been corrupt I still thought that they had been armed with the power of doing mischief. Though I was ready to declare my confidence in the integrity of the Directors, there were many parts of their system of which I could not approve, &c.ᵃ &c.ᵃ.—This is very different from the report in the Chronicle,—but I understand that the reporters were most carefully excluded from the Court.

I hope the business at the College has been settled to your satisfaction, and that the result of the late unpleasant disturbance will give you some security against its recurrence in future.[1]

I conclude that you have quite finished writing the alterations and amendments which you projected for the new edition of your book.[2] When I last saw you I think you had made considerable progress and therefore it is probable that you may be already in the press. What point will next engage your attention? for I hope as Mr. Say says that you will travaillez toujours.—

Make my kind compliments to Mrs. Malthus.

Ever Yʳˢ

DAVID RICARDO

[1] The Committee of Directors who had the superintendance of the East India College had expelled a number of boys in consequence of the latest outrages (*The Times*, 1 Dec. 1815).

[2] The *Essay on Population*; cp. above, p. 289.

## 145. MILL TO RICARDO[1]
[*Reply to* 143.—*Answered by* 149]

Ford Abbey Dec.ʳ 22ᵈ 1815

My Dear Sir

Though you are yourself the best judge, as best ac- 22 Dec. 1815
quainted with the circumstances of the case, yet as your letter
appears to imply a kind of appeal to my opinion, I think it
necessary to send you what occurs to me.

Of the three practical points which you urge in your
discourse, the first, it appeared to me, was not only the most
important, by far, but that on which you laid the greatest
stress: viz. the regulation to pay Bank of England notes in
bullion, not in coin. That is not affected by the principles of
any bargain of Perceval. The last of the points, relating to the
division, (among the proprietors) of the savings of the bank,
is equally exempt from its influence. So that there only
remains the point which relates to the surplus payment
which the bank receives from the public.

Now if Perceval did make a bargain which sanctions this
improper, and, as towards the public, unjust remuneration,
it would be something to expose that bargain, and shew that
it was such a bargain as ought never to have been made. If
I were in your situation, I should go further, and say it is
a bargain which ought to be cancelled. There is utility in
making bargains between individuals strict, unless where
fraud appears to have intervened. There would be utility
in holding all bargains between the public and individuals
nul, in which the interests of the public are sacrificed. The
law even recognizes such a principle; since all grants by the
executive power in which the interests of the public seem
to be sacrificed, are reducible, on the averment, that the King

[1] Addressed: 'David Ricardo Esq / Gatcomb Park / Mincing Hampton / Gloucester Shire'.—MS in *R.P.*

was deceived in his grant. But whether you urge this point or not, viz. that the minister was deceived in his grant—the bank ought to be stimulated on the score of honour—and told that having inveigled the public with an improvident, and shameful bargain, it is infamous to seek to take advantage of it; and join the crowd of those who wish to grow rich upon the plunder of the people: that they are avowedly receiving from the public, year by year, a great sum of money, which they ought not to receive; which, if the interests of the public had been taken proper care of, they would have been well prevented from receiving; and that decency—common decency—would recommend it to them to give up this undue advantage—against a people oppressed by public burthens. I should treat all the excess above the due remuneration for their public services, as money got upon false pretences, which the law treats as swindling. And without violating the mildness and forbearingness of your own disposition, I think you may put this whole view of the matter in question in a strong and vivid light.

After all, you are the best judge of what, upon this subject, the public are likely to attend to, and hence to be the better for—all that I have been able, or can pretend to do, is, to suggest the above, as among the matters which your judgement has to work upon.

The gratitude which you express for what I did in regard to your M.S.—though far above any benefit you would derive from it—and even any trouble which it gave to me—I am yet highly pleased with—because I am happy to receive any opportunity of improving your regard for me.

Now for still more of the old subject. In anticipation of the M.S. which I expect soon to receive, as part of the great work, I have been reading once more your last pamphlet.[1] And it

---

[1] *Essay on Profits.*

has suggested this to be given to you, as an advice; which is, that you should all along consider your readers, as people ignorant of the subject; and never set down any material proposition without its immediate proof, or a reference to the very page where the proof is given. You must never leave any such proposition to be inferred, through a number of steps, by your readers themselves, from some distant principles. It is this which has made the pamphlet, in question, be reckoned obscure, and not unjustly, as regards the state of mind of almost everybody in regard to the subject. I have resolved on this account to set you an exercise. You have stated repeatedly this proposition, That improvements in agriculture (suppose in such a state as that of England at present) raise the profits of stock, and produce immediately no other effects.[1] But you have no where stated the proof. You have left it to be inferred from your general doctrine, as to rent. The additional produce cannot be received as rent, which is limited by another circumstance. And it cannot go as wages, because they too are otherwise limited. Therefore it must be received as profit. But what I wish you to do, is, not to content yourself with this inference—but to shew by what steps, in practice, the distribution would take place. As for example—By improvements, all the capital employed on the English soil becomes more productive—the same quantity of corn is consumed in cultivating the land; a greater quantity is returned: What, in their order, are the effects which follow? On this subject, I ordain you to perform an exercise—a school exercise: in other words, write me a letter. That is to say, provided you understand what I propose to you. My meaning is, that you should successively answer the question, What comes next? First of all is the improvement. What comes next? Ans. the increase of pro-

---

[1] See above, IV, 11, n. and 19, n.

22 Dec. 1815 duce. What comes next? Ans. a fall in the price of corn. What comes next?—and so on. I shall then see what next is to be proposed to you. For as you are already the best *thinker* on political economy, I am resolved you shall also be the best writer. It wants only capability, and industry—of both of which, in your case, I am assured. All that is required is that you should resist some of the most frivolous of social calls; such calls as you have all your life long resisted for business, and which you ought now to resist for study. For example, you never thought it necessary, for the sake of your friends, to give up to them your mornings, and keep away from the Stock Exchange. So now—give up to your friends cheerfully all that remains of the day from the dinner hour— and when you must go to see them at their houses, you must add as much more as the time necessary to go. But your hour, before breakfast, and before dinner, should be your own, for study, as it formerly was for business. As soon as people know this to be your rule, nobody is offended at. They rise in their respect and esteem, for you, by knowing that you are doing, what so few people are capable of doing. Conducive to these ends, it should be a rule never to stay late at any persons house; and if any body stays late at yours, that you, without noticing any body, disappear at a particular hour. Never mind a little shame at the thought of a little singularity—singularity is always a sign of weakness, when it respects a matter of no importance—always a sign of strength when it respects a matter which is really worthy of it, and which cannot be attained without it.

You must not tell Mrs. Ricardo how I am thus acting the pedagogue over you. She will think (what I think myself) that my impudence truly is not small.—We are still here— and if your letter is ready within a fortnight, it may safely come here. But I shall write to you, before we go, that you

may exactly know. I hope you are all well—and about to   22 Dec. 1815
have a merry Christmas.

Yours truly

J. MILL

## 146. MALTHUS TO RICARDO[1]
[*Answered by* 150]

E I Coll Dec.[r] 22. 1815

My dear Sir,

    I see your name in the papers today as a speaker among   22 Dec. 1815
the Proprietors of Bank Stock, from which I think I fairly
infer that you are in Town. I fear I have no chance of
seeing you on saturday here, but I expect to be in Town
tuesday or wednesday next for some days, and I shall be
much pleased to hear that you are not leaving Town immediately, and that I shall have a chance of meeting you, before
you [leave][2], particularly as I am apprehensive that it will not
be in my power to reach Gatcomb this vacation.

    I should have written before but have been overwhelmed
with College business and able to do nothing, on account of
these foolish disturbances, and the necessity [of][3] constant
councils, Reports &c: The term is ended now, and I can
breathe again; but I have latterly done little to my Edition.[4]

    I think the principal difference between us relating to the
subjects we have last discussed, is, your opinion that General
Profits never fall from a general fall of prices compared with
labour, but from a general rise of labour compared with

---

[1] Addressed: 'D. Ricardo Esqr /
Stock Exchange / London'; redirected 'Gatcomb Park / near
Minchin Hampton / Gloucestershire'.

MS in *R.P.*
[2] Omitted in MS.
[3] Omitted in MS.
[4] Of the *Essay on Population*.

prices. I own, I can see no reason for this opinion. It is only true in reference to the working of the precious metals, and in no other case. In purchasing them from a foreign country, if labour and stock fall in the purchasing state, more labour and more produce will be given for them, and labour will fall in price instead of rising or remaining stationary.

I believe I assented in pa[rting][1] to the proposition that in the successive cultivation of poorer land, the price of labour would rise as well as the price of corn. When however the rise in the price of corn is occasioned solely and exclusively by the necessity of cultivating poorer land I am now convinced that the rise must be very small, and as the real price of labour must fall, I see no reason why the nominal price of labour should rise. How can such a country purchase the precious metals so as to occasion a general rise in the price of labour. Of course I suppose that it has no peculiar advantage in manufacture. If it had, its corn and labour might both rise from a different cause. This, if true, would make an alteration in your view of Profits.

I hope you succeeded to your satisfaction in your speech. I was sorry to see it given so short.

How goes on the pamphlet.[2] I hope that you have found it again, and that it is ready for the press. Mrs. M desires to be kindly remembered.

Ever truly Yours

T R MALTHUS

[1] Covered by seal. Possibly should be read 'in part'.

[2] *Economical and Secure Currency.*

## 147. RICARDO TO TROWER[1]

[*Reply to* 141.—*Answered by* 154]

Gatcomb Park Minchinhampton
25th Decr 1815

Dear Trower

Since I received your letter I have been in London. 25 Dec. 1815
I attended the Bank Court, and even ventured to give my
opinion on the subject under discussion, which I did with
considerable agitation to myself, but which I believe was not
apparent to those whom I was addressing.[2] You appear to
me to have got over the first difficulties of public speaking[3]—
I have them all to encounter, and they really assume too
formidable an array, for me to dare to wrestle with them. As
I am busily employed on my MS with a view to publication,[4]
and as you will there see my sentiments on Bank affairs,
I shall not make them the subject of my letter. So much has
already been said on the Bullion question that I have thought
it better to say very little on that subject. I may therefore be
permitted to express here my entire assent with your opinions
on the prices of bullion and other things.

I have very little doubt but that there has been a considerable rise in the value of money which I think has been
effected by the many failures of country Banks, which has
increased the use of Bank of England notes in the country,
both as a circulating medium, and as a deposit against the
alarm which always attends extensive failures in the country.
I believe too that bullion has had a real fall, which has also
contributed to bring it nearer to the value of paper. The

---

[1] Addressed: 'Hutches Trower
Esqr/Unsted Wood/Godalming/
Surry'.
    MS at University College, Lon-
don.—*Letters to Trower*, VI.
[2] See above, p. 335, n. 2.

[3] Trower was a frequent speaker
at the meetings of the Court of
Proprietors of the East India
Company; see *Letters to Trower*,
pp. 4, 11.
[4] *Economical and Secure Currency.*

bullionists, and I among the number, considered gold and silver as less variable commodities than they really are, and the effect of war on the prices of these metals were certainly very much underrated by them. The fall in the price of bullion on the peace in 1814, and its rise again on the renewal of the war on Bonapartes entry into Paris are remarkable facts,[1] and should never be neglected in any future discussion on this subject. But granting all this it does not affect the theory of the bullionists.

The description you give me of the mode in which you pass your time leaves me nothing to regret on your account. You have exercise both of the body and of the mind, you are living in a healthful country,—do not know what ennui is—are surrounded by a charming family and must necessarily be a happy man. Do not however imagine that emulation and ambition are extinct in you, they are only dormant for a time, or perhaps they may have only changed their field of exercise. The love of distinction is so natural to man that he never relinquishes his title to it if he sees it clearly within his grasp, and notwithstanding your present humble system of philosophy you have yourself been stimulated, and do not fail on every occasion still to stimulate others, by the rewards which are held out to successful exertion.

I am glad not to hear any complaints from you of the low price of produce, though you must suffer from such low price in common with all other land holders. Those who have their property in land will not I think for a considerable time regain the advantageous position in which they stood during the war in relation to the rest of the community,—yet the price of corn appears to me unnaturally low and their

---

[1] On the Peace of 1814 the price of gold had fallen from 108/- per ounce (1 March) to 90/- (28 June); on the return of Napoleon in 1815 it rose from 89/- (28 February) to 107/- (4 April).

situation will on the whole improve from the present state 25 Dec. 1815 of depression. In every change from peace to war, and from war to peace, there must be great changes in the distribution of capital and much individual distress. In the present case I fully expect that it will be followed by a rapid and brilliant course of prosperity, notwithstanding the disadvantages we labour under from the pressure of our enormous debt. I am every day becoming a greater enemy to the funding system.— Besides its other evils it disturbs so cruelly the prices of commodities as to give us a serious disadvantage in all foreign markets. If the supplies were always raised within the year, and if in consequence one class of the people were obliged to borrow from another in order to discharge their quota of the taxes,—a debt as large as the present might exist, but the effects would in my opinion be beyond all comparison less injurious.

But I am getting on high matters at the fag end of my letter and have barely left myself room to request you to give the united regards of Mrs. Ricardo and myself to Mrs. Trower.

Ever truly yours<br>DAVID RICARDO

## 148. MALTHUS TO RICARDO[1]

[Reply to 144.—Answered by 150]

London Dec<sup>r</sup> 28<sup>th</sup> 1815

My dear Sir,

I saw your name in the papers, and wrote immediately 28 Dec. 1815 to the Stock Exchange,[2] hoping to catch you before you left London, and indeed thinking it possible that I might find you in Town the next week. I conclude from your letter

---

[1] Addressed: 'D. Ricardo Esqr / Gatcomb Park / Minchinhampton'. MS in *R.P.*          [2] Letter 146.

28 Dec. 1815 that you set off the next day, and that mine has not yet reached you.

It would, I assure you, give me great pleasure to fulfil my engagement at Gatcomb, but circumstances are not favourable to it. I am in Town with Mrs. Malthus and the children, and cannot possibly leave them till they return; and then I shall be so behind hand with regard to my own business, and so likely to be involved in College affairs, that I fear it will be quite impossible for me to leave this neighbourhood. I have been so much interrupted already by College business, that I have made very little progress in my edition since I saw you, and I find it will require altogether more time than I expected. By the by I wish you would mention to me any passages in any part of the work, which may have struck you as objectionable. I still doubt as to the additions which I ought to make to the new chapters you saw. If I complete the subject, and say what I meant to say with respect to Restrictions on the importation of foreign corn, and the effects of high prices on foreign commerce, I fear I shall be led into too great length, and yet if I shorten it I shall probably be thought obscure. It would have been better perhaps in many respects to leave out the whole of the practical question relating to Bounties and Restrictions.

I am glad to hear you have recovered your manuscript, and that it is likely soon to appear in public. You would naturally feel a little agitated in speaking for the first time in the Court, but you are so much in the habit of speaking correctly, when you do speak, and have generally so good a command of words, that I should never feel any apprehension about your acquitting yourself well.

I am writing from Town and among all the children who are reading aloud so I hardly know what I say. In my last to the Stock Exchange I said something on our old subject.

I much fear I shall be called upon to write something about 28 Dec. 1815
the College, which will be very inconvenient to me. Mrs. M
desires to be kindly remembered to Mrs. Ricardo

Ever truly Yours

T R Malthus

## 149. RICARDO TO MILL[1]

[Reply to 145.—Answered by 151]

[Gatcomb Park, 30 Dec. 1815][2]

My dear Sir

A passage in Mr. Percevals correspondence with the 30 Dec. 1815
Bank, which I had overlooked when I last wrote, and which
has been since pointed out to me, gives such a limited character to the agreement that he entered into with the Bank,
that I have now no scruple in recommending its being
annulled—so that I have been again at work on the MS.
I have added to various parts of it and it now waits for your
friendly eye, and I hope unfriendly, or rather unbiassed,
judgement, to decide whether it shall be sent to the printers.
If it is published it is material that it should appear about the
1st of feby, (the meeting of Parliament), and I conclude from
your last letter that you will be in London time enough to
allow of its being printed by that day. If you think you shall
not I can send it to you in a parcel from London where I shall
be again the week after next,—about the 9th Jany. You will
perhaps oblige me with a line here before I quit home.

I am obliged to you for suggesting to me what might have
been said in favour of laying this agreement aside, if it had

---

[1] Addressed: 'J. Mill Esqr / Ford
Abbey / near / Chard / Somerset-
shire'.
MS in Mill-Ricardo papers.

[2] Inscribed by Mill: 'Undated,
but Recd 2d Jany 1816'. Minchinhampton postmark, undated.
Cp. the end of the first paragraph;
30 December was a Saturday.

all the character of durability which I at first attached to it. There are in fact two agreements with the Bank, one which expires next year, and refers to the deposits only; the other regards the management of the debt. The latter, tho' prodigal, is not sufficiently so to justify its being cancelled on the plea of being an improvident and shameful bargain—the former has I think much more of that character. When you see the MS you will be so good as to tell me what you think of the short argument I have used on this point, and will perhaps suggest some little addition to that part of the subject.—

I am much pleased with the idea of having a task set me on which to write, and I would immediately begin on the one which you have given me if my mind was not rather anxious about the MS. Whilst it is with me I am incessantly looking it over to see whether my powers can do any thing [1] more for it. I have seen so much of it that I sometimes fear I rather mar than mend. As soon as I get rid of it I will begin on the proposition which you require to be proved.

I know I shall be soon stopped by the word price, and then I must apply to you for advice and assistance. Before my readers can understand the proof I mean to offer, they must understand the theory of currency and of price. They must know that the prices of commodities are affected two ways one by the alteration in the relative value of money, which affects all commodities nearly at the same time,—the other by an alteration in the value of the particular commodity, and which affects the value of no other thing, excepting it ent[er][2] into its composition.—This invariability of the value of the precious metals, but from particular causes relating to themselves only, such as supply and demand, is the sheet anchor on which all my propositions are built; for those who maintain that an alteration in the value of corn

---

[1] In MS 'think'.          [2] Covered by seal.

will alter the value of all other things, independently of its effects on the value of the raw material of which they are made, do in fact deny this doctrine of the cause of the variation in the value of gold and silver. You shall find me a tractable and I hope an industrious pupil.

I had already before I received your letter begun to practise the right of secluding myself of a morning. Some of my brothers have been staying here but they have seldom seen me after breakfast till dinner. I am persuaded that I shall not get on with any work if I suffer my mornings to be broken in upon.—

My sister Mrs. Porter relapsed again and was nearly as bad as ever, when at the wish of her friends she placed herself under the care of Mr. Scott a surgeon and apothecary at Bromley in Kent of whose success in disorders of the skin we had heard much said. She has been there 2 or 3 weeks and her progress to recovery appears miraculous. All her wraps are thrown off—opium is discontinued—she can walk 3 or 4 miles a day—every part of her body is healed except the inside of her hands,—and they are mending every day— her nails are growing and she has rejoiced us here at Gatcomb by a letter in her own hand writing. You may judge how happy she is, and how happy that charming girl Esther is— who is still her constant companion. We are all delighted.

Y<sup>rs</sup>

D Ricardo

# INDEX OF CORRESPONDENTS
## 1810–1815

*denotes letters not previously published*

[1] For letters to Malthus formerly published as of 1810, see under 1813.